Global Business Analysis

Colin Turner

Global Business Analysis

Understanding the Role of Systemic Risk in International Business

Colin Turner
Edinburgh Business School
Heriot-Watt University
Edinburgh, UK

ISBN 978-3-031-27768-9   ISBN 978-3-031-27769-6 (eBook)
https://doi.org/10.1007/978-3-031-27769-6

© The Editor(s) (if applicable) and The Author(s), under exclusive license to Springer Nature Switzerland AG 2023

This work is subject to copyright. All rights are solely and exclusively licensed by the Publisher, whether the whole or part of the material is concerned, specifically the rights of translation, reprinting, reuse of illustrations, recitation, broadcasting, reproduction on microfilms or in any other physical way, and transmission or information storage and retrieval, electronic adaptation, computer software, or by similar or dissimilar methodology now known or hereafter developed.
The use of general descriptive names, registered names, trademarks, service marks, etc. in this publication does not imply, even in the absence of a specific statement, that such names are exempt from the relevant protective laws and regulations and therefore free for general use.
The publisher, the authors, and the editors are safe to assume that the advice and information in this book are believed to be true and accurate at the date of publication. Neither the publisher nor the authors or the editors give a warranty, expressed or implied, with respect to the material contained herein or for any errors or omissions that may have been made. The publisher remains neutral with regard to jurisdictional claims in published maps and institutional affiliations.

Cover image: Andriy Onufriyenko@gettyimages

This Palgrave Macmillan imprint is published by the registered company Springer Nature Switzerland AG
The registered company address is: Gewerbestrasse 11, 6330 Cham, Switzerland

Preface

Having taught International Business for over 30 years I found myself examining whether the subject was facing an existential crisis. The progressive onset of globalization meant that all business disciplines were integrating an international dimension into curricula. Thus areas that would have been in a conventional International Business course were now covered elsewhere. In pushing the study of International Business as an adjunct of Strategy, I became increasingly interested in evolving its curricula to focus upon the dynamics within the International Business Environment and how such processes impact upon the formation, structure, and operation of business models. This allowed the curriculum to begin to stress a set of broader themes from subjects as diverse as geopolitics towards climate change. Students were responsive to such themes removing them from being treated as peripheral issues to ones that were at the core of understanding how the businesses they sought to enter were going to evolve. It is to those students that this book is dedicated. I have long touted a book of this nature to academic publishers. However, it was not until after the COVID-19 pandemic that interest in a book focusing upon risk within global systems really began to take off. It was this point where the combination of global pandemics, the lasting legacy of the global financial crisis, and a more critical perspective on the nature of global systems has led to an increase in professional and academic interest in global risk. The book was written against the context of a global economy coming out of COVID-19 pandemic and entering the new systemic instability created by the Ukraine–Russia conflict. For that reason, the book does often draw upon these as examples of the risk process within the global system and how events cascade across different sub-systems. Ultimately I hope the reader of this book finds the process of comprehending global risk as fascinating a subject as I did when writing it.

Colin Turner
Edinburgh, UK

Contents

1. The Nature of Global Risk 1
2. The Global Business Model: Business and Embedded Global Risk 29
3. The State and the Global System 57
4. Geoeconomic Risk 89
5. Geopolitical Risk 123
6. Ecological Risk 153
7. Global Social Risk 189
8. Technological Risk 227
9. Infrastructural Risk 265
10. Conclusions: Analysing Global Business In a Complex Environment 297

Supplementary Information
Index 313

Abbreviations

ASEAN	Association of South East Asian Nations	NIS	National Infrastructure System
EU	European Union	OECD	Organization for Economic and Development
FAO	UN Food and Agriculture Organization	SAARC	South Asian Association for Regional Cooperation
FDI	Foreign Direct Investment	SIDS	Small Island Developing States
GDP	Gross Domestic Product	TSMC	Taiwan Semiconductor Manufacturing Company
GIS	Global Infrastructure System		
IMF	International Monetary Fund	UN	United Nations
MNCs	Multinational Companies	WEC	World Energy Council
NGOs	Non-Governmental Organizations	WEF	World Economic Forum
		WTO	World Trade Organization

List of Figures

Fig. 1.1	The risk assessment matrix	5
Fig. 1.2	The global system and its component sub-systems	12
Fig. 2.1	A simplified business model framework (Adapted from Osterwalder et al. [2005])	31
Fig. 2.2	The embeddedness of the business model	33
Fig. 2.3	A simplified value network	34
Fig. 2.4	Business model endogenous risk framework	39
Fig. 2.5	Internationalization risk and business model evolution	45
Fig. 3.1	The strategic trade-off for states (after Rodrik, 2011)	67
Fig. 3.2	State strategy spectrum	67
Fig. 3.3	Liberal capitalism and state-based risk: a virtuous cycle	76
Fig. 3.4	Authoritarian model of country risk	77
Fig. 3.5	The PESOE risk framework	84
Fig. 3.6	Japan's PESOE risk profile	86
Fig. 4.1	The four dimensions of globalization	93
Fig. 4.2	The centrality of geoeconomic risk to global system risk	102
Fig. 4.3	Cascading effect of asset bubble bursting on global flows	115
Fig. 5.1	Multi-scalar impact of macro-level risks	127
Fig. 5.2	Four geopolitical states	134
Fig. 6.1	Business risk in Anthropocene	156
Fig. 6.2	The physical impact of climate change	161
Fig. 6.3	Climate risk scenarios	163
Fig. 6.4	The water–energy–food (WEF) security nexus and climate change	166
Fig. 6.5	Global water usage by sector (2020) (*Source* WEF)	169
Fig. 6.6	Global share of energy production 2020	176
Fig. 6.7	Energy mix in 2050 under net zero scenario (*Source* BP [2021])	177
Fig. 6.8	Renewables by type—share of total renweable energy production (Other—includes electricity generated from geothermal, biomass, and other sources of renewable energy) (*Source* BP [2021])	178
Fig. 6.9	Rates of moderate and severe food insecurity (2014–2020) (*Source* FAO [2022])	184
Fig. 6.10	The global food system	185
Fig. 7.1	Major types of global systemic social risks	196
Fig. 7.2	The ageing of developed states 1970–2020 (*Source* OECD, 2021)	198
Fig. 7.3	Share of global working-age population by region, 2000 and 2030 (percentages) (UN, 2022) (*Source* UN Population Division)	200
Fig. 7.4	The trend in old age dependency ratios (UN, 2022) (*Source* UN Population Division)	202
Fig. 7.5	International Migration 1970–2020 (Percentage of Total Global Population) (*Source* IMO 2022)	206
Fig. 7.6	Youth unemployment (UN, 2022) (*Source* UN Population Division)	209
Fig. 8.1	The main fourth industrial revolution technologies	237
Fig. 8.2	Jobs at risk from automation (*Source* Office of National Statistics)	241

Fig. 8.3	Average monthly number of serious cyber attacks (*Source* Centre for Strategic and Information Studies)	246
Fig. 8.4	Intenet usage by individuals 2021 (%) (*Source* ITU [2022])	255
Fig. 8.5	Usage of internet by gender (*Source* World Bank [2022])	256
Fig. 10.1	The complex links between the global sub-systems	300

List of Tables

Table 1.1	Strategic/operational risk matrix	4
Table 1.2	The multi-scalar nature of risk	7
Table 1.3	Global sub-systems and risk profile	18
Table 1.4	Examples of sub-systemic links in a complex global system	19
Table 1.5	Systemic resilience	23
Table 1.6	Resilience action at different levels	25
Table 2.1	Business model component and risk type	38
Table 2.2	Drivers of business model globality	42
Table 2.3	Broad global business model typology	48
Table 3.1	Alternative views on state discretion and globalization risk	61
Table 3.2	State-based risk and globalization	65
Table 3.3	Facets of major state strategy types	68
Table 3.4	State rankings across a range of economic indices (as of 2022)	72
Table 3.5	Stages of state competitive development	74
Table 3.6	The categorization of state risk within the PESOE framework	80
Table 4.1	The relative share of economic activity across global regions	91
Table 4.2	Geoeconomic risks and its cascade effects in other systems	99
Table 4.3	The Sino-American dominance of the global economy	103
Table 5.1	Multi-scalar nature of political risks	125
Table 5.2	The interface between political risk and other sub-systems	127
Table 5.3	Nationalist states (as of July 2022)	144
Table 6.1	The impact of water scarcity upon non-ecological global sub-systems	170
Table 6.2	Comparative energy security	174
Table 6.3	Global sub-system risks from the energy transition	179
Table 7.1	The Interface between social risk and other sub-systems	192
Table 7.2	Total global fertility across selected regions and groups of countries	198
Table 7.3	The different generations	203
Table 7.4	Main types of risks created by high and sustained youth unemployment	211
Table 7.5	The multi-scalar nature of global health and wellbeing	215
Table 7.6	The public health dimensions of the UN's sustainable development goals	216
Table 7.7	Global pandemic risks to global sub-systems	220
Table 7.8	The most and least health secure states (out of 195)	225
Table 8.1	Recognized types of technology systems	229
Table 8.2	Phases of development of technological system	230
Table 8.3	Impact of technological system upon other global sub-systems	231
Table 8.4	Overlapping innovation cycles and industrial revolutions	232
Table 8.5	Major multi-scalar 4IR Technological Risks	239
Table 9.1	Multi-scalar infrastructure system	267
Table 9.2	The hierarchy within critical infrastructure systems	270
Table 9.3	Examples of infrastructure risks across global sub-systems	272
Table 9.4	Global bottlenecks in international logistics	278

List of Case Studies

Case Study 1.1:	The Strange Case of Kim Jong Un's Weight Loss	8
Case Study 1.2:	Globalization and Superspreading—The Case of COVID-19	14
Case Study 2.1:	Apple's Global Value Network for the iPhone	35
Case Study 2.2:	Chinese SME Internationalization	54
Case Study 3.1:	Why Afghanistan Matters	71
Case Study 3.2:	Mapping State-Based Risk: The Case of Japan	85
Case Study 4.1:	The 'Excessive Globalization' of Rare Earths	112
Case Study 4.2:	The Economic Shock of COVID	118
Case Study 5.1:	Geopolitical Risk in Global Business: Russian Divestment and the Russia-Ukraine Conflict	135
Case Study 5.2:	TSMC and Geopolitics	140
Case Study 6.1:	BP and the Energy Transition: Moving Beyond Petroleum	164
Case Study 6.2:	Water Risk on the Nile and Ethiopia's Grand Ethiopian Renaissance Dam (GERD)	172
Case Study 7.1:	Social Media and Social Risk	193
Case Study 7.2:	Japan's `Super Ageing' Society	201
Case Study 7.3:	Global Obesity and Social Risk	218
Case Study 8.1:	India Moves up the Tech Value Chain	261
Case Study 8.2:	Google and China	262
Case Study 9.1:	The Ever Given's Disruption of the Suez Canal	280
Case Study 9.2:	The Nord Stream Pipelines	285
Case Study 9.3:	China's Malacca Dilemma	293

List of Boxes

Box 1.1:	Twenty-First-Century Events That Impact Upon Global Flows	20
Box 2.1:	The Legacy of Global Complexity: The Universal International Business	43
Box 2.2:	Global Value Networks (GVNs): The Global Interconnection of Business Models	49
Box 3.1:	State Types	62
Box 3.2:	The Return of the State	77
Box 4.1:	From Connectivity to Hyperconnectivity within Global Economic Systems	100
Box 4.2:	The Great Moderation	105
Box 4.3:	The Strategic Challenges of China and US Decoupling	109
Box 5.1:	Global Governance Architecture: The Main Global Co-ordinating Institutions	131
Box 6.1:	Climate Change and Small Island Developing States (SIDS)	158
Box 7.1:	Agricultural Pandemics	220
Box 8.1:	The Dark Web	260

The Nature of Global Risk

Reports that say that something hasn't happened are always interesting to me, because as we know, there are known knowns; there are things we know we know. We also know there are known unknowns; that is to say we know there are some things we do not know.

Donald Rumsfeld

At the end of this chapter the student will be able to understand:
− The role of risk in business analysis.
− The structure of the Global System.
− The form and nature of Global Risk.
− The difference between trends and events in risk analysis.
− The importance of global system resilience.

Introduction

We live in world characterized by uncertainty. Any act undertaken at any level (whether the state, the corporate entity, or the individual) involves a risk. That such risks—linked to any action—have always existed is indisputable. However, what is new is an awareness that the consequences of actions can create risk through ever more opaque channels. In International Business, the actions of states and business (the primary focus of the analysis within this book) takes place against a global system that exhibits high degrees of complexity. This renders the effects of any trend or event (over both the short- and long-term time frames) unpredictable. For business operating in a global system this increases operational and market risk increasing the uncertainty of functioning across multiple states. This chapter seeks to explore the nature of this strategic challenge. After initially examining the nature of risk in general terms, the chapter moves on to assess how the evolving global system is shaping the operating and market risk environment for business. In so doing, the chapter provides the basics for the analysis that follows within the rest of the book.

The Nature of Risk

At its core, risk is about the uncertainty of actions. It reflects the probability of some (known) event occurring that has the potential to impact negatively upon the agent undertaking the action. The magnitude of exposure to risk is reflected by an assessment of the probability of an event occurring and the extent to which the event poses a threat or opportunity to the objectives of the agent (be it a business, state, or individual). The attitude to risk will be shaped by perceptions of risk and return; that is the likelihood of the event occurring and its consequences against the benefits should any potential event not occur. In business terms, it is about how the actions of a corporate entity in pursuing their strategic objectives to promote its commercial sustainability engages in actions that both knowingly and unknowingly exposes the corporate entity to phenomena that have the potential to erode future corporate wellbeing (in financial or other terms) or in extreme cases threaten the survival of the business. The exposure to such risk can be the result of both strategic intent (that is defined aspirational plans) or simply as an inevitable consequence of routine, day-to-day business operations.

This allows for the categorization of strategic risk into two categories:
- Discretionary risk: those risks and uncertainties to which the business is prepared to be exposed to which are created through the desire of the corporate entity to pursue a specific objective which is expected to support and enhance corporate sustainability.
- Mandatory Risk: those risks to which the firm's value creating system is naturally exposed as a consequence of the firm's existence within a given context. Such risks are largely out of the firm's control with a limited ability to mitigate any ecological consequences. Its main parameter of action is to reshape its corporate configuration (see ▶ Chapter 2).

Just as risk emerges as the natural or intentional by-product of strategy so it can also be categorized as to whether the primary source of the risk is internal or external to the value network of the business model. This bi-modal division of operational risk can be defined accordingly.
- Internal risks: are those threats to the financial sustainability and performance of the business sourced from the operation of the extended value network of the corporate body. That risk is sourced from the wider value network and not just to the boundaries of the firm itself reflects the high degree of permeability of firms borders and that the value creating/destroying forces from firm operations can lie at a distant from core operating functions of the business (see ▶ Chapter 2).
- External risks: are those threats to the sustainability and performance of the business that lie beyond the boundaries and control of the business and its extended value system. This reflects the high degree of dependency between the corporate value system and its macro/meta operating context (see below). It is these external risks that will form the focal point of the analysis within the remainder of this text.

◻ Table 1.1 brings these two types of business risks together to identify the differing types of strategic and operating risks that corporate entities can face.

This simple matrix reflects that discretionary risk measures can create their own risks as a result of resistance to the processes of strategic change initiated by the business. These could be HR related but could also be created by loss of fitness of the business model to their operating context that causes the value network to be impacted. Similarly discretionary risk actions can also create external risks as core stakeholders could react negatively to the intentional actions of the business in promoting change. Similarly rising internal and external risks can create new discretionary risks in the choices firms adopt to respond to the challenges posed by alterations in these shifting internal and external operating environments. Similarly, the mandatory risks that businesses face can also alter internal and external operating environments. This could be through changing regulatory frameworks, shifting customer sentiment, etc.

As previously indicated, risk is tied intimately into notions of uncertainty. Uncertainty reflects that knowledge with regard to future events and processes is lim-

Table 1.1 Strategic/operational risk matrix

		Strategic risk	
		Discretionary risk	Mandatory risk
Operational risk	Internal risk	Typical Risk includes: • HR issues/strike action • Finance issues created by choice of financing model • Negative internal stakeholder sentiment to changes • Accidents, human error	Typical risk includes: • Regulatory changes that reshape operations • Competition • Changing costs
	External risk	Typical Risk includes: • Negative external stakeholder sentiment to changes • Obsolescence of pre-existing technology • Reputational risk	Typical risk includes: • Change in political and economic sentiment • Legal risk • Natural events

ited and that whilst firms can have some idea of future scenarios and how they might evolve these are nonetheless subject to unpredictability. This exists alongside conditions of uncertainty where the nature and the extent of outcomes are unknown. This signifies the fact that the future is uncertain and—as such—it cannot be predicted with any degree of accuracy. Overall, given the dynamic nature of the business' operating environment, there can be no section of the firm's business model (see ▶ Chapter 2) or its operating environment that are not subject to uncertainty. The combination of the rapidity of technological change and legacy of hyper-globalization are just two of the factors driving this process. Kay and King (2020) argue that the upshot of these trends is a situation of 'radical uncertainty' that is the notion of conventionally dealing with risk through assessment of probability is mistaken as the likelihood of any given outcome is unknown. This is especially so given the complexity of the system and the emergence of random events (see below).

The link between uncertainty and risk underscores the desire for businesses to have as much predictability within their internal and external operating environments as possible. Thus, as we shall see as the analysis within this book progresses, businesses prefer systemic stability (both internally and externally) as a precursor to commercial predictability and lower risk. Stability makes decisions easier and can therefore act as a public good by facilitating investment. This can make businesses agnostic (or even resistant) to emerging trends within their operating system that can undermine this stability. It can also create corporate social responsibility (CSR) issues where businesses could prefer the desire for stability and predictability over taking a position on social/political issues. This has been an evident problem for western businesses doing business with China where aspects of this state's behaviour have contravened western consumer sentiment. Whilst taking an agnostic stand may work for business stability over the short term (keeping Chinese authorities' content); over the longer-term reputational damage in western markets may harm corporate financial sustainability.

The Nature of Global Risk

Paradoxically stability can be destabilizing in those systems that are stable and are not changing and evolving creating endogenous risks and tensions that build up within the system. Thus, systems are as vulnerable to endogenous as well as exogenous risks. Both of these effects can have amplifying effects. These are identified as systemic risks where these processes (both internal and external to the system) create a challenge to the proper functioning of the system. There is the potential that these risks can even create an existential risk to the system itself where the logic underpinning the system is undermined.

The extent to which the existence of risk acts as a constraint upon business is a reflection of where on the spectrum of risk acceptability and anticipated reward/impact any event lies. Such decisions are formed against the aforementioned uncertainty as expected impacts of any event will be based on experience which could be an unreliable guide to future events and processes as well as their impacts upon the business. Thus, the extent to which the business is risk averse given the extent to which an impact of an event is known with certainty, doubt, or ignorance will form expectations with regard to the acceptability of the risk. ◘ Figure 1.1 represents the conventional matrix of risk assessment for business based upon the action that follows dependent upon the relative assessment of the risk in terms of probability against impacts upon business operations. This broadly defines four broad types of risk:

Contextual Risk: these are events with high probability of occurring, but which will have minimal impact upon the business. These would impact upon the broad commercial environment but to which the business system could easily adapt and would prove resilient. This could be due to a single piece of infrastructure failure where its capacity can easily be replaced.

Existential Risk: these are events that can be very likely to occur and when they do, they pose a threat to sustainability of the business. These include events such as a recession, the loss of key suppliers, etc.

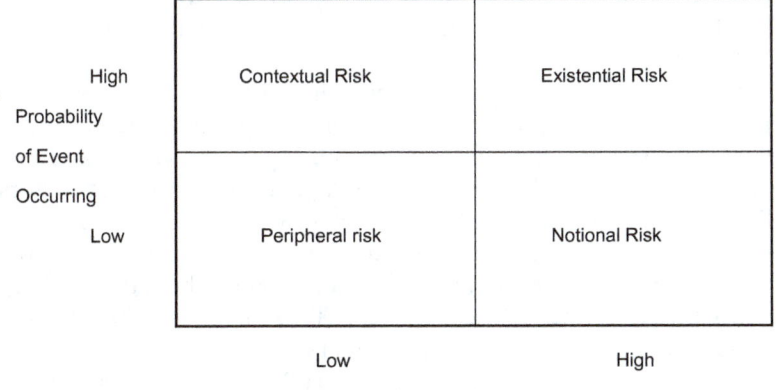

◘ **Fig. 1.1** The risk assessment matrix

Notional Risk: these are events where the impact is high but where the probability of the event occurring is low. Thus, the firm can largely ignore. This would include events such as nuclear conflict.

Peripheral Risk: these are risks that are low likelihood and also—should they occur—would tend to have a minimal impact upon the sustainability of the firm. This includes certain natural events such as extreme weather or localized public disorder.

The Systemic Nature of Risk

Much of the narrative surrounding risk tends to treat it as a standalone phenomenon based on singular events that impact upon a single agent. Though it is important to stress that the complexity of business and its interaction within its environment is unlikely to render any event a singular episode with no cascade effects upon other parts of the broad commercial system within which the firm operates and in which it functions as an interdependent and interconnected component. Furthermore, such analysis also understates the extent to which singular events are part of longer-term trends. For example, an extreme weather event could be indicative of climate change or where industrial unrest is symptomatic of broader social-political change. This link between events and processes in risk analysis is explored more fully below. A starting point in recognizing the systemic impact of these events/processes is recognizing that they have the potential to be multi-scalar. That single events can impact upon other scales. ◘ Table 1.2 begins to address the nature of this trend of risk operating between and across scales. The scales of analysis used within this book are:

- Micro: this is level of the individual agent (normally—in this work—the corporate entity).
- Meso: this is the level of the network and of the interactions between notionally independent corporate entities.
- Macro: this is the level of the nation state based on the notion of it occupying a territorially demarcated space over which it exerts territoriality.
- Meta: this is the level of inter-state network and interconnectedness.

The logic of systemic risk is that interconnections within and between each of these levels shape the form and nature of risk as well as its broad systemic impact. Thus, future events and trends impact upon the wellbeing of the system and the efficacy of its operation as well as that of the agents operating within it at multiple scales (see ◘ Table 1.2). It raises the prospect that micro-level events can have meta-level consequences but more important—for this work—how meta/macro trends can impact upon micro- and meso-level performance where the latter are a source of trends/events that alter the risk environment. These highlight that the impact and adaptive strategies taken can impact upon other levels.

The embeddedness of businesses within broadly developed business ecosystems (see ► Chapter 2) underlines they do not operate as standalone commercial entities but exist as part of a broader local, national, regional, and global business system. The firm as a component of this system interacts with other agents within this

■ Table 1.2 The multi-scalar nature of risk

Systemic operating level	Impacted agent	Nature of risk	System impact
Micro	Business, individual	These are small systemic risks largely confined to the borders of the business or to individual actions	Failure of component of business network can impact upon meso-level operation and macro performance
Meso	Business, NGOs, Public sector	These are risks within value networks (see ▶ Chapter 2) shaped by the inter-relationships between businesses within mutually supporting value creating relationships	Meso-level events impact upon micro performance through disruption to value creating relations. Macro-level impact possibly felt at regional or national level by impact on employment, output, etc.
Macro	States, Businesses	These are systemic risks emerging from within the territorial boundaries of a state (including their relationships with other states) that have the potential to radically reshape the operating context of a business	Change in macro environment by shift in regulation or policy can impact on meso-level operation and therefore onto micro level. This can also impact on other states and create potential meta-level impact
Meta	Businesses, states, international organizations	These are universal, global trends emergent to impact upon all agents operating within the global system	States adapting to these trends can impact on macro, micro, and meso levels

system creating interdependence between themselves and the other components. Self-evidently the weight of any singular agent in this system will vary but what is unvarying is that the impact of—and adaptive response to—events upon and by one agent can impact upon others. Clearly the more salient the agent is to the operation of the system the more severe these systemic risks will be upon the overall efficacy of that system. Thus, the legacy of systemic risk is that no single component of the system can be viewed in isolation and that any risk to any single component (and the impact and the impacted agent's adaption to such a risk) can impact upon other parts of the system. It is also true that just because any single component of the system is exhibiting stability it does not mean that every other component of the system is stable or that such stability is true of the system as a whole.

The link between different scales of impact (see ◘ Table 1.1) and the creation of systemic risk is the existence of feedback loops within the system. These are endogenous to the system created by links between agents within the system where a share of the systems output impacts upon the systems behaviour. Such loops can be either positive or negative for the operation of the system and work through amplifying and/or adding velocity to any impact upon any single agent and cascading it through the rest of the system via the interconnections and interdependencies between them. For example, the root cause of the 2008 Global Financial Crisis was a two per cent loss in the US sub-prime mortgage market: the same as an equivalent fall in the US stock market. On its own this would have been shrugged off by the financial system. The fact that this fall (and consequent losses) exposed the losses of certain investors, with consequences for their balance sheets and liquidity as well as exposing the otherwise unknown interconnections between market players. These reflected how imbalances had been allowed to build up generating a loss of confidence in the backing system as normally secure financial institutions found their balance sheets compromised.

The legacy of this complexity for risk analysis is that outcomes can be both unintended, unanticipated, and unpredictable. This combined with the probability that these effects could be damaging to the system and stimulating further events in other linked systems. Finally, there is the possibility that their origin and trajectory are often unknown creating an opaque set of risks that need to be addressed. This is driven by the fact that these are global in nature created by systemic interconnectivity leading to complex causal structures with the result that the cause-effect relationships are often uncertain based on ambiguous catalysts. Finally, these systemic risks are stochastic means that more than one outcome is possible. Thus, complexity enforces the notion that not only can systems be damaged by singular events but that they can also be damaged by a complex set of self-generated complex chain of events.

> **Case Study 1.1: The Strange Case of Kim Jong Un's Weight Loss**
>
> King Jong Un is the Supreme Leader of the North Korea and has been so since the death of his father in 2011. Like his father and his grandfather before him, Kim Jong Un runs North Korea as a totalitarian dictatorship based upon a strong cult of personality. Alongside this strong degree of control, King Jong Un has sustained—as far as possible—the global outsider status of North Korea fostering a strong sense of isolation from the rest of the global economic and political system bar China with whom it engages with trade in core essentials such as coal and food. Alongside this isolated status, North Korea—under the Kim dynasty—has also pursued an aggressive militarization strategy with a long-term objective to acquire a nuclear capability with its on-going missile tests unsettling its neighbours notably Japan and South Korea. Ultimately, the unpredictable nature of the Kim regime allows it to play an outsized geostrategic role within the global political arena. All of this depends upon the continuity of leadership provided by Kim Jong Un.
>
> Thus, when Kim Jong Un appeared on North Korean state television in mid-2021—after a sustained absence from the limelight—having appeared to have lost a substantial amount of weight specu-

lation grew within western intelligence agencies as to health of Kim. This appearance led to a large volume of speculation as to whether this weight loss was due to ill health and if this could lead to a power struggle with North Korea something that could have long-standing ramifications for regional stability given its stock of chemical and nuclear weapons. Of course, there was speculation that the opposite was true namely that this slimmed down appearance reflected a more health-conscious leader who was aiming to prolong his reign. Whatever the reason, this uncertainty reflected not simply the secrecy that surrounds the state but also how little outsiders truly understand the power dynamics within it notably that there is no obvious succession plan should Kim Jong Un die. Thus, whether this change was for health or for more ominous reasons, the slimmed down appearance mattered for geopolitical reasons.

Kim Jong Un is renowned for unhealthy lifestyle with a penchant for both cigarettes and alcohol and comes from a family with a history of diabetes and heart disease. Thus, many governments have looked for clues as to the leader's health to provide a guide for how the state develops. Prior to 2021, on his visits abroad Kim was watched closely with intelligence estimating that he was severely obese with a body mass index of over 40 (where below 25 is considered healthy). The secrecy surrounding his health has led to the use of a special toilet when he travels to ensure no samples of his detritus can be taken. This ambiguity over his health rose with the pandemic where overseas travel (most importantly diplomatic exchanges) both in and out of North Korea became even more constrained. It is evident that Kim Jung Un is keen to maintain (outwardly at least) an appearance of health should any evident decline be seen as weakness by both domestic and foreign adversaries.

What this rather—at first sight—rather benign case demonstrates is the complexity of the global system where speculation regarding the health of a leader has the potential to create speculation with regard to future developments within the region. Whilst Kim Jong Un is a rogue and unpredictable leader there is a sense that he could be contained, there is concern was to where the state would go should he suddenly die. Would there be a power vacuum? Would there be internal unrest? Would the resultant leadership be more hostile to western states? What would their attitude to the long-standing conflict with South Korea be?

The Global System

At the core of the analysis of this book is the global system and the risks within it and how it is reshaping the broader business environment. A very broad-based definition of the global system sees it as a construct emerging from the globalizing political, social, and economic forces in which the main human created (both tangible and intangible) and naturally occurring resources exhibit globality. This global system is shaped by the interaction between a series of agents operating at the multiple scales (see above) namely states, corporate entities, international inter-governmental organizations, and non-governmental bodies. The systemic approach imbibes a belief that these interactions (whether tacit or explicit) stimulate mutual interdependence between agents operating (both implicitly and explicitly—see ▶ Box 2.1) across political borders. This ties the existence and sustenance of the global system to the broad-based process of globalization. Whilst globalization is normally assumed to be defined in economic terms, these commercial drivers have rippled out of the economic system into other sub-systems (see below). Moreover, the late twentieth/early twenty-first-century trend towards hyper-globalization based on the interface between rapidly evolving technology and liberal markets which increased the penetration and speed of efficacy of these forces with the respective sub-systems (see below). The trend towards hyper-globalization towards the latter stages of the twentieth and the formative stages of the twenty-first century was characterized by the intensification of global flows across a wider space and broader range of activities at faster speed than previous episodes of the process. These will be addressed more fully within the respective sections below.

The logic of the development of these links was that globalization is a public good. The form and intensity of international links and the speed with which they can occur can deliver social and economic benefits through opening up these systems to outside influences and knowledge promoting innovation and change. This belief underscores how the diversity of ideas can alter the trajectory of human development. It is these global links that spread human knowledge. It also—by creating the opportunity for distributed development—sought to promote system resilience allowing for the global system to have recourse to alternative resource should one component of the system or sub-system fail (see below).

At the core of globalization (and thus of the process of a global system) is global interconnectedness. However, it is not simply that spatially disparate parts of the global system are interconnected (there has to greater or lesser degree been some interconnection) it is that these links are wider (across more forms of activity), deeper (i.e., impact upon more states and socio-economic strata within any state), and faster (i.e., that these interactions happen with ever-increasing velocity) than ever before. This highlights that globalization is not an either-or process but a graduated process that varies across time and space. Levels of inter-state protectionism can ebb and flow with domestic political sentiment and whilst the technology facilitating the velocity of flows is established it can run up against border barriers which also inhibit its ability to penetrate state space. Globalization is also a process without an end state. A truly global economic, political, and social systems are for a mix of practical as well as political economy reasons elusive. Thus, the state of and volume of interactions within the global system is variable over time and space. The global system—due to the nature of globalization—has been characterized of varying levels of intensity between and within the component sub-systems. Importantly links between the sub-systems and agents are not random and intermittent but frequent and structured. This reflects we live in system of flows where those flows are recognized as legitimate and based on end-to-end certainty and reliability.

It can be argued that the global system is again at a turning point with the seeming inevitability of hyperglobalism (i.e., ubiquitous and ever intensifying global interaction) being challenged with a more restrained process. In part this has been driven—as we shall see throughout this book—by the risk created by this hyperglobalism for civil society, states, and businesses from this process. What is emerging—as a consequence of this altered risk perception—is a more managed form of globalization as a direct result of agents (mainly state based) seeking to manage and control the risks that emerge from it. This contravenes the hyperglobalist consensus that the state is rendered irrelevant by the power of the market- this consensus has been eroded by on-going crises (see ▶ Box 1.1) and emergent risk scenarios within the hyperglobal systems (see the respective chapters within this book). Though, of course, the reality was always that markets were never as unconstrained and as all powerful as the narrative suggested. These were only as legitimate so far as the consensus that underpinned them held. The notion that the globalization is driven by modernity and the export of western (market-based) capitalism is being challenged by new forms of globalization based around alternative (increasingly state based) forms of globalization. This will change the form and function of the global system. The global system can be analysed along two dimensions: structure and operation. The former looks at the different components (or sub-systems of the global system), the latter at the interactions within and between these sub-systems.

The Structure of the Global System

It is widely accepted that the global system comprises of five sub-systems: four developed by human activity the other naturally occurring but heavily influenced by those developed by humanity. These sub-systems are as follows.

The ecological system: this comprises the atmosphere (air), the biosphere (life), the hydrosphere (water), cryosphere (frozen water), the pedosphere (soil), and the troposphere (topography). These components interact with each other for the purposes of the exchange and transformation of the materials and energy within each sub-system. It is these interactions that form the basis of the aforementioned ecological system. This ecological system is at the core of human activity for it is the habitat humanity occupies and whose state is a main driver in human existence and development.

The economic system: this is the conventional focus of business analysis and comprises those commercial activities by agents (business, consumers, governments, etc.) that take place within and between demarcated borders of states. The systemic component reflects that economic activity within and between states occurs through the interaction between these agents to create economic goods and services. The preference is for the economic system to be stable and predictable; the more it veers away from these facets the more the spillover into broad systemic instability becomes an issue. This spans both domestic and international economic systems as economic flows are at the core of the borderless hyperglobal system.

The technological system: this exists as the interface between human and natural systems and comprises the intentional designing of components to perform a specific activity with the purpose of negating further human input in terms of design or any other action. The global dimension reflects that such technology operates across borders both by design and functionality. This functionality is based on the capability of the interacting technological components to transform, store, and control both naturally occurring and human created resources (both tangible

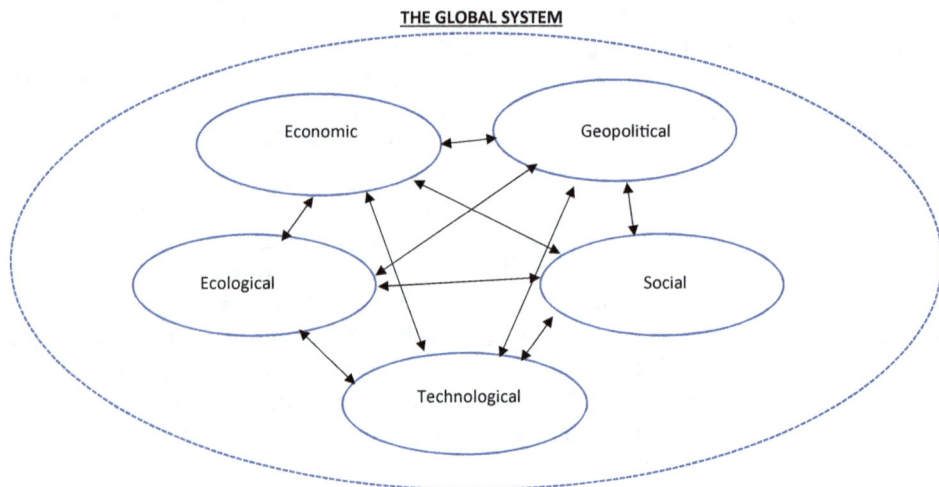

Fig. 1.2 The global system and its component sub-systems

and intangible) to enable the fulfilment of a given task. The technological system is on an unknown trajectory with still unknown impacts notably how it influences the evolving human condition.

The social system: this represents the sum of human interaction and the rules and institutions that govern and provide order to such relationships. In a global system, these social systems are normally defined with regard to issues as culture which are shared by group nominally defined as the nation. These systems extend internationally as humans migrate (permanently or temporarily) but also as shared cultural norms and trends cross borders and extend into overlap lapping domains between states.

The political system: in any state the political system represents the collective set of formal institutions that shape the process of governance. This process decides how decisions are made and implemented and who makes them. This reflects not just the formal institutions of the state but also the rules under which the state functions. The systemic elements of the political system reflect the interaction between and within these institutions of the state to shape governance and control of the system. The nature of international relations is that these national political systems interact often through inter-governmental organizations to aid the management of the global system.

These sub-systems are underpinned by an infrastructure system that provides the physical links between these systems that facilitates the interaction between them (see ◘ Fig. 1.2). These infrastructures include economic (transport, energy, and information), social (education, healthcare), and social (for example governance rules). These are important as disruption to these disrupts flows and global connectivity. These infrastructures represent a second level risk as their disruption is often a legacy of an event within one of the main sub-systems identified above such as shifting political sentiment, extreme weather, terrorism, etc. Nonetheless this is an important risk in its own right (see ► Chapter 9).

The Operation of the Global System

There are two components to the operation of the global system. The first is that it is characterized by complexity and—second—by concentration.

Complexity

The complexity of the Global System is born of the aforementioned understanding that none of the above sub-systems exists and operates as a standalone system but interacts with other components of the system. Notionally this is created by the intensity, extensity, and velocity of the cross border interactions and that these interactions create interdependencies not just between the different sub-systems but also across multiple scales within and across the component parts of the global system. In this sense, complexity refers to a structure with multiple participants each possessing multiple links with a multitude of other parties who in turn have links with a multitude of agents and so on. The conceptualizes the operation of the global system as a network of multiple agents engaged in on-going multiple interactions in a multitude of locations engaged in a multitude of tasks. From any single point in the global system, an agent is subject to processes within first order links (i.e., direct links) but also becomes vulnerable to impacts upon successive links where indirect links (I.e., those links to the first firms order links) are central to agent performance and wellbeing.

The dynamics of the global system reflect that it is subject to an on-going process of change created by events that change dynamics within the system. These have been encapsulated via the notions of the butterfly effect and defect created by positive and negative feedback loops. These feedback loops within the Global System reflect actions, trends, and events within one system spread into another sub-system creating a range of outcomes within each sub-system but also for the system as a whole. Such interconnectivity between systems at multiple scales underscores that accounting for how this complexity impacts upon individual actors within it becomes difficult to assess. Whilst these global forces can offer benefit in terms of system resilience (see below) it can also become difficult to disentangle cause and effect within economic, political, and social systems. Thus, as a result complexity makes risk within systems more difficult to predict.

Concentration

Notions of complexity are suggested of a global system that operates in a self-organizing, decentralized fashion with no central means of control. No centralization does not mean that there is no concentration of activity within it and that all parts of the system are of equal importance in its operation. Concentration within the Global System refers to the manner with which system (or sub-system) operation depends upon a single component within it to sustain global flows within and between components of the system. This is reflected in the extent to which the efficacy of certain aspects of the operation of sub-system depends upon activity which is concentrated in a limited number of hubs with a high intensity of interactions between them. The emergence of such hubs can be market driven, the result of geostrategic expediency or simply a result of geography. In economic systems, these effects are most evident notably in terms of global logistical, energy, finance, and information systems where resources and capacity are heavily geographically concentrated with more activities and agents all located in close proximity. The benefit of concentration is that it allows for the benefits from economies of scale. These hubs can act as a direct simulant to cross border interactions by enabling ease of connectivity across national political, economic, and social systems. Thus, where human activity becomes concentrated, so complexity follows. This has to balance against the fact that these hubs can create negative systemic effects if their capacity to process global flows was disrupted. The more concentrated a set of interactions are, the higher the degree of risk of complexity catastrophe where singular events create systemic cascades as a higher share of the systemic interactions will be impacted (see Case Study 1.2). This means its cost on the efficiency of the Global System will be higher. These are explored in more detail in ▶ Chapter 9.

> **Case Study 1.2: Globalization and Superspreading—The Case of COVID-19**
>
> Globalization was- according to a prevailing narrative—meant to be always and everywhere a good thing. It is evident that such sweeping statements have fallen into disrepute under closer examination. This was evident within the 2019–2022 COVID pandemic when the forces of globalization were seen as a major driver behind the rate of expansion of the virus. The spread reflected systemic risk within the global system created by the physical expansion and intensity of interaction across transportation systems. One of the major drivers behind the rapid spread of the COVID virus was the existence of `super-spreaders'. These are locations (or hubs) within the global transportation systems where there is a high degree of interaction between, and turnover of people combined with their rapid dispersal throughout the global system. These are airports, train stations, and seaports where several routes converge to a single point where passengers then change vehicles and/or modes for their onward journey. The close and rapid interaction between large number of people allowed for the rapid transmission of the disease (a higher transmission than would normally be expected) and allowed it to rapidly spread spatially at a quicker rate than would normally be expected. This was compounded by the fact that in using transport systems users spend a sustained period in proximity to other users. The more and longer a space is shared the higher the risk of transmission especially where these spaces are enclosed.
>
> Aviation has long been seen as a super spreader of viruses simply due to the nature of the mode of travel and of the infrastructure used at termination points. What the global system learned from COVID—and its rapid spread—was that as much as transport hubs can aid the rapid mobility of people, they also have a negative side where they allow the detrimental effects of globalization to be rapidly spread throughout the system. These trends were also evident in cruise liners and other passenger intensive maritime systems where the high level of interaction between users in an enclosed and isolated environment was a prime source of the spread of COVID.
>
> In the initial phases of the spread of COVID, it was evident that those locations with a high degree of connectivity to China were initially the largest states impacted. The central role of global transport hubs was highlighted that as

the disease spread there was a surge in cases in the United Arab Emirates which was out with what was normal in the region. This was due to the existence of the Dubai air hub. The sharp rise in cases in Iran was more due to point to point interactions between Iran and China. The spread of COVID from China therefore reflected patterns of trade and investment. Those states that had higher levels of interaction with China in trading terms saw higher levels of infection than those states that did not. Thus, functional proximity rather than geographical proximity drove the nature of the spread. That is where there was intense interaction with the state at the source of the spread there were higher rates of infection. This reinforced role of hubs as sources of infection as these were places where globalization intensified where meetings were held, etc. The spatial organization of globalization drove the patterns of the diffusion of COVID.

There is little doubt that COVID-19 was the first pandemic of the global era. It used established global connectivity accelerated through transportations super spreaders to gain a rapid speed of transmission. The pattern of transmission reflected the nature of the globalization. The circulation of people especially where they converged on major transport hubs enabled the rapidity and shaped the pattern of this spread. At the time of writing (Autumn 2021), the long-term legacy of this impact upon the movement of people has yet to be fully understood. There are doubts as to the extent that the hyper mobility of the hyper-globality will ever be able to return unchecked.

Global Trends and Global Risk

These short-term dynamics of operation are also underpinned by long-term processes of change within the global system. Global trends are meta-level processes emerging from within and as a result of the operation and inter-operation of the global system and its component parts. These trends are meta in the sense that impact upon multiple states and other agents irrespective of their locality. These trends are known or anticipated processes of change within the global system (and its sub-systems). These trends are likely to evolve in an expected fashion (and impacted agents can be expected to adapt accordingly with the system exhibiting the necessary resilience in expectation of the trend (see below)) but can be subject to sudden ruptures when tensions within it build up creating a 'tipping point'. Such events can reinforce anticipated trends, speed up its anticipated evolution, or potentially open up new paths for the evolution of the sub-system and thus for the global system as an entirety. If the event is large enough it can cascade throughout and change system functioning and/or structure. These processes are only a risk to the extent the effects are unanticipated and the extent to which they stimulate the need for a response to which an agent cannot and will not adapt. This recognizes that the global system is subject to change and that this change can occur in both an evolutionary and revolutionary fashion.

The nature of the trends is shaped by the evolution of complexity and concentration within the respective sub-systems of the global system. These trends can emerge within a single sub-system but connectivity between these systems means that they can shape pattern of evolution within other systems. Thus, for example,

US-China rivalry has direct links between the evolution of global economic and political systems but has spillover effects upon technological and ecological systems. Of course, the underlying trend shaping the analysis of this book is the globalization of the respective systems. Much of the popular narrative has surrounded the globalization of the economic system but this process has overlapped with increased globality within the other global sub-systems. Alongside these are those trends within sub-systems where globality is built-in notably ecological systems. These processes highlight that these processes can emerge both as a result of discretionary acts (i.e., the act of removing trade barriers) as well as those that binding upon the agent by the nature of the structure and operation of the sub-system.

All agents are embedded in the global system, and they seek to evolve with this system to ensure the sustainability and persistence of their actions. The need to maintain fitness with their environment whilst seeking to anticipate how that environment is changing creates an adaptive tension for agents. It is within this context that the interface between global trends and global risk starts to be formed. These are largely through five processes:

- That firms do not adapt to their changing context causing adaptive tensions to rise and inhibiting agent development and create self-imposed risks of operation.
- That trends continue in an anticipated manner until a tipping point is attained which generates a sudden unanticipated process of change.
- That anticipated trends evolve in an unanticipated manner creating a new trajectory for the known trend.
- That knowledge of system structure is not fully understood and where singular non-descript event creates unanticipated cascade effects.
- There is shock to the system created by a random unanticipated event that—through sub-system connectivity—spreads throughout the rest of the system across most if not all agents at all scales.

The nexus between global trends and agent adaption begins to define the nature of global systemic risk where failure to adapt, anticipate, and/or understand meta-level trends can—via inter-agent connectivity—create system wide impacts. Thus, whilst global connectivity offers benefits it can also raise risk within the system. Often such risks lie deep within the system and can emerge from seemingly isolated events. Goldin and Mariathasan (2014) refer to these as 'the butterfly defect' where moderate singular events cascade throughout the system based on feedback loops that accentuate their impact. The fact that these risks are not specific to a single agent or process but are felt across the global system and sub-systems underscores their systemic nature. These are driven by the aforementioned complexity and also by forces of concentration. These forces make risk within complex systems more difficult to describe and understand. This means agents face a major disruption to their activity which requires a major adaptation to their (as well as the systems) functioning. In extreme cases, the singularity could create an existential crisis for agents due to the rapidity and scale of the adaptation required. The challenge of such singularities is their unpredictability and rarity to the extent that they have a low probability of occurring that agent simply do not prepare for them. Risk is no longer linear. Instead, it is a series of events one perceptibly following on from the other to the extent that the effects and processes were predictable and avoidable.

Complexity changes this relationship. This reflects how hyperglobalism (and its alterations to the speed and depth of cross border interactions) has radically altered the risk landscape where global risk can be accentuated and accelerated even before it is fully understood. Thus, single point failures can create contagion of failure throughout the system that threatens its stability, structure, and/or operation. These risks are termed by Goldin and Mariathasan (2014) as vector risks created by the increased interaction between agents.

Alongside these interactivity driven vector risks are those created by the density of specific, core global activity within limited localities which open up the prospect that the disruption to one will disrupt the entire system or sub-system (see issues of concentration above). This density driven risk pattern has also highlighted the role of 'super-spreaders' as a catalyst for contagion throughout the system which channels and accelerates these risks through the system as flows are concentrated at a single point that then disperses then throughout the rest of the system (see Case Study 1.2). These systemic risks are highlighted by both their intensity and extensity and by the speed with which they can be transmitted throughout the system. It is not just the volume and intensity of links within global systems (be it aviation, trade, logistics, data, finance) but also that this intensity is growing in its extensity with new nodes being added to these systems all the time whether it be through interconnecting cities, logistics hubs, data centres. Thus, risk within system increases the more activity within a globally complex system is concentrated within a limited number of nodes. For example, the more aviation is concentrated in a few core hubs, the more data is stored within a limited number of data centres, etc. This concentration reflects the benefits of global scale within the global system but also exposes vulnerability to the system as the more limited specific activities are located within a limited number of geographic centres the more that the system is vulnerable to disruption to singularities within a specific location and that location specific shock generating systemic impacts. These themes are reflected within ◘ Table 1.3.

The Nature of Global Risk

These operational and structural issues and their nexus with global trends allow for global risk to be defined as those endangerments (both known and unknown) to state, corporate, and civil society activity sourced from the operation of the global system. These are risks that cannot be isolated to a single global sub-system (or a component of one) and which spill over not only between these sub-systems but will also significantly impact upon agents at multiple scalar levels both within and between the component sub-systems. The rise in global risk has become more evident as there is increased interaction between these systems as human population grows and the resultant activity impacts upon these other systems. The larger the demographic concentration in any given space the greater the impact upon the natural, social, political, and economic systems.

When viewing global risk, the focus is upon singular events that disrupt global system operation. Individual events emerge from within the system and have the potential to become transmitted, accelerated, and accentuated to become systemic risks. These events have the capability to temporarily disrupt the normal operation and/or structure of the global system or could even be a precursor to long-term

Table 1.3 Global sub-systems and risk profile

	Indicative concentration risk	Indicative complexity risk
Economic	Financial activity focused on three core centres (New York, London, and Tokyo)	Logistic transmission depends upon a flow through a number of core bottlenecks (see ▶ Chapter 9)
Ecological	The Amazon rain forest—a major carbon sink—destruction makes a major contribution to the emission of Carbon Dioxide and contributing to global climatic instability	Global Atmospheric systems create localized risks through extreme weather events
Political	Geopolitical power becomes concentrated in a single state creating risk for states that are hostile to its hegemony	Political instability within one state creates localized events in another state
Social	Increased concentration of populations within cities increases the risk of epidemics	Increased level of diversity of population leads to threats to social cohesion
Technological	Semi-conductor manufacturing is concentrated in South Asia notably Taiwan	Products are based on modular components operated via Just in time systems

change within it. These may be related to broader trends or may simply be the result of a singular event that is unrelated to any other process on-going within the global system such as unique human behaviour or localized topographical event (such as a landslip or flood). These singular events can often be caused by long-term events. This is not to discount the possibility that singular event can be totally random (especially at the micro level) but the cascade effects of high scale processes (i.e., those formed at meta and macro levels) are arguably more evident through connected events. That these processes are known and the singular events unanticipated reflects a key adaptive tension within the global system.

Frequently the impact of an event (its scale and severity) can be through the failure of the firms to fully adapt business models to the process (see ▶ Chapter 2) suggests that the risk is known but that its timing is ambiguous. Table 1.4 highlights the link between trends and events in the Global System. This underscores that no single event can often be treated as isolated but is created as a derivative of broader set of processes. Single one-off events that are unrelated to systemic processes tend time limited 'disasters' that are collectively experienced delivering negative impacts upon all parties. Of more longer-term duration are crises which are on-going processes that are often short term in duration that can impact upon system operation. The challenge for business in each of these events or processes (even if they are anticipated) is a loss of fitness between the business model and its operating context (see ▶ Chapter 2). This results from the unpredictability of the operating environment where the timing and impact of events and processes are unknown as discrete meso-level interconnections can render inter-firm links ambiguous.

Risks are normally defined by the sub-system within which they emerged. Nonetheless there is no universal categorization of risk partly because any single risk can

Table 1.4 Examples of sub-systemic links in a complex global system

	Ecological	Economic	Political	Social	Technological
Ecological		Climate change leads to economic disruption due to extreme weather events	Extreme weather leads to political unrest due to water shortages and food supply constraints	Exposure to climate events and processes leads to social disorder	Climate forces process of change by eroding old technological paradigm
Economic	Increased economic activity causes ecological degradation		Economic instability can fuel political unrest	Rising social risks created by high levels of economic inequality	Increased trade has increased utilization of information networks for data exchange
Political	Increased political uncertainty leads to ecological damage	The rise of populism can give rise to economic instability through erratic policy actions		Political agitation can fuel social risk and disruption	Extremists use of technology to sow political unrest
Social	Expanding populations place pressure upon natural environment as competition for resources increases	Increased migratory flows increased risk of global transmission of diseases resulting in economic lockdown to limit transmission	Social unrests and political uncertainty can be directly related. Populism has been facilitated by social issues		The challenge of how social media can be used to ferment social unrest, or the social disruption caused by attacks upon critical infrastructure
Technological	The need for rare earths to support new technology can lead to ecological degradation but can also militate damaging effects of activity upon ecological systems	Spreads and increases risk of economic contagion	Can reinforce social exclusion by limited access to digital technological cresting a digital divide	Technology aids political messaging to support or supress political activity	

have multiple impacts across a number of the sub-systems with the tipping point occurring across more than a single sub-system. The book uses as its base analysis the five most commonly identified risks (i.e., economic, political, technological, environment, and social). On top of these five widely accepted risks is added a sixth—infrastructure—which reflects the embedded links between and within these systems upon which these respective systems depend for their operation. These broad categorizations are defined as follows:

Economic Risk: typical of economic risks are asset bubbles, economic downturns, commodity prices shocks, and generic price instability (see ▶ Chapter 4).

Ecological Risk: these include extreme weather events, damage to the environment from human activity, and loss of biodiversity (see ▶ Chapter 6).

Geopolitical Risk: these risks include terrorism, inter-state relations, and the spread of weapons of mass destruction (see ▶ Chapter 5).

Social Risk: these risks include pandemics, social fractures, long-term unemployment, and intergenerational conflict (see ▶ Chapter 7).

Technological Risk: these risks include cyber risks, digital exclusion, and the failure of digital infrastructure (see ▶ Chapter 8).

Infrastructure Risk: these risks include the failure of state-based critical infrastructure system, global logistical channels, and core transportation hubs (see ▶ Chapter 9).

Box 1.1: Twenty-First-Century Events That Impact Upon Global Flows

Over the past two decades, the seemingly relentless progression of globalization has hit a few potholes that raised doubt about and has stimulated on-going debate with regard to how far globalization should progress. Anyone of these events was unlikely to be examined as a singular event that undermined the legitimacy of emergent globality, but each added to an emerging view that there were limits to the progressive onset of globalization and that each called into question how far the globalization of factor and product markets should progress. Whilst the list below is far from definitive, it does underscore key events that have drafted an increasingly hostile narrative to the forms of globality.

Security Crisis 2001
The catalyst of this crisis were the 9/11 attacks upon the US. The importance of this event for the global system has only really been evident in the years that followed the 9/11 attacks. The first and immediate consequence was how the US effectively shut down large parts of the international airspace as a security measure as it grounded all flights within and heading to the US. The medium-term legacy was the US that was more hostile to international flows. The US saw global logistical system as a security weakness and increased the policing of this process under its Container Security Initiative. Moreover, it was openly hostile to investment in its critical infrastructure from states that it judged were actually or potentially hostile. This was evident in the attempted acquisition of US ports facilities by Dubai Ports which was blocked by the US government. This was important as the US was the economic superpower which drive the progressive globalization throughout the twentieth century. Longer term, there

has been increased hostility to migration and overseas investment and trade. The legacy of the 9/11 attacks is arguably an increased suspicion of the globalization and how this process has weakened the US both in terms of economic and political security. This is something US populists have openly capitalized upon.

Global Financial Crisis of 2007–2009

The Global Financial Crisis (GFC) represented the end of the high watermark of globalization. It underlined more than any other single event the risks embedded within global systems. Whilst the causes of this crisis have been explored extensively explored but were ultimately sourced from the sub-prime mortgage market in the US where falling house prices within this market—due to the securitization of these mortgages—led to the values of these assets being worthless than the loans held upon theme which rapidly eroded the balance sheets of a few financial institutions creating liquidity problems creating a banking crisis. The state had to enter the system to support these banks in so doing added substantially to public debt. In this way, the financial crisis led to a sovereign debt crisis the interdependence between financial and state sectors created a 'doom loop' as banks bought the debt issued by the state to support the banks which fell in value as more was issued which then fell in value which worsened the bank position which required more support from the state. The legacy of this crisis was a loss of confidence in the operation of the global system especially when its behaviour was difficult to predict. It was also raising issues with regard to the popular legitimacy of the global capitalist system which took excessive risks and managed to private the profits but socialized the losses. The result was a popular movement to limit the excesses of the system.

The COVID-19 Pandemic of 2019–2022

Emerging from the wet markets of central China, this respiratory disease spread rapidly across the globe aided by the global transportation system and the consequent rapid movement of people. From the first outbreaks in November 2019, the disease spread quickly to other states to the extent that was declared a global pandemic in March 2020. By October 2022, there were an estimated 618 million cases and 6.54 million confirmed deaths globally. The immediate impact of this pandemic was to severely curtail economic activity as lockdowns inhibited social and economic interactions both within and between states. In terms of international business, the most immediate impact was a curtailment of international travel severely hitting the tourist and hospitality industries. The global logistics sector was also impacted as the initial reduction in demand led to a mothballing of capacity which only slowly resumed though with periodic issues of congestion due to China's zero-COVID policy leading to a reduction of capacity at its major container ports. The longer-term impact is still difficult to determine as the system is still adjusting to the new health requirements for cross border movement. The crisis further underlined the vulnerabilities to states created by the hyperglobal system and the rapid and expansive movement of people engendered within it.

The Russia–Ukraine Conflict—2022–Present

The final crisis to be examined is the current (at the time of writing) conflict between Russia and the Ukraine. The source of the conflict was long-standing hostility between these states which resulted in Russia invading Ukraine in early 2022. What was quickly evident was that this seemingly localized conflict would rapidly spread into the region and out into the broader global system. The most immediate impact was upon energy systems where the EU—which took a hostile stance to the invasion—depended upon Russia for a large share (40 per cent) of its energy. Russia's immediate countermeasure was to begin to restrict supplies of energy to Europe to seek to change its attitude to the invasion by precipitating an energy crisis. This occurred as Europe rapidly sought to wean itself from Russian energy. This had a knock-on effect of rising energy prices globally as Europe's rush to find new sources bid up the price globally. Thus, a regional energy crisis became a global issue. This energy problem was compounded by the fact that both Russia and Ukraine are major suppliers of commodity foodstuffs and fertilizer. This supply was curtailed by the conflict causing these flows to be disrupted creating a spoke in commodity food prices. These problems were especially acute for many developing states. Whilst the conflict is still on-going at the time of writing, the legacy for global systems already appears clear. It is already evident that the global energy system will fragment with many states moving towards increased domestic generation. This trend is also evident in other areas where firms were forced to divest their assets in Russia and where states will also seek increased domestic security in food production.

All these (both in singularity and in combination) have highlighted the vulnerabilities to states, businesses, and citizens from the operation of the global system. This is not to argue that the system is inherently flawed but that its management requires a recognition of its complexity where single events can spread throughout the system. The long-term effects upon these events are difficult to discern but they have driven a sustained push against the forces of hyper-globality. As such, we should expect a new restrained globalization system to emerge where states concern with regard to security, control and cohesion are at the forefront of state strategy.

Systemic Resilience in the Face of Global Complexity

There is no inevitability that these events and trends need to disrupt the system. There is the possibility that the system could adapt to adsorb these challenges without a fundamental rethink to the nature of this operation. Much of the concern as to whether the system can adapt to these challenges is based upon the notion that pre-existing forms of governance are not always appropriate for the evident complexity for the global system. This is compounded by the perception of powerlessness by individual agents or groups of agents in the face of this complexity and is a powerful factor shaping global risk (see Table 1.5). The belief that conventional methods cannot or have limited impact upon such complex forces has been a powerful factor in agents seeking to reassert control over the global system through state-based mechanisms of change. This is a pushback against globalism and a passive acceptance that these forces could work to the advantages of all. These forces are addressed elsewhere, but they do reflect aspects of resilience as to how systems

◘ Table 1.5   Systemic resilience

Sub-system	Nature of resilience
Economic	Capability of economic system to maintain and/or resume economic interactions and structures when challenged by external threat to the extent that expectations of prosperity and growth/development are maintained
Political	Sustenance of political stability and certainty when faced the internal or external threats
Ecological	Capability of natural ecosystems and habitats to sustain their behaviour and condition when faced with the impact of human activity
Social	Maintenance of social cohesion when challenged by shifting economic, political, and technological threats—ability of group and communities to cope with external threats
Technological	Ability to maintain acceptable technological competences and capabilities when subject to severe disruptions to its critical processes and the systems which support them

adapt from the bottom up to the possible legitimization crisis. The need for the resilience to such pressure creates further adaptive tensions upon the global system.

Resilience refers to the capability of the global system (or component sub-systems) to resist, respond, and adapt successfully to the pressures places upon it by unanticipated events and trends. Resilience means that any event or process does not fundamentally alter system stability, operation, or form for any prolonged period of time. Resilience is normally expressed in terms of some sense of normal/acceptable functioning being maintained or restored within a set time frame. Thus, resilience is the capability of the system to adapt to the pressures upon it from changes within and between the sub-systems so as to promote system stability and continuity in a context shaped by dynamic change which has the capability to alter/impact any part of the system. This revolves around one or more three facets:

— That the system to robust and resistance to events and trends to this extent that its operation is essentially unaltered by them.
— The system is impacted by change but that it can recover back to usual means of operation within an acceptable time frame.
— Adapting its operations to the changes in the contextual condition in which it operates and thus develops new features/facets accordingly.

Overall, the degree of resilience is dependent upon the efficacy of an event/trend, where within system it impacts and the preparedness of critical component. This is often created through systemic redundancy to enable the system to cope with pressure on capacity/capabilities elsewhere within the system. Resilience does not simply reflect redundancy as a spare resource within the system to mitigate any disruption but also the ability of agents operating within the system to utilize available resources to militate against the risk to the system from events and/or processes. This reflects that resilience comes from effective governance; the ability to know what to do in the face of a disruptive event. This indicates the logic of governance for the system lies at the metalevel or between states. That fragmented systems undermine systemic resilience. The need to avoid different agents pulling in different directions. The inability to deal with the risks created systemic risks—so-called governance gaps—has drawn in a more diverse array of civil society agents often NGOs to deal with the consequences of these risks. As noted by the array of NGOs involved within the refugee crisis for example.

Resilience reflects a desire to make the system more predictable and of knowing how to act when the unpredictable happens. Whilst trends can be anticipated and actions planned accordingly, events (whether related to these long-term trends or whether existing as singularities) are more difficult as they are by their nature characterized by higher levels of uncertainty. Thus, any event creates a scenario whereby the changes in the condition of the systems operation means it is less effective and desirable than before then it will not be deemed resilient. Such definitions are evidently subject to preferences about what is desirable. Also, the process of desirability in one sub-system might create undesirability in another. Thus, adapting to sudden sharp rise in unemployment might have consequences for the natural environment. This reflects that resiliency is complicated by the fact that complexity makes resilience difficult due to conflicts between sub-systems.

Global risk suggests that resilience is a system issue, and it is shaped by the resource availability of agents operating at all levels. Though not all parts of the system are given the same attention as global risk is a derivative of the adaptability of critical components of the system where flows are concentrated and exhibit interconnectedness with other parts of the system. In short, not all parts of the system are created equal. Not all parts will need to exhibit the same resilience and nor will each attract the same degree of attention amongst policymakers. It is about ensuring the vulnerable part, so the system is prepared (e.g., flood proof or earthquake resistant, etc.). For the global risks, this implies meta-actions between governments, etc., as states cannot isolate themselves from the advent of risks. These then become an issue at all levels within and between states and these events cascade there impacts throughout the system. The ability to develop a system wide response depends upon multilateral solution as any risk by nature would spread across borders and between agents irrespective of their location. This depends upon activities at micro–meso, and macro levels all having capabilities to adapt their strategies actions and have a long a degree of preparedness to any global event that occurs within a given time frame. In a fragmented system, risk could normally be managed on a state-by-states basis or on a firm-by-firm level. Rising interconnectedness means that risks cannot be isolated at any level and spill over between levels (see ◘ Table 1.6). These themes are reflected upon in the conclusions in ▶ Chapter 10.

Systemic Sustainability

Whilst notions of resilience reflect the short-term issues with regard to capability of the system (and of sub-systems embedded within it) to cope with crises within them, with regard to longer-term issues the focus is upon systemic sustainability. Naturally issues of sustainability will reflect short-term resilience issues but they also reflect a long-term capacity of the system to adapt to longer-term trends which are known and understood but whose impacts are not always easy to ascertain. In its simplest terms, the notion of sustainability reflects the capability to persist and

Table 1.6 Resilience action at different levels

Level	Primary focus	Example of adaptive action
Micro	Firm, individual	• Render core facilities (factories, etc.) immune to known risk (fire, flood, etc.); • Share information with key stakeholders
Meso	Firms, value networks	• Mutual co-operative agreement to create space capacity within value system so as to improve value system architecture; • share information on impacts which depends upon intensity of links and availability of alternatives (e.g., in supply chains)
Macro	State	• Create redundancy within critical infrastructure systems; public information campaigns
Meta	Inter-state	• Create international norms of actions for all states to ensure uniform response

exist. This links the ability of the agent to adapt to the environment to maintain fitness with it. This is often framed in terms of the net contribution or loss of resources (natural, financial, social, etc.). The notion of sustainability is that the system and the actions of agents within it either makes a net contribution to systemic resources or is at best neutral. This reflects the capacity to adapt to the pressures that operate within a system thus issues such as changing political sentiment, economic behaviour, ecosystems, technology, and social processes can all later the operating context of business. To be sustainable, agents need to adapt to these processes.

Consequently, the concept of sustainability is underpinned by the notion not simply of on-going systemic evolution but also of stability of the system to sustain the population of agents within it whether they be economic, social, and/or political agents. Thus, adaption and change within systems should:
— Adopt technologies that promote resource efficiency.
— Utilize natural resources so as to not lead to a net depletion and therefore undermine its ability to act as a habitat for multiple species.
— Have social systems that facilitate the formation of social capital enabling stability and cohesion.
— Engage in activity that enhance the availability of economic resources.
— Adapt activity to allow social networking and maintain development of social capital.

Through these adaptations the aim is for the creation of a sustainable system who attributes stay within an acceptable range of states. Thus, the process of sustainability reflects that any system does not consume too much or produce too little resource. As much as resource depletion can undermine systemic sustainability it can also be challenged by growing too fast and consuming too many resources over a short period of time. The other danger is that—due to the mutually supporting nature of these systems—the promotion of sustainability within one will create unsustainability in another. This has been at the forefront of the green movement where economic growth has been at the price of sustainable ecological systems. Ultimately unsustainability emerges when a system burns through resources quicker than they can replenished. The fear is that a high burn rate of resources leads to the potential collapse of these systems. This is fed by instability and uncertainty with regard to the operations of these systems. Ultimately unsustainability of the systems will be driven by:

- Sustained net resource depletion.
- Limited resource renewal that occurs at that is below resource depletion.
- Resource generation below expectations and/or requirements.
- Resource starvations and deprivation.
- Overuse of existing resource.

These challenges for the sustainability of the system can be a number of drivers such as ignorance of the adaptive tension promoting unsustainability, poor human capital, obsolescence and senescence of the agent, too much complexity and separation from contextual drivers. These themes on systemic sustainability are reflected upon in ▶ Chapter 10.

Conclusion

Risk has become embedded within the global system as it has grown more complex. The risk is evident at all levels within the interdependent multi-scalar sub-systems which form the global system. This renders the global system a much more difficult system to predict in terms of the nature of its operation. This has become evident where seemingly random events can generate a cascade effect that can impact upon multiple levels within multiple systems. Each sub-system can be a source of risks that impacts both upon its own and inter-related system functioning. The ability of the system to adapt to the risks is shaped by inbuilt resilience which enables the system to maintain functioning and move towards long-term sustainability.

Discussion Questions

1. Do you agree the proposition that business is facing increased level of risk?
2. Do you think that risks within the global system could increase scepticism towards globalization?
3. How could businesses seek to militate the risks they face?

Activities

Taking a business with which, you are familiar, identify the main risk that business faces and how it seeks to lower its exposure to such threats.

Summary

This chapter examined the form and nature of risk within the global system. The chapter noted that with high degrees of interconnectivity, that risk is embedded within the global system and can spread easily and rapidly within the system. This reflects the nature of how the global system has evolved across the main sub-systems which are at the core of how the system is structured. This risk does not merely occur across these sub-systems but also occurs across multiple scales within them.

Key Readings

Goldin, I., & Mariathasan, M. (2014). *The Butterfly Defect*. Princeton University Press.
Held, D., McGrew, A., Goldblatt, D., & Perraton, J. (2000). Global Transformations: Politics, Economics and Culture. In *Politics at the Edge* (pp. 14–28). Palgrave Macmillan, London.
Kay, J., & King, M. (2020). *Radical Uncertainty: Decision-Making for an Unknowable Future* (p. 2020). The Bridge Street Press.
OECD. (2003). *Systemic risks in the 21st Century: An Agenda for Action*. OECD.

Useful Web Sites

World Economic Forum. (2021). Global Risks report. Available at ▶ www.wef.org

The Global Business Model: Business and Embedded Global Risk

© The Author(s), under exclusive license to Springer Nature Switzerland AG 2023
C. Turner, *Global Business Analysis*,
https://doi.org/10.1007/978-3-031-27769-6_2

The nature of the global business environment guarantees that no matter how hard we work to create a stable and healthy organisation, our organisation will continue to experience dramatic changes far beyond our control.

Margaret J. Wheatley
American writer, teacher, speaker, and management consultant

By the end of the chapter, the reader will have an understanding of:
- The form and nature of business models.
- The nature of business model adaptation and resilience.
- The nature of business model risk.
- The structure of business model globality.
- Risks created by business model globality.

Introduction

The business model is at the core of the analysis within this book. It is through this configuration of tangible and intangible assets that the pressures generated by global trends and risks manifest themselves through altering the business' value creating capability. This chapter introduces the framework of the business model and outlines the need for these commercial configurations to be adaptable and resilient to the external pressures upon their commercial sustainability. The chapter then moves onto examine how globality (defined here as the conditions under which firm value creating capabilities are shaped by global processes) impacts upon business models. This is not just simply through an examination of form but also in understanding how these value creating configurations are adapting to global trends and risks.

The Nature of the Business Model

At its most very basic conceptualization, a business can be best understood as a self-sustaining commercial entity. That is, it generates sufficient resources from its activities to cover costs and generate sufficient surplus to ensure corporate sustainability Baden-Fuller et al. (2010). The business model effectively tells the 'story of the business', it informs the observer how the firm seeks to generate value through the interaction and interdependence between the component parts of the business to promote corporate commercial sustainability. Value is—of course—a flexible concept which can be defined by shareholders (i.e., rising share price and capital values) or—as is more likely—a broader set of stakeholders (i.e., not just shareholders but a wider set of parties impacted by the business' commercial activities).

Any business model for any enterprise is unique to that concern reflecting what the business believes is the best way of not only generating value to customers but also in stimulating a transaction because of consumers deciding to value the products and how best the firm can organize itself to ensure this process is maintained and sustained. Thus, the business model represents a flow of resources (both tangible and intangible) within the business and between the business and its operating environment. The value of the business model framework lies in the offers a holistic framework in understanding how the different components of the business fit together to facilitate value creation. The core (highly simplified) model that underpins the analysis within this work is reflected in ◘ Fig. 2.1. This simplified structure seeks to reflect the dynamics within the business system and the mutually supporting nature of this process.

The simplified model of the business model is based around three separate components each of which is linked to the other by resource flows or in its configuration to ensure they are mutually supporting and—therefore—facilitate (or offer the prospect of) commercial financial sustainability. Briefly, the components are as follows.

- *The Value Proposition*: this really is the raison d'etre for the business and is essentially what it offers to its customers that is deemed of value to them as a precursor to stimulate a transaction. This offers a sense of competitive differentiation for the business through facets such as novelty, quality, price, brand, etc. This reflects that the value proposition can be quantitative and/or qualitative and is mutually dependent upon the conditions of, and context set by the operating and marketing dimensions.
- *The Operational Model*: this is the key infrastructure of the business and represents the tangible and intangible assets (including human, financial, physical, and intellectual) that are central to the business enabling and realizing the core value proposition. These include assets such as manufacturing capacity and capability as well as internal processes and procedures that enable the firm to operate for the process of creating value via the initiation and development of prod-

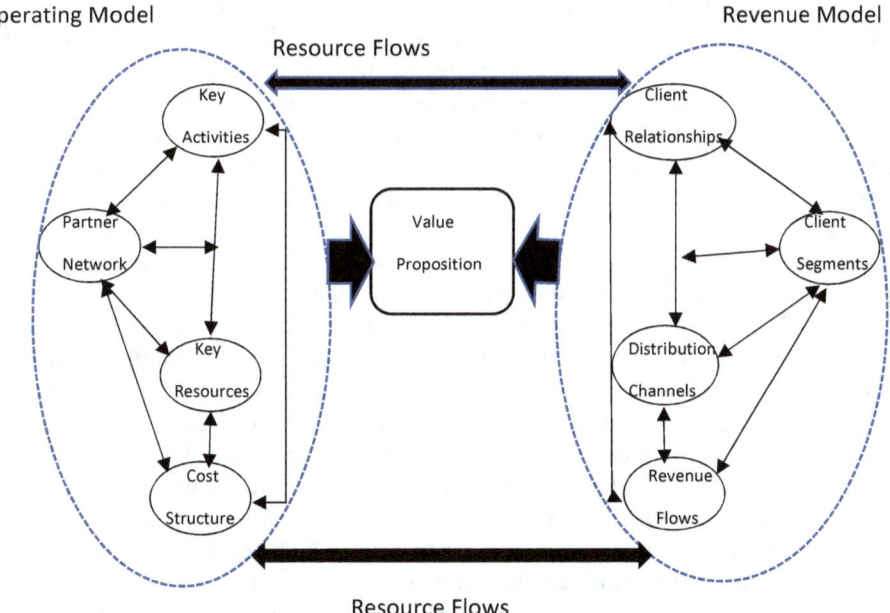

◘ **Fig. 2.1** A simplified business model framework (Adapted from Osterwalder et al. [2005])

ucts/services. This dimension overlaps with an awareness of firm core competences and capabilities that are leveraged through this operating dimension. Increasingly integral to this operating environment is the value networks (see below) in which firms are embedded. These can be extensive and are used by the business to militate risk within the business model enabling the firm to focus upon its core activity. These are explored more fully below.

— *The Revenue Model*: this is the resource generating side of the business. The business uses this aspect to stimulate transactions with its targeted group of customer segments which generates a financial flow from the customer into the business. The flows generated by the interaction between the business can also be extended into flows of information regarding consumer sentiment, after sales service and the creation, maintenance, and development of channels through which the business and its customers interact (such as online and delivery channels). These feed through into the ability to generate sustained revenue streams into the business which in turn reflect the strategies developed with regard to the marketing mix (i.e., pricing, promotion, product, and place). These revenues feedback into the business to support and enable the operational dimension and the credibility/legitimacy of the stated value proposition. These channels reflect that the marketing dimension imposes a transaction cost upon business; thereby underlining the interaction between operational and marketing dimensions.

As business models are transparent and therefore replicable with varying degrees of ease there must be a degree of alignment with corporate strategy to ensure it reinforces and sustains competitive advantage and differentiation. This means that the business model must be configured to support and enable that strategy (e.g., that low-cost strategy has to be supported by low-cost operations, etc.) and that this configuration has to evolve as the strategy evolves. This reflects the importance of adaption in the process of business model configuration and reconfiguration (see below). Thus, a core focal point of strategy is to facilitate the evolution of the business model. Thus, it takes a longer-term perspective between business model fit and its changing environment and seeks to adapt the model accordingly. The business model may be the source of competitive advantage if its components are hard to replicate due to intellectual property right protection, system opacity, or network effects for example.

Business models do not exist as standalone entities but are embedded in more diverse underpinning business systems. This is reflected in ◘ Fig. 2.2 which underlines the links that the business model has with its broader value network (see below). It is worth considering the role of the firm within its broader business ecosystem. This notion of the business ecosystem reflects the dependence of the value creating process of the business model upon organizations to whom the firm has no direct links, but which nonetheless can impact upon its financial sustainability. It underscores the complexity of the firm operations and how the business model needs to coevolve with these actors. In terms of risk, business ecosystems take on an increased salience as they are means through which meta trends and associated risks can be transmitted into the business model. This also underscores the permeability of boundaries of the firm to external events, processes, and actors. These ecosystems are an extension of the notion of the networked enterprise business model where the influence of actors upon the business model extends deep beyond the

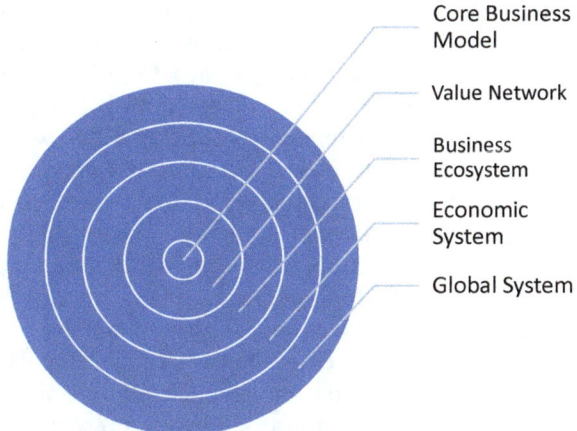

Fig. 2.2 The embeddedness of the business model

first and second order customers and suppliers. This is a holistic, more loosely integrated system of interacting agents. The fact that stakeholders are integrated into the broader business ecosystem reflects holistic approaches and how agents that might otherwise be disconnected or distant from the value creating capabilities of the business can be an influence upon the process.

In reflection of complexity, Fig. 2.2 highlights the mutual embeddedness of business models within the broader economic systems which is turn embedded within a broader global system. This reflects the multi-scalar process of value creation and reflects parallels with the multi-scalar approaches. This embeddedness reflects broader risk context within which businesses operate. It reflects also the multi-scalar nature of value creation and the dependence of this process upon a range of actors and processes beyond the borders of the business model. With regard to the outer layers of the system, the notion of the economic system reflects that business models are embedded within this system and their efficacy as a value creating entity depends upon broad macro conditions within this level of activity. This in turn is influenced by processes within the global system which can create cascade effects into economic system and impact upon the efficacy of the business model.

Value Networks

As per notions of complexity, businesses and their enabling business models do not exist as standalone entities. Businesses are integrated into a wider business ecosystem with which they evolve. More salient are business links to other businesses that form part of or are integral to the value creating process. These are reflected within the existence of value networks based upon interconnection and mutual dependence between business models. Firms utilize these links to collaborate and employ their respective resources and capabilities towards the development and delivery of a good/services that offers value to the end user. In so doing, this enables all parts of the value network to create value. These networks are a firm's constellation of links where there are first (i.e., direct) and second (i.e., indirect) links between the firms creating a mutually dependant value creating system with each firm being a node within this system. First order links are those that have a direct relationship with the firm's business model at the hub of the network; second order relationships are customers of customers, suppliers of suppliers, etc., who do not have a direct relationship with the firm's business model but can impact upon who impact upon its operation through indirect means (see ▶ Box 2.1). As such, value networks can be conceptualized as an ecosystem of companies operating in a strategic configuration to support a given value proposition. The fact that all businesses operate in support of an agreed value proposition indicates the existence of formal agreements between the component business to ensure sustained alignment of objectives.

For the firm, the value network can include a range of partners from suppliers, customers, coalitions, and distribution channels all of which have the capacity of extending the enterprise and its resources. These represent intimate and intense interactions between partners that interconnect their respective business models. These will be unique to the firm and are an exercise in risk mitigation to the firm by seeking to add certainty by creating unique relationships that are known and predictable. It also militates against the need for the firm to fully integrate its value relationships and incur the financial and operational risks that are likely to result from such a structure. This position of the firm within its (as well how it is configured) value network is central to the business model. ◘ Figure 2.3 reflects a simplified value network where strategic vendors and partners integrate to work together (via contracts) to enable the business value chain. These links will involve both tangible and intangible flows to mutually support their own contribution to the value creating process between these businesses.

Value networks represent a shift away from the firm centred business models identified above. They are based upon the creation and embeddedness of a network of businesses. They reflect the dynamics of exchange between businesses and

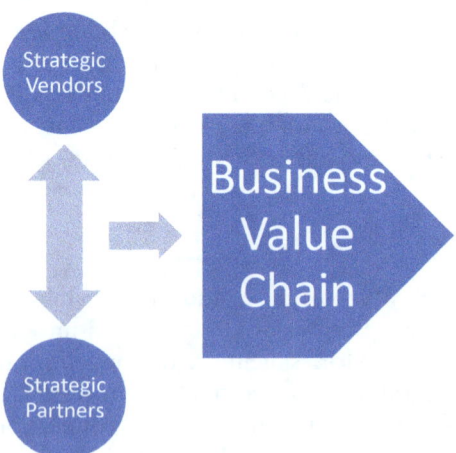

◘ **Fig. 2.3** A simplified value network

how these networks themselves are dynamic as pressures upon them by their operating environment shift. It also reflects the interdependence between firms' respective business models within a process of mutual value creation. The complexities of the business ecosystem could mean that the parameters of the value network could be difficult to define. This reflects the value creating system as identified in ◘ Fig. 2.3. Which reflects that the firms and the extended enterprises are embedded into and have links into a broad business ecosystem and that they need to coevolve with these processes. The more accessible the network is the more the network is open to innovation and change. Evidently closed networks could run the risk of obsolescence if they become unresponsive to external trends and processes. For this reason, there is a need to differentiate between first and second order links.

Case Study 2.1: Apple's Global Value Network for the iPhone

The iPhone was launched in 2007 to much fanfare but behind this high-profile product is an extensive value network that extends across 43 states and six continents. The extensive value network reflects that each product is built from hundreds of different parts each of which is manufactured by a different supplier. For the firm, the advantages of such an approach are based upon maximizing efficiency of supply chains and minimizing inventories. Using specialist suppliers also enables the firm to focus its core competence of design and leave the development of specialist components to other firms who are better able to deliver to the quality expected. Thus, for the iPhone, for example, the camera and screen are developed and manufactured in Japan, parts of battery in China, and key software in Germany.

The challenge for such an extensive value network lies not so much in seeking out the right partners—wherever they maybe—but to develop the product that Apple wants to develop and to ensure that the diverse range of partners interoperate in a manner that appears invisible to the end user. On top of this, there must be sufficient influence over the value network by the firm that the network can adapt to the pressure exerted upon it without undermining the core value proposition to the end user. For the iPhone, this is reflected within the on-going updates to the product to ensure added functionality with each iteration of the product. On top of this, this value chain must handle the surge in demand associated with the introduction of a new version of the iPhone.

The design of the iPhone takes place at Apple's headquarters in California. The manufacture of the product takes place overseas based upon ready-made components and established assembly processes. Manufacturing of components and assembly is also a disparate process with the company acquiring components from its diverse supply network which it then transports on to the final assembly plant (which is also a third-party manufacturer). From this point of assembly, the final product is then shipped to wholesalers and retailers all over the world. The configuration of the value network is not fixed and readily adapts to the pressure that is exerted upon it. For example, rising labour costs in the Far East have led Apple to move some of the manufacturing processes back to the US—though it still does depend upon a significant input from specialized components suppliers.

The high volume of sales of iPhones means that surplus products and components is rarely a problem. Moreover, by treating every product as having its own 'use by' date it is able to meet surges in demand facilitating adaptive products and processes whilst limiting waste. Moreover, Apple has sought to keep its supply chain lean and efficient by reducing the number of component suppliers from over 100 to 24 thereby encouraging competition between them and incentivizing these suppliers to innovate to keep their Apple contract. This has also been supported by the reduction in the number of Apple warehouse to further limit the risk of over stocking.

Whilst Apple is experienced in the development of such extensive supply chain, it is not without its risks. One of the highest profile were the reputational risks created by the working conditions at some of its suppliers. At one, its assembly plants run by Foxconn, there was a spate of suicides in 2010 in the face of poor working conditions that to some bordered-on sweatshop conditions. These allegations have persisted despite Apple seeking to limit the damage to its reputation from such actions. Foxconn's response was to deny the allegations but has been gradually replacing labour with robots to further remove the company from any concerns. These reputational risks are also evident as Apple needs to defend the ecological impact of its products and how it needs to adjust its value network accordingly. As such, one of the main actions undertaken by the company is to reconfigure its value network to increase the use of recycled materials and components within the process. It is also seeking to ensure that these products are resource intensive throughout the entire process of production and consumption. Like other companies, Apple became exposed to the impact of COVID within its value network. As the disease spread throughout Europe and China, it led to a halt to the manufacturing of key components and it hit the assembly process as factories were shut to contain the outbreak. Many of the factories (notably in China) remained closed for several weeks leading to longer shipping times especially on the more specialist build to order products. Overall, the lasting impact of COVID was a short-term reduction in device shipments throughout 2020. The development of the latest iteration of the iPhone was also hit by the travel restrictions upon employees that occurs prior to the launch of a new product to ensure processes are fit for purpose. These delays eroded the time available to secure orders of the components needed to ensure the product could be launched on time.

Business Model Risk

Expressed in terms of the logic of the business model developed above, risk can be expressed as those events and processes that directly and indirectly inhibit the capability of the firm (and its extended value network) to maintain and sustain its value creating capability and therefore the credibility and legitimacy of the value proposition, the sustenance of the business infrastructure, customer facing issues and financial sustainability. Risk is integral to the form and nature of such value creating systems due to their modularity and embedded complexity. As business models exist as dynamic entities it is important to stress that this risk context represents a constant process of evolution both within the firm and its extended value network but also by its interaction with its broader operating and commercial environment as defined by the broad sub-systems which it occupies. As per ▶ Chapter 1, two broad types of business model risk can be identified (see ◘ Table 2.1); endogenous and exogenous risk.

Endogenous risks reflect the way the business model is constructed and formed meaning that the value proposition might not be credible, that the components within the system are not aligned, or that the entire business model does not deliver value when configured. This can be due to a multitude of factors such as human error or failure to evolve to changing market dynamics (see below). Based on the business model configuration offered in ◘ Fig. 2.4, the simple business model risk framework is offered by upon the interface between operational and marketing/revenue facing aspects of the configuration. These reflect the broad risk context of the business given the tension that is placed upon the two core components of the value creating system. This interface between these two will in turn directly impact upon the credibility/legitimacy of the core value proposition. Briefly, these types of endogenous risks are.

— *Negligible risk*: this is a scenario where both revenue and operational risk are low. This is due to certainty with regard to revenue flows from target markets and that there is low risk with regard to the extended value network notably with regards first and second order suppliers. This is a business model that can be categorized as resilient where any threats to either operational or revenue can be easily countered.
— *Market risk*: this is a scenario where operational risk is benign the firm faces high degree of risk upon the revenue side of the business. This can be due to high competition, a failing value proposition, price pressure or some other marketing driven pressure operating upon the business that places pressure upon the systems revenue model through impeding the transaction process. These risks due to the dynamic nature of the business model will feed through into resources being deployed back into the operational side of the business.
— *Fulfilment risk*: this risk is sourced from operational insecurities. These are created from increased risk within the firm internal infrastructure and production process and/or first/second order suppliers. This poses a challenge to the firm's value proposition by potentially undermining its capability to deliver the product/service. This in turn is likely to generate a revenue risk as the firm will be unable to complete transactions.
— *Existential risk*: this is a high-risk scenario where both the operational and revenue models of the business are subject to high degrees of risk due to factors mentioned above. This could be created by contagion effects between operational and revenue risks that feed off each other. The core issue is that these—if they are maintained—are likely to undermine the commercial sustainability of the business model in its current configuration (◘ Fig. 2.4).

Exogenous risks are risks that are largely external to the value creating system largely created by the broad commercial context in which the firm is positioned. Exogenous risks are likely to be shaped by a range of factors the not least of which

Table 2.1 Business model component and risk type

Risk type / BM component	Endogenous risk	Exogenous risk
Value proposition	• Quality risk and uncertainty factors • Availability and maintenance factors • Data risk • New technology risk and uncertainty • Risk of innovations	• Divorced from shift in ecological context • Sentiment render value proposition obsolete • Regulatory constraints upon value proposition • Rival products/services • Changing customer expectations • Rivals offer better value
Operating dimension	• Failure of physical assets • Obsolescence/senescence of infrastructure • Operating failure • Human error • Legal risk • Loss of key staff • Employment practices • Poor activity execution • Performance risk • Fraud • Unanticipated variable costs	• Poor maintained public infrastructure • Disputes over access to core raw materials • Bottlenecks in core infrastructure • Theft of intellectual property • Investment risk • Ecological concerns with regard to production methods • Externally imposed cost increases
Marketing dimension	• Inability to meet customer demand • Customer relationship risk • Customer solvency • Customer access • Failure to adapt to customer needs • Pricing risk • Reputational damage due to poor product and failure to meet customer expectations • Cost increase in customer relationship management	• Disruption to distribution channels and third-party logistical systems • Quality of sales channel • Payment disputes • Taxation issues that impact upon revenue model • Regulatory constraints • Changing customer profile • Changing demography • Economic turmoil lowers market size • New rivals' lower market
Value network	• Partner disputes • Failure of second order supplier • Problems with second order customer • Partnership fails to deliver expected results • Benign/malign neglect of relationship	• Lack of trust • Misalignment of partners • Defection to rival network • Rivals reduce pool of available partners
Business ecosystem	• Failure to acknowledge/respond to stakeholders • Ignore regulatory instructions	• Resistance to business by proactive stakeholders • Competition policy • Political risk

Adapted from Brillinger et al. (2020)

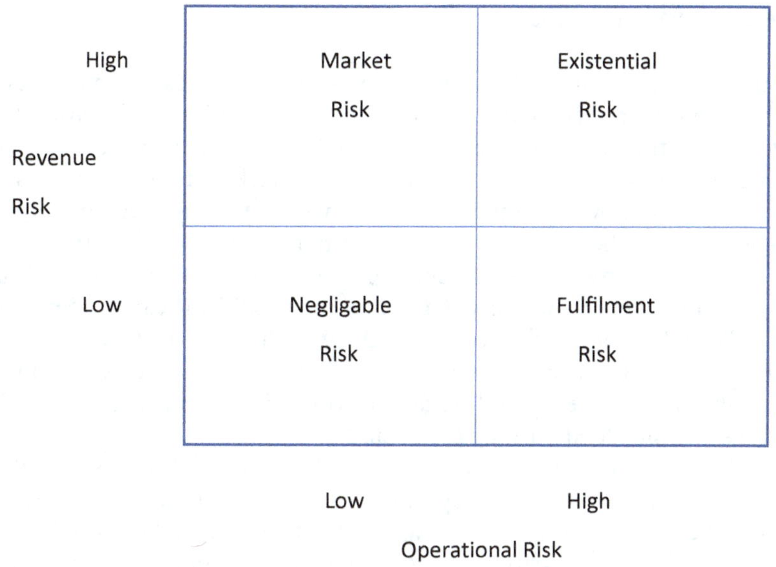

High	Market Risk	Existential Risk
Revenue Risk		
Low	Negligable Risk	Fulfilment Risk
	Low	High
	Operational Risk	

Fig. 2.4 Business model endogenous risk framework

is that no business model is irreplicable and that the loss of differentiation could undermine financial sustainability as copy-cats emerge. Further factors could be shaped by the erosion of interconnections between the partners within the value network and the possibility that key strategic partners and vendors could switch to rivals or lose responsiveness to the needs of the core value proposition. Other risks reflect a failure of the business model to innovate (see below) and where—as a result—it becomes focused upon a narrow resource deficient niche as they have failed to adapt to their changing context. This also reflects a risk that the firm simply becomes too divorced from its contextual drivers leading to a misalignment between the business model and its operating environment. Given their existence within complex systems there is always the risk that the business model could be subject to cascade effects within the system where the high degree of interconnectivity between agents causes a failure within one component of the system to spread to all other parts.

For simplicities sake, the form and type of each of these risks is reflected in Table 2.1 which maps the type of risk to a particular component of the identified business model component as well as broader aspects of the process namely the value network and the business ecosystem.

This conceptualization of business model risk leads inevitably to the need to address risk within these value creating systems draws attention to two further topics that address the notion of how these systems deal with risk. The first of these is Business Model resilience; the second is business model adaption. These reflect both the competence of current model but also its flexibility under adaptive tensions. It is worth considering each of these themes in more depth.

Business Model Resilience

As identified with ▶ Chapter 1, at this scale the notion of resilience reflects the ability of the business model to absorb the pressures placed upon it without any fundamental disruption in its operation nor challenge its core value proposition. It reflects not simply a situation of organizational slack but where processes can be adapted simply to known and unknown risks within the value creating system. The more rigid the links between the component parts of the system; the less able the current system can absorb the pressures placed upon it. Thus, although interconnectivity can increase adaptability if the link is inflexible, it can hinder adaptation. This reflects that configuration of resources with limited slack will be vulnerable. Thus, the focus on lowering costs and removing spare capacity accordingly might be more subject to concerns with regard to operating a resilient system. This sees resilience as an embedded cost for the business.

Organizational slack reflects that there is a function of diversity of links, redundancy, and spare resources. These systems are more able to absorb external shocks. Resilience reflects a learning capacity within the firm to enable it to adapt to events that will shape its value creating capacity. This reflects upon adaptability to overcome adversity. These adaptations are also linked into the innovative capability of the business allowing it to not merely adapt but also to anticipate the risks and trends that firms might face within their operating context. The notion of building up resilience within the business model must be core to its configuration that allows resources to be built up to allow it to respond to unforeseen events.

Business Model Adaptation

Alongside and interlinked into notions of resilience is the concept of business model adaptation. This is a process of conscious adaptation to at least one of the value creating dimensions in response to or anticipation of changing levels and form of risk. Their existence within a complex system of global interactions means that business models are under pressure to adapt to the pressures placed upon them by their fluid operating environment. As we shall note below, globality is one form of innovation that results from such processes. This underlines the need for business models (as well as associated value networks) to be constantly reviewed and—where needed—reconfigured to maintain fitness with their environment and their notion of value creation. Innovation in this context reflects the desire to access new suppliers and customers as well as value network components across political borders to maintain and enhance value creation. This examines innovation driven adaption less through technology and more through the process of market scanning. The fact is exploiting these opportunities can often mean reconfiguring/redesigning the pre-existing model spatially and operationally. This is reflected within innovation driven models of internationalization (see below). This reflects both adaption on potentially both the operational and marketing dimensions of the business model.

This role of adaptation within business model reflects that the system is impacted by two core facets namely openness and users/supplier responsiveness. Openness reflects that the borders of the firm are permeable and that the firm is open to learning about shifts in its context and thus is not wedded to the status quo. Also reflected in this openness is that the firm is responsive to user/supplier pressure that that their nature of what they value about the business can alter. The shift in the value network to which the firm must respond is a core driver of change. Business model reconfiguration can broadly be of three types:

- Seeking new sources of revenue (new markets, products, etc.).
- Seeking new means of operating capabilities.
- Assessing the role, the firm plays within the embedded value network.

The failure to adapt is often due to a mix of factors such as management mindset which will shape the perception of threat by the business and path dependencies within the business model configuration. The nature of adaption is to ensure the firm business model remains aligned to the trends within its environment. This is a risk-based action as it involves a change in the business model configuration with uncertain outcomes. Adaptation depends upon whether the trend is perceived as a risk or an opportunity. The more severe the treats the more the pressure is upon firms to adapt.

Globality and the Business Model

Business model configuration is a fluid structure based upon decisions by firms about what it needs to do itself (and what it can outsource) and where it can do these activities to maximum value creating effect. This involves a model that can integrate spatially dispersed product and factors markets and what aspects of these markets the firm needs to integrate and those it keeps at more distant relationships. These can reflect the need for the firm to access knowledge that is spatially dispersed and to leverage that to alter the efficacy of the business model. These processes are also about addressing risk issues in operating globally enabling the firm to more fully understand and adapt to the global context in which they operate. The driver of business model adaption within the context of globality can be subdivided into opportunity and risk mitigation drivers. These can be a mix of active (i.e., opportunity exploitation and risk mitigation) and passive drivers. These are highlighted with ◘ Table 2.2.

Globality—in this context—is defined as a state whereby the value creating capabilities of the business are heavily influenced if not solely determined by its interaction with and interdependence on the global system. This reflects the notion that the global intensity, extensity, and velocity of cross border flows have bred a spatial interdependency within value creation. Thus, globality is not (as it often conventionally understood) the end point of globalization (i.e., the creation of a single global economic, social, political, and ecological space) but the commercial reality that at a point in time the firms value creating capabilities are heavily influenced by the state and operation of the global system and its position within it. The presumption is that this value creating process becomes more spatially complex with the progressive process of globalization. In terms of the business model framework offered above (see ◘ Fig. 2.1), the process shapes value through one or more of following:

Table 2.2 Drivers of business model globality

Opportunity driver	Risk driver	Passive driver
• New growth markets • New sourcing opportunities • New revenue generating opportunities for existing value proposition • Capability to adapt value proposition to different context • To access spatially dispersed value creating resources	• React to actions of rival • Value network senescence • Obsolescence of value creating system • Maturity of current markets • Cost pressures of business • Erosion of value proposition in domestic market	• Following migration of users • Second order suppliers are non-domestic • Involuntary reconfiguration of value network • Extended business ecosystem • Shifting customer pressure/sentiment • Emergent globality of client segments

— A value proposition can be transferred between and adapted to non-domestic markets.
— Porous political borders enable the freer enablement of cross border operations and transfer of resources.
— Access to non-domestic customer segments and distribution channels allowing non-home transactions to be stimulated and realized.

Authors such as Tallman (2017) have identified that these value creating opportunities are driven by the amalgam of several meta-level drivers namely:

— Global connectivity (which is both intense and rapid) facilitated by a rapidly evolving digital infrastructure and enabling ecosystem enabling closer and more intense value networks to be created and sustained which allows for more flexible systems of value creation.
— Technological change that has facilitated embedded globality within business models and fosters the aforementioned global connectivity within often narrowly defined product and/or customer niches often through highly flexible manufacturing systems.
— Geographic expansion of trade and investment facilitating reforms which lower the transactions costs associated with cross border interactions thereby enabling the easier creation and operation of cross border business models.
— The acceleration of global factor and product flows has further lowered the barriers to the efficacy of the operation of business models that operate across multiple political domains.
— The enhanced access to global (tangible and intangible) resources has enabled the extension of global sourcing of factor inputs. This is especially important with regard to improved data analytics allowing better information with regard to markets.
— Emergent state activity to secure own systems that impose restrictions upon activities.
— Increasingly footloose consumers.

The Global Business Model: Business and Embedded Global Risk

These pressures place adaptive tensions upon the business model to adapt with the pace and impact of these drivers being shaped by the legacy of hyperglobalism and the extent to which the process constrains/impacts upon corporate decisions, leads to re-organization of value creating system, penetrates deep into the value creating process, and shapes the speed with which these events may need to occur. Indeed, these trends have created more innovative business model configurations characterized by facets that outlie conventional globality within business models namely by asset light entry, distributed production, etc. These all underline the intimacy between globality and technological change that allows businesses to have intensive penetration and extensive reach at relatively rapid speed. These trends underscore the rise of intangible international business (based on the increased digitization of business ecosystems) where the value lies in performance rather than in physical product. This has been enabled by divorcing reach and scale in business models where easier cross border collaboration allows for extensive and intensive reach without the cost of multiple market presence. These ecosystems through collaboration are subject to more fluidity and change. This is compounded by enhanced data collection and technology allowing global providers to higher degree of customer intimacy with highly adaptive value proposition to reflect the bespoke nature of the offering. This reflects how data within these hyperglobal business models facilitates multi-segmentation within the marketing dimension of the business model. This has also enabled more flexible manufacturing system where the need for scale is diminished in favour of the benefits of locality. This allows lower scale production to be more adaptable to consumer preferences. The fluidity of such technological developments runs up against the desire of states to increase local content of what is delivered by the global system. The response of companies to these pressures is to adapt to these pressures by more local content and adaptability with a stronger sense of locality throughout the business also enabled by proactive non-market strategies and strategies and activities that maximize impact on the local level through employment, etc.

Such narratives tend to paint a very positive image of how hyper-global systems can add value to business and create more fluid and adaptable value creating systems. This analysis tends only to apply to a limited niche of companies namely those with high levels of technological sophistication and global outlook. The risk within such approaches through technological risk for example is left underexplored within such an analysis. If does offer scope for how data does change nature of globality for businesses.

> **Box 2.1: The Legacy of Global Complexity: The Universal International Business**
>
> Arguably the most enduring legacy of hyper-globalization is the realization that international business is not a separate sub-set of the broader population of businesses but that—to the extent that all businesses are impacted by global processes, trends, and risks—all businesses are international businesses. Thus, internationality can be passive in the sense that it is felt through daily commercial pressures (such as changes in the prices of commodities) or proactive where the

firms knowingly expose themselves to these processes as a result of strategic decision making (such as aggressive overseas market entry).

These global effects can be exhibited through one or more of the following channels:

First order effects: these are intra-firm effects created by the cross border configuration of the business model where operating and marketing dimensions are spatially dispersed across political borders.

Second order effects: these are created by direct interconnections by the firm across political borders as part of the value creation. These can be non-domestic suppliers or customers and directly impact upon the firm's value creating capability, its revenue model, and cost structures.

Third order effects: these are indirect interconnections across political borders where—for example—domestic suppliers have overseas suppliers or the non-domestic customers of the firm's direct customers. Linked to the state of the broader business ecosystem.

Systemic effects: these impact upon first, second, and third order levels of the commercial system. These are events that can spread across borders and can do so at speed. These can be events that originate in the economic system or one that has spread from another sub-system. These effects and impacts are especially difficult to predict.

Internationalization and Business Risk

Internationalization as a process reflects the existence of risk within globalizing the business model. The gradual process of extending geographic reach reflects the uncertainty involved within the process as the lack of knowledge and the persistence of commercial ambiguity defines the trajectory of change within the business model as it spatially expands its reach. Risks within internationalization models are seen as largely endogenous, driven by the absence of internal knowledge with regard to the targeted market. Thus, firms are expected to make a resource commitment with regard to international market entry in the face of incomplete knowledge. However, it also must be recognized that the process is not shaped by risk per se but by the firm's propensity to take risk but also their tolerance of such problems within their actions. The latter is assumed to be dependent upon the availability of resources to counter the realization and financial impact of realized risks. Tolerable risk reflects other factors such as allowable risk of loss of resource.

The process reflects both a process of implicit and explicit risk and it also underscores how the business model evolves with organizational learning. Risks within the process are generated by firm specific and contextual considerations. The basic 'steps' model to internationalization is reflected in ◘ Fig. 2.5. It underscores how virtuous cycles of learning and experience (through the conduit of organizational learning) push firms deeper into the international system. The gradualism reflects the risks within the process and how the perception of this risk alters as the process matures and as the firm learns of the opportunities. Within the basic 'Steps' model, risk is encapsulated in terms of the financial commitment to be made by the firm (relative to presumed available resources) in the formative stages of the process (see Johanson & Vahlne, 2009). Presuming therefore that this process is driven by smaller, more resources constrained entities with limited knowledge with regard to the operation of and within international markets.

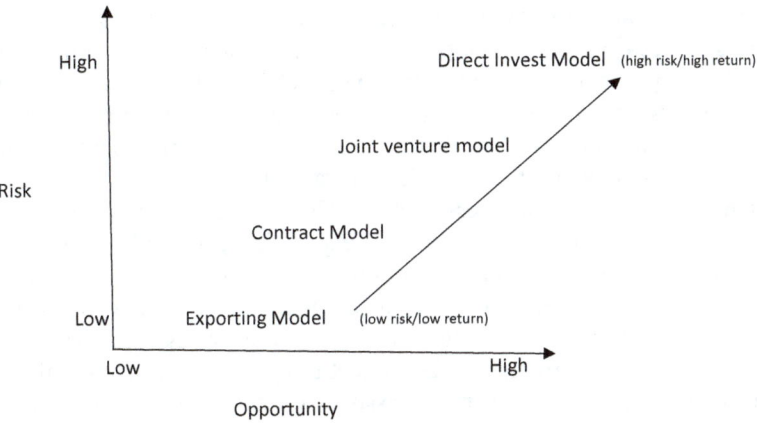

Fig. 2.5 Internationalization risk and business model evolution

Implicit within the steps framework is how the shift in the attitude to risk leads to the business model—that serves the firm within and between markets—evolving. These patterns reflect lower endogenous risk as organizational learning is supposed to lower the internal uncertainties associated with the process. This enables the firm to manage, understand, and mitigate the risk and/or see them subside as it develops the competence to undertake the process with more certainty. Thus low-risk models involve minimal final engagement with a business model configured with a high domestic operating dimension with varying degrees of engagement with the international marketing dimensions depending on whether the firms undertake direct or indirect exporting with or without a third party. The model presumes that the degree of operational engagement increases with the market as risk are reduced and familiarity with markets increase. At the final point of this process of evolution, the firm develops its own distinct operating dimension with the market. This does not presume that risks are mitigated as exogenous risk will still be evident within such business models.

These exogenous (market) driven risks are assumed—at the formative stages of the process—to be created by ambiguties created by the liabilities of newness, foreigness, and networking which create inbuilt advantages vis-a-via incumbents, national value networks and where the value creating capability of the firm within this new context is either not differentiated sufficiently, not understood or simply has limited efficacy within the new context. These theories suggest that risk increases with cultural distance as it increases the cost associated with the process. Risks are also seen to be positively related to economic distance due to the problems in accessing local stakeholders though these can militate by levels of economic development and access to a talented, abundant labour pool. There is also possibility that businesses could also find non-internationalization as risky where failure to adapt to rivals' actions could lead to long-term decline.

The balance of risk and opportunity within the internationalization has found expression within the 'S'-curve hypothesis. In suggesting that international strategy faces impediments in both its formative and mature stages suggests that there are evident risks in the formative stage of business model evolution to new geographic markets and that geographic diversification of the business model faces risk driven by the aforementioned liabilities of newness, foreignness, and exclusion. Thus, risks emerge where its faces contextual problems in its market entry process driven by a mix of misunderstood value proposition, powerful incumbents, culture, and possible exclusion from host value networks. These reflect risk not simply due to knowledge and understanding but also due to reactive strategies and competitive risks associated with the process. These risks are mitigated as the firm gets more experienced or that any risks that do exist are more than compensated by the opportunities presented by geographic diversification. However, internationalization is not an on-going process with all firms on an ever-expanding geographic reach. Eventually, opportunities relative to risk start to fall and the risks of entering new markets start to rise as market attractiveness declines as the firms move beyond the most lucrative markets to ones with more uncertain return. These ambiguities will be driven by factors outlined in ▶ Chapter 3. These reflect not just exogenous but also reflect endogenous risk created by co-ordination issues as the firm gets more complex.

The emergence of the born global reflects an embedded globality within the value creating system that mitigates against any hesitancy shaped by the perception of risks from the process of internationalization. Better information availability shaped by more widespread information infrastructure systems can help resolve uncertainty or simply that the founders have extensive international experience at the point at which the firm is formed. Thus, the expected pattern of risk might not apply (see Case Study 2.1). The focus of these firms upon narrowly defined cross border niches about which the firm has a high degree of experience, and which exhibit higher degrees of standardization of wants across spatially dispersed markets also facilitates this more rapid process of internationalization. It also mitigates against disadvantages of scale. These are enabled by their niche products being highly differentiated thus mitigating the need to compete on cost. These firms can often use extended value networks to integrate risk of going international these are strong and intimate links between suppliers and consumers. The business model becomes embedded within international value networks to enable internationalization and mitigate risk and uncertainty associated with the process. The Born global tends to be highly embedded within international business ecosystems as a precursor to their rapid process of internationalization. These links are born through links with knowledge intensive actors such as universities these links are further enabled by the links the firm seeks to build with local suppliers and customer bases to secure high degrees of customer intimacy to create some degree of lock in with these partners.

The fact that risk is an inherent part of the process of internationalization is highlighted within the process of de-internationalization. These reflect that firms retreat from a market or develop a business model configuration with a less resource intensive configuration. These can be created by a shifting context in which the firm operates within a single or across a variety of markets. This process could also be driven by changing attitudes/perceptions of risk by the firm in its operating and marketing dimensions. These actions are easier when the resource commitment to the market is less intense. This process could reflect ignorance at the point of entry and that the risk taken at this point turned out to be disadvantageous to the business. These reflect internal and external dynamics within the host economy that leads to the value creating capability of the firm within the market being undermined. These can be created by pre-existing risks that were no evident at the time of entry and/or those that emerged during the lifetime of the firm's involvement within an economy.

Types of Global Business Models

The simplest divide in the developing a typology of global business models is between those that have a physical international presence and those that do not. Thus, the conventional analysis is of a binary split between exporters and MNCs (see below for formal definitions). This binary divide was formed in an area before hyperglobalism and emergent complexity. Thus, types of global business models are more complex with them varying by degree of passivity/proactivity, asset light/heavy, tangible/intangible value creation, and emergent global value chains to name just a few delineators. As such, the global business model can be highly differentiated often cutting across the conventional binary format. Indeed, because of the drivers mentioned above, there has been the emergence of global (in terms of reach) business models based upon adding value through several facets namely offering cross border services, asset light market entry, value adding software, the creation and development of global digital ecosystems, global personalization, multi-local manufacturing, developing multiple national identities. In a work of this nature, we can outline the main forms. This dimension of globality within value creating system is also extended beyond the borders of the firms notably with the increased salience of global value chains in which many businesses operating globally are positioned. Thus, for the purposes of identifying types, firms are broadly categorized across the three dimensions of the global business model aligned to the framework offered (◘ Fig. 2.1) above and will differ by:

- The degree of globalization of operations.
- The degree of globalization of marketing model.
- The degree of adaptability of value proposition.

Business models for global markets differ by these dimensions. The conventional model is the multi-national corporation (MNC) but there are many types of MNC models thus simply defining a model by defining it as operating in more than one state is inadequate to capture the diversity of business model configurations. However, the MNC is not the only model for accessing the global system. Not only is there the conventional exporting model but more innovative models have emerged that have divorced scale from extensive overseas operations. As suggested above, the more complex this configuration of resources the greater the risk attached to the model. This section will not review the theory of MNCs but will examine them through the lens of business model risk. ◘ Table 2.3 offers a broad categorization of the main types of business models evident within global systems. These are all proactive in their approach to engagement with the global system. As mentioned above, some firms are more passive internationalizers by dint of their position within global value networks.

There is no single explainer of the MNC other than it exists as multi-national configuration of networked resources. Why it is configured as such reflects the idiosyncrasies of the firm. As suggested, the MNC model captures many different strategic configurations with many best conceptualized as networks of businesses each of which is networked into its specific operating (national) context with its value network with which it evolves. Thus, the MNC is a network of networked businesses. These networks of businesses are normally co-ordinated across borders

Table 2.3 Broad global business model typology

Type of IB model	Business model configuration
Passive internationalizer	These business models are based around domestic configuration but exhibit second order links via suppliers/customers which create an exposure within its value creating system to international forces possibly via their positioning within a global value network. These are in addition to contextual drivers that can impede upon the firm's value creating capability
Export	These are a relatively low risk, proactive international business model based upon domestic operating dimension serving both home and overseas markets. This model involves a degree of internationalization of the marketing dimension with the firms largely seeking to extend home-based value proposition into overseas markets. To mitigate the risk of this process the firm could possibly use in indirect exports where third parties with intimate local knowledge or it could seek to develop this dimension itself
Micro-national/Born globals	These are business models (often for small-scale enterprises) which have a strong, proactive global dimension from their inception (or very soon afterwards). These are businesses that undertake (or have undertaken) a rapid internationalization process based on a value proposition that occupies a defined global niche based on global, asset light operations. These can often be firms offering common technology platforms across multiple localities
Multi-national	This is the classic wide-ranging definition based upon the business possessing physical assets in at least two states where one of these is its home country. In business model parlance, these are firms with tangible operating and/or marketing dimensions in non-domestic locations based upon a network of subsidiary firms (which can be fully or partially owned). The population of MNC is a diverse grouping of business of varying sizes. Attempts have been made to categorize these firms in terms of variances expressed within the integration responsiveness frameworks that identify four strategic types of MNC. Even within this definition, there can be further variances as more firms deploy asset light models

which tangible and intangible resources flowing between these businesses. The difficulty of co-ordinating such relationships through the marketplaces incentives the firm to internalize these transactions via the network of overseas subsidiaries.

Whilst Table 2.3 highlights that the MNC is just one broad type of business model within the global system, it has long been recognized that this model faces adaptive tensions as it seeks to operate across diverse markets where differences in contextual issues in areas such as culture, economic systems, logistical systems, and ease of doing business create complex operating environments whilst the firm is simultaneously seeking to scale up operations to generate operational efficiency. To reconcile these apparent contradictions within the operating and marketing dimensions of the business model, the integration-responsiveness framework offers a stylized framework to understanding how businesses seek to capture value from glo-

bality. These reflect how the firm will seek to configure itself across a number of territories via several limited strategic types namely:
- Global/standardization Strategy—global marketing and operations and uniform VP across all markets—tight coordination of operation and marketing dimensions—standardized close links.
- Transnational strategy—global reach but localized production and marketing—differentiated value proposition—looser and discretionary acts by localization of operations and marketing dimensions.
- Multi-domestic Strategy—loose configuration of resources, highly locally responsive value proposition builds strong links between interdependent units to facilitate flow of intangible resources e.g., learning and knowledge.
- International—export-based strategy—domestic production—international marketing dimension—limited variation between domestic and overseas value proposition.

This list is not definitive as business models can seek to extract value through assorted (often bespoke) configurations. There are those for example, that—for varying reasons—eschew any sense of the home market. These have precedent with the 'free standing' companies of the nineteenth/twentieth-century colonial era where MNCs emerged from a state (normally in this case the UK) but with limited or no activity within that home state (Wilkins, 2013). There has also been a focus upon meta nationals which are seen as an emergent type formed in a knowledge intensive sector where the configuration of the business model is designed to tap into spatially dispersed pockets of technology and know-how. This model seeks to diminish the link between the home and host with embedded globality of the value creating system which is built upon sensing, connecting, and exploiting spatially dispersed tangible and intangible resources. This divorces the firm from the conventional home to host trajectory based upon the firm leveraging domestically formed competences in their formative period of international expansion.

> **Box 2.2: Global Value Networks (GVNs): The Global Interconnection of Business Models**
>
> This is used as a catch-all term to explore an array of network-based arrangements to extract value from the spatial dispersion of tangible and intangible resources. These GVNs are dispersed value creating systems operating across political borders but often within and beyond the borders of the firm. These can be a network of firms that create a vertically disintegrated concentrations of economic activity that stand in contrast to the MNC which is based upon the creation of a vertically/horizontally integrated series of assets within the boundaries of the firm, but which operate across political borders. These have generated global connectivity between different business models to create globally modular value networks based upon interconnection between a range of businesses. In this sense, these configurations are seen to supersede that of the TNC as a business model.
>
> GVNs represent a network of business models supporting a central value creating capability through connect firms both functionally and territorially. These con-

figurations have been enabled by contextual drivers namely rapid ICT development and economic liberalization. Often these networks are built around a 'flagship' firm that drives the creation of this extended value network and around which other firms adapt to support. The active involvement by firms within GVNs can help the process of internationalization and stimulate globality. These can aid risk mitigation by making it more asset light and to share uncertainty. These GVNs allow for both passive and active globality within BM as second order will adopt globality through pre-existing partnerships. These configurations of firms underpin that complex value creating system depend upon both first and second order suppliers and customers within the value creating constellation. The role of the lead firm and of the needs of rims to align to this suggest an adaptive tensions upon these businesses to adapt their systems to the pressures placed upon theme by the lead firms. This reflects the asymmetric nature of power within the global production networks.

The emergence of GVNs reflects that the configuration of business models will seek to tap into location specific advantages to support value creation. These value creating capabilities are also shaped by place which creates adaptive tension upon the value network. These—in turn—are shaped by regulatory pressures that can affect these value creating contexts that can cascade across the network. States can be proactive in this process and but can also represent a risk to this process (see below). Firms are embedded within these value creating systems with each offering a specific function as part of this process. These have taken on various terms but reflect a trade away from completed good towards value added, task, and/or capabilities based on the trade in intermediate (i.e., semi-completed) goods. This has been generated by the vertical and horizontal specialization of firms within these value creating configurations. These create value created by utilization of respective value creating capabilities of the partners for the purposes of mutual benefit.

MNCs and Macro-level Risk

As much of the rest of this book examines the risks associated with international business functioning, this section will only briefly touch on such themes. The theme here will seek to address international risk contextualized within the framework of the business model rather than assessing them in a broader generic, contextual sense as later chapters will do. The narrative within this section will seek to address how international business inform and adapt to the risk environment. Notionally, the long-standing supposition by many of the champions of globalization is that the process through creating convergence of consumers tastes, market conditions, and investment rules leads to a less risky commercial environment. This convergence would—it is supposed—overcome any friction to interactions created by inter-state ambiguities. The logic is of intense interaction created by freer flow of resources leading to an approximation of market conditions between states. These pressures are compounded by a supposed unwillingness by states to vary from the 'norm' due to a desire to sustain flows of investment into their economy.

Such arguments have proved to be excessively simplistic and understated the complexity of the global system (see ▶ Chapter 1) and of the desire of states to sustain such divergences. Thus, the process of global homogenization and its risk mitigating impact have been over-exaggerated. Nonetheless—as the ▶ Chapter 3 indicates—investors do require specific conditions to make investment notably transparency. This transparency reflects that risk can—to some degree—be mitigated in the face of uncertainty by the capability of the system to remove ambiguities through enabling the business to identify gaps in their knowledge and be offered the means of alleviating such uncertainty.

Ultimately risk within global business models reflects an evolutionary process as these businesses cannot only be subject to exogenous risk but can also—in a number of cases—(either tacitly or directly) shape the form and nature of the risk environment in which they operate. In the latter case, this evolutionary risk process will vary with the business model deployed and impact will vary on size of firm relative to host. These reflect a long-standing position that international business (notably MNCs) can have mixed impact upon hosts and that such activities can create risks for the business as well as opportunities. Not surprisingly much of the narrative surrounding the interface between international businesses and risk has been based around the larger scale MNCs. Much of the literature upon the risk for business from the process of international engagement is shaped by interface between the business and the host and how this interaction shapes both the host state and the business. These risks are shaped by a number of factors with regard to how the firm configures its business model to the new opportunities presented by globality. These risks can reflect the following:

— The degree of cultural diversity between home and host states which inhibits the ready transfer of the firm's value proposition between states; misreading or misunderstanding this diversity could lead to commercial risks.
— Not understanding how operational systems need to be adapted across states.
— Different underlying technological infrastructures and capabilities which lead to divergent connectivity issues.
— Overstating cultural approximation in consumer behaviour and tastes and preferences.

All of these reflect the challenges businesses face in adapting to the reality of complexity in the process of developing an international presence. These are risks shaped by uncertainty and a degree of ignorance at the point of entry but also of the desire to operate across multiple states which divergent political, economic, social, and technological contexts. As suggested above, firms are keen to configure their operations across borders for both operating and marketing reasons. Such configurations can come at a price. Risk extends beyond this to mature operations and how the adaptability or otherwise of the business model to host conditions can be a powerful factor shaping risk conditions. These effects can be seen across political, economic, and social processes.

Political

One of the more controversial elements of MNC risk shaping behaviour is their perceived ability to alter political risk within a state. In many cases, these non-market strategies will be an act of necessity where—for example—it faces a closed political system with embedded corruption. MNCs will seek to use what political power they may have to shape host market business conditions towards that which best enhances its value creating capabilities and also protects its investment within a host. There is not a sense—as reflected in ▶ Chapter 6 that an MNC has a particular preference for a type of political system. It is more that the business wants a system that is stable and predictable in terms of regulation and any other decisions that can impact upon its value creating capability within any given host state.

These benign drivers exist alongside more malign concerns. The fear is that MNCs—due to their economic weight relative to that of the state's institutional system—can effectively capture key components of the political and/or regulatory system of the host state as a means of lowering its own political risk and possibly increasing the degree of risk faced by rivals. The fear for states is that dependency upon MNCs could lead to a loss of control of power towards these bodies. Whether such fears are apocryphal or not has formed substantial debate within international business. These processes tend to be especially prevalent where the state has an inherent political instability and where governance is weak. The power of the MNC can be especially strong in shaping political risk within a state where there is dependency by that states upon the activities of the MNC. Indeed, the very desire of states to attract inwards investment by MNCs may end up making them more vulnerable to MNC political influence. This can reflect a concern that MNCs can engage in 'regime shopping' where they can use the threat of relocation to get the policy outcomes that they desire.

Any general perspective on the ability of MNCs to shape political risk within a state is difficult due to the sheer complexity of processes both within the host, the MNC as well as the broader global systems. For example, there is also the possibility that MNCs could inadvertently decrease levels of political risk within host states through their investment in local infrastructure and other facilities that enable the political integration of states. MNCs to their investments in these systems have a direct impact upon enhancing political cohesion. These are especially evident in transportation and energy systems and their broader political effects.

Economic

The evolution of host state risk and the MNC has been formed around a consensus of mutual reinforcement namely that low host risk encourages FDI which reinforces and embeds low risk within that location. The perception is that inwards FDI into a state represents an economic good and which through its ability to promote growth and development lowers the level of risk associated with that economy. These reflect a belief that FDI has a broadly catalytic effect upon states to stimulate the creation of low-risk environments. It is also supposed that the desire to attract footloose investment moving around the globe that states will seek to create the conditions in which returns on inwards investment can be realized as a means of incentivizing this inwards flows. Thus, states—to attract inwards investment—will develop a set of flanking policies that seek to lower both micro- and macro-level risk. This can be through measures such as infrastructure development or through the use of financial incentives. The hope is that this FDI creates a virtuous cycle of risk reduction which operates a platform for growth and development. This can be felt through better know-how with regard to exporting that allows local firms to tap into these capabilities. Thus, the positive effect on risk is felt through positive spillovers with local businesses. Thus, MNC investment can work through multiple channels but the supposition that through promoting growth they lower economic risk where risk is seen as being negatively related to economic growth; though of course risk can rise where growth proves to be unsustainable.

The impact upon host state risk tends to vary on the type of states. Most developed states tend to low-risk investment locations whose development has been based upon being low-risk locations. For higher growth emerging states or for those at the lower levels of economic development the interface between the MNC and the host state risk can be more ambiguous. In some cases, the desire to be in a host (possibly to access a natural resource) means that the firm operates around and learns to cope with high levels of risk and seeks to operate in general isolation from aspects of the host economy. However, the sense that some of these businesses seek to be detached from the local economy (either for risk management or strategic reasons) can mean that they have little impact upon economic risk within the host state. Indeed, if these MNCs do not put down roots and limit autonomous development and exhibit no long-term commitment it could mean that this business could have net negative impact upon economic risk within host states. This could be compounded by these businesses outcompeting local firms and inhibit local entrepreneurship and if revenues earned within the host are repatriated out of the state.

Social

The final aspect of MNC activity upon host states is felt through their impact upon social systems. Often the central allegation is that MNCs in seeking to maximize their value creating capability locate in those states with lower levels of social protection. Beyond that there are concerns that MNCs ferment social risk by their attitude to human and labour rights as a consequence of their investment. Contrary to this are those positions that stress that these firms can improve social conditions within these states via the adoption of voluntary codes of conduct and that policing by a range of stakeholders holds them to this commitment. For many promoting social cohesion in a host state is seen as not just ethical but good business if it promotes lower political risk. This has been reinforced by product strategies that intentionally target the poorest groups in society and—as a result—can assist in improving the living conditions of this under-served group. The social risk that are created as a result of these MNC activity are shaped by a number of factors such as the existence of local civil society, effective governance at the host state level and the social capabilities of the host in terms of issues such as education, etc. These are also impacted by the level of intensity of competition and technological development/sophistication.

Case Study 2.2: Chinese SME Internationalization

Internationalization is conventionally seen as a gradual, incremental process of increased engagement based on experiential learning (see above). This reflects the risk embedded within the process reflecting the degree of ignorance and inexperience as well as resource constraints by the businesses seeking to engage in international markets. Increasingly SMEs have become a focal point of research in internationalization as more firms seek to be eschewing the conventional risk averse gradualist route for a more rapid process of internationalization. This is born of the role of networks in the process whereby firms can mitigate risk by tapping into pre-existing knowledge with regard to target markets. The development of these networks creates a dynamic business exchange through frameworks such as global value chains.

Increasingly the focus is turning to SMEs from emerging economies who are increasingly connecting into these networks to support their international activities. As these firms emerge from less mature business environments with less experience of global processes and generally weaker institutional environments, the engagement with networks can often be subject to risks created by fragile links, poor finance, and limited innovation. This latter point is driven by the fact that many emerging economy SMEs operate in low value-added manufacturing activities. It is evident that important to many processes of international engagement by emerging economy firms—to mitigate these risks—are strong interpersonal networks that span borders connecting widespread diasporas to facilitate ease of entry into international markets. In China, the importance of guanxi (i.e., social networks) to create the social capital to mitigate market entry risks. These network ties alongside the entrepreneurial drive of the businesses themselves have been powerful factors shaping the process of international engagement. These create both internal and external drivers to create the rapidity of learning within the firm to eschew some of the risk created by the process of internationalization. Though these networks could become a source of risk in themselves if they lead to a sense of mistrust between partners and create network instability.

As the Chinese economy began to liberalize so the SME sector of its economy began to emerge and follow similar patterns to other major economies where these businesses contribute significantly to GDP (over 60 per cent) and employment (over 80 per cent). Despite a large home market, these niche focused businesses quickly found that rising wages and limited opportunities within their niche were forces pushing them to engage in internationalization. The initial source of advantage was being eroded so these firms needed to move overseas to sustain cost advantage. It was evident that interpersonal networks were a main source of approaching this strategy in a more risk averse manner. These supported efforts of these firms to position themselves within GVCs. Also important in the process of network development were trade fairs where personal contact could be made with new customers but also finding out about best practice in an industry.

The experience of Chinese SMEs underlines how networks are used to speed up internationalization without increasing the risk associated with such a move. The links built with customers can offer firms

> more security with regard to new avenue for sales prior to the formal move. Thus, risk averse strategies are focusing upon becoming an insider in networks and GVCs to allow growth without creating too much corporate risk for the business in doing so. The firm's business model is centred upon enabling its role within the GVC.

Conclusions

Increasingly all business (irrespective of size) is directly impacted by the process of globalization. This impacts upon their value creating processes and highlights how within the contemporary business environment all businesses are embedded within the global system. This process is impacting upon the nature of the risk facing businesses of all sizes and across sectors of the economy. Across both the operational and revenue component of the business model, globality has become a universal shaper of value creation and destruction. In adaptation to this process of change within the global system, there are group of businesses proactively adapting their business models to take advantage of the opportunities the process of globality creates. However, this proactivism exposes these firms directly to macro and meso-level risk as they engage with global system.

Key Points

- Business Models explore how businesses create value and tell the 'story' of a business
- Globality has become embedded within business models as globalization has matured
- Globality is reshaping the risks faced by businesses in the value creation process.
- Many business models are proactively configured to take advantage of the globalization process.

Discussion Questions

1. How is value creation shaped by globalization?
2. How can globalization generate value destruction?
3. How could a multi-national company adapt to markets risk in its strategic decision making?

Activities

Taking a local business with which, you are familiar, map out the business is both directly and indirectly impacted by the globalization process.

Summary

Risk is embedded with the global business model where all businesses to a greater or lesser degree of directly and indirectly impacted by global events and processes. Dealing with risk within global business models is made difficult by the complex structures in which business models are embedded which can make risk difficult to accurately understand. Adapting to the risk context in global systems is often reflected within the processes and structures with which firms approach passive and/or active engagement with the global system.

Key Readings

Baden-Fuller, C., Demil, B., Lecoq, X., & MacMillan, I. (2010). *Special Issue: Business Models, Long Range Planning, Vol. 43, issues 2–3*.

Brillinger, A. S., Els, C., Schäfer, B., & Bender, B. (2020). Business Model Risk and Uncertainty Factors: Toward Building and Maintaining Profitable and Sustainable Business Models. *Business Horizons, 63*(1), 121–130.

Johanson, J., & Vahlne, J. E. (2009). The Uppsala Internationalization Process Model Revisited: From Liability of Foreignness to Liability of Outsidership. *Journal of International Business Studies, 40*(9), 1411–1431.

Osterwalder, A., Pigneur, Y., & Tucci, C. L. (2005). Clarifying Business Models: Origins, Present, and Future of the Concept. *Communications of the Association for Information Systems, 16*(1), 1.

Tallman, S. (2017). *Business Models and the Multinational Firm. In Multidisciplinary Insights from New AIB Fellows*. Emerald Group Publishing Limited.

Wilkins, M. (2013). *The Maturing of Multinational Enterprise*. Harvard University Press.

The State and the Global System

© The Author(s), under exclusive license to Springer Nature Switzerland AG 2023
C. Turner, *Global Business Analysis*,
https://doi.org/10.1007/978-3-031-27769-6_3

Globalization is going to bring us closer and closer together across nations and technology you can't stop.

John P. Kotter

At the end of this chapter, the reader will be able to understand:
— Understand the role of the state in the global system.
— Comprehend how globalization impacts the state.
— Be aware of how the state adapts to globalization.
— Identify the different forms of state strategy.
— Understand how the state shapes global risk.
— Comprehend what drives state success and/or failure

Introduction

The nation state (hereafter simply the state) is a core unit of analysis in international business where the whole process stems from the operation of commercial and non-commercial activities as well as global processes across political borders. The global system is based around the fragmentation of social, political, and economic systems generated by the compartmentalization of the earth's surface into 206 states each of which seeks to assert uncontested sovereignty over a designated geographic area. This fragmentation of space is a major contributing factor to the complexity of operations within the global system with each state reflecting frequently divergent cultures, business practices, economic, and political systems. The notion of these territorial entities as nation states means that this territoriality is linked around the premise that the inhabitants of a territory develop their own sense of self based upon their shared history and identity. The territoriality of this space is enforced by a set of political organizations/institutional system which set the rules for operating within the territory, facilitate distribution of resources within it, embed a governing ideology, and have the capacity to sustain control over this space. These are created and enforced by a range of actors around these institutions. Dealing with such diversity does not merely add to the complexity of international corporate activity but is also a major factor shaping the risk context of business not merely through the state's sovereign actions but also how these states adapt to the tensions placed upon them by global trends.

The State in International Business

Whilst they are relatively new phenomena, states are the most powerful organizations within the global system. They emerged from a diverse range of socio-political and economic interests and exercise power in very unequal ways (see Chapter 4). The state as a territorial unit claims certain sovereign rights over a space (see below). These sovereign rights are shaped by a jurisdictional remit based upon the exclusive right (recognized by all other states) to exercise power (in a uniform manner) over this space. These states' rights are also extended to resource rights related to the existence of exploitable material located within their recognized space. Finally, states have the right to control the movement of tangible and intangible flows entering and exiting as well as moving across their territory.

In terms of international business, that states (in theory) are free to exercise sovereign power over this territory in whatever way they want can affect business behaviour/performance accordingly. This state-based capability reflects that business in a state-based system must adhere to a myriad of rules that are necessary as a result of its exercising its choice of how to configure its business model across political borders. This suggests that firms accept such complexity as part of the conscious choice to engage within a non-domestic market. There are an increased number of exceptions to the totality of this sovereignty with new international organizations (see Chapter 4) but also the power of the business to attempt to circumvent controls upon their activity. This has given rise to the conventional understanding that the role of the state within the global system is one of diminishing sovereignty. The supposition is that sovereignty is a zero-sum phenomenon and that as globalization matures so the sovereignty of the state over its territory is eroded and transferred to transnational forces and actors such as non-governmental organizations, global corporates, and global governance systems (Strange, 1988). Thus globalization—as it matures—is expected to see the retreat of the state as a source of influence within the global system as its room for discretionary action is superseded by the need to acquiesce to the power of meta-level global forces. The power of the state has also been shaped by the rise of the global risk society, the power of identity politics to supersede the state and the rise of transnational civil societies, and the capability of inter-state conflict to be conducted over continents. These have been shaped by networks between actors and the multiple levels.

These narratives have led some to argue that the nation state as a key focal point of the international system is of limited lifespan and efficacy. The rise of hyper-globality meant that—in theory—the ease with which economic flows could move across borders and penetrate the space of each state renders notions of control essentially meaningless. In this context, states are seen as sources of fragmentation and divergence within the global system and therefore act as a constraint upon globalization. These state-based arrangements generate many of the transaction costs that inhibit global integration. These emerge not simply because of the barriers to flows imposed by states but also because the divergences between states that create discontinuities within the system. These reflect differences in operating environments for businesses which find that they need to use different currencies and engage in different and divergent regulatory regimes as part of this process. To globalists, these legitimize globality by enabling states to benefit from freer cross border flows at the expense of discretion where such discretion works—as globalists perceive it—against the interests of the state.

These hyperglobalist attitudes reflect a belief that states face the risk of economic exclusion from the global system if they do not adapt to market processes. In the logic of the 'race to the bottom', globality imposes upon states the need to continuously seek to improve the profitability of global businesses by continually lowering the costs of doing business within that state largely through lowering regulation and other cost increasing constraints upon business. The logic is that states who (the argument presumes) are largely powerless in the process compete to offer the lowest cost and therefore the most profitable location for this footloose investment (i.e., investment unrestricted in its ties to a location). The fear is that the desire for states to mitigate international economic risk of being denied investment increases the level of domestic risk by the gradual erosion of labour and environmental standards as well as eroding corporate tax base. Such arguments—as intuitive as they maybe—are rather simplistic and—as we shall see—understate the complexity of the process shaping welfarism in states.

Whilst this erosion of state power has long been predicted, the state does remain a focal point of the global system and—indeed—as the forces of globality wax and wane, so it is becoming more assertive. The notion of nationalism—as a juxtaposition to globalism (see below)—is rising as national identities retain their hold upon economic, social, and political spheres. Across the main sub-systems, the nation states retain its salience as a core organizing agent. Whilst there are new inter-state arrangements above the level of the state, it is still the state that retains the formal point of reference for economic, political, and social actors. This was reinforced by the state being the primary recourse in dealing with crises that emerge from within the global system. Thus, whilst states may be seen to be challenged by globalization, they have nonetheless been a powerful factor in shaping its stability and development (Rodrik, 2013). This reflects that global markets need a set of non-market factors to facilitate them (such as rules, infrastructure, etc.) and that only the state could provide these.

Thus, the state stands at a paradox of both enabling globalization but also being the force that stops it from deepening. This conflict was reconciled by domestic policy agenda which kept national and global systemic needs compatible. States managed the intensity of globality, but this was challenged with the trends towards hyperglobalism. This weakened domestic governance creating democratic issues as well as inequality though states are not powerless in the face of hyperglobalism and have a variety of capabilities to enable them to cope with the pressures placed upon them by such processes. Despite the strong narrative that underpins an inevitability with regard to the globalization process, national differences reinforce diversity within the system based upon state heterogeneity and a long-lasting desire for localization in many elements of production and consumption. Thus, lower transaction costs do not necessarily lead to an increase globally due to national preferences that are resistant to such pressures for geopolitical, security, or other reasons. Thus, the friction of distance in international interaction remains strong. Indeed, even where there are long-standing ties between states this does not equate to depth or loyalty between these long-distance links.

States still retain considerable discretion to militate against the potential social, economic, and political risk within their space caused—at least in part—by globalization. Indeed, making globalization work for the state requires such risk mitigation strategies such as those integrated into notion of the welfare state where the state compensates losers from the globalization process. Such notions often ran against the aforementioned constraints upon discretionary acts by states in global system where such strategies could be seen as eroding the competitive position of states. This was seen as especially salient within the context of the aforementioned 'race to the bottom'. This narrative implied—as we noted—the erosion of cost increasing welfare provisions as states converge on a global norm to render the state 'business friendly'. However, to simply argue for a race to the bottom is to ignore that discretionary acts by states that seek to shape the risk environment in an era of globalization through engaging in public policy that seeks to militate domestic social, economic, and political risk caused by the on-set of globalism. The logic is that these discretionary policy decisions work to legitimate the choice of globalism by counteracting any economic insecurity that emerges from the process.

Agnew (2017) argues that the states possess the capability to shape the environment beyond their borders and the form and nature of the global system. Global processes and the global system represent state interests so whether it is free mobility or fragmentation these forms of the global system take places through the prism of state interests. Sovereignty is more than territoriality. States are simply one form of territoriality and that others exist such as imperialism which is based on networked power of the state based less on the notion of contiguous space but on dispersed and projected power by the core state. Another is 'integrationist' where states cede sovereignty to a deeper integration process. A further type is the 'globalist' based on territorially unconfined networks such as a hegemonic state seeking to influence flows across multiple localities. In short, sovereignty is not bound to territory. Thus, as much as globalization runs counter to the power of the state in territorial terms, it opens up other notions of state activity.

Ultimately, discretion is the capability to choose or not to choose globalization and that if it chooses globalization what options is the state allowed within the process to mitigate against the likely domestic risk associated with the process (see Table 3.1). This reflects Rodrik (2011) and the existence of compensation hypothesis where the welfarism continues as means to mitigate against domestic risk rising when exposed to external pressures. These are compounded by the characteristics of national systems that drive welfarism as a form of compensation to those that lose from globality. Thus, any risk of lost investment from proactive welfarism is more than outweighed by any potential increase in social and political risk that emerges from globalization. Indeed, there is little evidence that investment is deterred by discretionary state expenditure at all. In addition, it has also been argued that the level of welfarism and globalism are unrelated as they operate in separate spheres with domestic factors driving the level of welfare provision. This is reflected within the 'varieties of capitalism' hypothesis and that the impact of globalization

Table 3.1 Alternative views on state discretion and globalization risk

Perspective on discretion	Nature of discretion	Risk interface
Efficiency hypothesis	This is based on the idea that globalization imposes discipline upon states and creates a race to the bottom	That the state risk losses due to non-adaptation to global norms. All risks feed off this potential economic risk
Compensation hypothesis	That states compensate losers from globalization via welfare system	Works to lower macro-level risk by mitigating socio-economic effects of globalism
Variety of capitalism hypothesis	Globalization has little effect upon welfare state as it is driven by each national idiosyncrasy	State manages risk through embedded systems and not impacted by external pressures

is filtered through the process of national institutions such as the facets of the electoral system, the form and structure of the welfare state, and the facets of the national labour market.

According to Weiss (2005) globalization has augmented the state and that state power has grown alongside that of globalization. Welfare states have grown alongside globalism reflecting long-term social change as many states are acting in a similar fashion to this form of external change. Indeed, the state becomes more important to social life. Weiss (2005) argues that the system is more transnational than global where the state is still an important actor but that its role has adapted with the process. Indeed, strong states are facilitators of globalization (as highlighted by the literature upon the competition state—see below) and states are effective in creating networks to enable this process. Some states—notably in East Asia—have proactive 'Go Global' strategy where states proactively seek international presence.

The interface between states and risk shaped by globalization are nuanced. Hyper globalization might reduce investment risk for example but also increase the state to systemic risks. Rodrik (2011) argues that there needs to be a 'sane globalization' which is more managed based around allowing the diversity for states in setting own systems to deal with the risk associated with globalization whilst allowing them to benefit from the process. This eschews the notion that risk minimization comes from harmonization but in fact sourced from intra-state system diversity. This all suggests that the state is not a passive risk taker created by the complexity of the global system. The state can be proactive in shaping these risks as well being active in demonstrating resilience to these processes.

Box 3.1: State Types

Whilst the narrative surrounding states tends to treat them as a homogenous grouping. States can be differentiated by any number of different categories. The most common differentiator is by level of economic development (where economic development is defined as the level of economic and social wellbeing of a nation). This is linked not solely to degree of economic growth and industrialization but also to more broadly defined modernization which is defined as adoption of contemporary economic, social, and political practices to support the welfare of a state's citizens. Broadly a number of different (frequently overlapping) categories of state can be identified where the differentiation between each grouping is defined by a variety of factors such as national income, quality of life, standard of infrastructure, and degree of industrialization though exact classification points are a point of discussion.

Developed States

These are the leading industrialized states characterized by their mature, diverse economies based upon an array of industrial and service activity. They have a high standard of living and/or per capita income and National income (as measured by GDP). These states also possess a diverse export base and are well integrated into the global economic system. As of 2020, the IMF has designated 39 states as developed/advanced economies. This includes Canada, the US, much of western Europe and parts of East Asia (though not China) and Oceania.

> *Developing States*
> There is no clear definition as what constitutes a developing economy. As a group of states, they stand as a juxtaposition of developed states in that they have immature industrial based with exports often being driven by a limited number of (often commodity) products. These have under-developed infrastructure systems and generally lower standards of living and quality of life than developed states. The classification includes a diverse array of states with many at differing stages of development facing differing growth prospects such as those that are landlocked or small island developing states. As such, getting an exact figure on the exact number of developing states is subject to debate though the IMF has identified 152 states (a figure which includes the 24 emerging economies below). This definition includes all of Africa, Latin America, most of Asia, and Oceania.
>
> *Emerging Economies*
> These are defined as those economies with low to middle incomes that exhibit certain characteristics of developed economies notably with regard to sectoral balance. These are often states in transition from exhibiting little or minimal integration into the global economic system exhibiting high rates of growth and rapid industrialization and are notionally attractive for inward FDI. The absence of diverse exports and/or technological infrastructure to support this sustained growth can often mean that these states can be relatively high risk and subject to elements of economic/political volatility often as they are also undergoing economic/political reform. As of 2020, the IMF identified 24 emerging market economies including China, India, Russia, parts of eastern Europe, and Latin America.

State Strategy

State strategy is based around the notion of this territorial entity coping with and adapting to challenges in the global system that shape their ability to act as a territorial agent or that can shape their position within the international system. This treats strategy as a set of actions followed by states that emerge from both within their own space but also across other parts of the global system and other states. Unlike notions of corporate strategy, notions of state strategy reflect a broad series of concerns that seek to sustain state power within a given territory. On top of this are those actions beyond the formal borders of the state where the state has a geo-strategic interest in shaping the behaviour of other states or other agents and which impacts upon its capabilities to secure its position either as a territorial agent or as a force for change or stability within the global system. This dual faceted (yet overlapping) dimension of strategy reflects the needs of the state to engage in actions to preserve its territoriality but also to shape those events and processes within the global system that impact upon this territoriality.

When viewed through the lens of global risk analysis state strategy emerges to seek to attain a couple of these objectives.

1. Promote territorial stability to ensure the state does not cause inter-territorial instability that inhibits the development and sustenance of an environment conducive to the desired form and intensity of international flows.

2. Engages in inter-state activities or activities within the global commons that seek to promote stability or to militate uncertainty within the sub-components of the global system. The logic of such action is that action will impact upon the state and potentially challenge its territoriality.

These in combination seek to mitigate macro-level risk acting upon state from forces within and beyond the formal borders of the state.

States—through their strategies—can impact upon the conditions within, and operation of the assorted sub-systems based on the interconnection between national systems. States have in-built incentives to strategize to reduce the risk attached to the engagement with the global system but also build territorial resilience to cope with territorial as well as system risk (see ◘ Table 3.1). This creates an incentive to engage in co-operative actions to mitigate such risks creating contagion effects. Thus, state strategies seek to promote the stability and smooth operation of the state-based system by both ensuring that no single state can be a disruptive influence over the system and its operation and that where an agent/state has the potential to be disruptive to the system inter-state action can seek to mitigate (see Chapter 5). Not all states are alike in terms of their systemic effects with some possessing the capability to create contagion effects throughout the global sub-systems via their territorial and geostrategic activity. This is especially salient if the state is politically and/or economically powerful or if it decides to go 'rogue' and contravene international rules for systemic stability (◘ Table 3.2).

State strategy—whether it is territorial or geostrategic—seeks to attain and maintain state territoriality. The underlying notion is that without these being attained and sustained there is a risk of state failure (see below). These are based upon Turner (2020) and reflect the need for the state to attain the following over the territory where it is sovereign.

- *Control*: the state needs to possess the capability to secure control over the territory. This is attained through the state possessing the sole right to assert physical force over the population should actions by a rival power within and beyond the borders of state seek to contravene and/or threaten the sovereign power of the state. In terms of risk analysis, the logic of the monopoly of control by a single body is to maintain territorial stability. To ensure that there is certainty with regard to decision making and that instability within the state does not create contagion effects throughout the rest of the system.
- *Security*: the state also seeks to ensure that the territory over which it is sovereign is secure. This means not just secure from external threats through both active border measures and military presence to both filter out harmful cross border flows and also to deter intervention by non-domestic powers. Security also refers to the capability of the state to secure sufficient access to those resources (such as energy and water) that are necessary for state functioning. As with control, the need for security reflects the need to promote territorial stability and certainty. An insecure state is one that cannot be controlled and one that will veer towards instability.
- *Integration*: overlapping with control and security is the need for the state to seek to penetrate all parts of the space under its jurisdiction as a means of integrating them under a single authority. This political integration goes hand in hand with the need for the state to promote the social and economic integra-

Table 3.2 State-based risk and globalization

	Positive effect	Negative effect
Economic	• Create new sources of vital goods • Open up markets to mitigate against domestic maturity • Enable economic resilience through diversity of sourcing	• Impact upon local firms and incumbents, systemic impacts from overseas dependencies • Erosion of discretion over economic policy • Systemic impacts • Vulnerability due to dependence
Political	• Multilateral agreement to manage risk • Reinforce state control through regionalism	• Energy insecurity • Reduce sovereign capability • Lower state control • Vulnerable to hegemonic pressure • Political insecurity
Social	• Social groups form across borders and territories reflecting international systems of beliefs and cultures. This can be created by religion or an extensive diaspora	• Rising social risk due to Potential unemployment • Inequality and social exclusion
Ecological	• Better access to goods and services that are less harmful to the natural environment • Less impact on domestic environment	• Global resource exploitation occurs as less developed seek to develop and degrade environment
Technological	• Better access to global know-how • Able to develop state domestic technological infrastructure by access to global technology capability	• Risk of external control of technological systems • Risk of corruption of domestic technological infrastructure from global sources

tion of the state. The logic is to seek to legitimize the sovereignty of the state through promoting greater equality of economic development and social opportunity across the territory. The promotion (if not attainment) of integration reflects that unequal territorial development, political influence, and social opportunity has the potential to alter the risk environment through challenging the legitimacy of the state amongst segments of the population who may feel remote and/or powerless.

— *Development/Growth*: arguably promoting the economic development and/or growth of a state is the primary function of the state. Promoting the economic welfare and prosperity of its citizens is central to the state sustaining and maintaining legitimacy amongst its citizens. Thereby growth can be seen as a core contributor to lowering the risk within a territory through improving the well-being of its citizens. These growth strategies have to be sustainable; boom-bust strategies where sudden surges in growth are followed equally by sudden declines in economic activity growth. The resultant economic instability could not only be a source of economic risk but could also contribute to social and political risk.

— *Sustainability/Resilience*: a final aspect of state strategy is the possessing of the capability to adapt to the challenges the states face with regard to processes and events. Sustainability refers to the capability of the state to fulfil other aspects of its strategic priorities in a manner that is conducive with the maintenance and improvement of its natural environment. Security, control, and growth are all heavily influenced by the state of the natural environment and what states do about it. As natural ecological risk grows, and associated events grow more common, so its associated risks are expected to grow. This places an emphasis upon the capability of the state to demonstrate resilience so as to absorb and—where impacted—recover from shocks.

In accepting the notion of the state as having power, there is also an acceptance (as mentioned above) that the state has limits upon its discretion. This was summarized by Rodrik (2011) in terms of the trade-offs needed by states as they seek to position themselves within a global system where the intensity of globality both within and across systems can vary over both time and space. In seeking to understand the choices made by states with regard to their positioning within the global system, a dichotomy of choices offered with regard to state strategy namely where the state seeks to position itself with regard to the balance between globalism and nationalism. When viewed within the context of risk analysis, the position reflects perspective taken by the state with regard to the most effective means of attaining the aforementioned objectives. In this context, it reflects how the state feels is the most effective means of dealing with risk generated by the global system. Thus, the state recognizes it exists within a global system it therefore needs to choose how to manage the resultant flows and the risks that result both directly and indirectly from this process.

In this context, the essence of state strategy in the face of the globality is the extent to which states are comfortable with reducing their degree of discretion in seeking to gain what are seen as the benefits of globalization. Whilst there are assorted policy choices, the essential one is between discretion and globality. As reflected in ◘ Fig. 3.1, Rodrik (2011) argues the choice is between three dimensions namely globalization, the nation state, and discretion. The state can have any two of these but not all three. Given this the state has a choice of restricting discretion, limiting globality, or globalizing democracy. Of course, the type of globalization encapsulated within this argument is hyper-globalization which is the more extreme form of the process. Thus, as the desire for discretion increases the intensity of globalization will diminish. That the loss of discretion is linked to the extreme forms of globality underscores that globalization and discretion are only opposites in the extreme forms. This process is also rendered more complex by the fact that some areas may exhibit more globality than others. The degree of discretion so varies with the power of the state within the global system.

The trade-off is if a state wants globality it can do so within the context of the national system but will do by limiting its discretion. Discretion with a global system implies a shift towards a multilateral system where the state seeks to steer the global system towards its preferences. Nationalism with a preference for discretion means eschewing globality. This is a restatement of the trilemma within the context of state strategy. These trade-offs reflect the risk environment and prevent discretionary acts by states generating system wide risks. Where discretion does remain

The State and the Global System

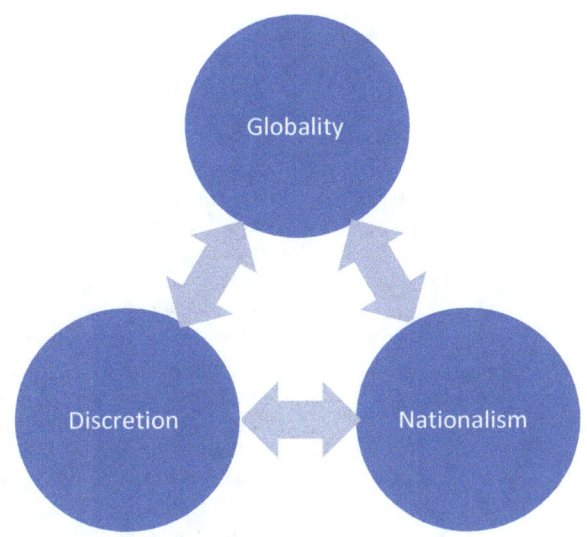

Fig. 3.1 The strategic trade-off for states (after Rodrik, 2011)

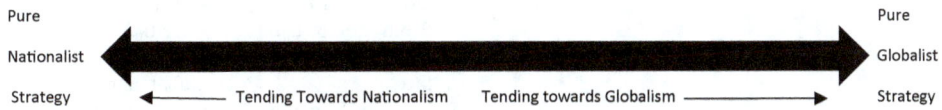

Fig. 3.2 State strategy spectrum

at the level of the state then it operates within a narrower sphere of activity. The desire to have lower economic risk within the state leads to lower political risk as a consensus emerges within and between political systems based on a consensual position with regard to reconciling national systems with globality. If states want globality then they must—in effect—render themselves obsolete and engage in shaping discretion at the inter-state level. State strategy is formed against a basis where—despite the rhetoric—actual formal integration is quite limited. There is within many markets a home bias which refers the local over the global. This has been reflected within the semi-globalization position.

In simple terms, the discretion over state strategy is reflected in where a state seeks to position itself on the nationalism–globalism spectrum (see Fig. 3.2). The state positioning within this spectrum reflects a range of policy choices over an array of policy impacting upon trade, welfare systems, economic management, etc. This position though does not simply reflect a decision taken in isolation but also reflects the state of globality within the system. This positioning upon this spectrum reflects a range of internal and external factors. Upon this spectrum the two strategic types can be defined (Table 3.3).
- Globalist strategy

This strategy is based on the state using its discretion to accept the globalization of the domestic system. This is normally reflected within the economic sphere, but this

Table 3.3 Facets of major state strategy types

		Strategy type	
		Nationalist	Global
Dimensions of state strategy	Control	• Strong centralized control; controlled cross border interactions • Interface between control, integration, and security	• Multilateral interactions to create common solutions to common control problems where freer movement inhibits full discretion
	Integration	• Promotion of social cohesion over globality • Strong regional dimension to territoriality • Strong interface between control and integration	• Focus on integrating all parts of a territory into global economy • Promote social policy infrastructure to enable coping with globality
	Security	• Strong control over cross border flows • Promotion of control-security interface • Discretion over de- and re-territorialization of flows	• Mutualization of security • Multilateral strategy to facilitate global flows whilst not comprising security/control interface
	Development/Growth	• Focus on national 'champions' • Limit intensity of domestic competition • Protectionism to promote security/economy interface • Discretion over economic flows	• Open to global competition • Limited domestic support • Global consensual rules accepted
	Sustainability/Resilience	• Promote localization as solution • Focus on national responses to global problems	• Address notion of sustainable natural systems as common problem • Mutual inter-state agreement

globalism will also extend to other sub-systems notably the political system where the state strategy will seek to replace discretion employed at the national level with that deployed at the global level. States accept restriction on discretion as rules of membership of global system. As a result, states will attempt to form coalitions and co-operation agreements to mitigate against the domestic risks faced by globality. Thus, states seek to steer this global system towards a direction that suits the state's geostrategic and territorial outcomes. As states are open to global governance as a mediating power, state discretion is used at international level though national systems are constrained but not rendered irrelevant. States have adaptive capabilities to the process of globalization. This reflects any constraints upon governments by the process are not absolute but relative.

The globalist strategy has found its most evident expression within the logic of the competition state (Cerny, 1997). This has growth/development as the focus of strategy through the proactive engagement with global forces as a driver for state competitiveness. The logic is that exposing domestic business to global competition can facilitate the success of domestic business. This could be a long spectrum from the creation of 'national champions' through to the reduction of barriers to trade to expose domestic firms to external competition. This is legitimized on the process of stimulating innovation and technological change and enabling domestic businesses to scale up but also by seeking to make the state an attractive location for inwards foreign direct investment. This strategy reflects Porter's notion of competitive advantage—where nothing is better for state competitiveness than competition itself. The effect is effectively globalizing the state's economic system and through this indirectly positively impacts upon political and social cohesion. The adoption of the competition state reflects those states competing for global capital, that will converge on global norm of policy to ensuring mobile capital is subject to low-risk context; this means keeping inflation low, fiscal restraint, and the extension of markets and the erosion of welfarism which is seen as a competitive disadvantage.

Despite this pro-global approach, the state remains central to the process as only it can stimulate and manage the necessary enabling policies that operate as a platform for successful integration of the economic base into the global system. Thus, the logic of state activity is not to replace the market or its failures but to make the market work more effectively and for that state's territorial and geostrategic interests. Thus, the globalist strategy is about managed globality within domestic systems. This management reflects a desire to mitigate the risks associated with globality not just economic (such as market foreclosure by powerful companies) but intervening to ensure socio-economic cohesion and the need to compensate the losers from the process. Moreover, the need for the state to provide the platforms for effective globalism increases taxes as part of global strategy as such actions support investment through the provision of public goods and services. Indeed, many states are still very proactive in the management of their economies despite their so-called powerlessness in the face of globalization. Many states form proactive industrial policies to allow their firms to operate within global systems. Thus, the state rather than being beholden to the forces of globalization is operating as a domestic catalyst for the process. Different states will develop different means of positioning with the global system with some seeking to scale up through regionalism, others seeking to use resource abundance to drive their position (such as low-cost labour), some may push 'go global' strategies.

Total globalism comes up against home bias (a natural preference for indigenous production and consumption) and the notion of semi-globalization. The notion of home bias remains strong both in terms of traffic volumes but also that there exist many sustained forms of fragmentation within the systems. These reflect transaction costs that add to friction within the global systems. These could be applied by the strategic intent of the state but may simply be driven by the nature of geography where the degree of globality of the state can be shaped by the distance it is from major markets. Semi-globalization reflects that hyperglobalism represents a theoretical extreme and that many states are in fact either by design or nature operate a semi-globalist which does not advance a national system by intent but simply through the nature of the activity. These reflect that globalism is formed against a basis of divergent national systems. This reflects that across many of the major measures of globalized activity (data movement, mobility of goods, services, people, and data), international flows are peripheral when compared alongside domestic flows. Indeed, across the flows, the global dimension is less than 10 per cent of total volume of such flows. In short, national flows dominate.

■ Nationalist strategy

This is a strategy that approaches engagement with the global system through the lens of national preference/determinism with a focus on unilateral, discretionary action. In its most extreme form, it would involve total non-engagement through a process of autarky which is based on national self-sufficiency and very limited international engagement. In practice, most strategies with a strong nationalist focus tend to be exhibited by higher degrees of protectionism and a penchant for national champions. This is associated with strong proactive approaches to welfarism to mitigate against the risks associated with excessive globality. This is more than simply compensating the losers but ensuring welfare by limiting excessive foreign competition by controlling cross border flows, by offering strong social protection despite what global forces say that the state should do and by nationalizing critical public services and infrastructure. This focus upon national determinism can often reflect a high degree of salience for security within national priorities. This desire for security leads to a higher degree of self-control in the specific areas of the economy notably those that are deemed 'strategic' which can involve a range of industries from food and broadcasting through to critical infrastructure. This represents a desire not to ignore globalism but to pick and choose intensity of interactions and to discriminate where it wants to protect its interests. Thus under the nationalist strategy the border remains a single salient definition of the market as it segments the state from all other states and the desire to monitor non-domestic flows impedes the penetration of the state by these flows.

Whilst the nationalist strategy can reflect a pushback against the domestic risks created by globality, it is not a strategy that is without risk. The trend towards nationalism is based upon the reintroduction of and/or sustenance of fragmentation within the global system as a defensive strategy by states to what is seen as the territorial threats from globalism. The strategy is not without risks. The reintroduction of barriers notably in areas such as trade and investment can lead to disconnect between domestic and global systems. This could have net welfare losses where strategies towards self-sufficiency occur where domestic systems are unable to replace imports either in sufficient quantity, quality, or at a price that would be acceptable to domestic markets. There is also the risk that disconnection (or even simply more discriminatory strategies) with the global system could impede upon economic growth and development through the discriminating state impeding the flow of knowledge into its economy. This could lead to long-term economic, social, and political stagnation as the state becomes detached from global knowledge systems.

Case Study 3.1: Why Afghanistan Matters

At first sight one might be forgiven for thinking that Afghanistan was geostrategically insignificant to the operation of the global system. The fact that this landlocked state with a population of 40 million straddles Eurasia and South Asia has often given it key strategic position within the global system. Historically the state has been pivotal in the main overland trade routes between Asia and Europe. It also become a focal point for many European states who were seeking to protect their Empires. These foreign powers sought to occupy and control Afghanistan but to no avail. These failed foreign powers include the Greeks, the Mongols, the Mughals, the British, the Soviet Union, and the US. This geopolitical turmoil surrounding the state reflects not simply this aforementioned central geostrategic position but also its recent form of governance has rendered Afghanistan a focal source of risk to the operation of the global system. Not merely through disruption to trade flows but also that the state has allowed extremist ideologies to ferment within its borders which have spread globally.

With the final retreat of the US from Afghanistan in 2021, the latest emergent superpower (China) has begun to show interest in the involvement in the state. For China, US involvement was—what they saw—part of a strategy of containment to encircle China with hostile states. Whilst this has diminished with US withdrawal China nonetheless looks at an unstable Afghanistan as a risk to its interests. China is especially worried that a power vacuum or civil unrest within this Muslim state (especially if more radical groups take control of the state) and could unsettle the already restive Muslim majority provinces of China (notably Xianjing) which Afghanistan borders. The fear is that any new Muslim regime could become a base of Muslim insurgents (such as the East Turkestan Islamic Movement) seeking to challenge China's control over these Muslim majority regions.

To this end, China is seeking to get involved with Afghanistan. It has begun to include the state within its high-profile Belt and Road Initiative in the hope that increased infrastructure in the state will help stabilize Afghanistan. This is a risk to China as Chinese contractors could be legitimate targets for insurgents and treated as merely the latest occupying power. Indeed, Chinese contractors have already been targeted in neighbouring Pakistan. The danger is that such attacks could lead to a spiralling involvement that sees China involved in a state that has already challenged preceding powerful states.

The reestablishment of the Taliban (a fundamentalist, militant branch of the Muslim faith) with the withdrawal of the US has re-affirmed concerns that Afghanistan could once again become a safe state for radical Islamic groups (in providing a haven for Al-Qaeda in the runup to the 9/11 attacks) to plan attacks on other states. Indeed, the accession of the Taliban saw increased levels of internal conflict rise between the Taliban and the even more radical Afghan version of the Islamic State (called Isis-K). Indeed, since the Taliban re-assertion of government, the Isis-K has been targeting minorities within the state and major al-Qaeda figures have also been successful in seeking refuge within the state. Ultimately, there seems to be little doubt that there will be a return to radical Islam within Afghanistan and that this has consequences for the stability of the state. For both western and Eastern states, this increases the level of security risk as this state has proved in the past that it can protect those bodies who seek to launch international conflict and commit terrorist attacks globally. The longer this goes on the more likely outside states will seek to get involved thereby creating the risk of another addition to the graveyard of Empires which has already claimed so many victims. Afghanistan remains a nexus of risk for the global system.

State Success and Failure

The underpinning logic of these strategies are that they promote the sustainability of the state within the global system. This is sustainability in the sense that the state secures the right to exist and persist. This in broad terms defines the success or otherwise of state strategy. The ability of the state to meet the criteria mentioned above (i.e., control, security, integration, growth/development, and sustainability) will shape the nature of success. That its capability to attain these objectives within a global system where it must make trade-offs with regard to discretion and its position across the globalist/nationalist spectrum forms the background to this strategy. This focus on strategy—as suggested—is not about treating states as companies engaged in a zero-sum interaction within the global economy but seeking to attain the strategic objectives.

Many measures of state success tend to be viewed through the narrow lens of economics. Measures such as DHL Connectivity Index and the World Economic Forum's Global Competitiveness Index (see web links below) tend to view state success through their engagement and positioning within the global economic system. There is a strong correlation between the perception of state success in terms of competitiveness and global connectivity. As Table 3.4 indicates five of those states that are the most connected are also the most competitive. This connectivity-competitiveness link is also reflected within the World Bank's Logistics Performance index (LPI) where the overlap is greater. In each case different degrees of connectivity are measured. In the case of the DHL index, it is connectivity not simply across trade but also across other measures namely data, people, and capital (see Chapter 4). The World Bank's LPI system is more narrowly defined in terms of trade flows, but they do give an indication of the ease with which goods flow across

Table 3.4 State rankings across a range of economic indices (as of 2022)

Top 10 global connected states (DHL)	Top 10 East of doing business	Top 10 states for logistics	Top 10 competitive states
1. Netherlands	1. New Zealand	1. Germany	1. Singapore
2. Singapore	2. Singapore	2. Sweden	2. US
3. Belgium	3. Hong Kong	3. Belgium	3. Hong Kong
4. United Arab Emirates	4. Denmark	4. Austria	4. Netherlands
5. 5Ireland	5. South Korea	5. Japan	5. Switzerland
6. Switzerland	6. US	6. Netherlands	6. Japan
7. Luxembourg	7. Georgia	7. Singapore	7. Germany
8. United Kingdom	8. United Kingdom	8. United Kingdom	8. Sweden
9. Denmark	9. Norway	9. Denmark	9. United Kingdom
10. Malta	10. Sweden	10. Finland	10. Denmark

and within borders of the state. The more successful states on this criterion can offer lower transaction costs for those businesses engaged in physical international interactions.

The WEF's Competitiveness Index takes a broader range of indicators (social, political, ecological, technological) to assess state economic positioning reflecting that competitiveness cannot be viewed in isolation from the broader themes of socio-political stability and quality of life concerns. The WEF ranking reflects the logic of the competition state driving a narrative that the state (in terms of the strategic themes) is pre-occupied with growth and development. The measures deployed by the WEF feed upon competitiveness as a driver of this process where competitiveness is defined by the state's relative total factor productivity. This seeks to measure how well resources are used within a given state. The drivers of competitiveness are based on how they effectively enable given resources to be developed and utilized. This is across several pillars which stress how state success is based upon the stability of institutions, the macro-economy, product/factor markets, and the financial system and the dynamics offered through social and economic infrastructure, health, skills, ICT adoption business innovation, and innovative capability. Thus, education and healthcare are not simply social goods but a means through which the quality of available resources can be enhanced. The index also makes a strong link between open democratic systems, open markets, and competitiveness (WEF, 2019). They stress how tangible and intangible components within a state interact to form a low-risk high growth setting. The more these are absent the higher the risk the lower the growth. These also suggest a strong link between growth and human development that growth is the means of poverty alleviation and stability.

This was also evident within the World Bank's Ease of Doing Business Report. This is an index of the extent to which any business seeking to or operating within a given state faces administrative, regulatory, and legal barriers within a given jurisdiction (World Bank, 2020). These measures by and large reflected the actual and implied transaction costs incurred by a business in each state context. It reflects the practicalities of both starting up and operating a business highlighting not simply the regulatory issues of gaining the necessary permissions in the creation of a physical operating unit but also of operating the unit in ensuring the ease of regulation and administration and understood legal frameworks. The narrative within the Ease of Doing Business Report was, first, about the speed of public administration decision making, second, about the predictability of the decisions being made and of regulations guiding this activity, thirdly, of the availability of enabling economic infrastructure, fourth, of the effective provision of reliable legal frameworks and finally of the ease with which products can be moved around the state and between the state and other states. This again reflects that success is based on open and predictable systems. These are systems that exhibit lower transaction costs in operational systems. Once again it is western market economies that are ranked as the states that are most business friendly with the exception of Georgia.

What is evident looking across these lists—aside from the appearance of the same states—is that they are the same types of states following the same types of strategy. These states are frequently small open developed economies for whom international interaction is almost an existential issue. Indeed, many of the most connected states have formed national strategies around positioning themselves as global hubs (notably UAE, Belgium, and Hong Kong). Irrespective of the size of these states, they also all tend to be liberal democracies where the allusion is that state success is driven by the combination of economic and political freedom. The logic is that these states are successful because they are open locations and that this openness leads to lower business risk.

These reflect the general conclusions of Porter (1990) who stresses market-based routes to competitiveness for states based on narrow economic objectives of seeking a high and rising standard of living. These market-based routes reflect that there are four bases for competition:
- Ability to sell based upon Price based competition and non-price competition.
- Productivity advantages which enable an ability to earn from investment.
- Innovation and flexibility that drives an ability to adjust.
- State attractiveness to inward investment.

These are all underpinned by the notion that there is nothing better for national competitiveness than the intensity of competition. The more intense the competition the more it will drive innovation and efficiency. Thus, states should seek to operate with minimal interference in the economy other than to work to preserve the intensity of competition between firms. Alongside these market driven factors, Porter is also keen to point out that factor conditions, demand conditions, and related and supporting industries can also play a role in the determination of competitiveness. According to Grant (1991) as reflected in ◘ Table 3.5, the dynamics of these processes led to the source of competitive advantage for the state changing over time. There is not inevitably that there is path dependency within these processes but highlight the stages a state can go through as they develop.

In terms of state-based risk, the logic of this analysis is that competitiveness drives national prosperity which delivers by default lower risk scenarios. If competitiveness is seen as a major measure of the success of state strategy based upon an ability of a state's firms to win market share based on good relative productivity, then this success is built upon non-market elements that lower the risk associated with entering the state namely the interaction between social infrastructure

◘ **Table 3.5** Stages of state competitive development

Development stage	Source of competitive advantage
Factor-driven	States compete on the basis of the availability of factors of production such as natural resources, labour, etc.
Investment-driven	When factor markets mature, rising demand within home market rises and stimulates increased competition which drives investment in human and physical capital
Innovation-driven	The combination of mature domestic markets, good factor conditions, intense rivalry, and meso links facilitate innovation
Wealth-driven	As economies mature and the former basis of competitive advantage declines, there is an increased focus upon managing existing wealth leading to an erosion of competitive advantage as innovation wanes, competitive intensity is lessened, and motivation declines

Source Grant (1991)

and political institutions and their interaction with micro and macro-economic factors. These are enabling factors that promote social-economic cohesion and mitigate against the excesses of free markets (see above). Acemoglu and Robinson (2013) reinforce this view stressing that it is open institutions that drive the process whereby the state creates the rights framework to allow markets to flourish based on open and accessible economic and political systems. The guarantee of rights on property, etc., stimulates innovation with the state engaging in basic market failure activities to support this process. These conditions for growth are not available in states with corrupt systems. The narrative stresses that the more broadly based political access the lower the risks are within a state (both political and economic) as decisions are more legitimate within this open system. These open systems generate political and economic stability as they are consensual. Systems where there is a narrow elite steering the economic system for their own benefit tend to be at higher risk. The longer the narrowness of this persists the higher the degree of political risk rises. This underlines the previous point that national prosperity—as a reducer of risk—lies not just in developing competitive firms but also in promotion of economic and social cohesion and political stability. Thus, social infrastructure is important not simply to supply industry with quality labour but also to promote social wellbeing and lowering state-based risk.

The overarching theme of this work is that the most successful states and those with the lowest risk are those liberal capitalist states. This pattern of growth through this method of lowering risk and that competitiveness being the driver of the process is reflected in ◘ Fig. 3.3. This reflects a virtuous cycle of the competitive, growing economy that acts as a basis for lowering risk across other sub-systems. Importantly, the model stresses that competitiveness is the catalyst of this process based upon a popular acceptance of the need by political system to accept the opening of the economy to global forces. This virtuous cycle can be broken if globalization breaks down as a source of growth. Indeed, populism as an expression of rising political risk was a direct result of rising social risks associated with the failure of economic impact of globality to deliver benefits throughout socio-economic strata (see Chapter 5). In this case, the political pressure based on rising social risk can put this cycle into reverse.

What About Alternative Cycles of Growth and Risk Reduction?

The flaw within the above analysis is that it can be ethnocentric arguing that western states are successful because they are liberal capitalist systems where the openness of political and economic not only generates growth and competitiveness but also work to limit social risks. There are other states (notably China) who do not conform to this model. These are states who push economic reform but without political openness and what economic reform does reform take place is heavily directed and controlled. This is a more state driven process where the state is proactive in driving those developments that will enhance productivity and that this instrument is closely linked to the nature of the state. There is belief that liberal capitalism will lead to under-investment in social goods that lower social risk but also add to enhancements in productivity. This is especially so in areas like social and economic infrastructure. In this case, the state needs to be heavily involved in directing resources to where the state's needs are greatest.

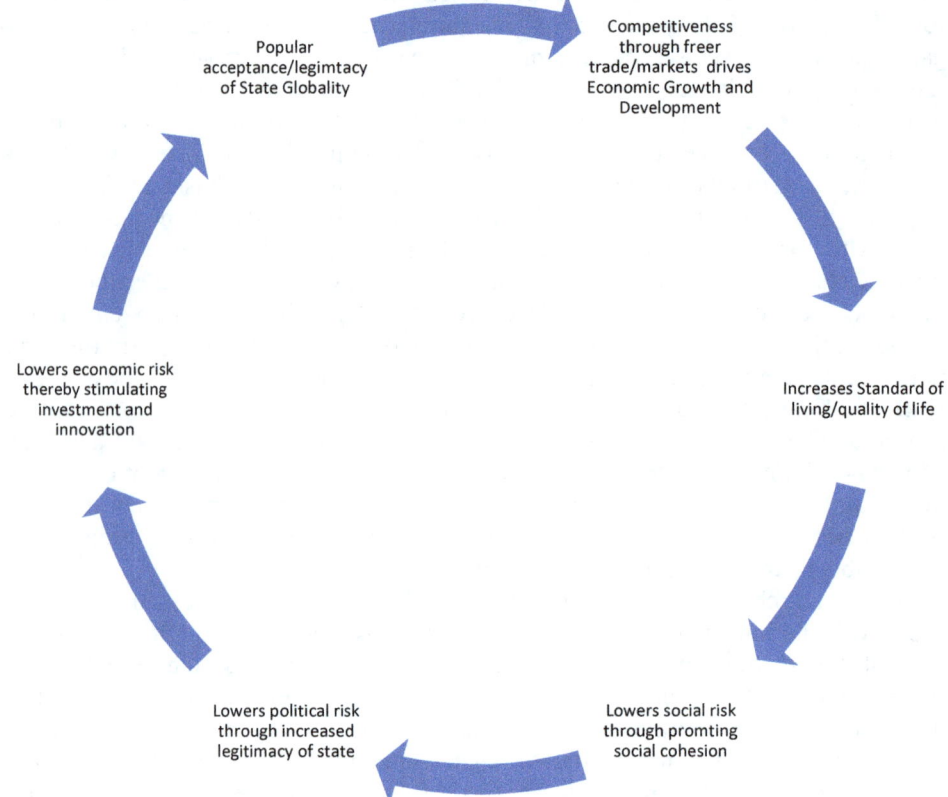

Fig. 3.3 Liberal capitalism and state-based risk: a virtuous cycle

This alternative risk reduction cycle is reflected in Fig. 3.4. This is a state focus on managing risk through political control. Markets have risk and the state needs to intervene to secure the necessary investment. Political control is the catalyst where the state manages international and domestic economic interactions. It seeks to make the state less dependent upon other states whilst seeking to increase dependence of others states upon it. The logic here is of the state being proactive in the management of risk so that disruptions/events in one area do not spill over into others. Thus, whilst the state might promote economic liberalization this process is steered to prevent the excesses of freer markets and market failure. The desire to use economic management of the economy to drive growth and legitimize power structures. The state does not want to turn economic freedom into political freedom and can only do so through delivering on rising standards of living/quality of life.

Alongside this the states' pushes managed globality so that openness does not align with loss of control or security concerns. The openness to overseas interactions is driven in part by a desire to not merely have a strong export driven strategy but also tap into intellectual property and know-how from overseas locations to feed into their growth model. Thus, the model depends upon controlled risk sce-

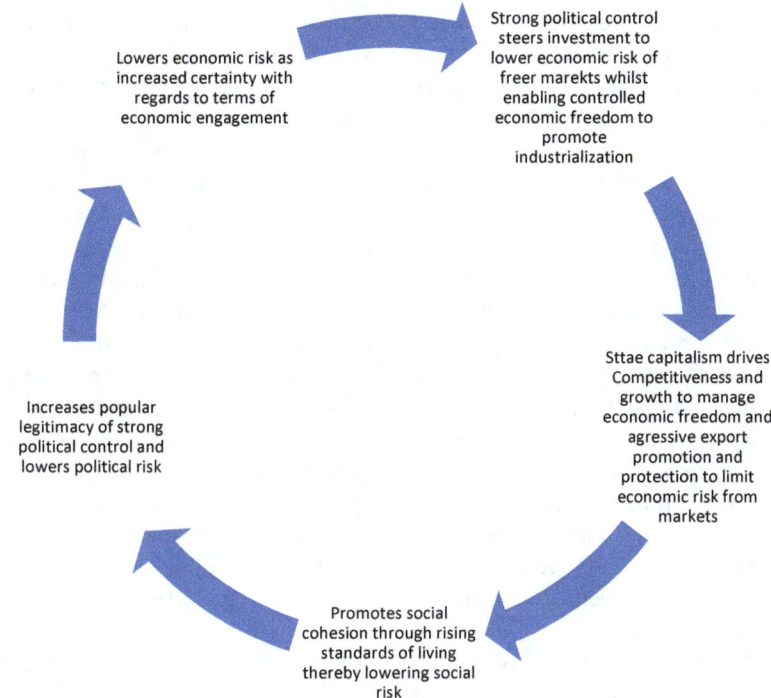

Fig. 3.4 Authoritarian model of country risk

nario where international interactions are managed and the globality of the systems controlled with a long-term emphasis of self-sufficiency where possible and international interaction where necessary.

Box 3.2: The Return of the State

For much of the twentieth and early twenty-first century, the role of the state was gradually diminishing. This was an era—whilst not exactly risk free—where there was confidence in global systems to mitigate many of the major risk facing states. However, this era is changing. There is increased level of political and economic risk within and between states and many citizens are looking to the state to mitigate many of these risks. Many of these risks were created by what many see as a misplaced confidence in the market driven global system to generate stability. Arguably the starting point for this sea change was the global financial crisis where the state had to intervene heavily within global financial systems when the risk within them was creating system wide risk threatening to spread from the financial system into the broader economic system. This spread (created a lack of liquidity in the financial system) could have led to the sharp rise of unemployment and business failure. There was heavy involvement by the state to bail out those financial institutions that could have created contagion throughout the system. Indeed, the US government spend some 4.3 per cent of GDP to bail out these failing firms.

The increased level of state involvement was also evident during the COVID crisis when demand for many businesses fell off a cliff edge. In this case, governments again offered a bail out of businesses. This time it was more widespread and covered a wider range of businesses to ensure that they would possess sufficient cash flows to secure their future beyond these extremely abnormal trading conditions. This led to lower levels of social risk as rises in unemployment were curtailed and political risks are mitigated as disposable incomes were sustained. This heavy intervention was also evident in the 2022–2023 energy crisis. Whereas in previous era, there was a greater degree of emphasis upon curtailing consumption in the face of restricted energy supplies and rising prices, in this case there was heavy direct intervention to cushion the effects of rising energy prices and to sustain disposable incomes and business cash flow. The heavy intervention of the state is also evident in the effect of other singular events such as weather events created by climate change where there is an exception upon the state to step in and cover the cost of regeneration.

These events in combination reflect how in a riskier environment the state has increasingly stepped into the secure systemic integrity. These reflect not just a response to market failure but also that the cost of doing nothing would simply be too much. There is still a tendency for the populous to look at the state as the actor of last resort should systemically risk rise. The rising levels of risk within the system have led to a more proactive state within the global system as each seeks to correct and mitigate the risk within their own part of it. Clearly in a global system individual action can only go so far and there are increased levels of co-operation between states where there is a mutuality of risk.

State Failure

The flip side of state success is state failure. These are generally territories where there is an absence of strong central control and/or low security and poor cohesion and represents a failure of the core tenets of state strategy identified above. These are states where social and economic infrastructure deteriorate and fail limiting cohesion intra-states interaction; where high crime rates and rival power groups within a single territory create social instability; weak economies and violence deter political and economic engagement. As such, the failed/failing state is an unsustainable territorial system. This unsustainability reflects the erosion of legitimacy due to their failure to deliver the public goods required of the state to provide. Citizens no longer feel secure with the state. These are also states that can no longer control their borders. In combination, these impact upon the territorial integrity of the state where another state might seek to gain control of parts of its space.

Thus, in terms of state failure the notion of whether it is competitive or not does not really figure in the debate. These are states with high political and social risks and that—as a consequence of such instability—economic development remains

The State and the Global System

subdued and often results in high economic instability. This tends to be indirect as investment is deterred by rising political risks and uncertainties within the borders of a state. As such, these states are largely peripheral to notions of international business. However, their impact upon the international business can be substantive if their failure spills over into geopolitical instability.

State failure can also be caused by cases of state capture. This reflects endemic corruption within the state in which the narrow private interests of well-connected elites override those of the broader population. The legacy of this is that state administration and bureaucracy becomes subservient to these non-state interests who have an excessive influence of how it functions so that it works to their economic advantage. This process differs from normal conceptualizations of consumption through the idea that state capture means that the outcomes of such influence are certain at the point at which influence occurs. Within corrupt systems, this outcome is far less certain. State capture is not necessarily state failure though they often do occur simultaneously, and the process can be deemed legal by the state. Failure in this sense is that the state fails to conform to what could be a business-friendly environment. Business under conditions of state capture run an increased risk of expropriation or interference with their operations should their activities run against the interests of the well-connected elite. This failure is more due to effective engagement with international norms that failure as defined above. State capture has been a common feature of states that undergone radical reform where the liberalization of markets (such as the ex-Soviet states) has led to an attempt by established elites to steer the process to serve a narrow group of interests through the granting of exclusive licences and other forms of economic preference.

PESOE Framework for State-Based Risk Assessment: Mapping State-Based Risk

Based upon the above analysis, the following offers an analysis of macro level within a state-based system. These are broad characteristics (also reflected in ◘ Table 3.6) as to what shapes risk within and between these criteria. Of course, the delineation of these is not clear cut as there is overlap between these macro-level risk drivers. Nonetheless each of these facets (both on their own and in combination) will shape the level and intensity of risk within a state. Each of these would normally warrant a chapter on their own so only short precis of the risks are offered. The rationale for these is to offer a mapping analysis to offer a holistic analytical framework to cover these processes to identify risk within a given state. These are reflected within the risk pentagon in ◘ Fig. 3.6 with allows each risk to be placed on a simple spectrum of low to high. This allows risks for each state to be mapped.

Political

Country level political risks are those uncertainties, ambiguities, and instabilities created by the functioning (or otherwise) of a state's political system. There is no presumption within such a definition that there any one political system (be it de-

Table 3.6 The categorization of state risk within the PESOE framework

	Low risk	High risk
Political	• Certain policy decisions • Open political systems • Separation of powers • Political Consensus at core of system	• Corruption • Closed political system • Narrow group of elites • Split polity
Economic	• Clear policy framework • Policy maker credibility/predictability • Certainty as to values of macro-economic indicators	• Unstable macro-economic indicators • Ad hoc policy framework • Loss of confidence in economic management
Social	• Good social infrastructure • Evident social mobility • Strong social cohesion/consensus • Strong, universal social safety nets	• Eroded/declining social infrastructure • Rigid social systems • Divided social/ethnic groups
Operational	• Minimal regulatory requirements • Certain and predictable legal system • High and reliable infrastructure systems • Ease of commercial engagement (both domestic and international)	• Discretionary regulatory system • Corrupt judiciary • Poor quality infrastructure • Excessive bureaucracy
Ecological	• Located away from natural hazards • Build-in resilience to operations • Low natural resource dependency	• High compliance costs with regulation • Physical location exposed to natural events • Low adaptation to localized risks

mocracy or autocracy) is better than any other but any system can only be assessed in terms of risk and the extent to which the system delivers a system that impedes upon effective business decision making and/or directly impacts upon the firm's activities within a given state. This will include the risks associated with the following:

— Bad governance: this can be driven by the failure of the centralized institutions to offer stable, predictable, accountable, and transparent decision making. The result can often mean that decision making can be arbitrary and legal systems only applied intermittently. This can often be created by poor economic performance and closed political structures.
— Corruption: often linked to poor governance, this reflects that elites utilize the political system for their own narrow personal benefit and is common within states that are defined as being kleptocracies (where political power is used to gain control of resources), narco-states (where a state relies upon illegal activity), and mafia states (based on strong links between states and organized crime). The challenge for business is shaped through the risk of expropriation by the politically well-connected and of making business difficult to undertake where policy can be changed on a whim.
— Political instability: this is where there is frequent and disruptive governmental change, the high likelihood and impact of political violence in society and/or a marked instability and unpredictability of public policy (as opposed to deeper regime change).

– Expropriation: this is the seizure of private assets by public authorities. This seizure could be linked to corruption, resource nationalism, or simply by a redefinition of public interest but the impact of the business is that its asset is involuntarily transferred to other owners.

The ability of rising national political risk to turn into geopolitical risk is based on the importance of the state to the global political system and the extent to which it is interconnected into and can shape this global system of national states. This rising political risk within a geopolitically powerful state is more likely to have global impact than other states. Where state failure (see above) or state capture by a hostile force that can spread across an inter-state region (such as Isis in Syria and Iraq) underpins how states that are largely peripheral to the political operation of the global system can have global impacts.

Economic

These risks are largely based upon macro-economic processes and events where micro-level risks are examined within operational issues. These macro-economic risks reflect how imbalances within macro-economic indicators can lead to an increase in risk for a given country. The typical set of inter-related indicators are:
– Unsustainable economic growth: this reflects that if growth is above long-term trend and fuelled by rising public and private sector debt then when that debt becomes unsustainable the economy faces the risk of dramatic slowdown leading to falling corporate profitability and lower consumer spending and firm investment.
– High and rising inflation: if inflation is high and rising then the economy faces problems are wages seek to keep up (causing a loss of competitiveness if there is no corresponding increase in productivity), that the real value of incomes is falling and inflationary expectations state to rise. As inflation rises and interest rates follow, exchange rates rise investment is deterred and export market share is also likely to fall.
– Budget deficits: this creates uncertainty through the impact on long run interest rates as states issue bonds to pay for the debt which—so some argue—limits the ability of the private sector to get access to funds. There is also the problem with how it is financed. If it is financed through an expansion in money supply, then it is inflationary. If budget deficits persist and lead to sharp increase in government debt, then investor might begin to doubt on the credit worthiness of the state leading to either rising interest rates or an economic crisis as the funds to support state activity dry up.
– Balance of payments issues: persistent balance of payments deficits place pressure upon exchange rates as it would be expected to fall to compensate for such imbalances. In these situations, states can find themselves in a lose-lose situation as either they increase interest rates to defend the exchange rate and risk recession or that allow the exchange rate to fall causing inflation as the price of import rises.
– Weak productivity: as noted above productivity is a leading indicator of competitiveness. As such any erosion of productivity is an indication of current and/or future economic difficulties as it is likely that the economy is losing competi-

tiveness, its firms losing market share, and an increased risk of future economic difficulties.
- High real interest rates: these are demand suppressants deterring investment, consumption, and—in keeping the exchange rate high—exports. These high real interest rates reflect embedded risks within the economic system but also create new risks due to their impact upon economic activity.

Social

These are risks created by a shift (either radical or long term) in the country's social structure created by a shift in culture or religious/social beliefs. They reflect those social structures are impacted by events and processes and that increases the risk of disturbance both within and across the different socio-economic groups that comprise the population. These disturbances can reflect especially the vulnerabilities/disadvantages of specific groups who can find themselves excluded or peripheral to the social system. There are many social risks that exist at the micro level generated as a consequence of business activity. At the macro level, the focus is upon society wide factors that can negatively impact upon the development and sustenance of social cohesion. These are also risks that can inhibit social connectivity that can directly inhibit the development of social capital which in turn can also limit the ability of a state to create and maintain a cohesive social system.

The challenge of this social change is not so much that the shift is widespread that can radically alter the underlying conditions/acceptability of the firm's activities within a location, it is more that the social shift is not universal and that as a result social stability is challenged. These social divisions can also spill over into political risk and can even cause geopolitical problems if they spill over into migratory flows between states. Overall, within any given state social risk will be driven by one or more of the following non-exhaustive lists of drivers:
- Divergent and conflicting ethnic groups: these are groups occupying the same territorial space who have long-standing or emergent inter-group conflicts.
- Social inequality: these create long-standing resentment and conflict between groups based upon unequal access to resources.
- Demographic change: long-term change in the composition of the population to which socio-economic structures need to adapt.
- Selective impact of technological/economic change upon particular social groups.
- Limited community resources to build social capital and cohesion.

Operational

These are largely micro economic processes that firms must incur as part of their actual or planned operations within a given country. They can indicate—in their simplest form—the transaction costs incurred as part of the business operations within a state. These can reveal the extent to which legal and regulatory frameworks within a state are stable and predictable and enable the efficient and effective undertaking of business from ease of starting to business through to insolvency. The more these activities are subject to the whims and discretion of policy makers the more the risks of operating within that country will grow. The risk is that the terms of business change whilst the firm is operating which can be created by legal uncertainties with regard to issues such as the enforcement of contracts. Thus, risk is related to ambiguity of laws and rules and the ease with which these can be changed at the discretion of well-connected policy makers. This degree of operational ambiguity overlaps with the levels of corruption within the country. Examples of operational risk include:

- Contract repudiation: these create legal ambiguity with regard to engaging with local partners and public bodies within the state.
- Confiscation of assets: the ease with which a well-connected individual or public body can seize an asset without adequate compensation will generate a hostile operating environment.
- Unreliable/under-developed logistics/infrastructure systems: these undermine the security of energy supply and the ease with which the firm's products can be moved around a territory.
- Excessive permitting requirements: the time required by business to meet all the necessary permits required to operate can add significantly to the costs. These include the time it takes to register a business, planning permission, ease of access to energy, etc.
- Poorly developed banking system: this can impact upon the ease with which a business can gain credit to support its activities and the simplicity with which this system can be navigated.
- Barriers to mobility across borders; modern value chains require ease of mobility of raw materials and semi-completed goods across borders the more bureaucracy a company faces when moving these factors across borders the higher the vulnerability of operation and transaction cost the firm faces.
- Immature tax system: the desires for a tax system that is stable and predictable and is also characterized by easy comprehension of the rules and simple paperwork.

Ecological

These are disruptions to business operations within a territory created by events and/or process occurring within the natural environment. These events/processes can be natural hazards (such as earthquakes) but can also be extended to ecological change created because of human activity (such as that exhibited by processes of climate change). These processes can cause damage to physical assets that inhibit operation of the business within a given location. Also included within this categorization of risk are the risks posed to the business by the policy response to the processes of ecological change within a territory. These ecological effects can also include effects that are more localized such as pollution and can also be extended to the depletion of natural resources (such as water) that support human activity within a country. The main ecological risks are:

- The probability of extreme weather events: this could be sourced from human activity driven climate change or from the location of a state which leaves it exposed to extreme events that can cause damage to firms' tangible assets or can impede critical infrastructure.
- Environmental regulation: in this case the business faces increased costs sourced from the regulatory necessity to meet minimum environmental requirements.
- Depletion of natural resources: the erosion/overuse of these resources can impede the operation of the business especially where the firm requires a large supply of that resource to operate.
- The prevalence of natural hazards: some states are in places which are naturally exposed to naturally occurring ecological risks (such as earthquakes). These places and businesses will have to incur costs to seek to militate against the risk of a high impact event damaging firms' tangible assets or impeding their operations.

Mapping State-Based Risk: The PESOE Pentagon

Based upon the main types of risks identified above, it is possible to develop a holistic framework to assess country-based risk. Based on an assessment of each risk, there can be a mapping where each risk is assessed on a spectrum of high-to-low. The highest risk states will be those whose profile offers an extended pentagon whereas lower risk states will evidently be closer towards the centre of the framework. The framework is designed to give an overarching perspective on the degree of risk faced within a country across a range of indicators. Evidently these risks will differ on a state-by-state basis. The example given in ◘ Fig. 3.5 indicates the two extremities of a high-risk state across all the available indicators and a low-risk state. Of course, these indicators alone will not solely shape the decision to engage with the state. The case of Japan below offers an exemplar of this risk mapping process.

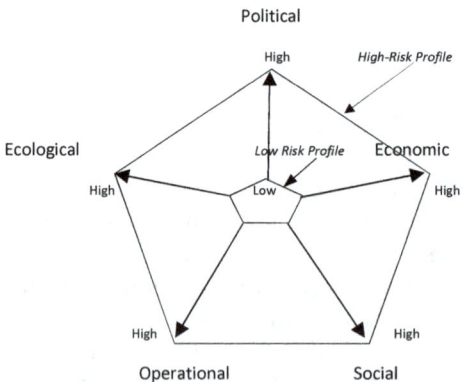

◘ **Fig. 3.5** The PESOE risk framework

Case Study 3.2: Mapping State-Based Risk: The Case of Japan

The following analysis is a brief exemplar of the PESOE framework used to identify mapping exercise for the country against the main identified risks.

Political Risk: Japan has a parliamentary government with a constitutional monarchy. Politics is dominated by the Liberal Democratic party which has been in almost continuous power since 1955 save for 1993–1994 and 2009–2012. Whilst there are several factions within the party, there remains broad consensus with regard to the main aspects of domestic, economic, and foreign policy.

Risk Status: Low

Economic Risk: Japan has a market economy-based system but has suffered low/stagnant growth for the past two decades since the bursting of the 1990s property bubble. As a result, inflation remains subdued with deflation being more of a long-standing problem as economic activity remains relatively muted. Whilst unemployment remains low, government debt is now over 260 per cent of GDP with the budget deficit being over 6 per cent of GDP (2021). Despite this the risk of default is minimal though geopolitical trends between the US and China are an on-going threat.

Risk Status: Low

Social Risk: Japan faces a rapidly ageing population with an estimated 60 per cent of the population being over 65 by 2060. This increases pressures upon social care as well as limiting the size of the working population. This is likely to have big implications for public debt. Despite this immigration remains low and society relatively ethnically homogenous.

Risk Status: Moderate

Operational Risk: Japan's supply side reforms have not advanced as much as other states. Indeed, its performance in the World Bank's Ease of Doing Business (it is ranked 29th out of 133) reflects that some aspects of business remain difficult notably ease of starting a business and ease of gaining credit. There are evident strengths in logistics though products and labour markets tend to exhibit relative rigidity.

Risk Status: Low

Ecological Risk: Whilst Japan suffers similar problems to other states with regard to the ecological effects of industrialization, the country is considerably more vulnerable to other natural hazards due to its position close to the meeting point of four tectonic plates. Japan has around 5000 minor and 160 moderate earthquakes every year. Whilst major earthquakes are rare (and the Japanese planning system has developed resilience strategies), they can—as the 2011 Tohoku Earthquake demonstrated—be extremely damaging to economic, social, and political systems.

Risk Status: Moderate

Based upon the cursory analysis offered above, the risk profile for Japan can be plotted on the PESOE framework. This highlights that social and ecological risks aside; Japan is a low-risk country (Fig. 3.6).

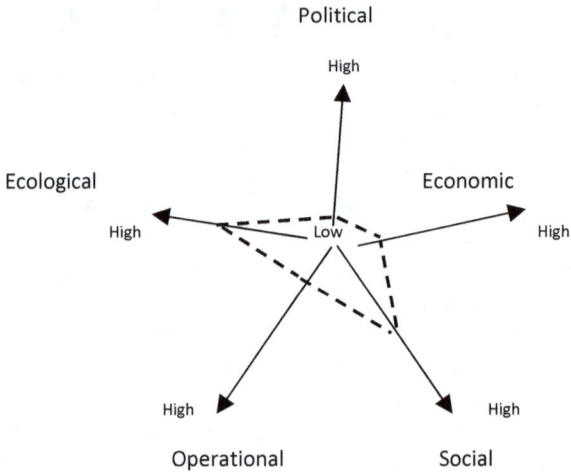

☐ **Fig. 3.6** Japan's PESOE risk profile

Conclusions

States are at the corner stone of the global system. It is the conditions within each state and the relations between them that set the conditions for the conduct and operation of global business. States (as mentioned) are very heterogeneous groups and differ by levels of economic development and political system to name just two parameters. As a result, states follow different strategies with regard to their position within and on the outlook of the global system. Therefore, level of risk across states is very divergent.

Key Points

1. States are central to the international system.
2. States are very divergent in terms of their strategies.
3. State success is often driven by their engagement with the global system.

Discussion Questions

1. What is the importance of the competition state to the global system?
2. How do you explain the rise of nationalism as a state strategy?
3. Does globalization challenge the power of states?

Activities

Choosing a country of your choice, undertake a PESOE analysis of that state concluding with a mapping of the risks within that country.

The State and the Global System

Summary

States are at the corner stone of the global system. These are not only a source of risks within this system but are also subject to these processes and events that can impact upon development and performance. To position themselves in the global systems states, develop a strategic narrative which seeks to balance the risks and opportunities created from managing the intensity of the globalization process. The resultant choice will shape the degree of discretion available to the state to pursue its own narrow interests.

Key Readings

Acemoglu. D., & Robinson, J. A. (2013). Why Nations Fail: The Origins of Power, Prosperity and Poverty.

Agnew, J. (2017). Globalization and Sovereignty: Beyond the Territorial Trap. Rowman & Littlefield Lanham MD.

Cerny, P.G. (1997). Paradoxes of the Competition State: The Dynamics of Political Globalization. *Government and Opposition, 32*(2), 251–274.

Grant, R. M. (1991). Porter's Competitive Advantage of Nations – An Assessment. *Strategic Management Journal, 12*, 535–548.

Porter, M. E. (1990). *The Competitive Advantage of Nations*. Free Press.

Rodrik, D. (2011). *The Globalization Paradox: Why Global Markets, States, and Democracy Can't Coexist*. Oxford University Press.

Rodrik, D. (2013). Roepke Lecture in Economic Geography—Who Needs the Nation-State? *Economic Geography, 89*(1), 1–19.

Strange, S. (1988). *States and Markets*. Bloomsbury Publishing.

Turner, C. (2020). *The Infrastructured State: Territoriality and the National Infrastructure System*. Edward Elgar Publishing.

Weiss, L. (2005). The State-Augmenting Effects of Globalisation. *New Political Economy, 10*(3), 345–353.

WEF. (2019). Global Competitiveness Report. ▶ www.wef.org

Web Links

The DHL Connectivity Index. ▶ https://www.dhl.com/global-en/spotlight/globalization/global-connectedness-index.html

World Bank. (2020). Ease of doing business. ▶ https://www.doingbusiness.org/en/doingbusiness

World Bank. (2022). Global logistics index. ▶ https://lpi.worldbank.org/international/global

Geoeconomic Risk

© The Author(s), under exclusive license to Springer Nature Switzerland AG 2023
C. Turner, *Global Business Analysis*,
https://doi.org/10.1007/978-3-031-27769-6_4

Our global economy is much more fragile than many of us realize.

Robert Kiyosaki

> At the end of this chapter
> The student will be able to:
> - Comprehend the global economic system.
> - Understand the nature of geoeconomic risk.
> - Understand the main drivers of economic risk within the global system and how they link with other systemic risks.
> - Identify the main forms of economic risk within the global system.

Introduction

The economic system is arguably the global sub-system where the forces of globality have had their greatest impact. Through the processes of economic liberalization, global economic flows have increased markedly over the past two–three decades creating rising economic flows of products (both finished and partially completed) and factors of production between states. Alongside these established and evolving interconnections between states are emergent forms of economic risk. These geoeconomic risks emerge because of economic interactions and interconnectivity between and within states but can spread throughout the global systems. This chapter will examine the form and nature of economic globalization before moving onto examine the main demand and supply side geoeconomic risks that are evident throughout the global economy.

The Global Economic Sub-system

The global economic system represents the totality of economic activity (i.e., those actions that involve the production, consumption, and distribution of products (goods and services)) within and between states. This economic activity is the result of the actions within and between economic agents (i.e., consumers, business, government) based around the engagement of commercial activity which has as its purpose the exchange of resources (be they financial or otherwise). In the capitalist system, this normally involves commercial exchange. Also involved within this definition is the means of management of the economic system as a means to influence the level of economic activity within the system (or a component of) so as to meet the broad set of objectives of the state or group of states. The focus within such a definition of so-called 'formal' activities is those activities that can be formally measured. In some states informal activity (often carried out due to it being illicit and therefore a desire to avoid formal monitoring) represents a substantial proportion of economic activity. In 2018, it was estimated the size of the 'shadow economy' was on average around 42 per cent of Global GDP and role to as much as 60 per cent in some states.

Thus, the global economic system comprises a complex set of economic actions at and between multiple scales but the focal point that drives analysis is the existence of interconnections between states which means that economic activity spills over between states and that—as a consequence—so does economic power. It means that any single interaction is increasingly comprised of a complex set of interactions that cross multiple borders multiple times in the process of an economic transaction being completed. The global economy is heavily skewed towards activity within developed regions with the relative shares (as of 2021) reflected in ◘ Table 4.1. This reflects that economic activity is concentrated in three regions (Europe, North America, and East Asia) which comprise over two thirds of all activity within the global system.

The economic system interfaces with the other major global systems and in so doing shapes the overall operation of the totality of the systems. The main ways in which the geoeconomic systems interact with the global system are as follows:

- *Political*: the performance of the economic system feeds into notions of the popular legitimacy of the system. The presumption is that a state and functioning economic system that delivers rising standards of living and national prosperity will attain political consensus. This logic applies to the logic of the global system where so long as economic globalization delivers benefits to the population so it will retain legitimacy. These arguments begin to fall apart under-conditions of economic instability, rising poverty, and inequality.
- *Social*: the global economic system is a core requisite of promoting social cohesion and stability. The more an economy grows the more the economy can invest in underpinning and enabling social infrastructure. If the economic system starts to facilitate and allow inequality the consequence is likely to increase social disharmony.
- *Ecological*: economic growth and development consumes natural resources with consequent long-term harm to the natural environment and to the conditions

◘ **Table 4.1** The relative share of economic activity across global regions

Region	Share of global economic activity (per cent) (based on estimates of share of regional GDP as a share of global GDP)
North America	20
Europe	21
Asia	49
Of which	
• North central Asia	2
• Middle East	5
• South Asia	9
• East Asia	27
• Southeast Asia/Oceania	6
South America	5
Africa	5

Source IMF (2021) World Economic Outlook Database

of human habitation. These concerns are especially acute in subsistence activity and in areas of rapid industrialization. As states develop economically so the social and political pressure increases to decouple the economic activity and ecological degradation.
– *Technological*: there is a strong causation between the nature of the global system and level of technological development. These links are mutually supporting in that economic development facilitates technological innovation which further supports economic change and progress.

The global economic system exhibits dynamics that have led its evolution from high openness but low intensity interaction of the pre-industrial era to the more intense more open interactions of the contemporary era. The modern economic system is based on interactions between states and the interconnectedness formed by the global networks formed by an array of economic agents from corporate to individual actions. Historically, the global system was based on interactions between states based on low intensity interactions which occurred with numerous hinderances to smooth cross border interactions. These were areas of system globality that exhibited low penetration within national economic systems and lower degrees of interconnectedness. Over the past two-to-three decades, this 'exceptional' system globality has been replaced by one where globality has become the norm for all agents at all levels. This change in the shape away of the global economy based upon more limited forms of international interactivity towards a more globally holistic system has been created by the increased normalcy in economic interactions associated with economic globalization.

The Nature of Economic Globalization

A crude indicator of the creeping globalization of the global economic system has been the increased share of global GDP comprised by the economic interactions created by global trade. Merchandise trade (i.e., trade in tangibles) offers the most visible manifestation of the globalizing system. Since 1970, global trade as a share of Global GDP has risen from 25 per cent to a peak of over 60 per cent in 2008; though it has fallen back since then to just over half of global GDP in 2020. Larger states tend to be less dependent upon trade with the US and China possessing a trade/GDP ratio of 23 per cent and 34 per cent respectively. For smaller states or where states operate a global logistics hub this ratio rises substantially to 320 per cent for Singapore and 293 per cent for Djibouti.

Economic globalization as the driver of the economic system globality represents the increased and increasing volume, speed, and penetration of economic activity between national economies as typified by the cross-border movement of goods, services, capital, technology, and data. The mobility of these factors of production reflects the globalization of economic activity where the creation of a value creating action and/or activity is based upon the intersection between value adding activities where resources and capabilities that are geographically dispersed and located within different countries. Evidently core to this production configuration working is the ease with which these respective value creating activities can be moved across political borders. This means that any single product is a result of a constellation of value creating activities (such as financing, production, marketing) resources (labour, finance, technology, etc.) and agents (corporates, consumers, governments) that are located in different countries.

The broad dimensions of economic globalization are highlighted in ◨ Fig. 4.1 and are briefly outlined below.

Globalized Production: This is based upon the creation of global value chains, corporate activity segments different yet distinct value creating activities across several different states. This creates a spatial vision of labour allowing firms flexibility in production (in response to changing consumer demands) which has been facilitated by technological change. The final product—therefore—is a modular construct of assembled distinct units from a diverse number of countries.

Globalized Markets: in terms of both business to consumer and business to business markets, the relevant market for business is no longer constrained by the physical parameters of the domestic/home market. Driven by a range of reasons (such as the need for scale and home market maturity), these forces drive firms into a broader range of international markets.

Globalized Business: this is based upon the existence of an array of corporate economic actors whose default setting for their business model is to operate in a global marketplace. These are businesses—as identified in ▶ Chapter 2—whose revenue and operating models are configured around the needs of the international market. These also reflect (as noted within ▶ Chapter 3) that domestic markets can be exposed to external competition as an intentional policy choice.

Globalized Technology: as stressed more fully below, technology is key enabler of globalization and therefore the opportunities can only emerge if technology is dispersed throughout the economic system. This is central to globalized production, business, and the servicing of global markets. Technological globalization is also central to the spread of 'know-how' throughout the global economy enabling commercial best practice to be spread widely.

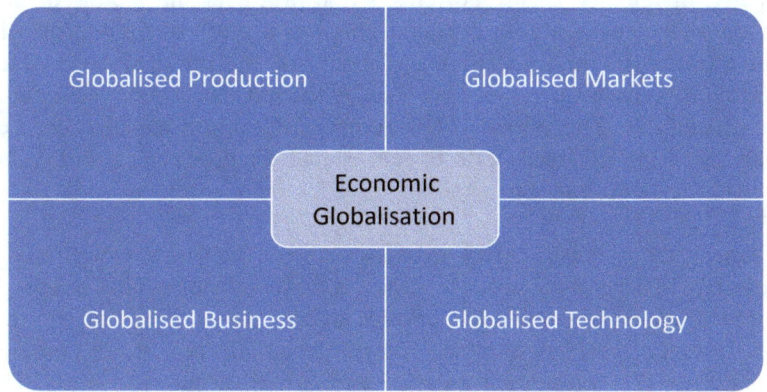

◨ **Fig. 4.1** The four dimensions of globalization

Drivers of Globalization

Economic Globalization has ebbed and flowed throughout global economic history. In its most muted form, it comprises the economic links formed between businesses and markets. Many of these links were the basis of the eighteenth- and nineteenth-century trend towards economic imperialism. Within a state-based system, the logic of economic globalism lies within the interlinked narratives of comparative, absolute, and competitive advantage where states specialize in those products, they are best at producing and use these as the basis for their economic engagement with the rest of the global economy in enabling it to access those products they would not be able to produce efficiently themselves if they could produce them at all. The notion of globalization is that such interaction becomes regularized and expanded and extended to a wider range of goods, services, and factors of production. The presumption of this is that the barriers to such mobility across space are lowered by states based on the belief that such barriers operate against the long-term economic interest of the state. Over time the nature of these economic flows have changed as they have:

– Increased in intensity; this is reflected in the sharp increase in the volume and value of trade of global trade over the past century where global trade has increased by more than 4000 per cent between 1913 and 2020. Indeed, exports are now 40 times larger in 2020 than they were in 1913. Over a shorter time period (between 1950 and 2020) the value of exports has risen from around $62 billion to nearly $ 20 trillion.
– Increased in extensity: this is reflected by the fact that what is actually traded and is subject to international trade agreements (either at a regional or a global level) has expanded markedly. Sectors that were conventionally protected for domestic strategic reasons have been exposed to international competition. This process has also been extended to sectors (such as services) that were conventionally seen as untradable. The other dimension of trade extensity is that fact that these international agreements now cover a wider number of states. As of 2020, the World Trade Organization covers the trading activities of 164 states; this is a sharp rise from 23 in 1947, 48 in 1964, and 123 in 1973.
– Increased in velocity: this trend reflects that products and factors of production can now move easily across borders. This has a physical dimension where progressive trade opening has eliminated many of the physical checks for a range of products. This has also been enabled by the automation of the remaining customs procedures. The velocity of economic interaction has also been enhanced by the extension of freer trade to services where production and consumption can be almost simultaneous.

These features of rising intensity, extensity, and velocity are symptomatic of the trend towards hyperglobalism within the economic system. This is based upon a virtuous cycle of ever-increasing economic interactions across borders that generates rising levels of inter-state interactivity, interconnectedness, and emergent integration between the component parts of the global economic system. These have been enabled by a number of drivers widely identified as follows.

Driver 1: The Triumph of Economic Neo-Liberalism

As identified within ▶ Chapter 3, a consensus formed since the 1980s of the benefits of freer markets not just within states but also between them. States have engaged in widespread economic reform that opened their economies to international competition. This consensus was based on US hegemony of the global economic system as it sought to export its model to other states. States based economic strategy around proactive engagement within the globalizing economic system in the belief that following this market-based system was more in its interests than being excluded from this rapidly evolving system. Thus—as noted above—more states engaged in the opening up of domestic markets to the discipline and constraints imposed by international competition. This was reflected within the policy prescriptions advanced by the Washington Consensus that stressed that successful states adopted market led economic reform, less state intervention/involvement in economic issues, and less generous social systems. The logic was to make these systems open to global capital.

Driver 2: Spread of International Governance and Regulation

Alongside this neo-liberal consensus was the emergence of various multilateral bodies which sought to establish global rules for state engagement with the global economy. Of the especial note has been the development of a set of world trading rules implemented latterly by the World Trade Organisation (WTO). This set core principles for trade based upon non-discrimination, reciprocity, transparency, and fairness. Over time—as mentioned—these rules have spread in both their spatial and sectoral extensiveness. Whilst they do not commit states to free trade, the rules do limit the freedom of action of states. Acting outside of these rules, can be expected to bring sanctions from other members. Also of note was the International Monetary Fund (IMF) whose primary function was to promote co-operation between states to foster stability within the international monetary system.

Driver 3: Finance and Capital Spread

Whilst capital has moved across borders for centuries, the most recent phase of globalization was characterized by a rapid easing on the controls that inhibited its spread throughout the global economy. These international capital flows included foreign direct investment, international bank lending, international bonds, portfolio investment, international equities, innovative financial instruments, development assistance, and cross border monetary flows. This promoted global financial integration where capital flowed to where the rewards were highest and enabling businesses to seek funding from whomever was prepared to finance their activities irrespective of their location. This also allowed financial assets to be traded internationally. These systems channelled finance from private citizens in one state to any other economic agents in any other states further deepening interconnection (see below).

Driver 4: Technology

The role of technology within the process of economic globalization has been mentioned above especially with regard to its ability to facilitate the process through the often-mentioned capability to promote time–space and cost-space convergence. This enablement function is underlined within the context of the other drivers in facilitating the intensity, extensity, and velocity of the process especially in areas like the global spread of capital and in enabling the speedier flows of products and factors of production across borders. This has been through technology lowering the transaction costs associated with engaging in international trade through, for example, lowering transport and communication costs. The spread of technology is key to enabling more states to engage with the international global system and—at a micro level—of promoting greater social interaction promoting greater cultural convergence.

Driver 5: Social and Cultural Convergence

The micro-level drivers mentioned above are to some degree determined by this process of socio-cultural convergence. Whilst the process has to a great extent been over played, it has been felt that global markets and global consumers are likely to emerge from the increased interaction of people across borders. The increased mobility of people, the export of cultural symbols, and the sheer power of US-based business—it was anticipated—generates a higher degree of cultural homogeneity that facilitates global markets.

These drivers have created a dynamic process of change within the global economy. For much of the past two to three decades, the consensus that surrounded economic globalization has viewed almost as an inevitable and irreversible process. This position has been shifting as the complexity of the process has exposed economic agents to unintended and unexpected risks (see below). These risks have emerged from the complexity of the process of interaction that has emerged as a long-term consequence of this process. This has been identified by four barometers of global interconnectedness (see below).

Global Economic Interconnectedness

Interconnection between national economic systems is important to identify and understand so as not merely to recognize the complexity of the processes but also the interdependencies that emerge between economic agents. It is through these interconnections that agents are connected to other systems and to the global economic system as a whole. These are the channels through which the economic interactions occur which underpin system complexity and the consequent performance of the system. These connections are uneven across space and time and reflect how connectivity varies and therefore how economic disruption can have uneven effects. These interconnections occur through four channels (trade, capital, people, and data—see below). This analysis takes on-going themes driving the global system to understand that these processes are variable over space and time. The degree of in-

terconnectivity (or a state's dependence and/or vulnerability) to global flows as a source of national wellbeing depends upon:
- The share of these flows compared to domestic activities. The greater that share of global flows the increased the dependence.
- The diversity of flows for the state that is the extent to which the state relies upon a limited number of states for the flows.

Trade Interconnectivity

The salience of the trade interconnectivity varies from state to state and depends upon the extent to which any given state requires such flows for the sustenance and rate of growth of its GDP. The convention is to treat exports as a major component of demand within an economy. Thus, if demand for exports falls the level of economic activity can also be expected to fall. The extent to which it does depends on the degree to which the economy is export driven and how any change in exports spreads throughout the rest of the economy impacting upon firm behaviour, etc. The higher the degree of trade connectivity the more the state will tend towards specialism though it trades this off against a higher degree of available product variety.

Capital Interconnectivity

One of the facets of systemic globality is that with financial globalization, states and businesses can draw upon more international sources of finance. This link draws the global capital markets closer together enabling FDI and international portfolio investment. The global capital system is concentrated on a few major markets (for example, New York, London, and Tokyo) who operate as hubs for global finance between which there are high degree of interconnectivity. Thus, the scope for diversity of funding is more limited but offers opportunities for a diverse array of savers to deploy their resources in a diverse manner. This interconnectivity becomes a problem when the resources within them become uneven or more limited in supply. Disruptions to these global hubs can spread throughout the global system as was highlighted the by global financial crisis in 2008–2009.

People Interconnectivity

This is linked to the ease of mobility of labour and tourists across borders. The ease of mobility largely due to absence of visas is seen as a positive factor. The ease with which skilled workers can move is a key integrator into the global system. These are economic flows due to the operations of business both with regard to internal business operations but also where states depend upon these flows for prosperity. For example, those states who rely upon short-term flows for the purposes of tourism or where states depend upon large volumes of expat or overseas labour to fulfil key roles within their economic model. This people connectivity overlaps with capital interconnectivity where a large diaspora generates large volumes of remittances for their home states. A final dimension of people connectivity is the movement of university students between states. These are important not simply for export earnings but also to aid the spread of knowledge.

Data Interconnectivity

As data becomes the nub of value creation within the global economy (see ▶ Chapter 8), so there has been an increase in the volume of data being moved across borders notably through the trans-oceanic cable system. This connectivity requires a reliable fixed infrastructure system with inbuilt redundancy to ensure that the disruption to any single route can easily be re-routed without any sense of disruption. On top of this the emergence of the cloud-based infrastructure system has highlighted the existence of these hubs as focal points in the global transmission of data. This data infrastructure is heavily focused upon developed states and underscores how data is (where allowed) stored and moved between states involving high velocity interactions and interconnectivity. This system seeks to draw on data harnessed from around the globe and globally distribute it for the benefit of relevant users.

***

Despite these channels for connectivity and interaction, in each case these forces are largely secondary to their equivalent domestic forces. Trade, data mobility, capital, and people movements are all dwarfed by their domestic equivalents. This highlights that despite the narrative of globality, the global economic system exists in a state of semi-globality where the domestic dwarfs the global. Nonetheless, these flows and their impact upon national systems is such that any disruption or impediment to these flows or—via some external event or processes—an event that suppresses these flows can generate geoeconomic risks. There is in truth nothing new about such links but what is novel is the tight coupling between these states with national systems often built around the objectives of exploiting these economic interdependencies. Thus, any sense of economic risk is defined by the extent to which these arrangements are endangered by economic events and/or processes that imperil this arrangement.

The Form and Nature of Geoeconomic Risk

The conventional notion of economic risk is based on an assessment of macro-economic risk. Within this definition the notion of risk reflects how trends in or events that influence key economic indicators that is inflation, economic growth, aggregate demand (and its components, i.e., investment, exports, consumption, and government spending), and exchange rates impact upon the investment and operating climate within a given state. Often the degree of economic risk is closely correlated to notions of political risk where sudden unanticipated shifts in economic policy undermine the viability of a business's involvement within a state to the extent to which these policy shifts drive a change in the aforementioned indicators. The catalyst for the shift can also lie within other systems aside from the political such as the social (unemployment), technological (cyber attacks), and ecological (singular events such as earthquakes) systems.

The notion of geoeconomic risk is that due to interconnectivity between national systems (due to the drivers noted above) any country-specific risk creating event or process has the capacity to spread beyond the borders of the country into other country/countries or upon the system as a whole. These geoeconomic risks can be broadly identified as one of two types:

1. Asymmetric: these are those geoeconomic risks that are country specific but have the capability to impact upon states where the geoeconomic risk is sourced. Generally, the ability of country-based event/process to impact upon other systems depends upon the importance of the country to the global system. Thus, for example, if the state is a major source of trade and/or capital flows any rapid deterioration in the macro-economic conditions in these states can rapidly spread throughout the rest of the system.
2. Symmetric: these those economic risks that will have system wide effects where the source of the risk is an event/process that effects a number of countries simultaneously though the impact upon each might be marked. These symmetric risks are generated by the interdependencies between countries with aspects of the economic system such as in global finance or logistics.

The notion of an event and/or process posing a risk to the economic system rests upon the extent to which instability and uncertainty is introduced into the system as a result of this process. Geoeconomic stability is seen as an economic good in that systemic certainty offers the basis for stable decision making and planning and therefore is a pre-condition for system efficacy. In addition to these intra-economic system flows, geoeconomic risk can spread out into other sub-systems. Exemplars of how rising geoeconomic risk infects other parts of the global system are highlighted in Table 4.2.

The notion of instability and risk within this context is that these events and processes spread beyond and between states and work to suppress activity within and between them. This could be a reduction in the level of economic activity within a state due to externally sourced or meta-level trends. The other side of this trend is where states or where these events/processes lead to a suppression of the

Table 4.2 Geoeconomic risks and its cascade effects in other systems

Risk	Geoeconomic risk interface example
Political	The pursuit of narrow economic aims can lead to rising levels of geopolitical risk due to rising levels of protectionism and other forms trade preference for example
Social	This exists where the pursuit of growth through hyperglobalism leads to increase social stratification where economic division increases leading to increased social risk
Ecological	The pursuit of growth and development often comes at the expense of the quality of the natural environment. This trade-off has long been accepted and is only slowly being challenged where there is a limited decoupling between growth and ecological degradation
Technological	As economies develop, they depend more upon advanced technologies which introduces new risks into the system

flows between state either by accident or design and which as a result lower the degree of interconnectivity and interdependence between states. The result is a risk to states that are impacted by this repositioning and a general deglobalizing of the system (see below). This is indicative of the power of economically powerful states to shape the performance of the global economic system.

> **Box 4.1: From Connectivity to Hyperconnectivity within Global Economic Systems**
>
> Connectivity within economic systems reflects the capability to engage with economic actors in other parts of the global system irrespective of their location. This was driven by the movement of trade, data, people, and capital across borders (see above). In the late twentieth century, hyperconnectivity began to be the norm for these economic flows. The gradation to hyperconnectivity from more basic forms of connectivity reflects that each of these sub-systems is in a permanent state of globality where the extensity, intensity, volume, and velocity of flows across borders renders these systems operating as a de facto single system where national resources and assets become subsets of a broader global system with the movement across borders being seamless and highly responsive to market forces. The salience of this trend towards hyperconnectivity is that the process becomes that much more difficult to govern. Thereby eroding the capacity of states to fully control the economic processes that are being undertaken within their respective borders. This reflects the interdependencies and outright integration between specific activities that take place within the global arena.
>
> The logic of hyper-globality is to render these global flows as normal rather than exceptional and in so doing to make these flows a permanent feature of the global economic system where fragmentation of the system (or any attempt to do so) would mean an economic loss for these agents wishing to curtail these flows. In so doing the logic of these moves was to eliminate all transactions cost involved in the movement of goods and services across political borders. This includes both tariff and non-tariff barriers. The trend towards hyperconnectivity within economic systems inevitably spills over into political and social spheres as the hyperconnected process impacts upon the performance and operation of these sub-systems. These inter-system globalizing effects were seen as a natural by-product of economic forces shaped by what was believed to be a social, political, and economic consensus with regard to the globalization process. Part of this was created by the perceived ability of large businesses to exert political power over states to minimize their socio-economic obligations.
>
> This consensus (which was largely commercially driven) towards hyperconnectivity reflected a belief that social and political systems passively accept these processes and simply adapt to them. This confidence in the adaptive capability of social and political systems was overstated as it understated the complexity of social systems within states and how hyperconnectivity would erode the connectivity within them and further erode social capital. As emergent hyperconnectivity began (both intentionally and unintentionally) to grow more complex and its effects became more explicit, these social connections became dis-

turbed through job losses and systemic instability which spilt over into political systems.

The combination of the COVID pandemic and the Russia–Ukraine conflict have served to erode this consensus. It was evident that both public health and security were imperilled because of the high degree of connectivity between states. Many see this as an era of deglobalization. Whilst there will inevitably be lower degrees of interconnectivity the more optimistic view is that new form of globalization will merge. Indeed, globalization has really been on the retreat since the global financial crisis and these new crises have accelerated the process. Hyper-globality was underchallenged as it struggled to manage the logic of specialization embedded within trade with the desire for states to diversify their economic bases. Thus, the free market logic of globalization conflicted with state intervention. Second, their evident inequalities were created by the process with states seemingly unable or unwilling to do much about it arguing that gains would trickle down. Third, globalization eroded the accountability of governments who argued that arguing against gravity was to argue against the laws of physics. Finally, it was eroded due to the innate contradictions between state security and international economic integration. The logic that states were too embedded with a global system to disrupt has been truly undermined.

As connectivity is lowered so narrative turn to what comes next. It is unlikely that autarky re-emerge. Despite this trend, it is possible that geopolitics comes to dominate the economic system where powerful states seek to shape the intensity and structure of global connectivity to serve their own interests rather than those of the system. What is likely to happen is that this phase of globalization will be replaced by a more managed system where the process serves national needs rather than those of the system. The hope is that the more states can control the openness of the system the easier it will be to attain a renewed consensus upon this process. To do this the system needs to ensure that national security within a global system does not create conflict. To militate against this threat a multipolar system. In short, geopolitics will be a major factor seeking to control and shape risk within the geoeconomic system.

Major Sources of Geoeconomic Risk

There are within the global economic system a large number of potential geoeconomic risks. This section will focus upon the main sources of risk within the system. These are based on the extent to which they offer the potential for geoeconomic disruption by impacting upon the economic growth/development of states. The broad framework for assessing risk (reflecting ◘ Table 4.2) is highlighted in ◘ Fig. 4.2 which underscores how many of the risks outlined below can spread into other sub-systems underscoring the core role the globalization of the economic system plays in the broader system as a whole. It also reinforces the point that no single risk can be seen in isolation from other risks both economic and non-economic. The list of risks addressed below is not definitive, but all have their catalyst within macro-economic uncertainty and ambiguity and how this feeds through into agent (notably states) actions and strategies to generate higher degrees of risk.

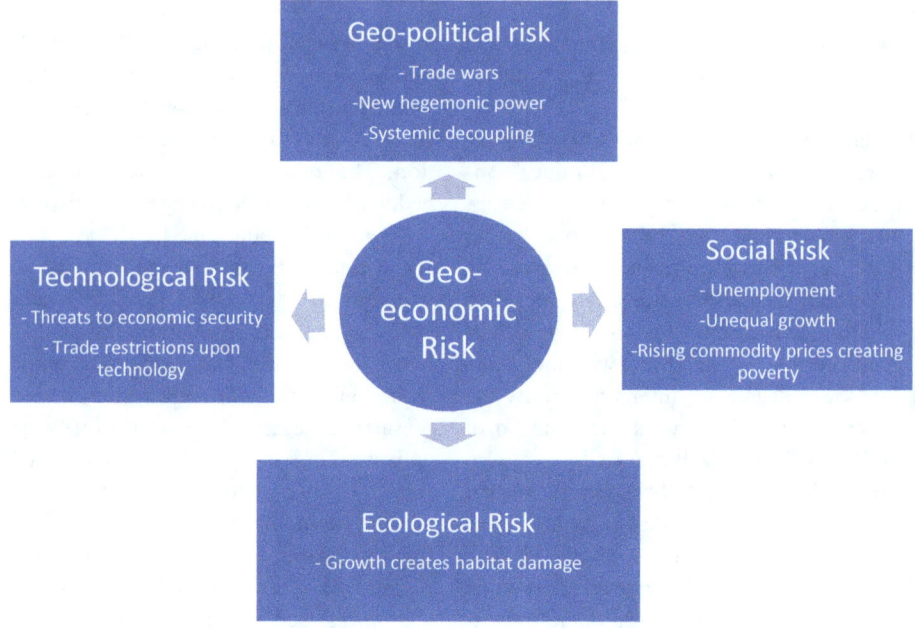

Fig. 4.2 The centrality of geoeconomic risk to global system risk

Dominant State Performance

The global economic system is a hierarchical system comprised of states with varying degrees of salience to the performance of the global economy. Very broadly these states can be categorized as:

- Core Countries: these are states that dominate the global economy both in terms of their share of economic activity and trade volumes. These are largely the mature industrialized economies of western countries but also should be included are established states in East Asia (notably Japan. Australia, China, and South Korea) who occupy strong trading positions within the global economy. In this sense, the core is essentially based around the three east Asian states, the EU plus three (Norway, UK, Switzerland), and Canada and the US. Thus, the core is a very narrow set of states. These states comprise over 70 per cent of global GDP in 2021.
- Peripheral Countries: all other states are contributing the other 30 per cent of global GDP. These peripheral states are the other 160 states within the global economic system. These comprise some large states such as India, Brazil, and Russia who represent over 7 per cent of global GDP. The other 157 states (i.e., all of Africa, Most of Latin America, and Asia) comprise the remaining 23 per cent of Global GDP. Indeed only 18 states have a share of GDP that is in excess of 1 per cent of Global GDP.

Whilst the dividing lines are not neat and over simplified, the division between these states underscores the asymmetry of power within the global economic system and where the greatest source of risk lies. Even within the core groups of states, there is a great degree of asymmetry of power as highlighted by ▫ Table 4.3. This reflects that—in effect—two states (the US and China) dominate the global economic system. This reflects more the rise of China than the outright decline of the US. Across this limited range of indicators, the economic dominance of China and the US is demonstrated. This dominance reflects a major risk to the global economy especially for those states that depend upon trade with these states to sustain their economic position. Large parts of Asia are dependent upon China and so it is with the Americas and the US. This concentration of economic power within these states represents a core economic risk throughout the global system. This leaves the global economy vulnerable not merely to the economic performance of these states but also disputes between these states (these are explored more fully below).

Some states are especially exposed. In North America, 37 per cent of Canadian GDP is from trade with the US and over half of Mexican GDP. Emerging economies are especially exposed to a slow down within the US. The same is also true of China where many Asian and Oceanic states (notably Australia) are especially exposed. The other key theme (as noted below) is the extent to which the US and China are interconnected. This tight coupling initially within trade highlights an asymmetric vulnerability within the system notably that if either the US and/or China suffered from an economic slowdown then the effects would spread. Initially, this would be through lower demand for goods and services produced elsewhere. The effect would be to create a cascade effect of lower demand throughout the rest of the global economy thereby creating a global economic slowdown or worse. These effects extend beyond trade and economic growth into FDI where an economic slowdown in these economies could curtail financial flows out of these economies. The financial dominance of these states highlights a further risk as these states (especially the US) are major magnets for global finance. Any downturn in corporate performance though could have ripple effects throughout the rest of the global economy. Financial difficulties within the US market could force US-based investors to withdraw their investments overseas to support their domestic business opening up the possibility of a liquidity crunch. This is also a possibility with many developing and emerging economies who have come to rely heavily upon inward Chinese investment (such as that funding the Belt and Road Initiative) which could also be curtailed or withdrawn during an economic downturn or change of strategic priorities.

Throughout much of the twentieth century, the US was by far and away the pre-eminent economic power with periodic challengers emerging in the form of

▫ Table 4.3 The Sino-American dominance of the global economy

	US	China	Sino-US total
Share of global GDP (per cent)	24.4	17.9	42.3
Share of global economic growth (2017–2020) (per cent)	17.9	35.2	53.1
Share of global exports (per cent)	8	15	23
Share of FDI outflows	13	26	39
Share of FDI inflows	17	14	31
Share of total equity value (per cent)	55.9	5.4	61.3

Germany and Japan. Whilst still important to the global system, the rise of China represents a more fundamental challenge to the dominance of a single global entity. Whilst the US was wary of the challenge from other 'western states' the rise of China represents not just an economic challenge but also a geopolitical issue. It does create new forms of risk especially where—as we shall see—it is leading to a decoupling process and fragmenting the global system (see below). This issue is not so much about the suppressing of global economic flows and performance but more about changing the fundamental nature of such flows.

Generalized Macro-economic Instability

Macro-economic instability are those processes that cause a rapid and unexpected oscillation in key macro-economic indicators (see above) that increase the level of economic uncertainty and risk with regard to the performance of an economy and/or interconnected economies. The higher risk indicators for any given state will reflect the likely outlook for economic growth, inflation, trade performance, government debt, and so on. These reflect that when these indicators behave in an unexpected manner there is an increased policy risk as states adapt (or are compelled to adapt) to the imbalance within their economic system. Thus, inflation may result in increased risk of deflationary policy actions which suppress demand; a trade imbalance runs the risk of a depreciating exchange rate and rising government debt runs the risk of an expanding money supply or austerity. For these reasons, macro-economic stability is seen as a positive strategic virtue with industrialized states showing the greatest degree of stability and predictability and developing states the highest degree of instability.

However, the economy is complex, and its performance is not always predicated with certainty. Thus, even in states where macro-economic stability is expected unanticipated events can throw an economy from its expected trajectory. Arguably the greatest risk faced by the global system is a symmetric economic downturn based on sharp falls (or even negative) in rates of economic growth experienced throughout the international economy. This effect is likely to be most pronounced when these downturns are felt uniformly across the major developed economies. These downturns and the level of interconnections between them would likely see a sharp fall in interconnectivity as lower global demand reduces the demand for imports or possibly as states react to lower levels of demand through increased discretionary trade discrimination measures.

Symmetric economic downturns can have multiple causes such as a financial crisis that leads to liquidity and therefore investment to dry up or a public health crisis (such as the coronavirus pandemic) which led to suppression of demand but with the common theme that both were unanticipated both in terms of occurrence, impact, and policy response. The extent to which any unanticipated event creates a system wide event depends upon the degree of resilience exhibited by the global system to counter deflationary effects of such events. This resilience reflects a capacity to absorb the reductions in aggregate demand from these events through countervailing measures such as government spending. Where such facilities do not exist then the risk of prolonged downturn is likely. Evidently this resilience is more likely in developed states. Indeed, the lack of resilience in developing states is likely to feed through increased social and political risks.

The emergence of macro-economic instability within dominant states has the capability of turning asymmetric macro-instability into rising symmetric system wide risk. The sheer dominance of the US and China (and to a lesser the EU) across the global economic system means that any macro-economic instability within any one of these economies has the potential to spread throughout the rest of the economy. For example, lower growth within these states has the capacity to rapidly spread throughout the rest of the global economy as these states are major export markets. There is also the risk that inflation within these states will also transmit across the rest of the system through rising prices within one state (and its counteracting measures) spreading throughout the rest of the economic system.

> **Box 4.2: The Great Moderation**
>
> The Great Moderation is the name given to a period for the global economic system (notably for developed economies) between the mid-1980s to 2007 which was characterized by high rates of economic stability and low rates of geoeconomic risk. This period stands in contrast to previous periods where economic instability became normalized. This low-risk environment was characterized by a low rate of instability within the system generated by:
>
> — Low inflation without trading off a rise in unemployment.
> — Stable and predictable growth.
>
> The stability of these macro-economic fundamentals led to the erosion of uncertainty within the system which led to greater risk taking. This latter point was generated by the fact that investors did not expect rapid oscillations in economic conditions or of economic policy (such as interest rates). The greater risk taking led to increased investment in both capital and financial assets fuelling a rapid rise in the prices of these (especially the latter in the case of house prices). These benign macro-economic conditions across developed states were fuelled by:
>
> — successful inflation targeting by independent central banks.
> — the ability to create and sustain non-inflationary growth.
> — falling commodity prices.
> — rapid advances in information technology and supporting infrastructure.
>
> These benign conditions—despite being driven by low-risk conditions and economic stability—really created the seeds of its own destruction by fuelling asset price bubbles generated by the aforementioned excessive risk taking. This led to rising levels of debt (notably by banks) as investors gambled on these rising asset prices and a gross understatement of the geoeconomic risks that were building up in the system due to debt led investment, rising trade imbalances, and artificially low interest rates. Eventually the over extension of investors and eventual defaults led to a scenario where the debt held on a set was worth more than the asset itself. This created a banking crisis as banks had too much debt on their balance sheets on assets that were falling in value. As the banking and other sectors were bailed out with state funds, a banking crisis became a sovereign debt crisis as risk became contagious throughout the global economic system as governments, households, and the banking system all found themselves with highly indebted balance sheets. The complex interactions between these became a core feature of the 2007–2008 Global Financial Crisis (see ▶ Chapter 1).

Global Decoupling

As mentioned at the core of the global system are the interconnections between states. One of the core couplings within the global system are those links between the two main global economic powers, the US and China. As China has emerged as an economic power of the past two decades so the interconnectivity between itself and the US have increased notably as trade and investment flows between these states has increased markedly. These interconnections between these states also extend to people where there are extensive tourist flows between these two states. As China has become more fully integrated into the global economy so trade and investment flows have increased markedly between these two states. This interconnectivity and interdependence between these states cut across three different dimensions.

- *Trade*: these states are their respective major trading partner. Outside of the North American trade agreement partners (Canada and Mexico), China represents the largest share of US trade at some 14.3 per cent of the total. This is just 0.2 per cent below the combined share of Mexico and Canada. Whilst total trade was (in 2020) $615.2 billion; exports at $164.9 billion were overshadowed by the volume of imports which were $450.4 billion. This asymmetry has become a major source of friction (see below). On the flip side, the US is China's largest trading partner comprising nearly 18 per cent of total exports.
- *Supply Chain Linkages*: the trade in semi-finished products comprises an increased share of global trade (about two thirds) and such links are also important to US–China trade links where the latter became the effective global manufacturing hub. The end result is that many US companies have become dependent upon Chinese manufacturing capabilities attracted by their reliability and cost effectiveness. Exact figures on the value of these links are difficult to attain but it is recognized that textiles, electronics, and machinery are thought to be especially dependent upon these links.
- *Investment Flows*: the financial links between these states involve both direct (i.e., investment in physical assets) and indirect (i.e., investment in non-tangible—often financial—assets). Direct investment in China by US businesses has risen substantially in the two decades to 2020. In 2000, the level of FDI in China by US business was just over $ 11 billion by 2020 this figure had risen to around $ 124 billion. The stock of Chinese FDI in the US was around $60 billion. Chinese citizens and government are significant investors in US financial assets. Its shares of total holding of US securities has varied over time but has generally oscillated between 9 and 15 per cent of total value of securities (many of which are government issued).

The catalyst for the pursuit of the advancement of decoupling between these two states was the persistent trade deficit the US has with China. Whilst the US had long complained about what it perceived to be China's unfair trading practices. It was not until the emergence of a populist (and protectionist) agenda emerged in the US in 2016 were their concerted actions to seek to remedy the issue. This trade issue was compounded by the perception of an emergent strategic threat to US business from China as the latter seeks to move up the value chain and produce more high technology goods. This strategy creates security concerns for the US as these business concerns overlap with those of the state. Thus, the US is resistant to the share of technology and know-how with a state that could be a potential economic and military adversary.

The systemic effects of this process are conjectural. The process does not intentionally seek to lower global interconnecting flows and thereby lower the intensity of globalization though that may be the long-term consequence of the process. Evidently the strategy decoupling is to lower the volume and value of flows between these states and redirecting them to between more aligned states. Decoupling has been aligned with strategies within both states to internalize value chains especially those for high technology. The effect of this decoupling will be to lower interconnectivity across the globe as states seek to internalize key activities that are central to state security. As such, across trade, investment, data, and people, there have been moves by states to internalize the flows. They create a geostrategic risk for the system as they can drive a suppression of economic activity between states and leaves states that are especially dependent upon such flows vulnerable.

Commodity Markets

A commodity is essentially (in its simplest form) a product that cannot be differentiated upon anything other than price, though—in practice—the quality of these materials can vary markedly. These have uniform qualities and applications irrespective of user. Within the international system commodities are generally equated with raw materials which function as inputs into the production of other goods and services. The fact that these commodities are globally traded means that the price of these inputs will be the same irrespective of the source of the material. The degree of openness of national commodity systems to overseas supplies and investment tends to vary with the price of commodity. When the price is low states tend to encourage FDI within this sector of their economy. When the price is rising there has been a tendency amongst some states to shift tack and move towards resource nationalism (see below). Arguably a major differentiating factor is the issue of supply and how this can vary (against relatively stable/predicted demand). This issue of supply depends upon local political economy, the availability of resource at a given point of processing/extraction and competition (or otherwise) between suppliers. The effect of discrepancy between conditions of supply and demand can be rapid price fluctuations, so-called commodity price shocks.

There are four broad types of commodity groupings:
- Energy: this includes the prices of oil, refined petrol, and natural gas.
- Agriculture: this includes the prices of staple crops and livestock produced upon on farms/plantations.
- Base Metals: these are metals used in manufacturing and production processes including copper, zinc, aluminium, etc.
- Precious Metals: these are rare, high value metals such as silver, gold, and platinum.

These shocks can be transitory or permanent. Transitory shocks are created by singular events that cause a short-term drop in the demand or supply constraint for commodity products. These transitory shocks can be created by a multitude of factors such as adverse weather, lower demand caused by economic recession within major export markets, or possibly human induced events caused by terrorism or human error. There is also the possibility that shocks can be permanently created by the advance of new technologies, processes, or knowledge that permanently increase the supply of or reduce the demand for particular commodities. These types of shocks are especially evident within the agricultural sector. Operating against these short-term shocks are the existence of commodity super cycles that reflect long-term cyclical patterns in the markets for these commodities.

One of the primary drivers behind oscillations in commodity prices is the shift in the economic cycle. Broadly commodity prices are closely and positively correlated to the state of the economic cycle. An upturn in the level of economic activity tends to increase the demand for commodities as output increases causing prices to rise. Economic downturns have the opposite effect. The era of the global pandemic (between 2020 and 2022) highlighted these trends over a short time span as rapid changes in economic activity caused a large shift in commodity prices. The initial 'global lockdown' caused a massive drop in many commodity prices notably energy where there was a sudden glut in energy supply causing a sudden almost 60 per cent drop in prices. These trends were also evident in other major commodity groupings such as agriculture (10 per cent), metals (15 per cent), and precious metals. In these cases, the prices rebounded quickly for as the economic stimulus took hold across the developed world, the prices of all these commodity groupings took off. This created an almost 'boom-bust cycle' for commodity suppliers where the bust of the initial lockdown was quickly overtaken by the rising prices as economies recovered as shortages of demand were overtaken by supply constraints.

These effects of this rapid cyclical change underscore the vulnerability of those economies that depend upon these products for export driven growth. For developed states, the sharp rise in commodity prices (notably in energy) underscores the inflationary risk from such price shifts. The legacy of this has been the actions by these states to lower their dependency upon these imported commodities (most notably energy) towards domestic production of these core commodities. Notably lowering the dependence upon oil in the transport sector by stimulating the change towards electric vehicles fuelled by electricity generated by domestically produced renewable. This is still for many states a long-term distant objective. Dependent upon whether these shifts are seen as transitory or permanent, the risk environment for the global system changes as inflation rises universally across all states and those lower income groups are adversely impacted. This is also evident across the system where many commodities importing developing states are more adversely impacted by commodity price rises and inflation especially incomes are static and employment uncertain. The sharp rise in food prices that has been created by supply side constraints (created by mixture of factors from rising fuel prices to climate driven production impacts) that pushed up prices is evidence of such pressures.

Nearly two thirds of developing and emerging economy states (this rises to 75 per cent for developing states) depend upon commodity exports and these rapid oscillations in price can be destabilizing and can cause big variations in economic activity within these states. A state becomes commodity dependent when at least 60 per cent of its merchandise export revenue comes from commodities. This leaves them vulnerable to a range of risks such as slow economic growth, macro-economic

Geoeconomic Risk

and political instability, poor governance, and high exposure to singular events that can radically alter the market conditions for the commodity product at a short notice. These problems become especially acute when the state relies upon a more limited range of commodities. Moreover, the sharp rise in prices can be a mixed blessing for whilst they can increase export earning, they can create the 'Dutch effect' where high prices push up the exchange rate and inhibit the development of an indigenous manufacturing sector.

> **Box 4.3: The Strategic Challenges of China and US Decoupling**
>
> One of the prevailing narratives surrounding notions of deglobalization relates to the gradual (and sometimes not so gradual) decoupling of the World economy's two biggest economies: the US and China. This decoupling relates to both informal and formal severing of economies ties between these economies so there is less co-dependence between them. On both sides, these processes are driven by issues of economic security; of depending upon a trade partner who is both an economic rival and (potentially) a military rival. Whilst China is developing a 'made in China' strategy by internalizing global value chains. The US is looking to 'friend shore' key strategic activities by seeking to move them away from China's sphere of influence into states with whom it has more cordial relations.
>
> Initially these efforts on decoupling were limited to areas of high technology and social media sectors. In part, this has been created by the desire of China to develop its own technology champions behind its own firewall as a means of seeking to control access to sensitive information. In the case of high technology, China is very keen to make up for lost time by rapidly developing high technology sector though this has often come by access to and—in some cases—duplication of western technology. For both commercial and security reasons, many western states and companies have sought to curtail access to such technologies. For China, such efforts are an attempt by western states to limit its rise further underlines its justification for such actions.
>
> Such efforts belie the long-standing and embedded interconnectivity between states which strategies of decoupling will struggle to quickly remove. There are many sectors from agriculture to raw materials to manufactured components where the links between these economies not only remain strong but are still actually growing. Indeed, in agriculture, China is the US' largest export market; an export market that is still growing. Whilst the trade deficit between the US and China has been falling (the size of the deficit was a major issue for the US), this was mainly done through China re-routing US exports through third states notably East Asian states where Chinese firms have a substantial presence. This is a trend that is also happening in happening in Latin America where there has also been a surge in inward Chinese investment.
>
> Similarly, US companies were sustaining and even increasing the inflow of investment into China. For US businesses, the narrative surrounding decoupling is not only unhelpful it is also impossible. Moreover, it feels that any policy to do so would merely feed the anti-US narrative within China. The more Chinese business the more de-

pendent China becomes on the US. Ultimately, this investment is sustained by the fact that such coupling with China is still very profitable. This absence of decoupling is evident on e-commerce platforms where the respective market leaders in each are still selling large amounts of goods from manufacturers from each other's producers. As the dollar rose in value throughout 2021/22, the coupling has only tightened as this process has lowered the cost of Chinese imports. As a result, many US businesses are importing products from China. Moreover, this process has also been driven by Chinese investors looking for a safe haven in US assets.

Nonetheless there is a strong anti-China sentiment in the US administration with an equivalent hostile positioning by parts of the Chinese government. Whilst business has sought to push back upon this hostility, populist sentiment is against it. As inflation rose within the US, there was a limited back tracking on this as the US sought cheaper imports. Moreover, as the US seeks to promote the energy transition it will need to import solar panelling from China which has a supreme cost advantage in such technology. However, China's asymmetric decoupling based on independence from the US remains an embedded policy.

These formal measures exist alongside those measures taken by businesses to divest their activities within China for reasons of corporate and social responsibility. Pressure these businesses face from a diverse set of stakeholders is placing pressure upon business to divest their activities within China where they are subject to concerns over issues such as human rights. Moreover, there is a long-standing trend by US businesses to seek to exert more control over their value chains by shortening them. This could also create more incidents of divestment in China especially in the face of rising political risks and uncertain logistics costs. In these cases, decoupling whilst ignoring long-standing connections remains fraught with difficulty.

Economic Nationalism

Economic nationalism is the tendency within states towards preference for domestic ownership, control, and supply of certain activities and assets and to eschew any sense of foreign control of key economic assets. These seek to prioritize national interests over international economic integration seeking to control and/or limit flows of trade, people, data, and/or capital. As such, this represents a discriminatory strategy deployed by states towards home-based agents and against overseas involvement within domestic economic activity. This can be expected to represent a fragmentary force upon the global system seeking to inhibit the intensity of flows between states. The logic of such strategies does not necessarily lie within economic hostility towards overseas involvement in domestic economic activity. Indeed, these forces can be driven by issues such as wanting to establish indigenous production and control for reasons such as ensuring and enhancing local inputs into the national economic activity for reasons such as economic security and mitigating the climate change effects of long-distance supply. Turning national preference into more overtly nationalist strategies has to reflect that the strategies are heavily skewed by themes of national determination, self-identity, and autonomy. Thus, national preference for reasons of strategic expedience differs from those actions taken that seek to explicitly positively discriminate in favour of national supply. Thus, economic nationalism in its most pure form involves reshaping the economic system to serve politically nationalist goals (see ▶ Chapter 5) and away from agreed global trading rules where they conflict.

This pure economic nationalism would promote global fragmentation by shifting towards protectionism, restricting immigration, placing constraints upon FDI, opposing globality, and global rules for economic interaction. The justification for the pushback against the on-going globality of the system is that these processes increase the degree of domestic uncertainty and risk. Thus, the process seems to trade off national risk created by globality for increasing global risk. This domestic risk reflects a desire to mitigate the worst effect of globalization in terms of employment, investment, and control of critical infrastructure, for example. They are also driven by the desire to create national champions in key areas of the economy. This reflects the desire to enhance the positioning of the national economy within the context of the global system. There is not expected to be any large-scale increase in economic nationalism largely since globality has matured to the extent that the interdependencies between economies make separating out the national from the international more difficult with many states seeing such economically nationalist strategies as ultimately self-defeating. However, this has not stopped many large states pushing towards greater degree of economic nationalism—to varying degrees—across all of the interconnector drivers identified above.

An expression of this trend towards economic nationalism is resource nationalism. This reflects a strategy by states who depend upon the extraction, development, and/or processing of natural resources (including all the types of commodities mentioned above) for exports seeking to ensure these remain under national control to ensure the profits from such assets stay within the state and not exported via the repatriation of MNC profit. Frequently, these debates with regard to resource nationalism have been shaped by the globally strategic important resources of hydrocarbons. These restrictions driven by resource nationalism begin to place restrictions on ownership and investment within these sectors. The logic here is not to restrict the flow as much as ensure that the rewards from these flows are directed towards the benefit of the state alone. The logic is that this material was derived from a territory therefore the resource should belong to that state. The assertion of state sovereignty over natural resources within their jurisdiction is a pragmatic more than an ideological strategy based on underlying market conditions. Though factors such as macro-economic difficulties, a misconception about costs and populism could also be contributing factors to the process.

Typically, the on-set of resource nationalism is driven by the belief by the state that the overseas investor is getting too good a deal for their investment. Whilst resource nationalism has been common within developing states it is becoming increasingly common within developed states such as Australia and the UK. The expropriation of foreign owner assets can be direct or indirect where the state can deploy a number of measures the state could increase the royalty rate (the fee paid by the overseas firm to extract the resource), increase taxes, alter licences, and impose new regulations. Resource nationalism tends to occur when:

− A state is over dependent upon natural resources for growth and development.
− The state has a fast-growing population coupled with a need to invest in public services for this expanding population.

- The politics changes and more nationalism pushes back against overseas control of assets of 'vital' national interest.
- There is a need to stimulate employment.
- There is a need for resources to develop/improve public infrastructure.
- The laws surrounding investment are antiquated possibly reflecting a colonial heritage/legacy.
- There is an absence of transparency or inequity within the tendering process for the concession to extract the resource.
- There is a belief/perception that the contract awarded was exploitative and was given on the basis of favours or desperation by the awarding state.
- There are high commodity prices.

The trend towards resource nationalism has increased since 2017 largely driven by the poor financial position of many states especially in the aftermath of the global financial crisis. This might not always involve direct ownership but can occur through other means such as higher taxes upon these businesses to cover any short fall in public funds. For business, these processes tend to increase the risk and uncertainty associated with international engagement increase as the certainty of global rules and norms are undermined and/or disavowed. It can lead to increased risk of expropriation, pressure to localize supply chains, and adapting to shifting local conditions. The risk level is also increased as there is also likely to be an absence of continuity in policy making processes and costs associated with involvement within such states are likely to increase. Thus, economic nationalism is closely correlated with political populism so economic policy is likely to be highly adaptive to changing public sentiment. The impact on business can vary on a spectrum from outright expropriation/nationalization at one end to creeping regulatory control at the other where the state seeks to steer align corporate objectives to its own.

The oil producing cartel of OPEC has proved a model for what nationalism can do if states seek to take a nationalistic stance in energy supply. Energy is 25 per cent of global trade by value so resource nationalism seeks to control the value of these flows by restricting value where necessary. Though the ability of resource nationalism to act as an effective strategy depends upon source of alternative (both actual and potential) competing/substitutable resources. Thus, the stronger the market control the more the resource nationalism works as a strategy. If an alternative exists, it will be of limited efficacy.

Case Study 4.1: The 'Excessive Globalization' of Rare Earths

At the core of the energy transition is the ability of leading industrial state to access what are known as rare earths. These are 17 metals that are used in electronic devices as well as new generation technologies such as electronic vehicles and wind turbines. The problem is that China controls the vast majority (over 80 per cent) of the accessible reserves. This becomes a geostrategic problem for western states given the strategic vulnerability of trade relations with China. The apparent oxymoron of these rare earths is not that they are rare at all; they are very common. The problem is that western supply chains have become reliant upon a single supplier (China) for these commodities thereby creating a potential chokepoint due to excessive concentration of supply.

The challenge in diversifying access to these rare earths means circumventing two challenges. The first is that accessing these rare earths requires that many more tonnes of aggregate and rock must also be removed to just access very small quantities of these commodities. This process can also lead to significant ecological degradation. Second, separating out the rare earths from other materials and preparing them for use requires high powered magnets and other energy intensive technologies. This is an area where China has a mature production and processing system that is significantly more advanced and efficient than rival sources. Thus, there is little direct commercial incentives for operators to seek to diversify supply without some impetus from states to do so.

The emergence of China as a global powerhouse for the extraction and processing of rare earths is a direct legacy of the long-term transfer of western manufacturing to China from the 1980s. Before this, states tended to rely upon domestic sources of these rare earths within their own abundant reserves. The transfer of this activity to China reflected the cost efficiencies that were evident from doing so. Chinese production of these material is up to 30 per cent cheaper than equivalent processes in many western states. As the energy transition began in earnest, there was a growing belief that states had allowed excessive concentration of these activities within a single state and that the resultant strategic vulnerability. Over the past decade Europe and the US have increasingly sought to diversify away from this dependence. In practice, progress has been slow. In the five years to 2022, the EU has only managed to lower the share of Chinese rare earths by 7 per cent to 90 per cent. This underlines the scale of the challenge.

Europe has set up new partnerships with new suppliers. The first was with Canada where the abundance of these resources combined with vast reserves of hydropower is opening this state as a supplier of these commodities. The other supplier with whom Europe struck a deal was Ukraine which also has an abundance of many of the rare earths. The positioning of Ukraine as a rare earth's supper power has been inevitably set back by the conflict with Russia. Russia was also going to be an alternate major source of these commodities. Given the harsh geopolitical conditions regarding these states, western states are now looking to further diversify from alternative suppliers in Latin America and sub-Saharan Africa both of which also face geostrategic risks in the processing of and the extracting of these commodities.

Asset Bubbles

Prior to the COVID pandemic there was no greater example of the economic risk created by globality than asset bubbles. These asset bubbles and the global flows of capital that generate such imbalances were a direct cause of the 2007/08 Global Financial crisis. Whilst the causes of this crisis do not need to be revisited here, their experience does highlight how the bursting of asset bubbles can spread globally. The development of global financial markets—as mentioned above—has allowed funds to be channelled globally to where the rewards are expected to be highest. Asset bubbles are created where the price of an asset (be it stocks, property, bonds, commodities, etc.) rises sharply in a manner that seems out of keeping with the market fundamentals of the asset (supply, demand). Thus, the price of an asset keeps rising due to speculation that the price of the asset will keep rising creating a demand that keeps pushing the price of that asset ever higher. There is long history of asset bubbles within the global economy and the bursting of these bubbles (where the asset price collapses to reflect its fundamentals) can exert tremendous damage upon the economic system as the collapse in value exposes investors to issues of debt and the holding of an asset that can often be worth a fraction for which it was bought. These effects are especially dramatic when these purchases were bought with debt by investors for whom such debt is substantive proportion of their wealth.

Whilst there has been a global dimension to a number of asset bubbles, the real estate bubble highlighted the complexity with which the 'bursting' of these asset bubbles can create global contagion as the failure of sub-prime mortgages left a host of national banking systems exposed. As the states sought to bail these banks out, what was a private sector debt crisis morphed into a sovereign debt crisis which fed into public sector austerity which contributed to rising populism. A direct cause of these asset bubbles has been the quantity of money created by central banks flowing into the financial system which is fuelling these purchases. Since the Global Financial Crisis, central banks have kept interest rates low and have engaged in quantitative easing to mitigate the global shocks to the system created not just by the bursting of the Real Estate Bubble but also to cushion the economic effects of the COVID-19 pandemic. This has driven a fear that new bubbles are emerging within the global system. Of especial concern is the risks within the Chinese property market which represents almost 20 per cent of Chinese GDP. By late 2021/early 2022, several large property developers were facing financial difficulties with no sign that the state was willing to bail them out. The fear is that if these collapse the effect upon the Chinese economy could create contagious effects upon the rest of the global system. There are also concerns with regard to the rapid appreciation of Bitcoin (a digital currency). Underpinning the extent to which these risks turn into rising global financial risks is the outlook on inflation. If inflation persists and interest rates rise persistently then the risk of an asset bubble turning into more exposed financial risk increases.

The Asset bubbles are not simply created by the complexity of interactions between agents and across borders but also by the complexity of the products themselves. Financial innovation has led to the emergence of new products that were too complex to effectively regulate that enabled financiers to engage in increasingly risky activities. The resultant collapse in the GFC underscored that multifaceted nature of complexity and that this complexity makes the financial system difficult to predict and manage. The experience of the bursting of the asset bubble is that it can create credit crunches as banks seek to lower their debt this means the supply of credit dries up limiting investment and is felt along supply chains as the credit that supports trade finance dries up. This spills over into consumption leading to a prolonged downturn. These reflect that asset bubbles are essentially a catalyst for a set of cascading effects that spread throughout the global economy. These are identified in ◘ Fig. 4.3.

Geoeconomic Risk

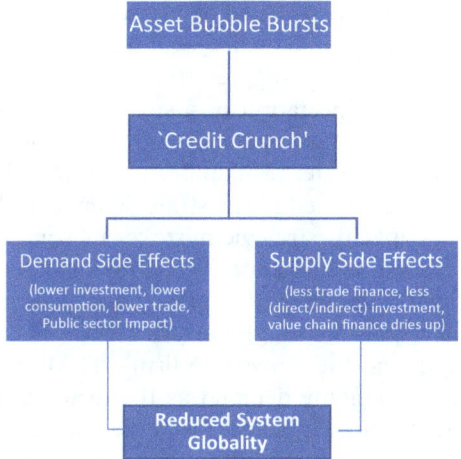

■ **Fig. 4.3** Cascading effect of asset bubble bursting on global flows

Supply Side Shock

This is a singular event that leads to a constraint upon the supply side of the global business system. This event can be localized created by unique events that inhibit the supply of a particular product. It can also be more generic where the supply side is disrupted through the transmission process between supplier and buyer. This can be created through blockages within the logistics systems where key hubs become restricted (see ▶ Chapter 9). The net effects of whether this disruption in supply comes through the production and/or the transmission process are an unanticipated increase in the price of a product. The more supply is concentrated within a given location, the more there are bottlenecks that can constrain the movement of these products across the globe the more pronounced these supply shocks—in terms of prices—these events are likely to be. The global aspect of the supply shock is created by dependence within the system upon a given place within the system for the production, transmission, and distribution. As a result—in terms of the global system—it is more accurate to talk in terms of a supply chain shock recognizing that the constraints can be caused by a multitude of processes (both direct and indirect) such as localized production difficulties through to geopolitics. The net effect of these events and processes is to reduce the volume of flows between states as trade and other flows are lowered due to production and transmission constraints.

An example of such difficulties was typified by the recent examples of constraints upon semi-conductor supply that emerged during the COVID-19 pandemic. The ultimate cause of the crisis is a lag between demand and supply where the latter has not been able to respond to a sharp uptick in the former. The period (2018–2019) leading up to the 'Global Chip Shortage' was actually one where there was a surplus of supply. This changed with the on-set of the pandemic and the demand for consumer products (as there was a sharp rise in people working from home and as the demand for gaming consoles increased) increased this was compounded by an increase in demand for chips from the automotive industry. Indeed, these semi-conductors chips are estimated to be around a fifth of the value of a new car. These unanticipated swings in demand were not matched by supply constraints within the industry as the industry adapted to the initial consequence of lockdown and curtailed production in expectation of a sustained period of lower even negative growth. This was compounded by localized disruption to production in plants in the US and concerns over water availability in Taiwan. These issues were compounded by structural issues related to the strategic impact of widely varying prices and the mothballing of capacity, strategic mistakes by some large producers in new product development, and broader geopolitical issues.

The global lockdown also exposed pressure points across the industry value chain where up to three quarters of global production is controlled by two firms (South Korea's Samsung and the Taiwanese firm—TSMC). On top of this supply cannot easily respond to changing demand as the sector has very high barriers to entry and long-time lags to move a factory from the planning stage to make it ready for production. With demand only expected to increase there is pressure to reform the sector's value chain to increase capacity. Moreover, the perceived strategic vulnerability of western states to Asia semi-conductor chip production has led some states to seek to localize the production of this key input.

These reflected broader concerns with regard to the operations of supply chains throughout the COVID pandemic which also adapted quickly to an anticipated slowdown in demand by mothballing capacity only to have ramp up capacity again when demand (aided by government stimulus) bounded back quicker than expected. This combined with enduring restrictions (especially within Chinese ports) led to a sharp rise in the costs of transporting goods between China and western economies with the price of containers rising manifold. This was compounded by rising traffic within importing ports which did not have the capacity to deal with the increase in traffic created by surging demand. These capacity constraints were port worker absences and shortages due to the spread of the pandemic and the availability of better employment conditions elsewhere. The legacy of these processes was increased waiting times and shipping delays at both ports of embarkation and disembarkation at core choke points within the system.

These two processes underscore the diverse nature of supply side shocks. These are essentially micro-level impacts created by meta-level processes. The broad macro impact of COVID highlighted within case study 4.2 underscores its complex effects and how the events surrounding the process became unpredictable and with unknown consequences throughout the global system especially so given the nature the spread of the disease and of the policy response to it. The pandemic—as a supply side shock—highlighted the vulnerability of global supply chains especially where firms operate upon 'just in time' production systems. This vulnerability was also evidenced when the Suez Canal was blocked for six days due to the grounding of the Ever Given container ship and how the close of this bottleneck within the global logistical system led to increase in prices and knock-on port congestion (see Case Study 9.3). This event underscores the complexity and vulnerability of such systems and how vast their impact can be upon the global economic system.

Singular Events

The final set of the economic risks to be considered are those created by singular events that occur elsewhere within other global sub-systems. These events create mostly secondary economic risks as they spill over into the economic system as a consequence of a primary event. Whilst these events are explored more fully in latter chapters, it is worth acknowledging the channels through which these non-economic events impact upon the economic system.

Political: this includes events such as coups, governance failure, and other sources of instability that are created by the political system either within or between states. Political instability of itself does not generate economic risk across the system though events on a local level can prove to be substantial. The impact of this instability within a single state depends upon the importance of the state to the functioning of the global economic system and its interconnectivity with the rest of the global economic system. Political events that generate instability in those states which are major trading states, providers of commodity products, or major conduits for the global logistical system. Thus, the impact of a political event depends upon the extent it will represent a retardant to international flows in to, out of, or across the territory. Thus, for example, in the supply of globally salient commodity, a key producer facing instability could lead to rising commodity prices. Moreover, a lean towards nationalism within key trading economies could also lead to a suppression of trade flows and impact negatively upon those states for whom the state exhibiting instability is a major export market. Where a state has low interconnectivity with the rest of the global system and there is a low dependence of the global system upon this state for economic activity, commodities, or logistics then the effects of any singular political event are unlikely to have any substantive economic impact beyond the state itself or the inter-state region where links are likely to be stronger.

Social: Events such as civil unrest fuelled by internal division within a state and another event that emerge from a state's social system also have the potential to spill over into rising economic risk. The salience of any social event impacting upon the economic system will (again) depend upon the extent to which the territory in question occupies a pivotal position within the global economic system. Moreover, the impact of the social event is likely to be felt through the political system where long-standing social grievances are felt through rising levels of political risk within the state which can then transmit into the economic system (see ► Chapter 6). The spillover effects of social risk can then be indirect into the global economic system and can often be more limited in impact. For example, the civil unrest in Myanmar reflects long-standing intra-group rivalry but its impact upon the global economic system tends to be limited as the country is not the source of major commodities or on core transit routes. The main threat is to foreign direct investments within the state. Consequently, its regional impact could be significant as Myanmar is a major transit route for hydrocarbons into Southern China. There could also be disruption in other southeast Asian states if the social unrest spreads into neighbouring states either through migratory flows or through an extended diaspora. These themes are explored more fully in ► Chapter 6.

Technological: this is an issue born of the fact that economic systems are increasingly dependent upon an underpinning technological system and that any disruption to this architecture can have far reaching impact upon the economic system. The major technological/economic risk has been created by the dependence upon cyber systems and how attacks upon this system can severely impact upon the operation of the economic system. Such violations of cyber systems have led to violations of intellectual property or simply a case where such attacks simply disrupt the smooth operation of the global economic system. That these are an Achilles Heel for the global economic system has long been recognized and any loss of confidence in these operating systems can be a severe retardant upon global data, trade, and capital flows. The interface between economic and security systems has led to increased trends towards the fragmentation of the global cyber system: again, something that risks inhibiting global economic interconnecting flows. These themes are explored more fully in ▶ Chapter 8.

Ecological: as ▶ Chapter 3 indicated state economic success is seen as directly linked to political and social stability. Thus, it is expected that social and political unrest would go hand in hand with economic uncertainty. What is less expected are ecological events which are far less predictable and can be much less discriminatory. Many of the world's major economies are increasingly subject to more unpredictable ecological events that can have a direct impact upon the global economic system. Japan is located close to a major earthquake zone and major events have had big global impacts. For example, the 2011 Tohoku earthquake and tsunami severely reduced Japan's semi-conductor manufacturing capacity for up to six months. This had a knock-on effect in terms of the global supply of semi-conductors which many manufacturers have now sought to mitigate by dispersing production away from such risky locations. Other businesses built long terms links with chip manufacturers to insure against such events in the future. The US' oil refining capacity is in the Gulf of Mexico—an area subject to extreme weather that seems to be of increasing frequency. In 2021, Hurricane Ida severely impacted upon these facilities with the US seeing a 20 per cent reduction in capacity due to storm damage. This caused a short-term spike in oil prices as global capacity was reduced. These processes are explored more fully in ▶ Chapter 7.

Case Study 4.2: The Economic Shock of COVID

As the COVID pandemic erupted in late 2019–early 2020, the response of the Governments to this public health crisis was to limit the extent of contagion through the introduction of social distancing. The immediate impact of this upon the economic system was to directly limit the flow of goods and people both within and between states curtailing both economic engagement, interaction, and transactions. Thus a public health crisis rapidly became an economic crisis creating a global suppression in commercial activity.

Due to the speed with which the virus spread the window for social distancing was limited and therefore the need to act quickly was vital. In the early stages of the pandemic, these early opportunities were missed as policy makers tried to work out the characteristics of the virus (such as the speed of transmission). This ambiguity was also evident with regard to how the virus would evolve. Thus, there was the risk that any attempt to quickly open economies to militate economic lockdown ran the risk of creating further outbreaks and lockdowns. At the point of the outbreak and of the initial spread so much with regard to the virus and its transmission was not understood. There was single pattern with regard to the impact of the economic shock and path with which economies took as they sought to close and reopen as the effects of the virus subsided.

Whilst the immediate effect of the crisis was a demand side shock as consumption was reduced through limited interaction, there was a good deal of adaption of firms moving activities online to maintain both business to business and business to consumer interactions. Longer-term issues with regard to the impact of the crisis depend more upon the supply side especially as many developed states sought to compensate for loss of consumer and business income through direct support. This was enabled by large demand side stimulus by many developed country governments. On the supply side, the impact created problems with regard to liquidity and capital problems. In the former case, central banks had to respond to the COVID pandemic by extending quantitative easing (i.e., buying government bonds to add liquidity to bank's balance sheets).

With regard to the real economy, several problems emerged on the supply side. First, it was evident that with large sections of the work force placed on furlough as an immediate consequence of the lockdown when the economy began to open a share of these workers decided not to return to the labour market. These labour problems were compounded by the rapid bounce back in demand as markets opened which highlighted a shortage of labour in several sectors and which increased wage pressures. Second, supply side problems were compounded by problems within global logistical systems. When lockdown happened many shipping companies lowered freight capacity to reflect what they felt was going to be a period of suppressed demand for containers. As demand shifted online much of this mothballed capacity was not easily restored creating congestion in global logistics systems and a sharp rise in prices for containers. This was also compounded by China's zero-covid strategy which persisted beyond the peak lockdown period in western markets which led to frequent reductions in capacity at the main Chinese exporting ports.

Over time, many of these shocks have been alleviated as the supply side begins to adjust. However, unforeseen effects have started to take their tool. One of the most notable of these were that the demand stimulus generated by governments to mitigate against the effects of COVID added to inflationary pressures within the global economy making many of these supply side problems worse as demand for manufacturers from China only increased as a response. The full inflationary impacts were compounded by the Russia–Ukraine conflict. Overall, the impact of COVID had a multifaceted impact upon the economic system. This was driven not simply by market dynamics and policy responses but also by the way the system has adjusted over the medium term to the pressures COVID placed upon it.

Conclusions

Arguably the most the high-profile form of globalization has been economic globalization. That has involved the globalization of markets and—consequently—of the interconnectedness between states. These interconnections between national economic systems are at the core of the global economic system. This system has—over the past two decades—been subject to increased levels of risk and uncertainty. This has been driven by economic imbalances building up within the system creating systemic flaws such as those that created the global financial crisis of 2007–2009. Already there are emergent geoeconomic risks emerging within the global economic system that are creating new forms of risk. These are created notably by rising geopolitical tension that is spilling over into emerging tensions within geoeconomics systems notably through pressures to decouple.

Key Points

- Geoeconomic risk is a major destabilizing force within the global system.
- The nature of geo-economic risk is shaped by the economic interconnectedness between states.
- There are several emerging economic risks to the global economic systems created by an increased economic and political scepticism of the value of globalization.

Discussion Questions

1. Is economic globalization always and everywhere a good thing?
2. What drives the high levels of risk within the global system?
3. Explore the notion that geoeconomics risk is driven by geopolitical factors.

Activities

Glencore plc is an Anglo-Swiss multi-national commodity trading and mining company. Using an analysis of the company's activities, outline what you believe to be the main economic risk the company faces.
    Company website: ▶ https://www.glencore.com/.

Summary

Economic globalization has become embedded within national systems as they engaged with the global system to promote national prosperity. Over time, there has been an increased trend to push back against the intensity of globality economic systems as these have tended to increase the level of economic risks within national systems. These risks created by complex economic processes exist on top of long-standing risks embedded within the system facilitated by long-term inter-state interactivity.

Further Reading

DHL. (2021). *Global connectedness index.* ▶ www.dhl.org.
Held, D., McGrew, A., Goldblatt, D., & Perraton, J. (2010). *Global transformations: Politics, economics, and culture.* Palgrave Macmillan.
IMF. (2021). *World Economic Outlook Database.* ▶ www.imf.org.
Medina, L., & Schneider, M. F. (2018). *Shadow economies around the world: What did we learn over the last 20 years?* International Monetary Fund. ▶ https://www.imf.org/-/media/Files/Publications/WP/2018/wp1817.ashx.
Tooze, A. (2018). *Crashed: How a decade of financial crises changed the world.* Viking.
Tooze, A. (2021). *Shutdown: How Covid Shook the World Economy.* Allen Lane.
World Economic Forum (WEF). (2022). *Global Risk Reports 2022.* ▶ www.wef.org

Useful Websites on Economic Risk

(1) The International Monetary Fund (▶ www.imf.org) is a good source of data and risk assessments.
(2) United Nations Commission on Trade and Development (▶ www.unctad.org) is a good source of data upon trade and investment issues.
(3) World economic Forum (▶ www.wef.org) offers a good overview of emergent economic risks.

Geopolitical Risk

© The Author(s), under exclusive license to Springer Nature Switzerland AG 2023
C. Turner, *Global Business Analysis*,
https://doi.org/10.1007/978-3-031-27769-6_5

Geopolitical impact is going to become one of the biggest risks for companies which are global.

Ritesh Agarwal

At the end of this chapter, readers will be able to understand:
- How political systems shape business activity.
- How political risk emerges and is formed.
- The form and nature of geopolitical risk.
- The major contemporary geopolitical risks.

Introduction

This chapter looks at the form and nature of political risk across the global system. This form of risk has become an increasingly focal point within global business analysis as many states push back against the forces of globality and—to a lesser extent—modernity. Initially this chapter looks at state level forces of political risk. Therefore, it will look at the forces of political globalization before moving on to examine the broad nature of geopolitical risk with the global system. Thereafter the chapter concludes with an examination of the main geopolitical risks faced within contemporary business environment.

What is Political Risk?

The salience of political risk is based upon its capacity to generate instability and uncertainty in the operation of the state and of the economic agents within and/or interconnected to it. This reflects upon the form and nature of the exercise of political power within a state. How this is done, the constraints upon, and the challenges to it will shape the certainty exhibited by any given political system. Thus, political stability as a juxtaposition to political risk reflects a system that is resilient to events that can cause disruption to the political process. Resilience reflects that any event or process does not fundamentally impact upon set power structures and decision making. States that are less resilient can find that substantive changes in the political context can have profound implications upon political structure which can have a deep impact upon the certainty that business craves from a political system.

Notionally there are four dimensions to the idea of political risk (see Table 5.1). The first is country level risk based on events and processes at the level of state. This is so-called macro-level risk. Second, are those risks developed through regulatory change and other legal methods that impact upon firm actions; these are broadly defined as micro-level risk. There are also meso-level risks created by actions within states created by frictions between groups (such as unions and employers, different regional groupings, etc.). The final type of risk is meta-level risk created between states' so-called geopolitical risks. This will form the majority of the analysis within this chapter. These dimensions are reflected in the recognition that political risk can generate instability and uncertainty through one or more of the following:

Table 5.1 Multi-scalar nature of political risks

	Governance risks	Instability risks
Micro-level risks	• Regulations • Risk of external influence/control	• Risk of damage to resources • Harm to staff deployed
Meso-level risks	• Overt prejudice against not favoured groups • Political discrimination	• Intra-group conflict • Internal violence • Domestic terrorism
Macro-level risks	• Instability of decision making • Absence of predictable process	• Erosion of control of territorial authority • Risk of civil unrest and social fragmentation
Meta-level risks	• Erosion of multi-level governance • Cross border disputes	• Geopolitical fragmentation • Inter-state conflict

- A change in government where the change represents a fundamental shift in the outlook of the government. The government could represent a powerful faction within the state and could highlight a breakdown in the consensus politics that tends to generate political stability within a state where any change represents a continuation of broad policy frameworks and strategy. Thus, the government system—with the erosion of this consensus—becomes more uncertain. This underpins that trust in government is central to political stability.
- Actions by legislative bodies which increase the hostility to and prejudice against non-favoured actors (both domestic and foreign). The most evident expression of this is through a system of officially sanctioned prejudicial public procurement which may favour domestic firms or where there is endemic corruption. In the latter case, risk is shaped by well-connected actors making the operating environment for less well-connected firms increasingly hostile. There are also those actions by regulators who can also render the operating environment unpredictable such as decisions regarding labour laws, trade tariffs, etc. Again, the efficacy of such actions reflects the unpredictability of such actions.
- The existence of internal political cleavages can also generate macro-level political risk where such divisions are focused around well organized political groupings. In these cases, where consensus is not possible, these groups will be vying for control of the territorial state leading to the increased risk of civil unrest within the state. These could lead to a mass breakdown in domestic law and order rendering the state ungovernable.
- Military control is meant to give the state order under threat of violence for those elements of the population who are deemed destabilizing. Military control—if it becomes established—can increase political risk due to on-going threats of violence, links to corruption, and lack of popular legitimacy. There is also the risk with military control is that this control begins to extend beyond political power into economic structures. Often the military will see the control of political power and economic power as synonymous creating an even more hostile environment for business.

The legacy for these criteria is that the degree of political risk reflects the extent to which the state can achieve a coherent and consistent policy process. These processes allow a sub-division of political risk between those that reflect a failure or—at least—a lack of certainty with regard to governance and those created by instability within the political environment, High levels of political risk within states are associated with:
- Low levels of political control by the centre over the territory where it is supposed to have jurisdiction.
- High levels of insecurity for both citizens and the state as a whole.
- Low levels of economic development due to the risk attached to the poor investment climate within the state.
- Low levels of socio-economic cohesion with rival states vying for influence in the absence of strong control.
- Low levels of sustainability due to absence of decision making.

Whilst the list is not an exhaustive one, it does indicate the main forms of political risk. It also highlights a need when differentiating between political risks that are firm specific (i.e., those that are created by the nature of a firm's operations) and those that a contextual (i.e., those that are generic and apply to all agents within a state). These standalone processes are formed against complex processes both within and between states. Political events and processes spread throughout the system and impact upon the activities of other agents and upon the functioning of the system as a whole. This can be through the following processes:
- Creating unstable and unpredictable commercial conditions within a state. The main concern is that political risk undermines the possible returns from an investment made within a state.
- Fracturing links between and within social groups within a state creating cleavages between them. The fracturing of inter-group links can lead to civil unrest where one group is disadvantaged compared to another group.
- Macro-level events spilling over into other states and creating systemic geopolitical instability (see ◘ Fig. 5.1).

The development and establishment of these risks do not develop in isolation from the other sub-systems. Indeed, there is a good reason to believe that its development is based on interactions with other global sub-systems. ◘ Table 5.2 offers some indicative inter-relationships between these sub-systems. The list is not definitive but does serve to illustrate that many of the political risks noted above and geopolitical risks noted below can have their genesis in other related sub-systems.

Political Interconnectivity

This macro-level risk within political systems has the capacity to spill over into other states and therefore create a meta-level risk. This meta level can be expected to occur at the regional level where political unrest spills across borders where space between states is contiguous and therefore—feasibly—into the broader global system indirectly. The other possibility for this transition is where a state is especially salient to the operation of the system and that political instability within that

Geopolitical Risk

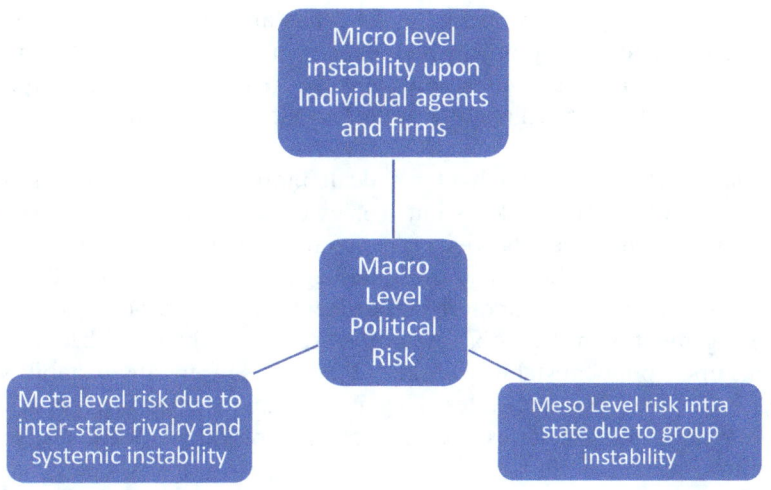

Fig. 5.1 Multi-scalar impact of macro-level risks

Table 5.2 The interface between political risk and other sub-systems

Sub-system	Political risk interface
Economic	• Economic inequality leading to political exclusion/inequality • Unemployment leading to mass protests
Social	• Long-term social exclusion leading to disturbances • Demographic change leading to changing political behaviour
Technological	• Use of social media to generate political unrest • Cyber-attacks upon critical systems leading to political unrest
Ecological	• Internal competition for resources spill over into political unrest • Events (flood, earthquake) leads to emergent political crisis

state can spread broader political unrest across other states. What underpins both of these spillover processes is the existence of political connections between one state and another based upon inter-relationships between the state and other states within the global system. The sources of these inter-relationships (either by design or by accident) can be sourced from the nature of the international political system (see below) and from political relationships/interactions formed as an indirect legacy of the interactions elsewhere within the global system. These connectivities are noted below.

Political Connectivity: this interconnectedness is driven by the nature of the political risk/uncertainty itself and that containing and managing the risk is not something that can be done in isolation. This could be due to the weakness of the state to be resilient to events/processes that are shaping political risk. It could also be—as mentioned below—that specific issues need co-operative solutions thereby fostering common actions. Other sources of political connectivity can be sourced from ever changing borders and past conflicts which create a legacy of inter-relationships across borders that foster co-operation. This has arguably its most salient expression in the trend towards political regionalism in Europe where strong historical and continuing linkages (as well as conflict) have created an emergent supranational system to reflect the high degree of political connectivity between states on certain issues.

Economic Connectivity: ▶ Chapter 4 dealt more fully with the nature of economic connectivity between states but it is evident that this form of connectivity spills over into political connectivity. As economic interactivity and relationships and possible dependence grows so the state begins to cede degrees of control over its territory. It begins to rely upon the attainment of its strategic objectives upon effective engagement with the global system. In so doing, the states become mutually dependent upon political stability within other states where any instability can disrupt economic flows between states. This gives states a vested interest in the political risk attached to other states and operates as a rationale for inter-state political co-operation.

Social Connectivity: aside from when social unrest in economically salient partner states spills over into the political sphere, the other major element of social-political connectivity is where peoples in other states have a strong allegiance or links to another state. These could be long-standing diaspora created by the reconfiguration of borders, refugees, and ex-patriot workers for example. What is relevant here is that the citizens with whom a state has an interest in securing their welfare and/or controlling do not all lie within the borders of the territorial state. Where a state has an interest in a social group beyond its territorial borders then it has an interest in fostering political connections with the state in which this social group is located.

Ecological Connectivity: the spillover between ecological and political connectivity are issues explored in later chapters. The interface between them can have a powerful factor driving political connectivity and shaping the risk environment. These links are especially evident where states share a common natural resource and where the utilization/treatment of that resource can impact upon another state. This can be evidenced where there are shared water resources such as a river that cross multiple territories or aquifers that span borders where to ensure effective management political connectivity is desirable to prevent inter-state conflict.

Technological Connectivity: the interface between technology and political connectivity can reflect several themes. The first of which is to ensure the flow of data between states does not compromise the interests of the citizens of the respective states. There are also connectivity issues that reflect the political economy of technological change where states trade hi-technology and where one state depends upon another for access to new technologies. This interface becomes especially relevant where the technology is essential to state security. In this case, strong political connectivity is desired to ensure sustained access and protection.

What these connectivity issues demonstrate is that within a global system of states with strong and resilient interconnectivity, is that sovereignty (i.e., the supremacy of domestic political processes and governance) is graduated. That is there are some areas where the sovereign political control is intact but there are others where sovereignty needs to be compromised or shared if the state's strategy objectives are to be attained. These reflect that the state (and businesses) operating within a subject to externally sourced political risks that could spread into the state creating the risk of instability in the state. This reflects the complexity of the operation of the global system where interconnectivity and dependence can cause political risk and uncertainty to spread across the system.

This reflects the notion of the state existing as a bordered power container is misplaced. Many aspects of what the state seeks to do can best be achieved through co-operation notably in areas like security, economic development/growth, control, cohesion, and sustainability. The connections necessary to enable these elements also expose the state to exogenously sourced risk and insecurity. This 'downside' of the global system has been something that fuelled populism/nationalism (explored below). As borders matter less so the security of the sovereign state is believed to become more vulnerable to erroneous cross border flows. Despite these challenges—as a political entity—the state remains the pre-eminent form of control within the global system. There is no other true alternative power to the state; not MNCs, not NGOs. Nonetheless such debates have been shaped by a trend towards political globalization.

Political Globalization

The legacy of this interconnectivity is the process of political globalization. This process reflects that whilst states remain the pre-eminent source of power within the global political system there are constraints upon their freedom of action. Thus, political globalization involves a nexus of a set of actors from governmental and non-governmental organizations as well as those bodies representing global civil society (such as international social and non-governmental organizations [NGOs]). The increased salience of such arrangements is conventionally seen as operating in a zero-sum relationship with the power of the nation state—that is that political globalization gains relevance at the expense of the sovereignty of the state. In practice, this is too simple an argument as it is just as possible to argue that this process augments the power of the state by allowing to have influence in non-domestic arenas where its interests are apparent.

Like other forms of globalization, political globalization is based around the intensification, expansion, and velocity of political relations between states. This creates new links or cements pre-existing to support the stability of the state-based system. This state-based system reflects a global system of territorially distinct states that interoperate to produce systemic stability based upon recognition of right of mutual co-existence. In short, they recognize each other's boundaries.

Also important to the process of political globalization is the emergence of global civil society. This represents the array of bodies operating across borders that are beyond the reach of government. These can comprise a very diverse set of actors including community groups, NGOs, social movements, labour unions, indigenous groups, charitable organizations, faith-based organizations, media operators, academia, diaspora groups, lobby, and consultancy groups, think tanks and research centres, professional associations, and foundations. The spread of such organizations and the diversity of interests that they represent has led many to see them as representative of the spread of democracy, but they have also advanced as the state involvement in many issues has retreated. In other cases, they can be used to express solidarity between groups of citizens located in different parts of the globe (such as International Aid Organizations). Their salience to the global system is reflected in their role in setting policy agendas, international law, and diplomacy cutting across a diverse range of issues from child poverty and famine through to environmentalism and human rights. These bodies—whilst increasing transparency and awareness upon their chosen issue—have had limited impact as they only tend to be influential where their activities are accepted. Thus, in states without a democratic tradition the impact of these civil society has been minimal.

There are several ways of looking at the process of political globalization. The first way reflects conventional understanding namely of the emergence of polycentric political system that facilitates the management of international interactions. The result can be an array of international arrangements from simple bi- and multilateral frameworks where states work together towards a common goal though there is limited transfer of sovereignty involved (such as is the case with the United Nations) towards deeper (though more spatially limited) arrangements (such as the EU) where there is a limited pooling/transfer of sovereignty towards transnational bodies. These can also be compounded by the emergence of NGOs that monitor state behaviour. Thus, political globalization also refers to the set of global governance arrangements formed largely to manage the economic system (such as the World Trade Organization (WTO), the International Monetary Fund (IMF), and the World Bank) (see ▶ Box 5.1). This form of political globalization is reflective of the emergence of global governance; a set of arrangements to coordinate the actions of all players (not just states) that shape the operation of the global system. The end point of this is a world government. The logic of the pursuit and attainment of global governance as a response to political globalization is that it can operate as a stabilizing force upon the global political system. The logic is that such global governance frameworks operate as an alternative to inter-state political disputes and possibly conflict. Thus, global governance has to be seen as a means of lowering the level of risk within the global system through establishing the means through which potential conflicts can be resolved. The rise of national populism (see below) has seen a pushback against the emergence of such arrangements.

The emergence of global governance as an adaptive response to political globalization reflects the increasingly complex operation of the global political system. It reflects that political events and processes cannot always be confined to the borders of the state where the source of instability occurs. This is created by the forces of interconnection mention above. It also reflects that some events/processes are international by nature and that—therefore—no single state can solve such problems in isolation from other states. In reflection of this process there is a recognition that power within the global political system is not symmetrical which raises the prospect that any single state's behaviour can be directly influenced by the actions of a more powerful other state. This is reflected within issues of hegemony below. It is on this basis that political globalization is rationalized. It is these events and processes at the national and international levels that have a multi-national impact and have the potential to alter the functioning of the global system that these processes seek to manage. Geopolitical risk is—as we shall see—endemic to the global political system.

Box 5.1: Global Governance Architecture: The Main Global Co-Ordinating Institutions

Below is a list of the main bodies that seek to develop and implement the global governance system throughout the global system; the list is indicative not definitive. In so doing, these bodies seek to foster co-operation between states (and other agents) and develop common rules and practices to which all participating states are expected to adhere. The existence of these rules is meant to operate as a constraint upon the freedom of action of states.

United Nations (UN): established in the aftermath of World War two, this is an inter-governmental organization that has the broad remit of seeking to maintain global peace and security by creating a framework for cordial relations between member states to facilitate co-operation and as a result a more stable and predictable geopolitical system. Over time, its role has diversified into related themes of promoting environmental co-operation, human rights, and humanitarian assistance.

International Monetary Fund (IMF): established in 1944, the role of the IMF is to promote and secure stability within the global economic system. Consisting of 190 members, the IMF works to promote co-operation between states to ensure systemic financial stability and stable conditions under which international trade and investment can occur relatively free of risk. In seeking to set the framework for policy for its members it seeks to lower the risk within the economic system that could occur due to errant state behaviour.

World Trade Organization (WTO): established in 1995, this also seeks to provide stability and certainty to the international trading and investment system through offering and managing an agreed framework in developing trade agreements. These multilateral agreements work to remove both tariff and non-tariff barriers to trade. These agreements are policed by a WTO administered dispute resolution system to ensure systemic stability by ensuring agreed methods to resolve trade disputes and to stop them from escalating. It has 164 members and largely prohibits discrimination between partners except where a state's core strategic goals are challenged by trade agreements.

World Bank: established alongside the IMF in 1944, the World Bank's job is as a complimentary function of promoting systemic stability through actions (largely loans) designed to promote economic growth and development in low- and middle-income states. It has over time shifted its portfolio to stress themes of ecological and social protection.

International Criminal Court: established in 1998, this inter-governmental body seeks to prosecute those individuals charged with international crimes such as genocide, war crimes, and crimes against humanity.

Regional Bodies: a common strategy by states over the past half century has been a tendency towards the creation of regional organizations. These are agreements between states that foster co-operation and (in several cases) explicit integration between these states. Frequently, these bodies are limited to fostering economic co-operation between member states to create free trade areas or even common markets between them. In some cases, outright economic union is envisaged. For states aside from trade and investment benefits of such agreements there are also potential geostrategic advantages by being able to counteract powerful states from allowing smaller states to act with a single voice. Examples include the African Union (AU), the European Union (EU), the Association of Southeast Asian Nations (ASEAN), and the South Asian Association for Regional Cooperation (SAARC).

Geopolitical Risk

Based upon the understanding of political risk developed above, the rest of this chapter will explore the nature of geopolitical risk. As argued, this is largely based upon macro-level political risk that spills over into the relations between states and into the system creating the risk of systemic instability. Initially this chapter examines the nature of geopolitics before moving on to explore geopolitical risk. Thereafter the main forces of geopolitical risk are identified and explored.

What is Geopolitics?

Geopolitics is based upon the notion of state interaction and that interaction generates political relations, processes, and disputes between these states. As these states are at the core of the international business system so disputes between them can have a powerful effect upon the global system by impacting upon the volume, intensity, spread, and speed of interconnecting flows. More especially, geopolitics is underpinned by the following principles:
- That states seek to maintain and sustain their established territorial space and its boundaries.
- That states seek to maintain the capability to influence and shape the action of other states through a series of actions from the capacity to wage a war through to co-operative bi- and multilateral actions that seek to mitigate any conflict.
- That interactions between states are a pre-requisite to secure their own respective interests and that these relationships need to maintain and be characterized by trust and reliability.

At the core of the notion of geopolitics is the idea of exerting influence over space and how that power is likely to evolve given the pressures that exist within the system. Thus, there is a need with geopolitical narratives to understand how states do and are going to behave given the stability of their interests (see above) as expressed within notions of state strategy (see ▶ Chapter 3). States need to assert control, maintain cohesion, attain security, and promote growth and prosperity. This they do—in part—through their relations with other states. These interests are expressed in terms of the framework provided by geography.

For international business, these geopolitical relations form the bedrock of the governance of global system. For amongst all the assumptions, several other issues need to be considered with regard to the operation of the system notably the following.
- Power between states is shared unequally. The resultant asymmetry of power gives some states greater influence over system functioning than other states. This asymmetry can reflect economic differentials and/or military efficacy but it does mean that some states have greater influence on the development of the geopolitical system than others.
- This asymmetry of power is not static and is always changing as powerful states ebb and flow in terms of their capacity to shape the political operation of the system.

- Less powerful states need to develop adaptive strategies to reflect the asymmetry of power. This can mean aligning with the power, seeking the development of a countervailing block comprised of like-minded states, or seeking to align with a potential rival power.

Thus a state's power within the global system and its ability to act as a stabilizing/destabilizing forces reflects an amalgam of four factors namely the possession of the capability and willingness to use military force against other states in a manner that challenges that state's very existence; the availability of surplus economic resources that enable it (and other agents located within it) to initiate, shape, and influence the interconnections both between it and other states but also in terms of third-party relations; that it is able to act as an ideological leader for other states to follow and finally that the state has a coherent and reliable system of governance. These reflect that a single state can use a range of hard (i.e., military, economic measures) and soft (i.e., persuasion) to shape and influence system operation.

Logically the more that these are concentrated in a single state, the more the system will tend towards stability. As noted below, the more there are multiple states exhibiting these characteristics the more the risk of instability within the system. The emergence of a polycentric system suggests multiple sources of power based around western and eastern alliances. What the system desires is a geopolitical equilibrium. This reflects a sense stability within the system where sources of power within the system are known and stable.

The Nature of Geopolitical Risk

Geopolitics is important to business as it desires rules of operation of the system and will shape its stability (or otherwise). The more the geopolitical system exhibits unpredictability, the more interconnectivity is deterred, the more globalization is dissuaded and the more the system fragments. These represent the core of the geopolitical risk for business. Geopolitical risk has been an ever-present feature of the business environment. As globalization ebbed and flowed through the centuries so geopolitical risk has altered accordingly. In the contemporary era, it is the perception of greater geopolitical risk driven by the complexity of the global system that has driven the issue up the corporate agenda. The direct and indirect interconnections between states highlight how any political disputes between states can impact upon business models.

Whilst geopolitical risk can be indirectly (as mentioned) stimulated by events in other systems it is the direct impact of political events and processes upon the activities and efficacy of the global system. The impact upon the firm or state is that the extent to which the geopolitical risk creates a loss of control either over the firm's assets within the host economy or the extent to which extra-territorial events impact upon the capability of the state to maintain territoriality. As with any risk, the degree of geopolitical risk reflects the extent to which any event/process will impact upon the welfare/performance of the state/company and the likelihood of that event occurring. In terms of impact, two levels of impact can be identified:

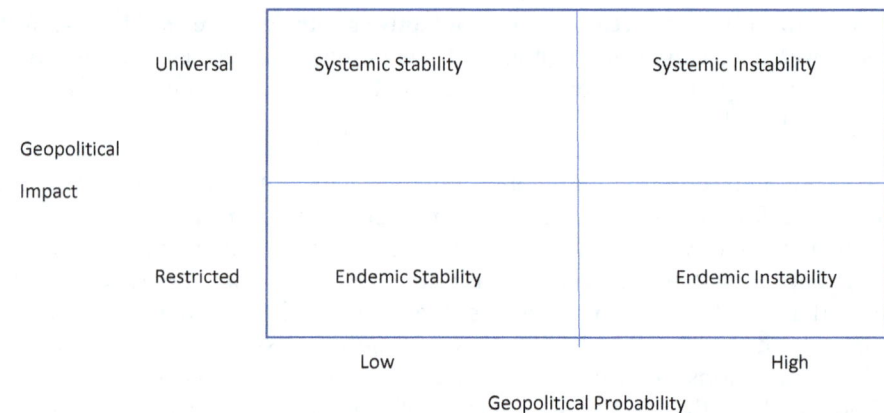

Fig. 5.2 Four geopolitical states

Universal: these are events/processes that will have a systemic impact and will—to varying degrees—impact upon all agents operating within the global system. The systemic impact will be greater than the extent to which the main players within the global system are impacted.

Restricted: at the level of the individual state or business geopolitical risk reflects the extent to which they are exposed to events and processes in non-domestic/overseas environments. In many cases, the restricted impacts demonstrate the strong overlap between political and geopolitical risk.

The impact of any given geopolitical risk depends upon the likelihood of that event happening. This places an emphasis within the system upon attaining geopolitical stability which reflects the probability of a destabilizing unforeseen event occurring. Thus, there is broad consensus amongst states and businesses (with exceptions noted below) towards promoting systemic geopolitical stability based on the avoidance of inter-state conflict. The interface between geopolitical impact and probability allows for the identification of four geopolitical states (see ● Fig. 5.2). These are not set but allow for the categorization of any single geopolitical risk at any single point in time. Evidently these risks vary by scale of impact and likelihood of occurrence.

These broad states can be defined as follows.

Systemic Stability: this is a desirable state where there are no evident threats to the operation of the global system. The global political system is characterized by systemic equilibrium where either a single power or interaction between multiple powers work to maintain the system's functioning through common agreement on rules of operation and what to do should those rules be infringed.

Endemic Stability: this tends to be a focus upon macro-level stability through such harmony may be driven by systemic conditions. This state represents a scenario where a single country exhibits low levels of political risk and high degree of political stability and certainty.

Systemic Instability: this will be the focus for much of the rest of the chapter (see below). It is worth noting here that this state is characterized by system complexity allowing any given event to spread rapidly throughout the system causing generalized instability.

Geopolitical Risk

Endemic Instability: this is reflective of the forms of political risk identified above. These risks tend to be isolated from the broader state of the political system and tend to be geopolitical in the sense that the business conditions within a non-domestic polity can generate a limited spillover into other states.

These conditions are not static, and risk can evolve and move between categories. Endemic risk can spill over into systemic risk if that event is in a powerful country or in a state that is core to the operation of the global system. This highlights the evolving nature of any given risk. It is the form and nature of these risks to which this chapter now turns.

Case Study 5.1: Geopolitical Risk in Global Business: Russian Divestment and the Russia–Ukraine Conflict

Russia has always been a difficult place to do business. With endemic corruption and a high risk of expropriation, businesses were always at risk of having their operations comprised by the whims of the political elite. With the invasion of Ukraine by Russia in February 2022, the vast majority of MNCs with investments within Russia were compelled to re-examine their involvement. Under pressure from both home governments and customers, businesses were obliged for a variety of reasons to scale down and eventually withdraw totally from Russia. In some cases, western sanctions made sustained involvement impossible. In other cases, commercial pressure drove the process. This often involved untangling complicated deals and came to many businesses with a substantive economic cost.

These divestments were across a wide range of sectors from consumer goods and retail through to energy and manufacturing. There was not an activity that was not impacted by these divestments. By Late October 2022, over 1200 western companies had voluntarily scaled down their operations within Russia. Despite this many businesses operating within Russia were determined to persist within the state. As of October 2022, there were 238 businesses that were operating a business-as-usual strategy in the state completely ignoring the geopolitical risk they were incurring. Some of these were from states (such as China) where sanctions had not been imposed by their home states. Though many of the remaining companies were US, Japanese, or European. On top of this there were nearly 160 businesses, who were biding time insofar as they were not actively seeking to increase their involvement within the state but still had substantive businesses within Russia.

For those firms that were holding out the pressure to divest has only increased. Danone (the French food company) initially ought to resist the pressure to divest arguing that it had a duty of care to its Russian customers. By October 2022, the company had relented and was looking to sell its assets in Russia though it would retain a residual presence in baby formula. Total (the French oil major) also resisted pressure to scale back its operations in Russia. Its strategy was to bide time, but it has come under pressure from non-governmental organizations who argue that its sustained presence in the state represents a war crime as its allegedly helping Russia in its invasion of Ukraine. This has arisen due to Total developing oil-based products in Russia that have fueled its fighter planes. Not surprisingly Total resists these claims suggesting it has little control over the assets supplying the fuel to these military assets. One business that has continued with a business-as-usual approach is TGI-Fridays (a US-based restaurant chain). This US-based business argues that as its business model depends upon local franchise agreements that it is up to these independent businesspeople as to whether these operations are sustainable or not. In making this decision, the company was keen to avoid any negative PR and donated all franchise fees owed to bodies providing food and water to Ukrainian refugees and to those suffering inside the state.

The experience of Russia for international businesses reflects the innate geopolitical risks in engaging with state where international norms are frequently not adhered to. For those states remaining either in partial or total form, the geopolitical risk that these firms are encountering runs the risk that these firms could suffer longer-term reputational damage through seeking to sustain commercial involvement with a state who has become—amongst many states—an international pariah.

Major Sources of Geopolitical Risk

The sources of geopolitics identified below do not represent a definitive list though they do represent what have been the consistent sources of systemic geopolitical instability throughout several eras. Indeed, a cursory scan of the contemporary geopolitical risk context can identify these risks as major sources of on-going geopolitical uncertainty.

Erosion of Hegemony

As mentioned above, despite the state being the core building block of the global system not all states are equal in establishing the governance of the global system. Thus, the support of the hegemon is essential for multilateral bodies to be effective in the governance of the global system. In the global system some states are more powerful than others with the most powerful state emerging as a hegemonic power within the system. The nature of the hegemonic state reflects that a single state (and allied states) operates as a legitimate source of dominance in terms of setting the rules for the operation of the global system. This dominance is based upon the hegemonic states' ability to shape the behaviour of other states due to its combination of economic, cultural, and political power. This rests on its power over global flows through operating as a focal point for international flows of capital, data/technology, knowledge, security, and trade. Thus it can exercise through economic sanction or preference or through the threat and/or exercise of military power. Through it can exercise structural power over the global system. Throughout economic history there have been several hegemonic states from the UK in the nineteenth century to the current position which the US has occupied since the formative years of the twentieth century. This power is exercised not just through direct government action but also through MNCs and cultural influence through agreed norms. The benefit of the power of the dominant state is to drive system stability through the attainment of inter-state consensus.

Notionally the exercise of hegemonic power is important to the predictable operation of the global system where the power through a mix of coercive and non-coercive power can ensure agreed rules are adopted and enforced. The key point is that for sub-ordinate states this power is legitimate. This legitimacy is born of the ability of the hegemonic state to guarantee one or more of core state capabilities through acting as a guarantor for security for example. The hegemon plays a key role in forming and shaping the risk environment for business. It is these dominant states that secure the process of international engagement to ensure that interconnecting flows are both secure but also guaranteed through mutually agreed rules. Thus, the legitimacy of the hegemon (and the fact that its power is unchallenged) is central to the systemic stability as states have little incentive to veer from these rules as to do so would incur sanctions. As a result, there is mutual benefit from the existence of a hegemonic state. There is the potential for increase from the emergence of a hegemon where lower power non-aligned states resent the power of the dominant state and form alliances to counter its influence (see Rogue states below).

The stabilizing force of the hegemon can mean that its decline and replacement can generate a period of instability within the global system. It has long been argued that the US is in decline as the global hegemon notably with the rise of Asian economic and political power. This was first exercised by the rise of Japan, but such debates have more latterly been focused upon China (see below). There are debates as to whether a single hegemon is needed for global stability or whether such lower risk contexts are compatible with multipolar systems. Contemporary narrative suggests that the incompatibility between existing and emergent powers can be an important factor.

At the core of US hegemonic strategy was the creation of a liberal internationalist order. This used a range of multilateral bodies to foster co-operation and co-ordination between states to create the rules to manage this system. The hegemon was central to this notably in terms of influencing states to agree to the membership and adherence to the rules of these bodies. Liberal Internationalism was based upon the globalizing of rules through co-operative mechanisms. In practice, this was used by the hegemonic state to attain consensus upon the pursuit of economic globalization and a strengthening of agreed global economic rules that developed a neo-liberal agenda especially in those economies that had limited exposure to international economic engagement. Alongside this were measured to legitimatize intervention in those states where there is a need to uphold global norms such as democracy and protection of human rights. Thus, a core agenda of liberal internationalism was the geographic extension of personal economic and political freedom, and the hegemon would intervene to secure these objectives. Moreover, the agenda of multilateral bodies were used to support the attainment of this agenda. Liberal internationalism sees economic freedom and political freedom as two sides of the same coin and that one necessitates the existence of the other.

The mutual inclusivity of economic and political freedom has been the corner stone of newly emergent hegemonic challenges to the US. For many states, notably those without democratic traditions, no such trade-off exists. Whilst it has long been mooted that US dominance is in decline, the rise of China over the past two decades represents arguably the greatest challenge to this hegemony as its political economy exists in sharp contrast to that of the US. This rise—unlike that of previous contenders like Japan and Germany represents a more fundamental challenge to the power of the US as it represents a totally different system based more on national-authoritarianism. This is reflected within debates upon nationalism below but with regard to the export of the model to other states, the challenge is based upon national interests above that of the global and an agnosticism towards individual liberty.

The challenge of China is driven by both its emergence as an economic power (see ► Chapter 4) but also by its emerging military prowess. Moreover, China has become increasingly politically assertive in areas of strategic interest to the US notably in Southeast Asia and its increasingly aggressive pursuit of a single China policy where it seeks to reclaim the 'rogue province' of Chinese Taipei/Taiwan over which it has long-standing territorial claims. The rise of China was compounded by US political system that has retreated from the liberal internationalism often following a more avowedly nationalistic stance. This retreat has allowed China to speed up the development of rival organizations to those established to govern the liberal internationalist student. The extent to which the rise of China poses a risk to systemic stability depends upon the extent to which its emergence:

— Leads to a fragmentation of the global system into rival power blocs based around rival hegemonic states.
— Leads to the establishment of uneven rules between these blocs resulting in more complex business operations.
— Leads to the erosion of multilateral bodies through the creation of parallel governance system.
— Leads to erosion of democracy as authoritarian states like the systemic stability offered by other authoritarian states.
— Generates a 'Thucydides Trap' where economic and political rivalry turns into military conflict as the emergent and established power are drawn into conflict. There are several potential flashpoints (not least Taiwan/Chinese Taipei) where conflict is possible.

Overall hegemony should stabilize the system resulting in lower geopolitical risk. Risks start to emerge when less powerful states start to push against this or when strategic missteps by the hegemon allow a rival to emerge. Currently much of the disputes between the established and emerging power are based around economics and technology. However, the rate of development of China means one cannot discount these conflicts deepening and expanding.

Rogue States

These are a set of states which are frequently non-aligned and are often peripheral to the operation of the global system but due to global system structure and/or operation are able to exert geopolitical power over the system which is disproportionate to their economic power or to the state of the global system. This disproportionate power combined with geostrategic intent allows states to promote systemic instability for their own geostrategic advantage. The term was originally used by the US towards those states that were a direct threat to systemic stability as defined by the norms of the liberal internationalist order. This potential for disruption is created by one or more of the following issues.

- A military prowess which exceeds economic power coupled with on-going belligerence towards neighbours.
- Acquiring or seeking to acquire weapons of mass destruction thereby allowing state to project power both intra- and inter-regionally.
- Repressing own populations thereby stimulating migratory flows into neighbouring states.
- The intent to sponsor disruption in neighbouring states to attain its ends.
- The control of raw materials which are central to industrial activity.
- The control of core logistical bottlenecks which could stymie global interconnectivity.
- Poor internal governance (or even failed states) with the result that systemic threats emerge within them (such as terrorism).

It can be argued that through the geopolitical lens of US aligned states, any state that challenges the US-based hegemony and control can be seen as a disruptor. In those cases, the definition can be extended to larger states such as Russia and China. Powerful states will seek to tame these rogue nations through a mix of hard and soft power to get them to fall back into line with international norms. These could include the threat of military intervention by a more powerful state, economic sanctions, or simple diplomacy. The ability to offer a coherent strategy upon this depends on consent as to the extent amongst allied states as to the nature of the threat.

In identifying the rogue state, it is important to look beyond the definitions used by the US and its defence of its liberal internationalism. These are states whose erratic behaviour threatens a more widespread instability. Whilst the list of rogue states has varied over time within the contemporary business environment the following states can be considered as being 'rogue' to the global system:

- *Iran*: as a theocratic regime occupying a position in a major choke point on oil transit routes, Iran has the capacity to disrupt the global economy. Furthermore, the long-standing Sunni–Shia split within Islam has led to financing operations within other states to spread disorder notably in Iraq, Yemen, Israel, and Saudi Arabia. This is further compounded by its open pursuit of weapons of mass destruction.
- *Syria*: from 2010, this state has descended into civil war as pro- and anti-regime factions turned on each other. In the resultant gap, Islamic State (a group advocating an extreme form of Islam) emerged. The risk of this failed state was that this group could as a platform be the global export of terrorism where there was a lack of internal checks upon its power.
- *North Korea*: an autocratic regime, North Korea has undergone rapid acceleration of the development of long-range missiles that post a threat not merely to its neighbours (notably South Korea and Japan) but also to the US. The state has become detached from nearly all other states bar China and the fear is that its erratic behaviour could lead to a US–China conflict.

— *Afghanistan*: Like Syria this state has a long-standing record in hosting and protecting extremist groups which have cultivated the spread of international terrorism. Whilst these groups were dispersed through US and allied intervention in the aftermath of 9/11, the reestablishment of the Taliban (an extreme Islamic group)—with the withdrawal of the US into 2020—has opened up the prospect of the state's link with international terrorism being established.

Whilst one state's enemy could be another state's ally, what binds these states is that they have the potential to disrupt the system for all states and indeed the system as a whole. In some cases, states may be deemed rogue due to lawlessness or capture by particular interests such as Narco states where the political system becomes captured by illicit drug interests.

Case Study 5.2: TSMC and Geopolitics

The Taiwan Semiconductor Manufacturing Company (TSMC) (founded in 1987) is the market leader in the manufacture of semi-conductors. It controls 84 per cent of the market for this product with a list of clients from Apple to Alibaba. For much of its existence it was involved in low value micro-processors. In 2012 with the launch of the iPhone it began to make ever more powerful chips as the company sought to create a competitive advantage through pushing to the limits of its manufacturing technology. TSMC's chips have powered the rise of smartphones allowing it to overtake Intel who once enjoyed a monopoly of this technology. As consumer and industrial products have grown more sophisticated so the demand for its semi-conductor chips has increased notably as cloud computing and rapid communication networks have become the norm. This rise in the level of demand for its products has led to the company investing substantial sums into chip research, development, and production to further secure its position within rapidly evolving technology systems. Its main rival—Samsung—has struggled to keep up especially as it continues to pour money into new chip factories.

This dominant position within the semi-conductor market belies the large geopolitical risk that this business faces as it seeks to serve both western and Chinese businesses with this vital component. In 2021, around two thirds of its revenue came from the US and around 20 per cent from China. This position between these states as well as its geographic location create especially large geopolitical risks as economic and political tensions between these states ratchet up. The long-standing geostrategic ambiguity of Taiwan lies at the heart of this geopolitical problem for the business. China has long claimed Taiwan as a rogue province that it wants to re-unify with the mainland. Whilst China has long sought a natural re-absorption of the island back into the Chinese state (along the lines of Hong Kong and Macao), the Taiwanese have shown no real appetite to want to rejoin. The result is that China has grown increasingly belligerent towards the island seeking to isolate it diplomatically, carrying out military exercise close to its territory and making increasingly hostile noises with regard to unification which the Chinese state sees as imperative. Indeed, China has refused to rule out taking Taiwan by force. However, the US has a commitment to defend Taiwan from any incursion by China. This sets the scene for rising geopolitical tension between these states that will impact upon businesses operating between these three states.

TSMC has sought to navigate these difficult relations by making itself indispensable to both parties. As already noted, both Chinese and US firms depend upon TSMCs products. TSMC is vulnerable to this geopolitical risk as it has kept much of its production on the island. It is encouraged to do by the Taiwanese government to limit any incentive for a foreign state to intervene in its affairs. Overall, 97 per cent of the company's assets lie within the island as well as 90 per cent of its staff. To keep both China and the US happy, TSMC has offered to invest more in the chip manufacturing capacity of these states, but these facilities will not be developing the cutting-edge technology. As the US grows more hostile to the economic rise of China so it is placing restraints upon those businesses that use US components to make products for Chinese firms that could pose a security risk to the US. This exposed TSMC which provides chips to Huawei (a Chinese smartphone manufacturer) which is currently barred from the US market. The effect is to limit what TSMC can do with Chinese firms. The risk is that this could lead to retaliatory measures by the Chinese. This has been compounded by strategies by many western governments to lower their exposure to TSMC through developing indigenous chip production. This increases pressure upon TSMC to diversify geographically into the US—some TSMC does not want to do. Nonetheless it is likely that the geopolitical pressures upon TSMC are only set to increase.

Nationalism

Nationalism conventionally stands as a juxtaposition to globalism (see ▶ Chapter 3). It is not so much that nationalism represents a pushback against globalism it is that states are increasingly assertive in doing so. That means that nationalism is pursued aggressively focusing on explicit discrimination against non-domestic forces. It also reflects that nationalism involves overt prejudice and the assertiveness with which it is pursued. After the consensus formed around globality within the global system since 1945, the formative decades of the twenty-first century have seen a resurgence within nationalism across many states not least of which are the global system's most powerful states—China and the US. In truth, China has been nationalist to some degree for decades but its entry into the global system has altered its potential for disruption as has the emergence of nationalism within the US since 2016.

At its core, nationalism reflects a truism about humanity namely that we are socio-cultural creatures that are born into communities through which we find meaning. Nationalism stresses the state, and the political unit are synonymous. The state is the nation, and the nation is the state. The state is the homeland that belongs to the nation. The two are congruent. There can be two broad types of nationalism. First is the benign nationalism which seeks to build identity and social cohesion but does not work to be discriminatory or exclusive and is often used to position a state within the global system especially where that state is newly established or seeking to establish a national identity in the aftermath of colonialism for example. At the other end of the spectrum is malign nationalism which is a fragmentary and discriminatory force through seeking to place the state above and beyond the global system. It is the latter issue which is at the forefront of the analysis within this section.

Whilst there are many different conceptions and drivers of nationalism (see below) what binds these different conceptions is a sense that peoples within a given territory are bound together by a common identity and that these citizens exhibit extreme loyalty to that state. In a more defined sense, this rather benign definition of nationalism is extended to involve the notion that the state as an expression/guarantor of this national identification and interest engages in actions that defends, secures, and enhances the national interest. This defines nationalism as working towards the exclusion—where necessary—of external concerns. Of course, (as mentioned above) not all nationalisms are discriminatory in many cases nationalism emerged (especially within the post-colonial era) as an anti-discriminatory logic and as a tool to bind otherwise disparate peoples in fledgling states together. In conventional political economy it is not nationalism per se that is the problem but those forms of nationalism that are discriminatory and exclusionary. It is these forms of nationalism that define the narrative within this section.

Generally, nationalism within the global system can be seen to increase the risks within it through a number of different dimensions namely:
- It increases the risk of systemic fragmentation as states seek to limit cross border flows in favour of domestic/national flows.
- It increases the risk of conflict between states as each seeks to assert—what is often—their mutually exclusive national interests.
- It increases the degree of formal and informal prejudice within the system by distinguishing between the national and the international.
- States pursue their own national interests and only align interests where the national and global overlap.
- States generate xenophobic/nationalistic views to promote their own survival and create systemic instability.
- States discriminate against non-domestic actors and flows in favour of their domestic/national equivalent.

In terms of the globalization, the narrative with regard to nationalism is that the state seeks independence from external forces and influences based upon a right of self-determination. Nationalism advances the notion of self-reliance and seeking to shape engagement with the system through the lens of the national interest. The legacy of this is that political harmony is based on some degree of homogeneity amongst a population based around some common identity. The legacy of this is that it can prove hostile to the legacy of globalism as expressed within multi-cultural and multi-national populations. Narratives embedded within nationalism sees these (and the process of globalism itself) as a direct threat to the sense of nation. This is evidenced through a belief that globality has tended industrialized economy decline as investment flowed to lower cost states. This was evident in the rise of populist nationalism (see below). As of 2022, there are number of readily identifiable types of nationalism across the global system. These definitions offered below are not mutually exclusive as states can exhibit elements of several forms of nationalism within their political system. The main types are as follows.

1. *Populist Nationalism* This has become a feature of mature democratic system across several industrialized states. The notion of populism reflects a strong anti-elite sentiment where there is a strong feeling that specific social groups have been left behind by globalism and suffered disadvantages due to the decisions of their leaders. This has manifested itself in pushback against globalism and a restoration of nationalism. This form of nationalism operates at the extremes of the political spectrum. On the right, this process has created a pluto-populist based upon the adoption of free market economics, political libertarianism, and social conservatism. This places a strong emphasis on identity over all other traits. At the other end of the spectrum is socio- or protecto-populism which focuses upon resisting the globality of national systems by counteracting and limiting international competition through aggressive state strategy and an increased degree of social liberalism. This type of nationalism has been evident in the UK and the US as well as parts of the European Union.

2. *Credo-Nationalism* This exists where there is a strong alignment between the predominant religion within a state and the political system. The main political parties openly espouse religious themes to gain support and legitimacy. Religious belief has influence over policy and such actions stand in contrast to secular system where political system and religion are kept separate. Thus, the congruence between the nation and religion can create exclusion effects creating a 'tyranny of minority' faiths. As a political strategy, parties adopt these credos to create strong alignment between the party, national identity, and religion. Credo-nationalism stresses a good national citizen adheres to these religious principles and infers that citizens that do not are less virtuous and potential enemies of the state. This form of nationalism has emerged where religion has a strong social basis and where it can be strong political cleavage between the population such as in South Asia. Other states have adopted elements of religious identity as part of national political strategy (e.g., Russia).

3. *Authoritarian Nationalism* These are states where there are either limits (artificial or otherwise) upon the degree of political competition or where such competition is explicitly banned. In some states, where there is single party control the state uses nationalism to legitimize its control. The strong control exercised by the state is rationalized as being in the 'national' interest where political competition can be destabilizing and therefore harmful to prosperity and where strong central control is necessary to curb social evils. The nation becomes interchangeable with the party. This trend is also evident in states that are notionally democratic and where there has been the rise of 'illiberal democracy' where the prevailing political powers seek to steer and control democratic political processes to ensure continuity of control stressing the role of external forces in seeking to challenge national identity.

The states that currently exhibit varying degrees of nationalist political strategy are reflected in ◘ Table 5.3. The US is a moot point as to whether it is still populist though given the clear electoral split between pluto- and socio-populists, it is fair to argue that the absence of consensus policies and the continuation of protectionist policies stress that nationalism is still strong. Across Europe, populism also remains

Table 5.3 Nationalist states (as of July 2022)

State	Nationalism type (s)	Potential for global systemic disruption
US	Pluto populist	High—engages in protectionism and disrupts liberal international order
Mexico	Socio-populist	Low—Possible impact on region and localized energy and migrant flows
Brazil	Pluto Populist	Medium—regional impact though possible global impact through increasing ecological risk
Venezuela	Authoritarian/socio-populist	Medium—regional risk increases through migratory flows but possible impact upon resource (oil) markets
Italy	Socio-populist	Medium—possible regional impact upon EU functioning and structure
Poland	Credo/populist	Medium—possible regional impact upon EU functioning and structure
Austria	Pluto Populist	Medium—possible regional impact upon EU functioning and structure
Egypt	Authoritarian	Low—though possibility of regional disruption
Morocco	Credo	Low—though possibility of regional disruption through disputes with neighbours
Uganda	Socio-populist	Low—though possibility of regional impact
Turkey	Socio Populist	Medium—occupies a key logistics conduit and has been proactive in regional geopolitics
Saudi Arabia	Authoritarian	Medium—possibility of regional instability and disruption to flows of hydrocarbons
Syria	Authoritarian	Low—possibility as a source of regional instability and international terrorism
Russia	Authoritarian	High—has promoted regional and global geopolitical instability for own geopolitical aims
India	Credo	Medium—has the potential for regional geopolitical instability
Pakistan	Credo	Medium—has the potential for regional geopolitical instability
China	Authoritarian	High potential to disrupt regional and global political and economic systems
Turkmenistan	Authoritarian	Low potential for disruption to hydrocarbon flows and regional disruption
Philippines	Socio Populist	Low potential for regional disruption
North Korea	Authoritarian	High—aggressive militarism increases risk of regional and global disruption
Vietnam	Authoritarian	Low potential for regional disruption
Australia	Pluto Populist	Low potential for regional disruption
Japan	Pluto Populist	Medium potential for regional and global disruption

strong and has proved resilient as a force throughout the pandemic even giving rise to vaccine nationalism where some states sought to limit no domestic access to COVID vaccines and/or its component parts as well as rising resentment against regionalism (notably anti-EU sentiment). The absence of political consensus means that nationalism as a source of geopolitical risk is likely to remain salient for the foreseeable future.

International Terrorism

Terrorism are those intentional acts of violence committed for political objectives where the targets are non-military (possibly random) targets (such as the general public) by groups acting in the interest of a sub-national group or possibly operating within the tacit knowledge of a state to destabilize another state. In a global system, such activity can cross international borders where terrorists located in one state seek to utilize the freedoms associated with globalization to disrupt the activities of another state or even the system as a whole. This form of risk emerges where the state has weak governance that allows these groups to flourish unchecked and to spread violence throughout the global system. In other cases, disruptor/rogue states can sponsor terrorism within a region or beyond to seek to disrupt the activities of rival states.

The main focal point of terrorist activity—either at a national or global level—is to destabilize the targeted system. This is not just to draw awareness to a cause but to seek to assert power over that system by altering its functioning as a direct consequence of their actions. At the political level, terrorism can impact how the state/states respond to the destabilizing threat this could involve:
- Military occupation of restive sub-region.
- Curtailment of civil liberties.
- Increase security at borders and key potential flashpoints.
- Proactive measure to promote inter-regional cohesion.
- Promotion of social cohesion.

These are a mixture of control, security, and cohesion as a means to limit the impact of domestic and international terrorism (see below) upon economic systems. Terrorism has both a direct and indirect impact upon economic systems through:
- *Direct economic destruction:* terrorism can target symbols of state political and economic power but can also be used to disrupt everyday economic activity through attacks on transport systems for example. This imposes direct financial and indirect opportunity costs upon states as they repair the damage and adapt to the threat.
- *Increased uncertainty*: in both financial and commodity markets increased terrorist threats and the potential for disruption can lead to sharp oscillations in prices.
- *Economic engagement:* internal terrorism can pose a threat to states' economic interaction with the global system. It can make FDI unsafe (especially where kidnapping of ex-patriot workers is a risk), it can stymy tourism where visitors do not feel safe, and it can lead to disruption of supply chains especially when insurance premiums as a legacy of terrorist incidents increase.

- *State failure:* as suggested above (see ▶ Chapter 3) terrorism is often symptomatic of poor governance within a state and terrorism compounds this problem. This can place the state's economic system under siege as governments react to the issue in terms of increased control and security.
- *Economic Impact of political response:* as noted above states respond to terrorism by increasing security. The impact upon business is that cross border flows are more heavily controlled and monitored and economic engagement with some states could be curtailed. The state is seen as high risk and hostile to international interactions.

Whilst there is a long precedence with regard to international terrorism, it has been enabled by globalization. Indeed, globalization has increased this degree of geopolitical risk and increased the vulnerability to disruption to these actions by the rising level of interactions. The increased movement of people, data, and resources have all been exploited by terrorists to create rising levels of geopolitical risk. These have allowed terrorists to build global networks with the aim of spreading disruption as widely as possible. These groups can use social media to recruit and radicalize individuals/groups of individuals to allow them to further spread the risk of international risk and disruption. Generally, these global networks of terrorism used globalization for the purposes of:

- Global fundraising: this is where the organization finances its activity through a global system of support.
- Global recruitment: through as mentioned social media but also using social systems (such as an extended diaspora) to recruit new members.
- Global networks are a form of social globalization as interdependence is created between disparate groups to form an interconnected group across multiple states.
- Global infrastructure to support their activity from dedicated transport system to their own IT systems.

On the flip side of this globalization enabling argument, it is also relevant to establish the fact that most terrorist attacks occur in places that are peripheral to the operation of the global system. Overall, the disruptive impact of terrorism depends upon where its interface with economic activity is strongest. As terrorism impacts more where an activity in centralized and where physical damage or restrictions upon flows can impede the degree of interconnectivity. Thus, terrorism will have its strongest impact on:

- Core logistical transit channels where transport is concentrated due to absence of other competing channels. This can include core conduits such as the Suez Canal or the Straits of Malacca (see ▶ Chapter 9).
- Core global hubs through international traffic are channelled through to other destination (such as hub air and seaports).
- Centralized data processing centres or oceanic cable landing points that drive international data flows.
- Centralized financial centres which can disrupt the operation of global capital.
- Attacks on global flows, for example, piracy on container shipping or IT system hacking.
- Attacks on state specific critical infrastructure which impacts upon state efficacy.

Overall, the interface between globality and the rise of international terrorism is ambiguous as most terrorism is local. However, global networks can ferment local unrest. At the business level, in certain states terrorism is an ever-present concern. This tends to be in less developed states. Attacks on developed states where the potential losses to business would be greater are significantly rarer as these risks are militated by better security, internal control, and social cohesion. Thus, the greater risk tends to be in states where there is—as a rule—less financial impact. The issue is the use of global networks to take local disputes onto a global stage. This renders the process a lot more uncertain.

Inter-state Conflict

The interface between globalization and inter-state conflict is nuanced. Intuitively greater economic and political interconnections between states should make the probability and desirability of inter-state conflict increasingly unlikely due to the costs to the state involved within the process. These costs are not merely direct in terms of damage of infrastructure, loss of personal belongings, etc., but also the indirect economic and political costs as states incur sanctions from non-combative states so as to seek to change the combative states behaviour and belligerence. As globalization has progressed so the cost of war has increased as the degree of interconnectivity with the global system has increased and as states do not want to forego the gains from trade. Overall globalization has reshaped and lowered the likelihood notion of inter-state conflict due to the following pressures.
1. States have increased mutual security arrangements as they have grown more aware of the political, economic, and social costs of conflict as well as the financial impact of military spending.
2. The intensity, extensity, and velocity of economic flows have increased the vulnerability of states to crises in even the most remote places of the global system.
3. As states get wealthier there is increased opportunity cost in terms of personal, corporate, and state losses from going to war.
4. The challenges to national security are no longer purely military as new threats emerge from multiple novel sources such as ecological, social, economic, cultural, criminal, illicit drugs, and terrorism to name but a few. These threats further increase the demand for international co-operation for mutual security.
5. Security within the state system is subject to the state of security within the global system as a whole where notably superpowers are able to assert dominant influence and seek to control the flows of weaponry around it.

Thus, there is a negative correlation between peace and globalization due to the above pressures. This has been compounded by a series of multilateral agreements between states to manage the potential for and outbreak of inter-state conflict. There are—for example—agreements of the global arms trade as well as agreements on the proliferation of weapons of mass destruction.

Since the end of World War II, there has been a sustained downward trend in global conflict. Whilst this coincides with the trends towards globalization there is no suggestion of direct causation. This trend has been especially marked in inter-state conflict where the retreat of colonialism has removed the pressure towards conflict. With the process of military globalization, the process of war becomes more complex. International alliances can mean that conflict with one state can mean conflict with many. This is compounded by the globalization of the arms trade and other forms of military interconnectedness that make inter-state conflict a more complex process than an inter-state bilateral conflict. These processes of military interconnectedness allow superpowers to assert global reach and offer mutually agreed security. This is also enabled by a dispersal of military bases by these states across the globe in areas where economic activity and global flows are vulnerable to disruption through inter-state conflict. This ensures that even if an inter-state conflict does break out in an area that is central to the operation of the global system, then the power of the hegemon can mitigate against its effects upon the wider global system. This is compounded by widespread co-operation in many states on issues of mutual security with many aware of the vast economic, social, and political costs of inter-state conflict.

As with other potential geopolitical disruptors, the impact of inter-state conflict upon the stability of and risk within the global system depends upon:
- The extent to which any given non-combative state has economic investment and political connections with the combative states.
- The extent to which the combative states are able to assert geopolitical and geoeconomic power over the global system and to disrupt its operation.
- The extent to which the inter-state conflict can disrupt global flows by disrupting transmitting flows between non-combative states.
- The possibility of the inter-state conflict spilling over into other states creating regional and potential global instability.
- The extent to which the conflict creates flows of migrants across borders into neighbouring states and beyond and how that fuels instability in the host states.

There is a flip side to the argument that increased globalization can actually be a catalyst for inter-state conflict. It has often been argued that intense globalization in the era prior to the First World War did little to prevent this conflict. Indeed, there is a case to argue that increased economic rivalry stimulated by globalization could spill over into increased political conflict and then into military conflict. Economic competition and grievances can lead to increased military conflict notably if these relations generate dependency and/or the relationship is unequal. There is also the logic that increased economic interconnection render states vulnerable to hybrid (or alternative) wars as powerful states seek to use competencies in the cyber system and resources to alter other states' behaviour and to even disrupt these states' internal workings. Thus, globalization has enabled differing sorts of inter-state violence. Ultimately the process of globalization has not removed inter-state conflict entirely though it has tended to move it to states which are more peripheral to the operation of the global system. These conflicts have often facilitated superpower (and allied) intervention.

There is also a belief that globalization can also increase the level of conflict notably through the means through which western power is exercised and through which it promotes social change. It also underscores that a distant event can have local consequences through cascade effects. Thus, the impact of globalization upon inter-state conflict does not always reflect a direct obvious process of causation. It is more obvious for some authors that where the benefits/costs of globalization are shared unequally then it has the potential to foster both inter- and intra-state conflict. In the latter case globalization through illicit trading can help ferment and sustain civil conflict through enabling its finance.

Global Governance Failure

One feature of the current liberal internationalist order is the plethora of multilateral bodies to foster global co-operation (see ▶ Box 5.1). As mentioned above, these bodies have evolved to offer multilateral solutions based upon agreement between states. These are formed around issues that cut across a state's borders. As globalization has matured and expanded so the global system has grown more complex, and more states enter the global system as the range of issues requiring global solutions increases. In the absence of a global government, this governance depends upon states interacting and co-operating for mutual benefit. Whilst this does not need a strong hegemon to create and enforce these rules it does help in terms of creating consistency amongst states with the rules to be enforced and adhered to within such bodies. The consensual perspective is that increased global connectivity increased the desire and need for more developed global governance frameworks as the range of issues that can only be solved through cross-border dialogue increases. The problem is that economic globalization always moved faster than political globalization. Moreover, the pushback against globalization happens faster within political globalization than in economic globalization. As a result, global governance systems always seem to be lagging behind the reality of the operation of the global system. As a result, some of the issues that need co-ordinated solutions are dealt with at the national level leading to a fragmented approach to global problems.

These are compounded by long-standing concerns regarding the structure and operation of the multilateral systems. These concerns have focused upon the inequity within the systems with hegemonic (and allied) powered tending to dominate the development of the rules that emerge from these global governance systems. This leads to a democratic deficit within these systems with many states being effectively excluded. The legacy of this is to potentially undermine the legitimacy of the global governance system. This can lead to systemic instability as rules begin to vary across the global system. As these under-represented powers begin to resent this the more rival systems can emerge creating a polycentric global system and fragmented global governance system. The less the governance system is representative of the nature of the global system the more it loses legitimacy. This discontent is growing as an increasing level of economic deprivation, declining public services, a sense of isolation from decision making structures, and other causes of social unrest are all undermining the legitimacy of the multilateral, co-operative system. Overall, it is widely accepted that global governance has failed to solve three problems to which it seems tailor-made namely promoting financial stability, ecological protection, and the promotion of greater equity. The result is that the system is failing the economic, ecological, and social systems. This has fuelled dissatisfaction with the system and the seeming unassailable dominance of neo-liberal logic as solution to global problems which makes things worse for some states.

The COVID-19 pandemic underscored the failure of global governance generated by reversals in the technology focused upon preventing communicable diseases this was compounded by increased levels of scepticism over the science of vaccines creating vaccine hesitancy. Moreover, failure to agree to limits on movement between states would have limited its global transmission. Failure was also evident in the inequity with which vaccines were rolled out with developed states seeking to prioritize their populations over a global roll out. This reflects an on-going concern (mentioned above) that global governance systems favour the strong over the weak. This was evident in the way in which economic policies were imposed upon developing states that reflected western preferences rather than the needs of the state seeking support. The Washington Consensus as a tool of international governance sought to impose western values upon non-western states. This reflected the power of the US over the international governance architecture. It also bred hostility towards how these systems operated and the asymmetry of power within the global governance system.

Aside from these long-standing asymmetries, the emergence of nationalism (see above) has led to states pushing back against the trend towards multilateralism. Indeed, with rise of nationalism states are often no longer willing to make the sacrifices to make the global system work to the benefit of all states. For example, many states have been slow to implement Climate Agreements and offered limiting funding to ensure a global vaccine programme. In addition, as states push back from this there is the risk that the system begins to fragment or that the system evolves into a polycentric international governance system possibly one a legacy of the western based system and the other developed around another powerful state such as China. Whilst such configurations are—at this point conjectural—they do underline how this fragmentation poses a risk to the system. This process will likely lead to:

- Uneven development of rules where there is a common interest.
- An incentive for states to engage in beggar thy neighbour policies in areas of common interest creating a risk of retaliation.
- Greater long-term risk as global solutions to common problems are shelved.
- The fragmentation of the global system of rules.

Thus, the global governance system is imperfect and needs reform to reflect a diversity of interests as well as changing power systems within the global system. Thus, without reformation it could lead to rising levels of risk as states' governance systems on common issues diverge.

Conclusions

If politics is about the distribution of power, then geopolitics reflects the relative power of states to shape the stability and performance of the global system. As such, geopolitical risk is created by the actions of a state and/or group of states that has the impact of challenging international political stability. For much of the past three decades, the US as the hegemonic power has been a stabilizing force upon the global system. However, geopolitical risks within the global system are increasing as the US' hegemony is being challenged by the rise of China.

Geopolitical Risk

Key Points

- Political risk is an on-going feature of business environments.
- Geopolitical risks reflect relations between states that can destabilize the global system.
- Geopolitical instability is rising due to the rise of China.
- Not all geopolitical instability is driven by states as terrorism can also destabilize the global system.

Discussion Questions

1. What is the geopolitical rationale of states decoupling?
2. Why does nationalism pose a geopolitical risk?
3. What do you think is the importance of the global governance architecture to resolution of global risk?

Activities

Explore the geopolitical risks encountered by Exxon Mobil in undertaking global energy extraction and production.

Summary

Geopolitical risk is widely acknowledged as rising throughout the global system. This has been driven by a pushback against global political processes and a renewed trend towards nationalism within states. This creates risks for business not simply through risk within and across any set of states but also by the risk that such political forces will result in a higher level of fragmentation across the global system. These processes will increase the transaction costs for businesses engaged in the global system.

Further Reading

Bremmer, I. (2012). *Every Nation for Itself: Winners and Losers in a G-Zero World*. Portfolio.
Bremmer I. (2022). *The Power of Crisis: How Three Threats—And Our Response—Will Change the World*. Simon and Schuster.
Jones, O., & Henisz, W. (2023). *Geostrategy in Practice: How to Manage Political Risk in a Shifting World Order Disruption Books*.
Munoz, J. M. (2013). *Handbook on the Geopolitics of Business*. Edward Elgar Publishing.
Rice, C., & Zegart, A. B. (2018). *Political Risk: How Businesses and Organizations Can Anticipate Global Insecurity*. Twelve.

Useful Websites

1. Blackrock (▶ https://www.blackrock.com/) is an international investor that publishes a geopolitical risk dashboard.
2. Kroll (▶ https://www.kroll.com/en/insights/) is a risk advisory business that offers a global risk assessment.

Ecological Risk

© The Author(s), under exclusive license to Springer Nature Switzerland AG 2023
C. Turner, *Global Business Analysis*,
https://doi.org/10.1007/978-3-031-27769-6_6

'The Earth is a fine place and worth fighting for'.

Ernest Hemingway, Author

At the end of this chapter, students will be able to understand:
- The form and nature of climate change.
- How climate change represents a risk to global business.
- Issues surrounding energy, water, and food security.

Introduction

Arguably, there is no greater long-term risk upon human activity and existence than those created by its interaction with the natural environment. Overtime humans have shaped and re-reshaped the planet to enable humanity—as the dominant species with no natural predator—to survive and flourish. This has manifested itself in rising levels of population coupled with increased levels of industrial and economic development. Increasingly the long-term consequences of these demographic and economic processes are being felt by the natural habitat that humanity occupies which is becoming less conducive to sustained human development and existence. In a chapter of this length, all the issues surrounding such linked events and processes created by human interaction and exploitation of the planet cannot be addressed. As such, the chapter will look at these interlinked processes through the lens of business risk and address how the shaping and utilization of natural resources and processes are driving this process. This it will do through an examination of key issues in the nexus between business risk and the natural environment namely climate change-driven risk and the legacy of the Food–Water–Energy nexus and how this is shaping issues of security concerns across these respective domains of human activity.

The Anthropocene

Whilst it is still an unofficial term, humanity is now accepted as living in the age of the Anthropocene. This is used to donate the period of time in Earth's history where human activity has begun to exhibit a telling and irreversible impact upon the planet's ecosystems and climate. The fact that the term is still unofficial reflects that there is—as yet—little evidence that humanity has had any sustained impact upon the Earth's rock strata (the lithosphere). The starting point for the Anthropocene is uncertain with some believing it began with the Industrial Revolution in the 1800s when large-scale emissions of gas (notably carbon and methane) were emitted into and began to change the atmosphere. Others place the date as later possibly at the beginning of the Nuclear Age (i.e., post-1945) where the dropping of nuclear devices upon two Japanese cities has—over the longer term—been detected in the lithosphere. It has been argued that plastic pollution might be the clearest example of this process. As plastic does not biodegrade it can be found in Oceans and Soils.

Irrespective of the official start date, it is established that sharp increases in human activity are having a significant impact upon the Earth's natural systems. The last 60 years have seen what has become to be known as the 'Great Acceleration'

where the impact of human activity upon natural systems has increased markedly across all of these systems created by the following human-generated processes namely:
- Carbon dioxide emissions: the burning of hydrocarbons for energy to power industrial, economic, and social development has led to a significant increase in carbon dioxide emissions which linger in the upper atmosphere.
- Global warming: the emissions of gases from human activity create a greenhouse effect warning the atmosphere which impacts upon established climatic conditions, oceanic circulation, and the habitats of flora and fauna.
- Ocean acidification: where carbon dioxide released by human activity is absorbed by the Oceans increasing its acidity and impacting upon its suitability as a habitat.
- Habitat destruction: the destruction of wild habitats for food and energy production has generated a reduction in viable habitats to support a diverse range of species.
- Extinction: the excessive extraction of resources beyond their ability to be replenished has limited the ability of other flora and fauna to survive pushing many species to endangerment and even extinction thereby lowering the biodiversity of the planet.
- Widescale natural resource extraction: the excessive extraction of natural resources for economic development has actively degraded the habitats of multiple species.

For business, it is the legacy of their activities that has been one of the main causes of these processes. Beyond a process of accountability and adaptation, the legacy of the emergent Anthropocene for business lies in how the alterations and functions of these systems impact upon their commercial activity. These risks from this process of change are based upon disruptive events caused by these long-term changes and also by the need for longer-term adaptions in business models as they have to adjust to a more hostile natural operating environment. They have also to adapt to changing customer sentiment that requires new sources of value creation. This risk context for business in the Anthropocene has three overlapping risks: market, operations, and policy. These reflect that business models need to adapt through:
- Adjusting to state policy programmes to militate effects of past, present, and future activities of a business that impact of natural system state and process.
- Facilitating policy measures that enable socio-economic adaption and response to events sourced from natural systems that impact upon human activity and its enabling socio-economic systems.
- Reflecting the shifting needs of customers and the broad value network within the products and processes undertaken by the firm so that these are not or are less harmful/disruptive to natural systems.
- Enabling recovery from climate-related processes and events that impact upon business operations and markets.
- Altering processes so that production and operational systems do not damage or interfere with natural systems.

These adaptions and risks reflect that the interface between business and the legacy of anthropocentric activity within natural systems reflects a mix of both proactive

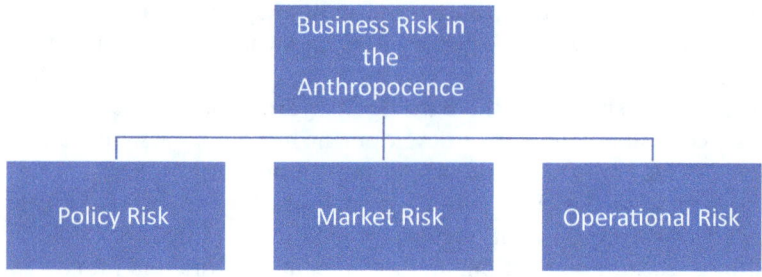

Fig. 6.1 Business risk in Anthropocene

and reactive measures (see Fig. 6.1). This reflects a need for businesses to become both resilient and sustainable in the expectation of challenges to its value creating processes but also to recognize that these processes by their nature change the process and understanding of value creation itself.

Climate Risk

This section addresses the main themes and risks created by the on-going process of climate change. This reflects a legacy of long-standing process of human economic and social development and how this development process has had a lasting impact upon the Earth's climatic systems. This has been caused not just by the industrialization process and the burning of fossil fuels but also by carbon released from the soil through the intensification of agriculture. Climate change has persistently been ranked by global business leaders as the main risk to be faced over both the medium and long term (WEF 2022). Climate risk has three channels of effects:
1. Climate drivers: these are the climatic changes occurring within a system that are the source of risks.
2. Transmission channels: these are the means through which these risks are transferred into other parts of the system.
3. Variability drivers: these are the localized factors that shape the impact of any climatic event or process upon a given location.

This section will briefly explore the nature of climate change and the broad risk it creates before more on to address the main two widely accepted forms of risk: physical and transition risks.

What is Climate Change?

This exists as a process of long-term change in the operation of the Earth's climatic system caused by the impact of past and on-going human social and economic activity. The nature of change is that greenhouse gases (carbon dioxide and methane) emitted into the atmosphere have had the effect of warming the Earth's surface. According to the IPCC (2021), the Earth's surface temperature was nearly 1.1 °C higher between 2011 and 2020 than it was between 1850 and 1900. These changes in temperature are larger over land than they are over the Oceans. This rise in temperatures has been especially marked over the Polar regions leading to physical changes on the Earth's surface as ice melt is causing sea levels to rise and promoting the increased of flooding and the physical degradation of land. These processes are also impacting upon ocean currents and large-scale circulation of air around the planet both of which are pivotal in channelling thermal energy across the surface of the Earth. The more these are disturbed the more weather becomes erratic.

The effect of these processes is that climate (which has always been variable) begins to increase in its variability and becomes a lot more unpredictable. Moreover, it also makes habitats increasingly hostile for many species due to the climate changing quicker than any genus' ability to adapt. The result is that the Earth's climatic system becomes increasingly subject to extreme weather events (such as droughts, heatwaves, floods, etc.), and the certainty of climatic conditions (given some degree of natural variability) is eroded. This runs the risk of eroding biodiversity, creating water risk, and promoting instability in social, political, and economic systems. In short, it threatens the stability and sustainability of existing global sub-systems. The impacts will depend upon the extent to which these systems exhibit:
- Resilience: that is the capability of this system to rapidly adapt to the extreme events of climate change so as to resume normal conditions of operation.
- Sustainability: the nature of how these systems adapt to enable them to sustain their operations within the context shaped by changing climatic conditions.

The degree of resilience and sustainability within the interacting global sub-systems frames the levels of risks within the global system. The nature of the climate risk is the degree to which any given hazard leaves any individual and asset (both natural and human created) vulnerable and exposed through its impact upon the persons/assets function in a normal manner without significant disruption to their existence, welfare, and physical wellbeing. This is compounded by the fact that climate change can impact upon systems through a number of channels for example, extreme weather can:
- Impact upon personal health through rising sunstroke, humidity, and exposure to increased precipitation.
- Undermine production through impacting upon food security.
- Hit productivity through increasing mental and physical deterioration of the workforce.
- Suppress economic growth as states spend to recover from the physical and non-physical damage.
- Create cascade effects as extreme weather in one state can impact upon others through for example food prices and extended global supply chains.

As suggested, the vulnerability of states to climate risk varies markedly across the global system. These states that are most subject to climate risk are not merely those that face the highest risk of disruptive hazards. This physical risk is combined with a vulnerability that is compounded by a low level of resilience and systemic sustainability. That is in the event of a climatic event the period between the event occurring and normality being restored is protracted for those states with low resilience and low degree of sustainability. This tends to render less developed states especially small island developing states as the most vulnerable states subject to climate risk (see ▶ Box 6.1). These are states that are subject to regular climatic events and for whom resilience is low.

Box 6.1: Climate Change and Small Island Developing States (SIDS)

SIDS are—as the name suggests—a group of 52 developing states that are small islands. These states are overwhelmingly located within the tropics and are uniquely vulnerable to the impact of climate change. The geographic location of these states renders them especially vulnerable to extreme weather events. On top of this SIDS are also more prone to the impact of rising sea levels. In combination, these extreme weather events, climate unpredictability, and rising sea levels could ultimately render many of these SIDS are uninhabitable. The location and climate of these SIDS are often central to their pattern of economic development and growth. Many of these tropical located islands depend upon tourism as a major revenue earner; others to a lesser extent depend upon their abundant fish resources. The dependence upon tourism for many of these states can create issues where climatic conditions render the state's habitability more vulnerable.

The vulnerability of these SIDS is not simply created by the increased risk of extreme weather but also but the development conditions in which such events occur. It is notable that these islands are characterized by:
— Limited natural resources and unsustainable human activity.
— High population densities and often high population growth.
— Freshwater recourses that are vulnerable to sea level changes.
— Comparative isolation from major markets.
— A high degree of trade openness and export dependency which increase the risk of external shocks.
— Limited physical size which can limit adaptability.
— Limited resilience and financial resources.

These vulnerabilities are reinforced by a high dependence upon external sources of critical resources such as food and water, low-lying areas that a vulnerable to flooding, and concentrations of population in coastal areas. Thus the challenge for these states is that their environment is changing and there have a very limited capacity to cope with these changes. The main impact of climate change upon these states will be felt through:
— A deterioration of already limited water resources as rainfall patterns are altered.
— Erosion of low-lying coastal areas is likely to inhibit the ability to undertake economic activity within these places.
— Increased heat stress within these states will limit options with regard to home-generated food security.
— There is likely to be a diminution of biodiversity because of these climatic changes.
— Local infrastructure is likely to be damaged by these changing conditions by being subject to more extreme conditions for which they were not designed.
— Deteriorating human health as changing climatic conditions led to more contagious diseases with which the local community does not have immunity.
— A reduction in the feasibility and attractiveness of tourism due to increased risk and failing hospitable conditions.

The challenge for these states to mitigate climatic risk is to create an adaptive capacity within them. This accepts that conditions are changing but that these states can adapt rapidly to these extreme events. This depends not simply upon more financial resources but also upon better governance and better data to fully understand the nature of the problem faced.

Overall, climate risk is based upon two inter-related risks:

Physical Climate Risks

The physical risks from climate change apply to both natural and human-created tangible assets that are impacted by climate-driven events. This includes changes to the hydrological and carbon cycles. There can be expected to be effects on both water and food security (see below) as traditional methods and sources are impacted by the long-term shift in climate. These physical risks are also likely to cascade down to increase socio-economic risk especially where such climatic events increase the physical damage which the state has a limited financial capability for redress. Developing economies are very dependent upon sectors that are specifically impacted by climatic-related events and processes. For example, tourism and agriculture (see ▶ Box 6.1). This vulnerability is created by a mix of economic (poor fiscal position, absence of economic diversification, and lower levels of development) and geographic (namely their location at lower latitudes and other physical characteristics) factors. Thus, these effects are going to happen unevenly across the planet meaning that the physical risk will be also spatially dispersed.

Broadly these types of risk can be categorized into acute risks (based on extreme weather causing wildfires, floods, storms, and heat waves) and chronic risks which are more long term and include phenomena such as droughts, sea level rises, landslides, and more variable precipitation. This all underscores that physical risk is also shaped by the socio-economic context in which that risk occurs that renders some parts of the global system more vulnerable than others. Typical physical risks incurred include:
— Damage to agricultural systems from wildfires and floods.
— Damage to critical infrastructure systems that are essential to state functioning.
— Damage to economic assets from extreme weather (such as storms).
— Damage to life and wellbeing from extreme and unexpected weather events.
— Damage to biodiversity from both short-term climate events and long-term processes.
— Damage to social fabric leads to migratory flows.
— Damages to asset value for those exposed assets.
— Damage from slow on-set events such as sea level rise and desertification.

Whilst such risk is long standing and a natural risk from locating within specific locations, the legacy of climate change is that such events are becoming increasingly frequent. These impact upon the economic performance of states and businesses as productivity, health, and production are impacted. Thus, the physical risks are both direct and indirect. These reflect that the physical risks can be created by cascade effects as physical damage in one locality or part of the system spreads into other parts. For example, the physical risk can create disruptions to global supply chains or energy production. These cascade risks also extend to the insurance sector which is liable for pay-outs to cover the damage from these events. As these events increase in frequency, so the impact upon the insurance sector and indeed upon the financial sector generally can be expected to increase. These indicate how climatic events can transmit to other systems and have multi-scalar impacts through the following processes.

- Micro-level processes—which are at the firm level where—for example—there is physical damage to the firm's assets which disrupts its operations and capabilities. This analysis can also be extended to households which are especially exposed to climatic risks.
- Meso-level processes—these are where there are impacts on the interactions between firms crated by a disruption to flows between them created by a climatic event or process.
- Macro-level processes—this reflects an impact upon economic growth, productivity, and other aspects of state capability by an climatic event.

These effects are not uniform across and within states reflecting that risk is subject to the following:
- Geographical heterogeneity—this reflects spatial differences in economic structures and the relative importance of vulnerable segments.
- Amplifier—these are feedback loops which accelerate, extend, and expand the impact of any single event/process upon another system. These are created by links between the sector and the climate risk events.
- Mitigants—these are actions that have been and can be taken by states to mitigate against the impact of any climate driver upon the operation of another system. This could be systems such as flood defences.

These processes created by physical risk from climate change are reflected in ◘ Fig. 6.2.

Adaptation Climate Risks

The adaptation risk reflects two trends within the process of the impact of climate changes upon the actions of states and businesses. The first is the risk associated with adjustment of physical systems to allow them to exhibit resilience and sustainability. With regard to the shift towards the creations of resilient systems, there are evident risks involved in terms of the costs and prioritization of adapting physical systems to the increased level of physical threat from the process of climate change. For example, this means having to increase flood defences and other social and economic infrastructures to enable them to cope with extreme events. This can represent a cost to businesses and states as well as a regulatory risk as businesses are forced to upgrade physical systems to adapt to the threat. The logic of enduring this risk is to minimize the economic and social costs of disruption created by extreme events. There is a risk that having made these physical adaptations that the anticipated events do not occur or that these changes place pressure on corporate and state budgets.

The second concern is the risks associated with the transition to a low carbon economy. These transition risks reflect the uncertainties created for individuals, households, and states by the transition towards an environment where economic and social activity has a less harmful impact upon natural systems. Very broadly these are changes within human-created systems designed to mitigate anthropocentric impacts upon natural systems. These are generally sourced from one or more of the following:
- Government policy, legislation, and regulation amendments to driver change in behaviour of economic and social agents towards their intended and unintended impact upon natural systems.

Ecological Risk

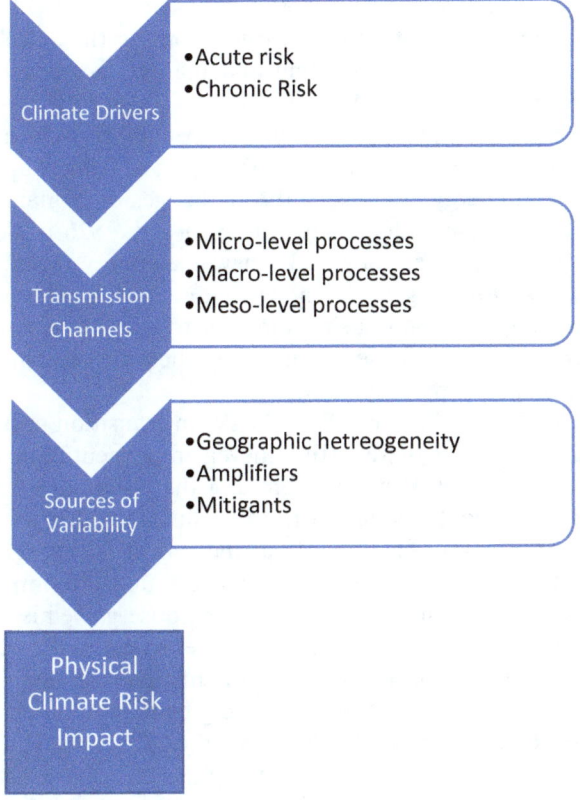

Fig. 6.2 The physical impact of climate change

- Cost of disruption from climatic events and the costs of adapting to this risk and resuming a state of normality.
- Costs both actual and opportunity created by pre-emptive actions by the state in anticipation of future climatic-driven events.
- Technological change is designed to facilitate less impactful human impact upon natural systems.
- Reputational risks are created by the failure to adapt to shifting ecological context.
- Market and customer sentiment establish clear parameters with regard to the tolerable/acceptable level of impact of human activity upon natural systems and how businesses must respond.

These drivers can create risk in terms of the ability of agents to adapt to these changes and the cost and pace of doing so (see below). The minimum level of transition expected of states and of business are reflected within international agreements upon climate change notably within the Paris Agreement which has sought to set multilaterally agreed curbs on greenhouse gas emissions within agreed time frames.

The technological dimension of the transition risk reflects the adoption of those technologies that facilitate the move towards low carbon consuming activity. This creates an adaptive tension upon business models not merely towards low carbon operations and revenue generation but also in adopting those technologies that facilitate resilience with business operating and market facing actions. These costs also reflect the risk undertaken in expectation of future events. States and businesses, etc., make a pre-emptive transition in expectation of future climatic-driven events. Overall, the IPCC estimated that it will cost $90 trillion up to 2030 to adjust urban, land use, and energy systems to the challenges of climate change. In terms of energy, the IEA estimates that there will need to be $26 trillion spent between 2015 and 2040 on energy efficiency and renewable energy technologies to achieve the internationally agreed targets for the curtailment of greenhouse gas emissions. Again, this places pressure upon business models to adapt to a shifting context. The utility sectors as well as businesses such as logistics who depend upon fossil fuel consumption are seen as especially vulnerable.

The WEF has addressed the issues and risks in transition and believes that one of the major threats is that there is the uneven implementation of the transition. This creates divergences between states limiting the potential for states to attain a co-operative and co-ordinated solution to the solution to this problem. This risk is as much about non-transition as it is about the transition process per se. This has been reflected in the unevenness with which some states have implemented internationally agreed targets for the reduction in greenhouse gas emissions. This delayed transition has been informed by the desire of states to recover quickly from the economic downturn created by anticipated and unanticipated events (such as pandemics and conflicts). As states prioritize economic growth so the objectives of addressing the needs of climate change get pushed further down the list of priorities. For both businesses and states, these lags in the deployment of transitioning can create reputational damage or increase credit risk as the agent may be deemed insufficiently resilient and/or sustainable to the risk of physical risks. According to the WEF part of the problem with the uneven transition is that the cost of the process is becoming more evident to both businesses and citizens with some sectors that are likely to bear the brunt of the transition actively pushing back on the process. This transition is also spilling over into geopolitical risk as states compete to gain access to key raw materials (such as those in batteries). These risks exist across multiple scales.

– Micro-level risks: there are those individuals and businesses that simply cannot afford the cost of transition. This could see the cost-of-living increase for many and increased cost of operation for businesses. This could result in a loss of market share for those businesses that move first within the transition and could leave firms with stranded assets rendered redundant by the transition process especially where the process is aggressively pursued.
– Macro-level risks: for states there could be a political backlash as a result of trends at the micro level. This could be compounded by resentment over differing levels of access to climate mitigating technologies within states. This could lead to increased levels of social risk within states as it implies that some groups will bear the brunt of climatic events more than others. There could also emerge rising levels of debt as states invest in the technologies to support the transition.
– Meso-level risks: the disorderly implementation of transition between interconnected states and across supply chains can undermine the sustainability and resilience of supply chains.

Ecological Risk

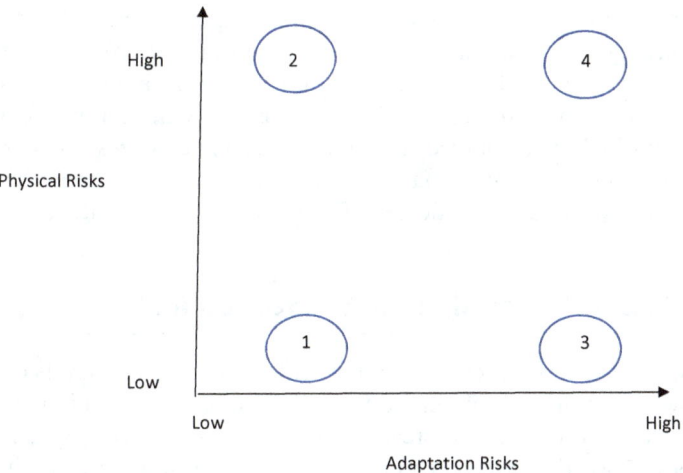

● **Fig. 6.3** Climate risk scenarios

— Meta-level risks: these have been explored above but the processes of transition can impact upon all other global sub-systems from geopolitics, geoeconomics, and natural systems.

Four Climate Risk Scenarios

Based on the interaction between transition and physical risks a number of climate risk scenarios can be identified (see ● Fig. 6.3). These scenarios are as follows.

Scenario 1: Low Physical/Low Adaptation Risk

These are agents where the potential for physical disruption is low and that as a result, they need to incur minimal levels of transition costs. These low vulnerability locations may reflect that these are agents that have made long-standing commitments to adaption to climate change so that even when an extreme event occurs there is an ease of adaption to any challenges that emerge. The low physical risk might not just simply reflect those idiosyncrasies of the location (such as low population density, etc.) but may also reflect that there has been a high degree of pre-existing adaption within physical systems. This long-term and on-going transition mean that the physical impact has either been anticipated or that the area—whilst not being exempt from the broader meta trend—has a low number of areas that will be subject to direct disruption to climatic events.

Scenario 2: High Physical/Low Adaptation Risk

These are agents which face a high degree of risk that climatic events have the potential to disrupt their functioning. These agents can also face a low transition cost as the acceptance of a high degree of physical risk has meant that there has been long-term strategy to invest in climatic events mitigation. Whilst these states will still face transition costs, large-scale spending has occurred to mitigate long-term events. These are evident in areas of low-lying lands with high population densities which have routinely been subject to flooding. States can seek to adapt these facilities to adaptions created by climate change. These states therefore have a high degree of resilience despite a high degree of vulnerability to climatic change.

Scenario 3: Low Physical/High Adaptation Risk

These are states that even though they face comparatively low levels of direct physical disruption from the risk of climatic events nonetheless face high transition costs. These high transition costs are created by an aggressive policy push to accelerate the transition towards a low-carbon economy. These are states with a low direct physical risk to climate change due to location but will nonetheless be impacted due to contextual pressure to adapt to change. These states will exhibit high degrees of resilience and sustainability so that any physical impact that is evident will have little impact upon states functioning.

Scenario 4: High Physical/High Adaptation Risk

These are the most vulnerable agents. These are subject to a high potential degree of physical disruption where the extent and degree of disruption are not known with certainty. These high degrees of risk impose big costs upon these agents not just in seeking to render themselves resilient to change but also in coping with any disruption that occurs. Thus, transition risk here also reflects the cost involved in responding to any events and in resuming normality as well as mitigating against any future risk. These agents will also face the same degree of transition risk created by the desire to adapt to a low carbon economy. These are states with a vulnerable geography where large centres of population are at risk of physical disruption this can be compounded by a low coping capacity should climatic events occur.

Case Study 6.1: BP and the Energy Transition: Moving Beyond Petroleum

For an energy company, there is arguably no greater risk than the transition away from hydrocarbons towards renewable energy. Over time, this process will gradually erode the revenue base of the energy business and render its business model obsolete. Of the largest oil companies, BP has arguably been the most progressive with regard to the adoption of the shift towards renewables associated with the energy transition. This reflects pressures from a range of stakeholders from regulators, investors, and consumers but also of the company to seek to create a lasting strategic differential between itself and the other oil majors. To this end, the company announced that in 2020, it would lower the production of hydrocarbons to meet these objectives. The aim is to lower, over the short term, its oil output by 40 per cent (around 1 million barrels a day) and replace this lost capacity increased investment in renewable electricity production by up to 50 gigawatts. This 20-fold increase is approximately the output of 50 nuclear plants.

To support the energy transition at the corporate level, BP plans to divest a significant chunk (about 13 per cent) of its hydrocarbon production. This has involved the disposal of both gas and oil fields as well as petrochemical facilities. The company would also postpone and cancel the proposed investment in potential sources of hydrocarbons. Alongside this divestment, BP has invested in several major businesses to support this process of change. This includes investment in solar energy businesses and other businesses involved in the charging of electric vehicles. However, these assets are taking time to make a significant contribution to the performance of the business. Indeed, though many of these 'transition-based' businesses are growing fast they are still a net drain on the cash flow of BP. Despite this, the business is increasing its investment in these technologies to $ 5 bn by 2030. This will involve not simply increasing the charging points for electric vehicles and acquiring more solar power facilities but also expanding its wind power assets notably in the US. The commercial rationale is the peak demand for oil has passed with new forms of energy required and that there is no long future for this commodity other than for those states who are lagging in the transition process.

Creating corporate slack to undertake this repositioning meant a loss of employment over the short term as its divested assets and caused suppression in its share price that was more extreme than its peer groups. BP is confident that revenues will increase over time as service station—for example—become charging points for an expanding number of electric vehicles. This market is expanding faster than anticipated with many automotive manufacturers accelerating the process of change within their own product portfolios. In addition, BP hopes that the revenues for renewables will be more predictable even if they are lower than the very erratic pricing that occurs within the oil and gas industries.

The concerns both within and external to the business were that the company was moving too fast in the process especially as oil and gas assets still have long-term revenue growth (something that became apparent in the aftermath of the Russian invasion of Ukraine). This problem could also be compounded if the firm stops exploration and ends up with a residual asset based (in terms within terms of hydrocarbon assets) that is of low value. Moreover, BP was seeking to sell assets when the market for such assets was not good. Thus, the company could find itself conflicted between investors' desire for growth and the short-term legacy of the energy transition especially if corporate profits suffer because of this action. Whilst other oil companies are making similar moves none has taken it as far as BP.

Water–Energy–Food Nexus

It has long been recognized that the supply of food, water, and energy are strongly interlinked. This reflects that:
- Food requires water and energy in order to produce.

- Water requires energy to be extracted and is carried virtually by food.
- Energy depends upon water for generation in many parts of the global system and food for the increased utilization of biofuels.

The links between these components to human activity are central to the interaction between humanity and the natural environment as obtaining secure access to supplies of each of these is central to sustainable human social and economic development. The sustainability of this cycle is being challenged through several trends notably demographic change as well as urbanization as the nexus must cope with increased demands upon its finite elements (i.e., water) and how this feeds through into the security of supply for both water and food. These notions of security are explored more fully below. In placing pressure upon the security of supply of these core components of human existence and activity so the risk environment is being radically altered.

On top of these demographic processes of change are those stimulated by climate change (see ◘ Fig. 6.4). This reflects not simply physical risks but also adaptive risks. In terms of physical risks, there is a fear that more uncertain precipitation patterns will impact upon the efficacy of the nexus to meet the demands of humanity with regard to the security generated by resources created by water, energy, and food. Thus, greater uncertainty in one dimension of the nexus undermines the salience of the other components of the system. Climate change will also impact upon other aspects of the nexus notably how rising temperatures can impact upon agricultural productivity and choices made with regard to energy production as well as the capability to generate water-based power sources. In turn, these events cascade out of the environment sub-system into other global sub-systems as the breakdown of the nexus can create:

- Increased social risk due to resource shortages and impact upon subsistence activity.
- Political risk as states and divergent groups compete for resources.
- Increased economic risk as resource shortages hit growth and productivity.
- Uncertainty over technological gains due to shorts of key inputs.

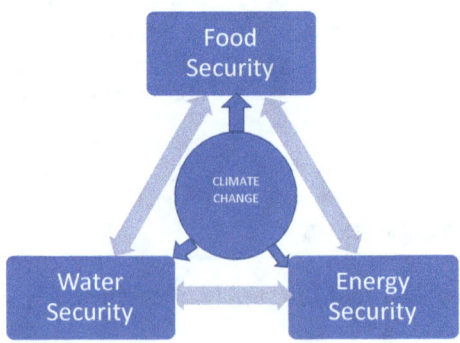

◘ **Fig. 6.4** The water–energy–food (WEF) security nexus and climate change

Ecological Risk

This global demand for resources is placing pressure upon each aspect of the WEF nexus as the demand for each is expected to increase alongside the legacy of climate change for the operation of the global system. The less secure the supply of each of these the greater the risk there is attached to these resources and to the operation of the WEF nexus. It is a legacy of the security of each of the pillars of the WEF nexus to which the analysis now turns.

Water Security

Notionally water is a finite renewable resource which flows around a naturally occurring hydrological cycle. Of the water available on and below the Earth's surface only 2.5 per cent is considered fresh water and therefore usable by human systems. These freshwater resources exist as either glaciers and ice caps (around 69 per cent) surface water (lakes, rivers, etc.) (about 1 per cent) or groundwater (about 30 per cent) (that is in aquifers below the earth's surface). It is this 1 per cent that is used to support both human and natural systems. On an annual basis some 4.3 trillion m^3 is extracted from ground and surface water resources. Of the water extracted, 60 per cent finds its way back to ground and surface water systems UN (2022). The rest is recycled through plant transpiration and evaporation. The need to have sustained access to this water to support and sustain human activity has generated human interventions within the hydrological cycle to alter the form and nature of flows to ensure and secure water supply. Human activity—and the need to be near water for economic and social reasons—has also shaped water environments by also seeking to build systems that are resilient to excessive flows. Across human activity the ratio of usage is agriculture 70 per cent; industry 19 per cent and households 11 per cent. These ratios do vary across the globe with industrial usage being 37 per cent in the US and agricultural usage as high as 90 per cent in India. These figures may understate the amount used by industry as a share of agricultural production as a share is used by industrial as an input.

Water is spread unevenly across the planet as much of the available fresh water is based in 410 freshwater basins. Of these around a quarter are deemed water stressed and account for 90 per cent of withdrawals from the freshwater system. Around half are located in the US, China, and India. Each of which has large demands for water. Water security is born of the perceived risks attached to the supply of water to states, businesses, and households. This is sourced from:

— A scenario where the level of water is too great for human physical water and natural infrastructure systems to cope resulting in flooding that is disruptive to human activity.
— A scenario where there is too little water resulting in a disruptive and even existential threat to human and natural systems.
— A scenario where the available water is of a quality that is unsuitable for consumption and/or utilization for agricultural/industrial usage due to excessive level of pollution as a result of human activity. It is estimated that 80 per cent of all wastewater (from both industry and domestic users) is emitted untreated into surface water systems.
— A scenario where freshwater systems are disrupted due to human activity or natural events.

These are also risks that cut across these themes such as those created by the lack of access to fresh water and sanitation. This is an issue involves water quality, quantity, and—possibly—disruption. As the demand for water rises due to economic development and rising global population of water security. Over the past century, whilst the human population has increased fourfold; water consumption has increased by a factor of eight. These pressures are created by:

- Rising demand for food where agriculture is still the single biggest user of water representing over 70 per cent of total demand. It is estimated that by 2050 the Earth will need 60 per cent more food. Available water suggests that this can only increase by 10 per cent.
- As economic development improves diets, households demand better diets frequently involving the wider consumption of water-intensive foodstuffs such as beef.
- Increased demand from industry as more water-intensive processes (such as steel, chemicals, etc.) expand.
- Rising levels of urbanization which place pressure upon water supply infrastructure and quality systems especially within developing states.
- Increased demand for energy generating wider use of hydroelectric and other water utilizing energy systems.
- Increased demand from households due to a rising middle class which also places pressure upon water infrastructure and sanitation. Currently, almost 1 billion people do not have access to a safe water supply with 2.5 billion not having adequate sanitation.

The net effect of these is that per capita water availability is on a rapid decline in many states. Globally between 1962 and 2017, there was a 57 per cent reduction in per capita freshwater supply. Some states in the Middle East have seen reductions of between 80 and 90 per cent with Kuwait showing a 99 per cent decline. On the flip side, some states in central and eastern Europe have seen average rises in per capita freshwater availability of around a third. These pressures are increasing water risk as more pressure is placed upon the existing water supply to support this rising demand meaning that it has to be circulated faster and be used more intensively and that—consequently—water quality is likely to suffer as a result. The result is that many states are extracting ground and surface water faster than they can be replenished. There is also the challenge that this pressure is exposing more segments of the global population to risks from flooding as they are forced to live in more intensively built developments close to water sources with erratic flows. This trend is reflected in ◘ Fig. 6.5. By 2030, the UN estimates that there will be a 40 per cent water deficit (where demand exceeds supply by this amount). This creates increased competition for resources at both micro and macro levels.

The notion of water security is based upon a given territory possessing the necessary water resources to support and sustain both human (including health, economic, and wellbeing needs) and natural (to support flourishing ecosystems) systems. Thus, security is based upon supply and demand within a state to ensure that these do not reach a state of imbalance to the extent that water security is challenged. These reflect not simply the notion of physical water supply and demand but also the availability of the enabling infrastructure to distribute, recycle, manage, and process water flows. It reflects the need to live with a degree of water risk.

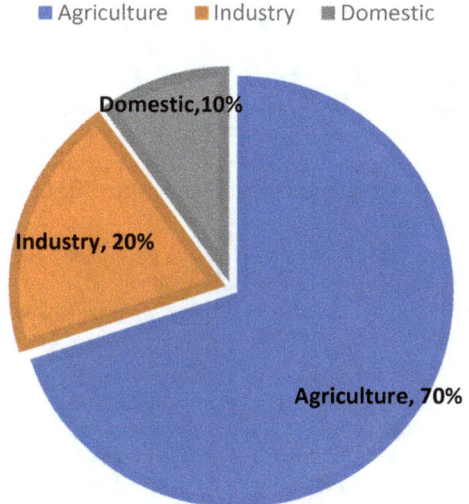

Fig. 6.5 Global water usage by sector (2020) (*Source* WEF)

Increased prominence—largely due to the link between food and water security—has been given over to the notion of water stress. Water stress occurs when there is a prolonged period of disparity where water demand exceeds supply. This is created by:
- Physical scarcity: this is where there is a deterioration or general absence of water availability due to local ecological conditions.
- Economic scarcity: this is created when there is a widespread absence or failure of water infrastructure to effectively distribute available resources.

Of course, these two drivers can overlap especially where a drought is combined with poor water governance. Not surprisingly, the most water-stressed locations are those in the most arid parts of the earth's surface but there are states like many in sub-Saharan Africa where extensive rainfall is not supported by a capable water infrastructure system. This pattern of water stress is increasingly fuelled by the process of climate change. This has been largely driven by the increased unevenness of precipitation patterns that inhibits the ability of core water sources (both manmade and natural) to be replenished. By 2018, it was estimated that two billion people lived in areas exhibiting signs of water stress; when considered on a seasonal level (i.e., that water stress is exhibited only over part of the year) then the figure rises to four billion. Whilst globally only 9 per cent of water is withdrawn from groundwater, this masks big discrepancies across space. In Europe, withdrawal is less than 6 per cent per year whilst in Asia it rises to as much as 20 per cent. This latter figure is assisted by conditions of water scarcity. In parts of the Middle East, groundwater extraction is in excess of 40 per cent per year. This is deemed critical. Globally it is estimated that by 2030, demand will exceed supply by 40 per cent in 2030. A disequilibrium exacerbated by climate change and by 2050 nearly 5 billion people will be subject to water scarcity (see Table 6.1).

Table 6.1 The impact of water scarcity upon non-ecological global sub-systems

Sub-system	Impact of water scarcity
Economic	Impacts upon agricultural and industrial productivity will subdue economic growth and creates risk of rising inflation due to impact upon production. The process may also limit trade as states seek to internalize the virtual water value chain. Finally, water scarcity can also impact upon domestic energy production
Political	Increased geopolitical tension as states compete over shared water resources especially as arid states seek to acquire land in less arid locations to supply the domestic market. Also, internal political tension as groups seek to access the same resource and states exhibit poor water governance
Social	Increased risk of social unrest due to poor quality and quantity of water. This can be created by the uneven development of water infrastructure between social groups. Solutions to water scarcity can often mean supplying one group at the expense of another through for example rural to urban water transfer. A further risk is created by large-scale migration caused by water scarcity
Technological	The risk to technologies reflects that many technologies (notably semi-conductors) depend upon high volumes of water in the production process. This could impact upon broad innovation competence. Technology can improve water management but is still underdeveloped and deployed. In addition, engineering solutions can cause ecological damage (see for example desalinization)

This scarcity of water is only expected to increase as the demand drivers noted above further increase pressure upon this finite resource. This rising demand against a fixed yet increasingly erratic supply means that water will operate as an increased constraint upon human activity and development. Water will increasingly be allocated away from agricultural production towards urban usage as urbanization expands major cities. Moreover, the disparity in the availability of resources is only going to grow more acute due to the processes linked to climate change. These processes are expected to make precipitation more erratic. Some places will suffer an increased risk of physical damage due to increased risk of flooding and other extreme weather events whereas others (such as in the Sahel) can be expected to suffer from increased bouts of water scarcity. Moreover, the process is expected to lead to an erosion of the availability of fresh water from snow melt and glaciers. It is estimated that around 20 per cent of global population depend upon water from snow melt and glaciers. As these sources of freshwater retreat and become more erratic so supply in these areas diminishes. This problem is especially acute in Latin America and Asia. These conditions make water scarcity worse as humans will respond to this more erratic precipitation and conventional resources by drawing fully upon groundwater and the more limited surface water. Water quality will also be impacted by climate change as higher water temperatures and lower levels of dissolved oxygen decrease the capability of water to self-purify. There is also a risk to water quality from the after polluting effects of flooding or by droughts leading to higher levels of pollutants in runoff.

It is estimated by around 40 per cent of the global population live in river basins that cross political boundaries. On top of this, it is estimated that 90 per cent of the global population live in states where river systems are international by nature. These nearly 300 international water systems represent more than half the global land area and comprise 40 per cent of the Earth's freshwater resources. The mutual need for access to these freshwater resources by multiple states requires cross-border co-operation but this can often be curtailed with collaboration turning into an outright competition between states. This is despite the existence of UN and regional agreements to mitigate against the risk of this competition. The risk is that this competition turns into increased risk shaped by conflict between states. There are evident concerns with regard to states disputing usage of Nile waters (see Case Study 6.2) and also the Indus basin where Pakistan and India have engaged in frequent disputes over the extraction of water for irrigation across their respective territories. These conflicts between states over water resources are not merely limited to surface water; there are also increased disputes between states where aquifers cross borders and where agreements between states on the rates of extractions are difficult to agree upon.

Business relies upon water in four ways. In the access of raw materials, production, suppliers, and usage. This reliance is especially high in sectors such as food production and also mining where water is a key input into the process whether it is extraction of raw materials or if it is needed as a key input in production (such as in food and beverages). It is also used extensively throughout all industries where it can be used to extract, cool, and generate products and processes. As water stress grows, so the risk to business in terms of the following risks:

- Reputational: these are meso-level risks emerging from an erosion of stakeholder confidence in the business' activities where such actions erode the efficacy of the water system. The effect of this reputational damage is to erode brand value/esteem, customer loyalty/perception, and/or create an existential threat if it stimulates a legal response.
- Regulatory: these arise when policymakers or other relevant governance systems seek to alter laws/regulations to alter firm behaviour. These can often lead to increased costs due to the need of the firm to alter operations to comply with the regulatory requirement. These risks are especially acute when such changes are random and unpredictable.
- Physical: these are created by either limit on the supply of water or the case where deluges create damage to a firm's assets due to flooding. The common theme is that they inhibit a firm's operations. This can also be extended to quality where pollution in water-challenged regions can also inhibit firm activity.

Too little water can halt production just as flooding can also do so. This risk is compounded by the state's seeking to rationalize water usage and compelling firms to adopt new practices/technologies. Moreover, a failure to do so might just not deliver regulatory sanction it can also provide negative reputational repercussions. Whether the risk is reputational, regulatory, and/or physical, the core theme is that the risk will impact upon the financial performance of the business either through increased cost or decreased revenues. Indeed, it was estimated in 2021, that was a risk of around $300 billion if companies failed to address water risk (CDP 2020).

Case Study 6.2: Water Risk on the Nile and Ethiopia's Grand Ethiopian Renaissance Dam (GERD)

In 2011, Ethiopia announced a plan to build a dam—the GERD—across that part of the Blue Nile that transverses its territory. The aim of this dam was not merely to generate substantial quantities of hydroelectricity for itself but also to enable it to operate as an exporter of electricity throughout the rest of Africa. In damming, the Blue Nile with a structure around 145 metres tall and 1800 metres across, it will create a reservoir which will be almost 1.3 times the annual flow of the river. Whilst it was designed to be completed by 2015, the reservoir only started to be filled in 2020.

This piece of energy infrastructure has created substantial controversy across East Africa and beyond. Egypt sees the creation of the dam as an 'existential risk' to itself as well as the Sudan. The development of the dam reflects long-standing disputes between up and downstream states upon the Nile. Ethiopia argues that it has the right to harness these waters as 85 per cent of the Blue Nile is sourced from the Ethiopian Highlands. Ethiopia argues that the GERD will not have a long-term impact upon flows along the Nile and that there are evident externalities with regard to the hydroelectricity generation for the region. In addition, Ethiopia argues that GERD will also allow for more effective water management of Nile discharge thereby mitigating extremity in flows. For Egypt, the Nile is a major source of its water security as it relies almost entirely upon these resources for household and commercial consumption. In the past (in both 1929 and 1959) Egypt has been successful in blocking any developments along the tributaries of the Nile. More recently Ethiopia has been able to secure the funding for this project largely through Ethiopians from home and abroad as well as investment from China.

The 1959 Agreement allocated the Nile's water to Sudan and Egypt but offered no rights to upstream states. In addition, the agreement gave Egypt a de facto veto over any future projects upon the Nile. Consequently, Egypt attempted to obstruct the construction of the dam. Ethiopia's failure to attain this led to Egypt shifting its position towards seeking to influence the pace at which the reservoir behind the dam would be filled and how the flows through the GERD would be managed in periods of water stress. These re-assurances over these flows were not forthcoming. Ethiopia wants to sustain the flexibility over the flows to meet its own not its neighbour's needs. There were also concerns from Sudan which find itself caught between the other two states. It is though less hostile to the GERD than Egypt seeing that there were development benefits from the development of the project though it does have concerns with regard to how the dam will impact upon its own dams.

The case illustrates the difficulties of governing water resources where a water basin is shared by more than one state. The case highlights the conflicts between states with regard to how they manage these resources. Egypt clearly relies upon the Nile for water security but the desire for Ethiopia to generate a ready supply of energy creates an emergent risk between these states that could possibly spill over into outright conflict.

Energy Security

The nature of business risk sourced from energy covers a wide range of areas. Within this section, the focus will be upon the overlap between energy security and the risk process with an especial focus upon how the energy transition will reshape the risk environment for the global system. One of the core facets of the global economic system over the past century has been the sharp increase in the level and intensity of the trade in energy. This has seen the energy system scaled up and transformed from what was once a highly localized system into one that is now highly international involving the global transmission and exchange of hydrocarbons. This globalizing of the energy system has come with risks linked to state-based notions of energy security.

The Nature of Energy Security

Energy security reflects an amalgam of demands upon energy systems to which they need to adapt to the pressures exerted upon them by a mix of socio-economic and political pressures. These are adapting both the demand and supply of energy within the global system. The strategy of energy security is set against a background where the demand for energy is expected to increase by 25 per cent up to 2030. This presumes some degree of suppression of demand through increased energy efficiency. Notions of security are normally built around the security of supply. Convention has evolved to stress a number of overlapping policy themes as being central to the attainment of energy security. These are based around the following criteria:

- Availability: this reflects traditional notions of security of supply based on the physical existence of a resource which can be utilized to deliver an energy source.
- Accessibility: this is focused on the notion that the available energy resource can be accessed not simply through means of physical access through technological systems but also through the notion that the resource is able to be supplied and the supplier is willing to supply it. This reflects both technological and geopolitical issues.
- Affordability: this reflects that the energy source supplied is available at prices that enable universal access to the energy created.
- Acceptability: this is based on the notion that the energy is acceptable to utilize for both ecological and social reasons. Reflecting that utilization does not harm the environment or worsen the social division.

These represent an ideal mix of concerns though there are evident potential conflicts between them for example with regard to affordability and acceptability. It can also be added that issues of steering users towards energy efficiency, replacement with green sources, shifting to secure (and away from insecure) sources, and suppressing demand also have to be part of the narrative with regard to energy security. Thus, energy security is based upon the idea of sufficient, accessible resource being available in an acceptable and affordable manner.

■ **Table 6.2** Comparative energy security

States with highest energy security	States with lowest energy security	States with largest energy resources/reserves[a]
1. Sweden	101. Niger	1. Russia
2. Switzerland	100. Benin	2. Iran
3. Denmark	99. Congo	3. Venezuela
4. Finland/UK	98. Chad (Democratic Republic)	4. Saudi Arabia
5. Austria/France	97. Malawi	5. US
6. Canada	96. Nepal	6. Canada
7. Germany	95. Madagascar	7. Iraq
8. Norway	94. Senegal	8. Qatar
9. New Zealand/US	93. Nigeria	9. UAE
10. Luxembourg/Spain	92. Zimbabwe	10. China

[a]This is calculated from the combined energy available from all hydrocarbon resources within the territory of a state
Source World Energy Council (2021)

Energy security and associated risks can be subject to a multitude of tensions from international terrorism to geopolitical upheaval. These can largely reflect the security of supply issues. This means that security is very rarely settled for many states for a protracted period of time. These vulnerabilities can be both internal and external and may also reflect the inadequacy of domestic and international infrastructure systems. At the core of the energy security system has been the concerted attempt by leading industrialized states to ensure continuity of supplies through the maintenance of reserves to ensure supply should this be disrupted. States in order to secure supply mainly do the following:

— Diversify supply both in terms of type of and sources/suppliers of fuels.
— Lower and even eliminate import dependence.
— Create resilience through space capacity on the supply side through the use of strategic reserves, refining capacity, etc.
— Ensure domestic systems are resilient to any potential disruptions in supply through storage systems and resistance to extreme climatic events.
— Promoting the stability of the global marketplace and of main supplier states.
— Gaining better information with regard to market trends and processes and therefore being able to anticipate further issues.

These principles of security have created less energy security based on independence and more security based on interdependence. Looking across the main measures of energy security namely availability, accessibility, affordability, and acceptability ■ Table 6.2 indicates (as of 2021), the most and least energy secure/risk states. This is ranked out of 101 states for which data is available. What is interesting is that those states with the highest levels of energy resources are not those that are the energy secure.

Integral to the notion of security is energy equity and the existence of energy poverty. In this case, energy poverty is defined by access to electricity and also by the extensiveness of biomass usage for cooking. This reflects the rights of all groups within the global system to have access to sufficient energy. As of 2022, there are 2.7 billion people that depend upon biomass for fuel with 1.4 billion exhibiting a lack of available electricity supplies. These are mainly in rural areas in developing states. In developed states there are pockets of energy poverty due to simple affordability of energy access and where an increasing share and unsustainable share of household income is spent upon energy costs. Energy poverty has many implications from enabling economic development, facilitating public health, enhancing productivity, gender equality, and ecological degradation. Within the context of risk and uncertainty, the salience of energy poverty depends upon the extent to which it creates social and political risk at multiple levels. The rising price of energy has in many states proved to be a catalyst for political risk. This has been evident for example in Egypt where attempts to remove petrol price subsidies have been extensively resisted. Energy prices have also been a contributory factor promoting social and political risk across many other states from Chile to the UK.

Energy is a sector that is especially exposed to the risk of resource nationalism. This could create a situation where the nation places its own energy security above those of other states REN (2021). This is not a process of simple expropriation but could also involve charging a higher price for exports to ensure that preference is given to domestic users. This creates a global risk for if there is any disruption to supply then it is likely that states will seek to service domestic customers first creating a supply/security risk for other states. This reflects that at its core resource nationalism reflects a struggle between domestic and foreign interests in energy markets. Whilst resource nationalism has been explored elsewhere within this book (see ▶ Chapter 9) it is important to stress that security can be the driver of this process. This is true where energy dependence creates a geo-strategic vulnerability to which states respond by seeking to acquire their own secure supplies sourced from within their territory or to assert control over those that are already developed. As supplies are accompanied by increased levels of geopolitical risk so there is a direct incentive to retreat domestic sources.

The Energy Transition and Security

The energy transition represents an adaptive risk by the global economic and political system to the legacy of the combustion of hydrocarbon fuels for the climate. The nature of the transition is to stimulate the large-scale shift away from carbon-intensive energy sources towards those that involve zero or low carbon emissions in their utilization. As reflected within the diagram below (see ◐ Fig. 6.5), these carbon-intensive fuels have generated around 80 per cent of energy consumed for multiple decades. The aim of the transition is to gradually lower this share of carbon-based energy generation to around 50 per cent by 2050. This process generates change within the risk context of energy security namely as it:

— Implies the increased localization and regionalization and decreased globalization of energy transmission.
— Increases the level of distributed generation based upon high pluralized generating infrastructure creating a more complex energy system.
— Will be accompanied by lower demand for carbon-intensive fuels due to shifting consumption patterns.

If the reduction in consumption of these carbon-intensive fuels follows the planned trajectory then it is hoped that any increase in global temperatures can be kept within agreed limits of 1.5 °C. This move away from carbon-intensive energy production signals a rapid increase in the deployment and utilization of renewable energy sources by 2050. This requires a shift away from the utilization of primary fuels (i.e., oil, coal, gas) towards an increased dependence upon secondary fuels (i.e., electricity). Renewable energy finds its main use in the generation of electricity where they account for around a quarter of generation. In practice, electricity represents less than 20 per cent of total energy consumption. This suggests that the core of the transition will be an increased use of electricity notably in areas such as heating and transport which are major users of hydrocarbons. In practice, rising global energy demand has tended to turn states to conventional sources to meet these pressures.

This transition is enabled by six drivers:
1. The rapid decline in the cost of renewable technologies where solar and wind technologies have fallen substantially in price. This is a process that is expected to continue.
2. Increased concern with regard to pollution and climate change.
3. Regulation and the establishment of renewable energy targets.
4. Technological change.
5. Corporate and investor action.
6. Public opinion.

As of 2020, the global fuel mix is reflected in ◘ Fig. 6.6. This demonstrates that as of 2020, the global energy system is still very heavily dependent upon the conventional fossil fuels with them comprising 83 per cent of total energy production in

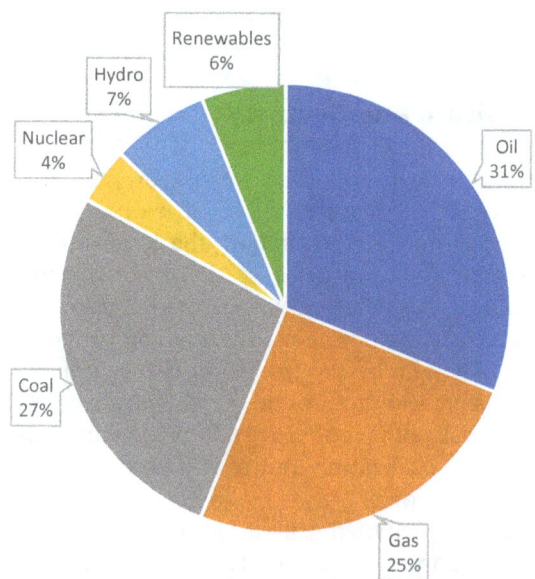

◘ **Fig. 6.6** Global share of energy production 2020

Ecological Risk

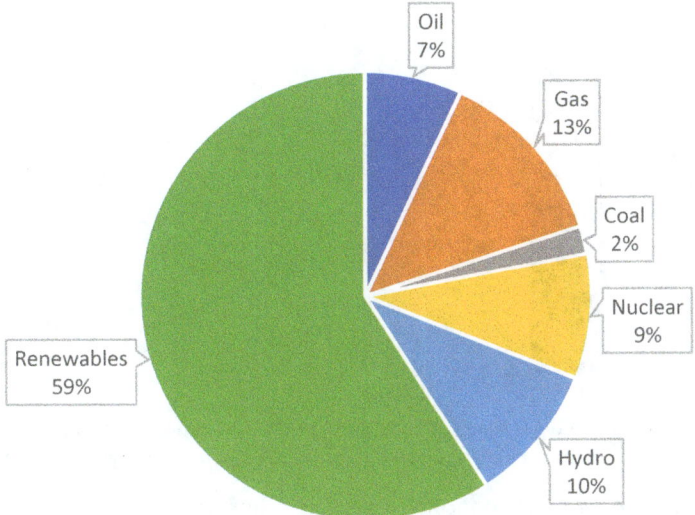

Fig. 6.7 Energy mix in 2050 under net zero scenario (*Source* BP [2021])

2020. Renewables (including hydroelectricity) are less than 13 per cent. In the decade to 2019, the growth rate for renewable consumption was just over 13 per cent and generation grew by 16 per cent. Whilst this represents around an increase, it does underscore the extent and scale of the transition.

This trend towards lower carbon energy production will cause a fundamental shift in the global energy system (as reflected in Fig. 6.7). Whilst hydrocarbons will not be phased out totally, they will be one choice amongst an increasingly diverse supply of energy sources. As the choice of fuels does grow increasingly diverse so the demand for these carbon-intensive fuels will diminish though they will not disappear and will continue to be a core to the energy mix especially in developing and emerging economies. In theory, this transition should create a more benign risk environment for energy security due to:
- More domestic generation.
- Less dependence upon potentially unstable suppliers.
- Less risk of disruptions due to transmission/logistics issues.
- More decentralized generation freeing the state from any abuse from a dominant supplier.
- The energy mix can closely match local context and priorities.
- Greater domestic control over energy systems.

The main focus within this transition is upon 'Net Zero'. This implies the sustained use of hydrocarbon fuels but in a much-reduced form. It implies that any carbon emissions will be counterbalanced by actions to remove an equal amount of greenhouse gases from the atmosphere. The use of 'Net Zero' as a strategy for mitigating greenhouse gases reflects that there are political and economic limits to the process. It signifies that this cannot simply be a top-down process but that the process has to change behaviour of households and companies through promoting develop-

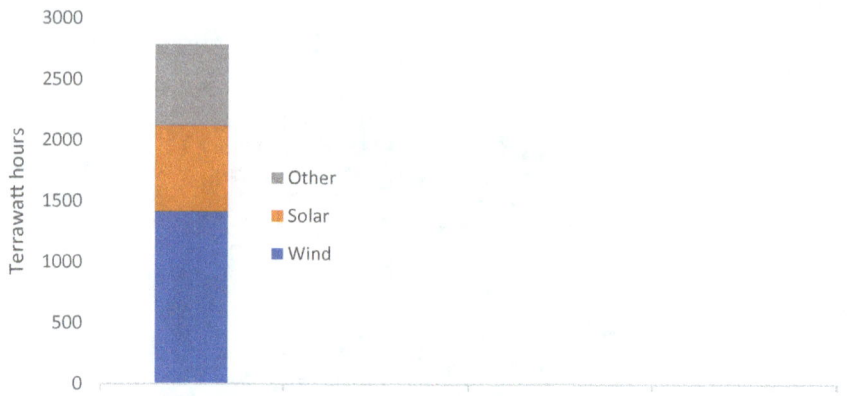

Fig. 6.8 Renewables by type—share of total renweable energy production (Other—includes electricity generated from geothermal, biomass, and other sources of renewable energy) (*Source* BP [2021])

ments such as the circular economy. There also has to be less resistance to the roll-out of low carbon technologies such as electric vehicles for example. Thus, the purpose is to nudge behaviour as well as a degree of compulsion there are bottom-up processes that will shape the transition process.

The rate of the growth in the transition has been hit by rising energy demand and accompanying rising prices that have led to users turning to fossil fuels to meet these pressures over the short term. In short, renewables were not available to meet this demand and not at the price that was desired (see Fig. 6.8). This has reflected that demand has not been met by increased pressures to increase energy efficiency.

The Risk Context of the Energy Transition

The energy transition has the potential to radically alter the risk context for business and the attainment and sustenance of energy security. This process does create a number of risks both to the energy system and to the form and nature of the global system beyond. The main type of risks across the assorted sub-systems are identified in Table 6.3.

Across these broad sub-systemic risks, there are a number of especially salient risks that can often cut across these sub-systemic risks. These are addressed below.

Investment Risk

The core technologies underpinning the transition (namely wind and solar power) have seen significant reductions in the cost of development and deployment over the past decade. It is estimated that solar power development and deployment has fallen by around 80 per cent over the past decade (up to 2022). Similarly, wind power has fallen by an average of around 50 per cent over the same period. This investment is set against four generic risks:

1. Demand and technology risks: these reflect the demand for the technologies that underpin the transition and the reliability of this technology. For example, the ambiguity with regard to the demand for electric cars and the need for the supporting infrastructure.

Ecological Risk

Table 6.3 Global sub-system risks from the energy transition

Sub-system	Example of energy risk
Economic	• Security, reliable, and affordable supplies • Cost of supplies • Threats to supplies due to human action such as strikes, depletion of energy reserves, and rising prices • Hit growth/development through more expensive energy sources
Political	• Shift in power away from hydrocarbon producers • Rise in resource nationalism with states promoting their own security at the expense of other states
Social	• Energy poverty; access and affordability of energy; effects of pollution upon health; and unequal access to green technology
Ecological	• Biomass depletes soil, pollutions of ecological sub-systems through energy use; clearance of forests for biomass; and natural events that damage energy systems
Technological	• Cost and effectiveness of new technology; transition technology • Capability of new technology to reverse climate change • Make existing assets redundant • Costs of deploying new technologies • Technical failure in power systems or cyber attacks on such critical infrastructure

2. Policy risks: these reflect the range of policy measures from subsidies, performance targets as well as direct regulation that shape firm and consumer attitudes to the transition. These policy measures can also impact upon risk by altering the timing and pace of the process of transition. This could leave assets stranded before they have been fully utilized and/or exhausted.
3. Market price risks: this reflects how the demand for complementary and substitute products will impact upon the process of the transition. For example, how the shift in the price of hydrocarbons can impact upon the process.
4. Other risks: these include legal and reputational risks and other business model impacts of the transition.

This process is subject to oscillations in the price of 'rare earths', and other commodities (such as steel) as well as logistics which has the capability to undermine these cost reductions. These technology risks have been compounded by increased financing costs as interest rates are on the rise across the global economy. This impacts upon the anticipated return on these projects. These risks are compounded by the potential for changing user and investor sentiment towards the deployment of green technology and its short-term costs. This is especially likely as cross subsidies and other surcharges to green technologies from conventional fuels push up energy prices generally. In short, the transition is seen as incompatible with cheap energy and is a cause of energy poverty. These can erode the political consensus around the transition leading to increased investment risks. These risks are compounded by the fact that corporate commitment to the transition leaves a firm with stranded assets (i.e., those assets rendered redundant by the process such as coal-powered fire stations). There is also the possibility that any future developments with regard to carbon-based fuel extraction incur a high degree of risk especially if the asset is unable to be fully exploited. This could also create a counter risk where the absence of investment in such assets go endanger energy security if public sentiment runs against the costs of transition.

These highlight that the transition readiness can vary markedly between states. This depends upon the availability of necessary infrastructure as well as policy and customer support for the process. The lower the degree of readiness the higher the degree of risk that is attached to the transition and the more protracted the process will be.

Geopolitical Risk

The pursuit of energy security by seeking to secure access to hydrocarbons has been a powerful factor shaping geopolitics over the past 50 years. The need for secure energy has been a catalyst for intervention by hegemonic states in those areas where hydrocarbons are abundant and accessible, but which could be disrupted by political unrest and/or economic turmoil. This has its most evident expression in the Middle East. More recently such concerns have led to disputes between the EU and Russia over the supply of gas. The energy transition—should it happen as planned—would radically alter the geopolitical context of business and alter risk. Risk has conventionally been associated with the fact that energy rich states could use their energy reserves as a geopolitical weapon to shape the geostrategy of those who depend upon these reserves. A further risk of the transitions is that these resource states increase output (and increase emissions) in anticipation of a long-term reduction in demand. These states are seeking to use these extra revenues to refocus their economies away from their export dependence upon fossil fuels. These strategies are less available to developing states without supporting infrastructure.

As renewables are in theory ubiquitous (as opposed to hydrocarbons which are distributed unevenly across the planet) the ability of a set of states to shape other state behaviour is clearly diminished. This also lowers the risk of disruption to the global system where the global energy system becomes less vulnerable to disruptions caused by blockages in core logistical bottlenecks (see ▶ Chapter 9). In practice, the intermittency of solar and wind means that new interconnections will need to be formed meaning that states will not be able to totally localize energy production. Also wind and solar are of varying intensity across the Earth's surface. These drivers are also compounded by the prospect that more distributed energy production changes the power structure within the energy sector.

There are also geopolitical concerns with regard to the aforementioned rare earths (such as lithium and cobalt used in batteries for electric vehicles). These are distributed unevenly across the earth's surface with those states with abundant supply possibly replacing those oil rich states as major players within the global system. The threat is that the desire for access to rare earths has led to a global scramble as businesses hunt globally for alternative sources to those that are concentrated in states such as China that might be strict to restrict the supply of these resources for their own geostrategic objectives (see Case Study 4.1). This is also true where some states are becoming increasingly powerful in the renewable value chain through for example controlling the supply of solar panels.

The risk could also be shaped by the relative energy security of the major states. With the US self-sufficient it has less need to intervene to secure non-domestic flows. China's more limited energy resources will also be aided by the wider deployment of renewables. In practice, the risk is less from the demand side and more on how the main suppliers adapt to these changing market conditions. The sudden loss of revenues for those states that depend heavily upon energy exports could be a catalyst for increased political unrest as budgets are cut as a response. This is especially a risk where states are highly exposed and have low resilience to the loss of demand for this export. This is especially the case for major oil and gas exporters in sub-Saharan Africa. Many Middle Eastern states are seeing the end of these exports and already have plans to diversify. Where there is both high dependence and high youth unemployment then these states are seen as especially vulnerable.

Alongside these states' decline is the emergence of energy superpowers. These will be states with high technological capability combined with the right climatic conditions. These states could become the new energy superpowers and exports of electricity globally. This includes states such as Australia and Chile. Moreover, there are those states (as mentioned above) that are resource rich in those rare earths needed to secure the transition. This could see states such as the Democratic Republic of Congo and Bolivia increase in geopolitical heft. Finally, those states that are big manufacturers of technology that underpins the transition will also gain influence. This could lead to technological dependence and dominance.

As electricity gains in usage and major generation capacity (notably renewable) comes on stream so new risks emerge where the interconnection between national girds creates new vulnerabilities where supplies can be cut off or states denied access to core technologies where there is a lack of alternative supply. Thus, as the role of oil and gas as a geopolitical weapon is reduced so the global system could emerge electricity as a geopolitical weapon. There is also emergent risk within the supply of biofuels especially if this production becomes concentrated in a few states. Thus, where it can be expected that oil and gas-related conflict might decline new sources which can emerge in areas such as cyber systems that underpin functioning electricity grids as well as potential conflicts over access to the aforementioned rare earths.

Geo-Social/Economic Risk

In addition to this geopolitical risk there are risks created by the transition to geo-social systems. These occur as there is an inevitability that the process will be uneven over space and also causes short- to medium-term losses for some states or social groups within states. Inevitably given the investment needed to promote the transition it will be developed and the leading emerging economy states that can be expected to lead this process of change. This has two implications. The first—as suggested above—is upon those developing states who rely heavily upon hydrocarbons for export strategies. A rapid and aggressive transition within these states' major markets will lead to these states possessing assets of limited marketable value and with little capability to replace these lost exports with other activities. This could lead to increase decline and macro-level risk within these states (especially in sub-Saharan Africa). These uncertainties could spill over into broad regional increased risk levels. This is especially so if the demography of these states (with relatively young populations characterized by high levels of unemployment) is not able to absorb this process of change. On top of this structural change within the energy system, there is also the risk that the rapid process of the energy transition will further cement and accentuate technological gaps between developed and developing states. This runs the risk of creating inverse technological risk within the system where the system cannot operate as an integrated whole due to the unevenness of the technological system between states.

There is also the possibility of increased macro and micro-level social risk within developed states. This largely comes from the social and economic costs of the transition upon individual regions. There is the risk that social deprivation could increase with the rapid transition away from coal for example that could render communities that are dependent upon the extraction of this energy source especially vulnerable where there are no compensating alternative forms of employment. There is also the risk that short-term policy measures to promote the transition could lead to pockets of energy poverty. This could occur as carbon taxes and other such methods increase the price of fossil fuels upon households and businesses for whom transition is a substantive cost especially where energy bills represent a significant share of household income/business turnover.

Food Security

The third and final aspect of risk context shaped by human interaction with its natural environment is food security. Food security stands as a juxtaposition with food sovereignty. In the case of food security, it is a state strategy based upon proactive engagement with the global food system where the supply of foodstuffs entering a state is delivered through the trading of these agricultural-based products. These would be supported through poverty alleviation strategies to support those groups that lose out as a result of the process of global engagement. Food sovereignty exists as a strategy of the state seeking to secure the necessary foodstuffs through the development of indigenous food systems with no more interaction with the global food system than is necessary. This strategy is often supported by programmes to support the territorial rights of minority groups.

In terms of the macro-level risk context, the notion of food security is underpinned by faith in global markets and that these global markets are predictable, stable, and will offer a secure supply of food under different operating contexts. This operates under the assumption of low risk and that both foodstuff suppliers and consumers have a direct incentive to maintain food system stability. The notion of food sovereignty presupposes the opposite scenario that the need to sustain a supply of food is to risk leaving to global markets and that the best means of attaining security of supply is to assert control over domestic production through the prioritization of domestic production. This can reflect both that some states are more risk averse than others but also a perspective that the global food system is too unpredictable to ensure reliable food supplies.

The distinctions of food security and food sovereignty are more nuanced than suggested. As food security will never depend totally upon overseas supply and that these non-domestic supplies are often used to buttress domestic production. Similarly, food sovereignty strategies will also need to interact with global systems to ensure diverse supplies. In the era of globalization (and especially of hyper-globalization), there was a consensus upon the efficacy of the global food system to deliver food security based on interconnectedness between national food production and distribution systems.

Nonetheless, food security reflects that trade in agricultural goods increases food security by enabling food to flow from those states where there is a net surplus of foodstuffs to where there is a net deficit. This raises the incomes of both exporting and importing (though lower prices) states. These concerns have to be balanced against a strategic vulnerability driven by the possibility of dependence upon non-domestic sources of food. There could also be a negative impact upon low-income producers that are damaged by the rise in exports.

Looking aside from these geostrategic definitions of food security/sovereignty, a more practical definition offered by the UN (FAO et al. 2021) which defines as UN (FAO et al. 2021) 'Food security exists when all people, at all times, have physical and economic access to. sufficient, safe and nutritious food that meets their dietary needs and food preferences for an. active and healthy life'.

This reflects four dimensions of food security:
1. Food availability: the existence of food in sufficient quantity via domestic production and/or imports.
2. Food access: the capability of individuals to access food through the existence of sufficient resources to acquire a nutritious diet.
3. Utilization: the capability to gain sufficient physical and mental wellbeing through the ability to utilize foodstuffs through the existence of clean water, sanitation, healthcare as well as an adequate diet.
4. Stability: that access to foodstuffs is consistent across both space and time and that there are low risk and low instability attached to food supply.

Thus, food insecurity exists when segments of the global population do not have access to the necessary foodstuff to enable them to flourish on a sustainable basis. On that basis, the 2021 FAO reports that food insecurity is on the increase. The UN estimated that in 2020 around 30 per cent of the global population was enduring some form of food insecurity with 12 per cent (nearly 1 billion people) suffering severe insecurity. These figures were driven in no small effect by the impact of the COVID pandemic upon the global food system. The rates of severe and moderate food security are reflected in ◘ Fig. 6.9.

These levels of crude insecurity as indicated by levels of malnourishment reflect systemic on-going problems and risks within the global food system (see below). They reflect how events and their impact upon the affordability of high-quality food sources. The attainment of this is a key UN sustainable development goal. These issues are not simply limited to the attainment of the necessary quantity of foodstuffs in developing states but also the ease of access to quality foodstuff in developed states. This issue is set against a perspective that food production will need to increase by 50 per cent to cope with the expansion in population up to 2050. This is set against increased with regard to the prospect of increased production.

At the core of this system of security is the global food system (see ◘ Fig. 6.9). This represents the complex set of activities across the globe that enables the production, distribution, and consumption of food. This system is more than simply the process of growing food and moving it to the market. This comprises all those

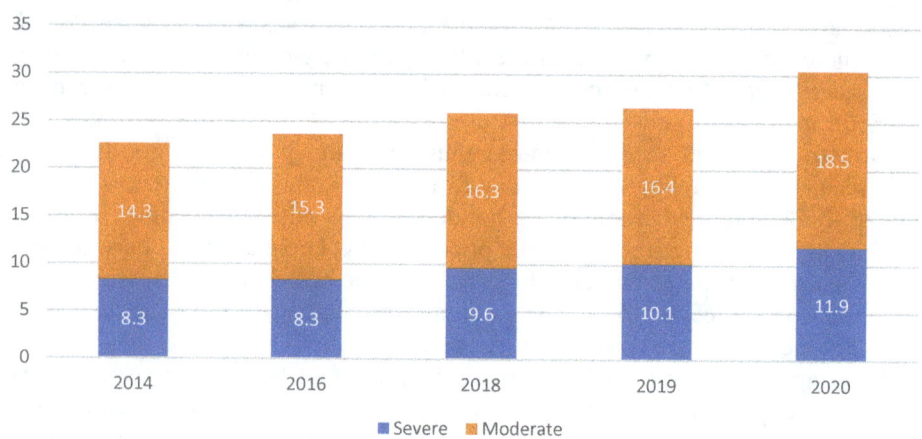

■ **Fig. 6.9** Rates of moderate and severe food insecurity (2014–2020) (*Source* FAO [2022])

processes involved in the processing of food as well as the underpinning infrastructure that enables this processing and distribution. This also comprises the notion of how the system deals with the waste products created from the production, distribution, and consumption of food. This system approach reflects that the condition under which food is grown and processed varies across the globe and that not all components are distributed equally (relative to needs) across the global system. The result is that the global system is interconnected based on the transmission of processed and unprocessed foodstuffs to reflect the differing dynamics of food security across and between states. However global trade is only a fraction of total agricultural production. Indeed, the food surplus states only export a fraction of their total production. Indeed, it is estimated that less than 10 per cent of commodity foodstuff is traded. Where food is traded the exported foodstuffs tend to be highly concentrated. 85 per cent of what exports are from just nine states and 90 per cent of rice exports are from just six states.

The value of the global system as conceived within ■ Fig. 6.10 is valuable as it underlines the complexity of the food industry but also it highlights where within the system risks can be generated. These risks extend beyond (as noted more fully below) simple issues of growing enough food to the underpinning market and logistical dynamics that shape the capability of the global system to feed itself.

Food Security Risks

The main challenges with regard to the global food system can cut across a number of the themes identified within ■ Fig. 6.10. The list that follows is not exhaustive but highlights the main challenges of food risk.

Geopolitical Risk

Conflict both within and between states raises the risk of disruption to the global food system especially where the political upheaval is focused upon states that are

Ecological Risk

Fig. 6.10 The global food system

major suppliers of food production. This has been evidenced in the cases of the 2022 Ukraine and Russia conflict. In this case, the main impact was on production as these states were major wheat suppliers but also major suppliers of fertilizers. This struck at the very base of the global food system. Inter-state conflict can have broader impacts upon the food system where these internal or cross border disputes can cause a disruption to the flow of food both within and between states possibly leading to malnourishment. This could either be a by-product of the conflict or an act of intent. In some states, notably in the Sahel region of Africa this has led to outbreaks of famine. Generally, these impacts are felt through internal rather than inter-state conflicts with 80 per cent of malnourished children living in areas of high political risk. The geopolitical dimension can be sharpened by migratory flows that arise as a result of famine or the broad absence of food security.

Climate Risk

This is seen as a significant risk factor over the medium to long term with political stability being seen as central to the effective operation of national and global food systems. Indeed, it is already seen as a major driver in food risk across the global system as many dimensions of the food systems are being impacted by erratic climatic conditions and extreme weather. This is more than simply about production. It is also about impacting upon storage and waste of damaged food and inhibiting processing through constraints such as water shortages where water can be a major input into the processing of raw foodstuffs into consumable food. There is a risk with regard to the loss of biodiversity, pressures upon both renewable and non-renewable resources, and risks created by deforestation. There is also the potential risk impact upon transport and distribution systems from increased climatic unpredictability. On the positive side, areas within temperate latitudes can be expected to increase food production as their growing seasons can be expected to increase as a result of global rise in temperatures.

Economic Risk

These can also be key drivers behind food insecurity where the price of food is not matched by rises in incomes. The problem is especially acute where there a generalized downturns in an economy—with corresponding declines in income—that lead to consumers switching away from healthy diets. There is seen as a direct link between the state of an economy and the widespread accessibility of healthy diets and nutritious food. These economic risks extend beyond markets and purchasing into pressures upon food processing through rising input costs as well as less time spent on preparation. For example, rising energy costs may sway people towards more pre-prepared food that involves less domestic energy consumption. The global food system is also prone to logistics risk where disruption to core systemic chokepoints can impede the flow of food from surplus states to deficit states (see ► Chapter 9). There are 14 major conduits whose disruption would represent a serious challenge for the operation of the global food system. Finally, there are risks upon food systems created by rising economic development. As economic development increases so pressures upon food systems increase as diets change towards more protein (notably beef and cattle) intensive diets. Such diets place increase pressure upon supply chains to supply the high resource intensive production methods to supply such dietary requirements. This also places pressure on land and water use increasing the risk of ecological degradation as a consequence.

Social Risk

Linked into the above are social consequences of rising food insecurity especially where food becomes unavailable and/or unaffordable. This is especially so when healthy diets become unaffordable. This can result in widespread consumption of unhealthy foods with consequences for public health through obesity and other long-term conditions. These are on top of the social legacy of poor diets through issues such as stunted growth and development. The source of these social pressures can exist throughout the food system from supply to increased processing costs. These conditions tend to be concentrated within lower income groups. In addition, there are also social risks created by the rising price of food if it leads not simply to the decline in not just the quality of a diet but also where it leads to a decline in the quantity of food eaten and an increased dependence upon charitable donations to make up any short fall in food availability. These social risks can also feed through into political risk where rising food prices and deprivation lead to political unrest. This was evident during the COVID-19 pandemic where the loss of economic welfare led to rising levels of social risk whereas the loss of income led to rising levels of social risk as some group's dietary requirements become unfulfilled. It also increased levels of social deprivation as social food distribution systems were disrupted notably for those groups that rely upon the education system for the distribution of necessary foodstuffs. There are also risks that the push towards food security comes at the expense of large-scale operations outcompeting and rendering obsolete small-scale subsistence-based operations. Social risk is also informed by inequality where the inability of all to access food in the necessary amounts. This is derived from levels of inequality between and within states. This can be compounded by rapid oscillations in food pricing.

Technological Risk

Technology has often been a key enabler of energy security where research has increased the productivity of food production systems and enabled mass processing of foodstuffs at low costs. This process can also involve risk too. There is, for example, the devotion of too much agricultural land to the generation of biofuels could have a knock-on effect upon food prices. There is also the risk that excessive planting of certain types of crops could lead to monocultures and the extensive use of fertilizer could lead to externalities upon both human and natural systems as these chemicals feed their way through the food chain as well as river systems for example. There is also the possibility that the increased centrality of cyber systems to the increased complexity of food systems renders them vulnerable to attacks and human errors that could disrupt the operation of this system.

***

These risks reflect that both the system is under a process of long-term change due to climate and demographic change. The system is also subject to shocks where there is a sudden change in the operation where a single component fails and spreads throughout the rest of the system. This could be a production shock or a disruption due to logistics issues. These shocks could be short term in occurrence but could have a sizable long-term impact.

Conclusion

Climate change is an existential threat to humanity. The gradual degradation of the atmosphere renders the earth a less suitable habitat for the sustainability of our species. For business, the impact—over the short term at least—is derived from disruption created by extreme climatic events and by the policy response to the risks created by climate change. In longer term, all agents have to adapt to the consequences of climate change and the policy measures to counteract it through issues related to the triple long-term securities of food, water, and energy.

Key Points

- Climate change represents an existential threat to humanity.
- Business is exposed to the risk of climate change through multiple channels.
- A legacy of climate change is on-going water risk and food insecurity.
- An adaptive response to climate change is the energy transition.
- The energy transition creates the risk of rising energy insecurity

Discussion Questions

1. Critically examine the proposition that the solution to climate change lies in market-based solutions.
2. How can businesses best mitigate the effects of climate change?
3. Examine the view that the solution to climate change lies with consumers, not business.

Activities

Undertake an examination of Coca-Cola's business model to determine its exposure to water risk. Also examine, the countervailing measures it is taking.

Summary

Climate change can have a substantive impact upon business through a mix of operational, market, and regulatory risk. Over the longer term, the greater risks emerge from the impact of this long-term change upon the food–water–energy nexus. This nexus is key to the sustenance of human activity. However, climate change places pressures upon this system at a number of points.

References

BP. (2021). *Annual Energy Report*. ► www.bp.com
CDP Worldwide. (CDP). *Global Water Report 2020*. ► www.cdp.com
FAO, IFAD, UNICEF, WFP, & WHO. (2021). *Brief to the State of Food Security and Nutrition in the World 2021*. ► https://doi.org/10.4060/cb5409en
FAO. (2022). *The State of Food Security and Nutrition in the World 2022*. ► https://www.fao.org/documents/card/en/c/cc0639en
IPCC. (2021). *Climate Change 2021: The Physical Science Basis*. In V. Masson-Delmotte et al. (Eds.), *Contribution of Working Group I to the Sixth Assessment Report of the Intergovernmental Panel on Climate Change*. Cambridge University Press.
REN21. (2021). *Renewables 2021 Global Status Report*. REN21 Secretariat.
United Nations (UN). (2022). *The United Nations World Water Development Report 2021: Valuing Water*. UNESCO.
World Economic Forum (WEF). (2020). *Water Security: The Water-Food-Energy-Climate Nexus: The World Economic Forum Water Initiative*. Island Press.
World Economic Forum (WEF). (2022). *Global Risk Report 2022*. Available at ► www.wef.org
World Energy Council. (2021). *The Energy Trilemma Index*. ► www.wec.org

Useful websites

1. Intergovernmental Panel on Climate Change (► https://www.ipcc.ch/) hosts a series of reports and offers data on the process of climate change.
2. United Nations Climate Action (► https://www.un.org/en/climatechange/) offers an array of material on the process of climate change.
3. Skeptical Science (► https://skepticalscience.com/) offers debates on themes related to climate scepticism.

Global Social Risk

© The Author(s), under exclusive license to Springer Nature Switzerland AG 2023
C. Turner, *Global Business Analysis*,
https://doi.org/10.1007/978-3-031-27769-6_7

One of the great liabilities of history is that all too many people fail to remain awake through great periods of social change.

Martin Luther King, Jr.

By the end of this chapter, the student will be able to understand:
- The form and nature of social risk.
- How global interconnectivity is changing the nature of social risk.
- That social risk is based around issues of demographic change, health and wellbeing, and inequality.
- The issues of social risk can often reflect common social problems between states at similar levels of development.

Introduction

It can be argued that as a pressure for change upon global systems, social risk is secondary in that its effects are felt through changes in other sub-systems notably political systems. In practical terms, the impact of social change is more nuanced as it is not merely reflected through political pressures but is also driven by changes in geopolitical, technological, economic as well as intra-system social pressures all of which can impact upon social wellbeing and cohesion. As social risks tend to be localized, the global effects can be indirect in that they are driven by meta-level trends (such as demographic change) that can have divergent impacts at lower levels of systemic activity. This global dimension is also reinforced by not simply common trends with diverse impacts but also that these local impacts can cascade across systems. This creates evident global dimensions across the system insofar as it spreads across borders and can impact upon business operations across multiple localities. This chapter initially explores the form and nature of social risk addressing issues of globality within social systems. Thereafter the chapter explores the main social risks within the global systems namely those created by demographic change, health and wellbeing, and inequality as well as the legacy of social risk from economic change.

The Nature of Social Risk

Social risk is shaped by those processes and events (predicted and unpredicted) that impact upon human welfare and social wellbeing. Thus, for social change to turn into social risk depends upon its impact upon the capacity of the social system to sustain interpersonal relationships, a shared identity, norms, value trusts co-operation, and mutual support. These shared capabilities are enabled through tangible and intangible resources (i.e., common goods for a common purpose). Thus, the social risk is sourced from changes in the population that causes friction (and even outright conflict) to emerge within a social system. This reflects that any societal risk to a group (or sub-group) within a system is shaped by its capability to create a socio-economic and political response. The extreme event is that social fractures leading to civil unrest and/or open and outright discrimination and conflict between groups within a space where previously established networks of relationships were common and established. Accordingly social risk can be delineated across the following lines:

1. Conventional Social Risks: these are those risks that are driven by economic events and long-term term processes (such as insecurity of employment, long-term unemployment, downward social mobility, and work-based incidents) but also eroding and changing social structures (such as social exclusion, elderly dependence, and weaker social ties).
2. Health risks: these are those social disruptions created by health and wellbeing of the population. These are created by forces of addiction, rates of infectious diseases and epidemics. These are compounded by the existence of unsanitary conditions, food contamination, and illnesses linked to environmental pollution.
3. Social Stability Risks: these are public order issues created by increased levels of disturbance with social systems created by rising levels of terrorism, civil disorder, criminality, and online generated attacks.

These types reflect the innate nature of social risk namely that it reflects how human activity can directly impact upon the risks facing agents operating within a given context. It also reflects that these processes adapt in the form and nature with which humanity adapts to events and processes and that—as a consequence—these risks are always evolving. These adaptations occur within a social system that is both increasingly connected via information technology (notably social media) that enables all who are connected to potentially shape the process of adaptation. This disparate yet highly connected process reflects that all risks are different both in form and impact and that high social interconnectivity allows any event to be scalable through amplification. For example, how social media has been used to fuel social unrest in the case of the Arab Spring, for example.

What is evident is that social risk covers a diverse set of processes and events, but all are bound that the ultimate source of the issue rests within the form and nature of the population and how that population (either as a whole or a segment of it) is changing. Moreover, the impact of social risk can impact upon multiple scales with some social risks sourced from global trends whilst others are derived from micro- and macro-level activity. Many of these themes will be addressed more fully below. Looking across the global sub-systems, ◘ Table 7.1 indicates the assorted means through which the interconnectivity between social systems and other systems can shape the risk context within each.

The level of social risk at the level of the state can be seen through the proxy of the existence of social capital. Social capital is defined as the network of relationships amongst the population that enables its effective functioning. The core of social capital is that it generates a stabilizing force upon social systems as social connectivity delivers benefits above and beyond those from the simple act of engagement in such activity. It is this social capital that through the development of connectedness between social agents and groups creates community cohesion and social stability. The notion is that such connectivity drives trust between groups to drive social stability through promoting political engagement, economic growth, labour market participation, lower crime, and better health and wellbeing. These links offer stability by allowing both individuals and groups to become engaged

◘ **Table 7.1** The Interface between social risk and other sub-systems

Sub-system	Social risk interface
Economic	• Economic changes have a social impact through impact upon livelihoods, inequality of income, and opportunity; • social cohesion impacts if social change is uneven across social groups and geography
Political	• Political legacy of social change, demographic change upon political systems; • social risk impact upon voter behaviour; • populism reflects rising issues of social cohesion
Environmental	• Social unrest fuelled by the legacy of climate change; • migratory flows created by climate change can create social problems in both home and host states
Technological	• Risk of unemployment and or unstable incomes created by technological change where the new technology replaces labour in the production process

within social, political, and economic systems. This can also occur through the potential for social capital to act as a basis for consensus between social groups. This consensus is shaped by a range of factors from the existence of universal healthcare provision through to the feature of local demography. Not surprisingly social capital tends to be more advanced in developed states. The levels of social capital are highest within Nordic states though some large, developed states are seen as having eroded social capital due to eroding public services and social fabric (due to high crime and inequality) notably the US and the UK. Many African states have low social capital due to the poor provision of public services and high infant mortality.

The narrative upon social capital is underpinned by the importance of social cohesion within the global system. This notion of social cohesion is normally solely perceived as a macro-level phenomenon but the increased social interactions between states underpin that this can spill over into the global system more generally. Social cohesion reflects the strength of the relationships and perception of universal social solidarity between members of a society that allows them to co-operate to survive and prosper and to avoid the marginalization of any single sub-group. It promotes co-operation between citizens towards the attainment of common goals. In this sense, it reflects clear overlap with social capital and cohesion is a direct derivative of the sustained and harmonious interconnectedness within a social system. These lead to the development of social networks that enable a multitude of social support for members of a social system. Thus, social cohesion does not merely reflect social interconnectivity but that such links generate the shared values. Cohesion does not merely reflect shared values but also indicates issues of economic and social equality and the extent to which any such disparities prevent commonality being formed. This reflects that social cohesion is also characterized by the lack of any sense of any underlying potential for social conflict within the social system due to inequalities of assorted dimensions (see below). Without these, the notion that the social system is engaged in a common enterprise to address shared challenges is absent to the extent that it can be questioned that each operates within the community.

Importantly social cohesion does not imply the need for homogeneity of beliefs and/or cultures. The concept is about unity within diverse social structures and that different social groups do not develop in silos but connect. This social cohesion must:
— Include all members by seeking to integrate new members of society.
— Evolve with its context and reflect that it is a process not an outcome.
— Reflect that its cross different aspects of social systems notably economic, political as well as socio-cultural.

Case Study 7.1: Social Media and Social Risk

Social media is the common term used to denote those technologies, websites, and applications that focus upon direct user communication, community-based input, content sharing, and collaboration. They are used for many purposes, but the main usage is for everyday interaction within social groups (both personal and community). This interactive component of these technologies occurs through virtual communities and networks based upon the pretext of using these configurations for content creation and distribution. The user-centred nature of these technologies can offer many direct and indirect benefits. They allow for social connectivity to be maintained and even restored, they can allow for the dissemination of ideas, and they allow for the development of social capital to name but a few of the perceived benefits of the widespread utilization of these technologies. These are compounded by the high degree of reach of these technologies as well as frequency, usability, relevance, and permanence.

Whilst there are evident benefits to the social system from the wider utilization of social media there are also risks that are being created to social systems. These systems form four main areas:
— Disparity: the deployment of social media can reflect embedded social disparities with the better educated tending to have better social media skills which reinforces their capability to form networks, find out about opportunities and therefore improves both their standard of living and quality of life.
— Political polarization: social media can create higher levels of social risk and division by being used to selectively expose targeted users and limit their exposure to alternative perspectives. The resultant polarization can stir social unrest between divergent groups.
— Stereotyping: social media can reinforce prejudices about particular social groups which leads to further social division. An especial concern is how misinformation can be used to target groups or people holding a certain set of beliefs.
— Intra-group communication: social media can be used as a tool by elements within groups to assert negative power over other members within that group. Whilst this technology is widely used by the young, it can be used by elements within this group to assert peer pressure upon members of that group through bullying and other techniques of intimidation.

These issues are all reinforced by issues related to the integrity and reliability of the data offered within social media systems. There is a concern that it can create information silos with limited interaction between the respective platforms. There are also concerns with regard to how the data harvested from social media usage is harvested and mined and the implications that this has for user privacy. There can be little doubt that social media has been a factor in promoting social unrest. It was a factor in the mobilization that drove the Arab Spring and something that acted as a catalyst for the 2021 Attack upon the US Capital. Whilst there are undeniable pluralizing aspects to the utilization of social media and it can be a tool for social enrichment and engagement, it is also a tool that can be corrupted through its use by extremist groups and by others who wish to destabilize socio-political systems.

Globalizing Social Risk

Within the global system, social systems (and hence social risks) tend to be defined at the national (macro) level. As stressed within chapter three, one of the bases for the creation of the nation states was formally connected social relations between a group that allowed common norms and properties to be established. This means social capital is also developed within the context of the nation state. Thus, disruptions to these connections that disrupt the social system are conventionally expressed within the context established by the state and its social stability/instability. Increased connectivity across borders has created situations where social systems and—hence social risk—can cross political borders. These processes of international connectivity have been fostered by new technologies and mediums such as social media, the movement of people and ideas, and of the movement of capital that has had an inevitable social dimension. Thus, whilst there was always the potential of leakage across borders because of cross border day-to-day interactions, globalization's social dimension has fostered societal connectivity that allows social risk to spread across borders. This spillover of social risk across political borders arises through the three broad processes below.

Meta-Level Social Risks

These are social risks created as a direct consequence of meta-level trends that are common across the global system. These emerge either because of the high degree of social mobility across borders (as in the case of the dispersal of contagious diseases and the development of pandemics) or because of the accumulation and/or simultaneous development of common trends across several states. This has been evident—as noted more fully below—in areas such as demographic change. These meta-level trends can create cascade effects across social systems where they stimulate social flows and processes between states. For example, the extent to which divergent demographic trends across states lead to migratory flows between them which can run the risk of social disruption in both home and host states.

These meta trends can also be evident through the creation of global social capital through global civil society bodies. These seek commonality across borders based upon mutual support and advantage. These are network actors that push change from below. These are indicative of global social movements. These are also evidence of global social movements that create new identities utilizing social media to erode national identity. These reflect the existence of transnational and global networks that operate across borders. These breed allegiance in areas such as religion or other belief systems that supersede loyalty to the nation state. These can often be upon specific issues. These are based on new interconnections creating in some cases global social capital. These can—depending upon context—be both a stabilizing and destabilizing influence upon states.

Macro-Level Social Risk

These types of transnational social risks are created where macro-level risk spillover from one state to another due to close interconnectivity between them. These cascade effects across borders can be produced by the existence of shared social capital between states created by an extensive diaspora, by other shared socio-economic facets that generate intense interaction between states or by simple geographic proximity. In these cases, social risks are transmitted through the system. Such risk can be evident where high youth unemployment in southern and eastern Europe stimulated migratory flows into Northern European states. This can limit the formation of shared norms within host economies. The spread of macro-level risks has also been evident where high levels of mobility have allowed localized outbreaks of disease to spread across several states. Social risk at the state level can also be created by the behaviour by states that could leave its expat or diaspora communities disconnected within host communities. The risks from extensive diasporas can also cascade back to home state where it impacts upon remittances especially so where those remittances are core to a state's wellbeing. The source of the social risk in one state might lie ultimately with events in another sub-system such as environmental change or economic decline and that the consequence increase in social risk in one state eventually begins to be transmitted across borders. As events and processes impact upon a single state and the population's health and wellbeing diminishes so there is an adaptive response to this rising level of risk which can spill across borders.

Meso-Level Social Risk

Social risk also becomes evident through firm participation within inter-firm international value networks. In this case, the social risk to the business can emerge via proxy. The actions of business partners within value chains can impact upon other businesses within the value network. This can reflect a joint liability with regard to social risk. Thus, the action of a single firm within the value system to violate agreed or implied social standards and protocols for the operation of the value network can cascade through that system. This reflects any single firm's corporate social responsibility is for the actions of the entire value system and not simply for that component under their direct jurisdiction/control. This trend has been evident within large MNC value networks where third-party supplier actions have infringed the social norms of other parts of the MNC which has created reputational damage for the business. In this context, social risk is an indirect risk expressed through damage upon the firm's reputation and potentially its commercial prospects. This can be present with limits on the process of social upgrading (i.e., the improvement in worker rights and wellbeing). The more the firm neglects social upgrading the higher the degree of risk associated with global networks. The more workers become dissatisfied or where social degrading (both in relative and absolute terms) is evident the greater the risk to the business both in reputational and economic terms.

Micro-Level Social Risk

Arguably the common perception of social risk is that encountered by businesses who engage in multi-national activity. In this case, social risk reflects events and processes that—in line with the above—erode corporate social capital. At the corporate level, this is defined by the erosion of the goodwill and/or positive perception of the business by its stakeholders. This could result in the loss of sales and erosion of confidence in the business by suppliers who may not choose to supply. This risk is largely reputational with its impact felt through a decline in commercial performance. The danger for the business is the more it engages in multi-national operations of the increased danger there is to the erosion of social capital where co-ordination and co-operation between different national strategic business units becomes more problematic. These risks are seen as especially great where the action of the firm can directly impact upon local welfare issues either through health or employment issues. Thus, the parent firm becomes damaged by actions and strategies followed by subsidiaries.

Social Risk Within the Global System

These diverse impacts of social change and risk across multiple levels suggest multiple trajectories through which these effects can impact upon the global system. When considering evolving social risk within the global system the focus is upon those that directly and indirectly impact upon system stability. The main social risks that concern the analysis are those that are common across states and not isolated to a single entity. Thus (as indicated in ◘ Fig. 7.1), the rest of this chapter will examine social risk across three broad types: demographic, health and wellbeing, and inequality. These risks reflect a direct capability to erode social capital within and between states and therefore run the risk of creating social-based disruption to the system.

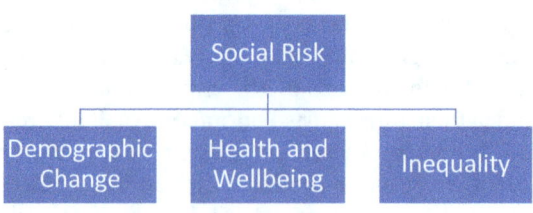

◘ **Fig. 7.1** Major types of global systemic social risks

Global Social Risk

These broad categories of risk reflect core challenges to social cohesion. These are forces that have the potential to erode the sense of commonality within a social system. The erosion of social cohesion represents a fundamental challenge (both long term and short term) creating divisions within and between groups, fracturing connectivity, and increasing polarization. This creates fractures not simply through inequality but also through divergences with regard to desirable social outcomes (as expressed for example in divergent attitudes to science and technology). In short, the erosion of social cohesion is the erosion of social capital as the social system fractures. This can be reflected with political polarizations as commonality between groups declines. This can be an international process where growing disengagement by sub-groups across states can lead to social disenchantment as groups occupying the same social system begin to resent or feel distant from one another due to inequality of opportunity and/or social progress for example.

Demographic Change and Social Risk

At its simplest demography is the study of populations at multiple levels. When examined at the meta and macro levels, it revolves around the characteristics of populations such as its size, composition (in terms of gender, ethnicity, and age profile), and its distribution. These characteristics are dynamic and the processes of change within them have a powerful factor in shaping the risk context for business. In this section, the main implications of demographic change for global risk are explored. These are examined as broad meta trends that impact upon the development of social capital and cohesion at the macro level. Whilst there are many impacts upon risk that are generated by the process of change these sections will focus on three interlinked themes namely the legacy of ageing process in developed/emerging economies; the intergenerational issues within both developed and developing states; and, finally, migratory flows.

Ageing

One of the more high-profile processes of demographic change is that of an increased ageing population within many developing and emerging economies. It has long been noted that many developed states are ageing rapidly. For example, in Japan the current share of the population over 65 is 25 per cent; this is expected to rise to 40 per cent by 2060. Similar trends are also evident across much of Europe. Indeed by 2050, the number of retirees is expected to be 1.5 billion people some 50 per cent higher than the 2020 figure (see ◘ Fig. 7.2). This trend is not restricted to mature, developed states as many leading emerging economies are also expecting similar changes within their demographic profile (see ◘ Table 7.2). In China, over 65s are expected to be 30 per cent of the total population (up from a current share of 20 per cent). Even states that are considered 'young' (such as India) are exhibiting signs of a maturing demographic profile. Globally, a clear trend towards ageing is evident. In 1950, the average lifespan was 47 years. In the intervening 70 years this has risen to 73 and is expected to rise to 83 by 2030. This increase in lifespan has also seen an unsurprising increase in the share of the global population over

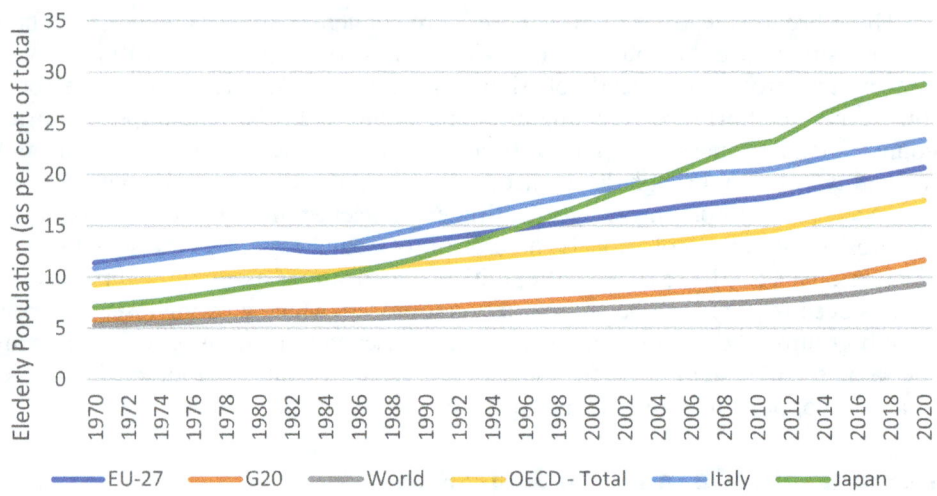

◼ **Fig. 7.2** The ageing of developed states 1970–2020 (*Source* OECD, 2021)

◼ **Table 7.2** Total global fertility[a] across selected regions and groups of countries

Region	1990	2019	2050	2100
World	3.2	2.5	2.2	1.9
Sub-Saharan Africa	6.3	4.6	3.1	2.1
Northern Africa and Western Asia	4.4	2.9	2.2	1.9
Central and Southern Asia	4.3	2.4	1.9	1.7
Eastern and South-Eastern Asia	2.5	1.8	1.8	1.8
Latin America and the Caribbean	3.3	2.0	1.7	1.7
Australia/New Zealand	1.9	1.8	1.7	1.7
Oceania	4.5	3.4	2.6	2.0
Europe and North America	1.8	1.7	1.7	1.8

[a]Live birth per woman where 2.1 per cent represents a stable population
Source UN (2022)

65 which will rise from its current share of just over 9 per cent (2020) to over 14 per cent by 2040. Overall, the populations of 55 states are expected to fall by over 1 per cent between 2020 and 2050. In some states (many in central and Eastern Europe) the fall in population is expected to be of the order of 20 per cent.

2018 was also a watershed year in the ageing process of state as for the first time, the over 65s outnumbered the under 5s. This gap is expected to increase whereby—2050—the over 65s will outnumber the under 5s by as much as 100 per cent. Indeed by 2050, the over 65s will also outnumber the number of adolescents (i.e., those between 15 and 24). Given a replacement rate of 2.1 to make the population stable, many states with falling fertility are now below this level. Moreover, the overall life expectancy is expected to increase to 77.1 years in 2050 and an increase on five years from 2020 through these rates do vary between states and levels of development.

This ageing represents an on-going demographic transition where states—as they develop—move from populations with high birth and death rates towards a demographic structure characterized by low birth and death rates where the lag in the decline by the latter relative to the former leads to natural increases in population (where birth rates exceed deaths rates). Populations stabilize over time as birth and death rates stabilize at lower rates. It has increasingly been recognized though that this is not the end of the transition. As argued above, many states move to a further transition where birth rates fall further to below the death rate leading to a natural decrease in population. These further declines in the birth rate have been driven by a range of factors both positive (for example, improved access to education, contraception, etc.) and negative (for example, cost of child rearing, economic anxiety). On top of this demographic transition, the spike in retirees is also driven by a large cohort of the population reaching retirement at the same time namely the so-called 'Baby boomers' (i.e., those born between 1946 and 1964) where there was a sharp uptick in the birth rate in developed states.

Overall, the global population is expected to increase to 11 billion by 2050. This increase in two billion in the thirty years between now and 2050 is expected to occur in very few states with the main growth areas being South Asia and sub-Saharan Africa (though the US is also expected to see population growth). This change is reflected in ◘ Fig. 7.3 which underscores how the balance of global population is shifting. This increase occurs against a background where the population in other states shrinks. The youth bulges within these states are expected to give these states a 'demographic dividend' as their working populations increase. This is expected to be especially evident in sub-Saharan Africa.

This process of ageing can be expected to radically reshape the risk environment at both the state and the global level. These also feed into further social issues below with regard to intergenerational risk and the potential for large-scale migratory flows. The main legacy of the process is as follows:

- Economic risks: these are created by a reduction in the working population and an increase in the dependent (i.e., non-working) population. In Europe, this ratio is expected to fall by 50 per cent between 2020 and 2050. This not only places pressure upon social welfare and tax systems but also upon the longer-term availability of workers within many developed states. Also, younger workers will need to work longer and increase their pension contributions to gain the same rights as current retirees. The surge could also see a reduction in savings rates, lower investment funds, and as a result lower economic growth.
- Social Risk: as suggested above, an ageing population places pressure upon welfare support systems especially those that are of universal availability. These could simply become unaffordable without radical reform or increases in taxation. This could also mean that future generations must work longer and will still be denied the same benefits as current retirees. These social risks are also created by increased prevalence of chronic disease as populations age as well as the increased need for social care. This either means increased taxes or reduced level of service.

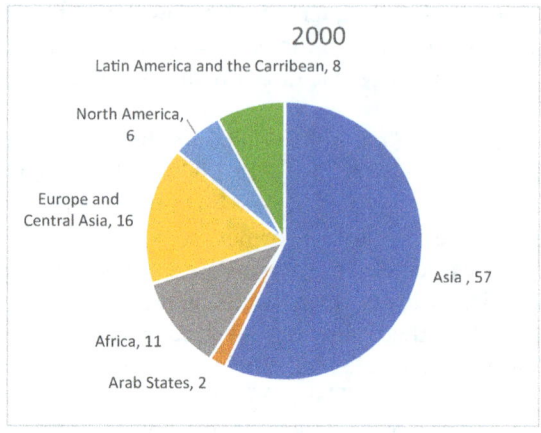
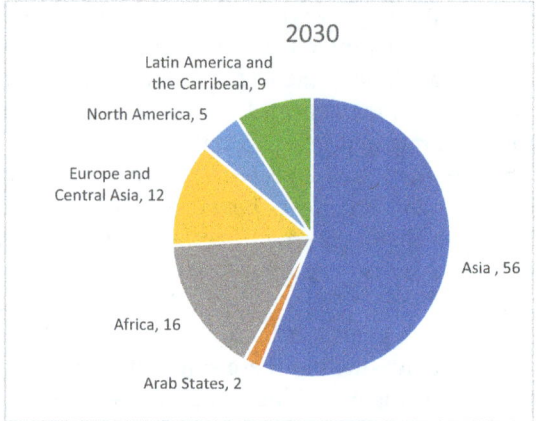

◘ **Fig. 7.3** Share of global working-age population by region, 2000 and 2030 (percentages) (UN, 2022) (*Source* UN Population Division)

- Political risk: the turnout amongst older voters tends to be higher thus raising increased risk of political upheaval as the system is geared towards meeting their needs over other groups.
- Technological risk: this could rise as states seek to address worker shortfalls with rising levels of automation. Indeed, there is already evidence to suggest that automation increases as populations age. This increases the degree of risk linked to the wider adoption of new technologies as an adaptive response to ageing.

Social risks from an ageing population can often be indirect and are shaped by both how governments adapt to this process but also how populations adjust to this shifting demographic profile notably in terms of economic and political behaviour. This—in turn—can shape the generational and migratory risks explored more fully below. For example, a response to an ageing labour force might be increased access to labour markets by groups otherwise excluded from it. This could have positive effects upon social stability. Many of the risks are currently shaped by debates viewed through the lens of economics. Thus, many of the risks examined within this chapter feed off (both directly and indirectly) this process of demographic change notably those that emerge as a direct consequence of increased economic and social consequences of rising dependency. As ◘ Fig. 7.4 highlights there is expected to be a sharp increase in the dependency ratio driven largely by an ageing process. This reflects the number of retirees (defined as those over 65) per 100 people of working age (i.e., those between 20 and 64). As the diagram reflects, across a range of states this dependency ratio is expected to increase markedly over the coming decades.

Case Study 7.2: Japan's 'Super Ageing' Society

Japan is ageing fast. It has a demographic structure where—in 2020—almost 30 per cent of its population (almost 40 million people) were over 65 with most of this age group being female. This share of Japan's population within this age group is expected to rise still further up to 2036 where over a third of the population will be within this age bracket. The legacy of this ageing process is that Japan's population is expected to fall from 127 million in 2015 to 88 million by 2065. This process runs counter to the logic that says that populations expand in periods of peace and prosperity.

The causes of this population decline lie within two processes. First, is a high life expectancy. In 2018, Japan has the second highest rate of life expectancy globally. This high life expectancy has been enabled by a healthy diet, access to clean water and sanitation, active lifestyles amongst the old, and universal healthcare coverage. This was compounded by a second factor namely a low fertility rate. Since the 1970s Japan's fertility rate has been below the replacement rate (i.e., the number of children required to keep the population stable) of 2.1. In 2019, the fertility rate was just 1.4. There is no single explanation for this trend but a mix of the embedded working culture (notably long working hours), an absence of opportunities for young men (important where women seek economic security in the choice of partner), and a shift in the gender balance in the division of labour are all thought to be explanatory factors. These are also reflected that the marriage rate in Japan is falling with a quarter of men and around 15 per cent of women at the age of 50 have never been married and that very few children are born out of wedlock.

The consequences of this decline in population are expected to be manifold. On the negative side, it is anticipated that this process could lead to an economic crisis due to a falling working population and increased budgetary pressures due to the rising pension and healthcare costs associated with an ageing population. Furthermore, there are already evident social problems created by rural depopulation and demographic inequality. On the plus side, there is a recognition that ageing populations present a problem for the Japanese state has stimulated increased rates of innovation in otherwise peripheral areas of the economy (such as social care). An area where this is already evident is the increased use of robotics to service the needs of the so-called 'silver economy'. There has also been the rise of vertical farming to address the labour shortage in agriculture. Efforts to militate against this labour shortage through increased levels of immigration have so far been limited as such measures are subject to widespread public hostility in a society that remains relatively homogenous. Another partial response to these problems is that the number of over 65s in employment is rising and is higher than economies at similar levels of economic development. The Japanese government (for whom ageing is seen as an existential challenge) is seeking to counter this trend with more family-friendly policies. It is increasing childcare support and pushing for wider adoption of parental leave. It is also increasing levels of free pre-school education.

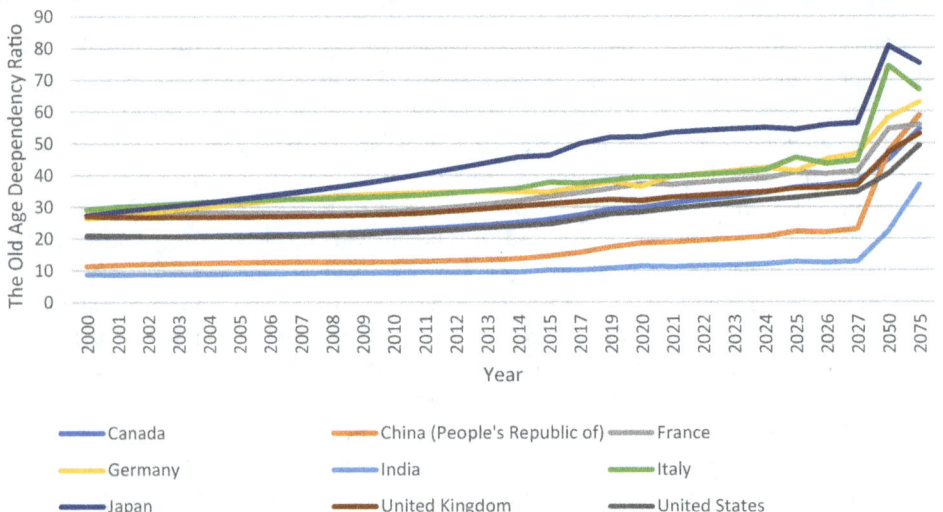

Fig. 7.4 The trend in old age dependency ratios (UN, 2022) (*Source* UN Population Division)

■ *Intergenerational division*

Linked to broader issues of inequality addressed below but more directly fed by the ageing of the working population and changes to demography mentioned above are the broader issues created by the impact of the ageing process upon succeeding generations. A generation is defined as a group of persons born at a specific time who encounter the same issues and changes. Intergenerational risks are defined here not solely as those risks that pass down from one generation to the next but as those tensions that emerge between different generations as a direct and indirect legacy of the process of demographic change. The core issue is that actions by one generation implicitly or explicitly impact upon the wellbeing of succeeding generations. This is largely through the increased risk attached to being a member of this succeeding generation due to the action/inaction of the preceding generation. In practice, the form and nature of these risks and their impact is uncertain.

Social systems are held together by mutual intergenerational dependence based upon the process that succeeding generations have at least the same or equivalent opportunities to those that preceded them. This reflects an implied intergenerational contract between generations that ensures mutual support and enablement between these groups. Broadly the nature of the intergenerational contract varies by level of economic development. In many developed economies it involves strong community support. In many developing economies it has a stronger familial support. This begins to break down when aspects of this contract become unaffordable or when economic prospects/opportunities between these generations begin to diminish. These reflect lower social capital formation, home affordability, and increased pension costs relative to preceding generations. Thus, in many developed states, the generations beyond the baby boomers are accumulating less capital and making less progress in income than previous generations. This results from increasing levels of intergenerational income inequality. In the cultures that generated strong familiar structures, the contract is being eroded through social change especially as families focus on the education of succeeding generations rather than the welfare of preceding generations. These pressures have increased as the number of family members to be cared for through familial ties increases as life expectation increases.

These pressures of an ageing population upon succeeding generations create the possibility of innate social risk and division fuelled by generational variations in opportunity as well as the pressures created as these generations are expected to care for preceding generations without experiencing the same levels of opportunity. Broadly, intergenerational divisions are commonly accepted as being delineated along the lines identified within ◘ Table 7.3. Much of the conflict is born between what are the perceived entitlements and opportunities afforded to the 'baby boomer' generation and those that are available to succeeding generations. Indeed, there is a widespread acceptance that the baby boomer generation has 'stolen' the opportunities for succeeding generating through dominating social, political, and economic life through their demographic dominance. In attaining and maintaining this dominance it is claimed that this baby boomer generation has not invested in enabling future generations. In effect, the intergenerational contract has been broken (see ◘ Table 7.3 for the categorization of generations). These concerns are greater where families are smaller and where there—is a result—greater dependence upon civil society.

◘ Table 7.3 The different generations

Name	Born	Age in 2020	Share of population in the US (per cent)
The Greatest Generation	Before 1928	92 plus	0.4
Silent Generation	1928–1945	75–92	6.61
Baby Boomer	1946–1964	56–74	21.45
Generation X	1965–1980	40–55	19.71
Millennial	1981–1990	24–39	21.93
Generation Z	After 1996	Under 24	20.35

The translation of these intergenerational discrepancies first really came to the fore in the aftermath of the 2007/2009 financial crisis where the millennial generation started to suffer rising unemployment whilst having to endure the rising cost of higher education which delivered lower than anticipated returns. Moreover, where this generation was able to find employment, it was often characterized by instability and uncertainty. Thus, whilst this was a generation that was more technologically literate, they became more economic outsiders especially within developing states (where 90 per cent of young people live) where there was more formal economic exclusion with many young people employed within the informal sector. Thus, in developing states, there is a need to create job opportunities at a rate which can absorb the annual expansion of the labour market created by an influx of young people. Most developing and emerging economy states are failing to do especially as the share of young people within their labour force is expected to double by 2050.

These more limited employment opportunities are compounded by the burden placed upon this generation by the social system whereby they pay increased taxes and other social costs to support the ageing population created by the longer life expectancy of silent generations and the expanding population of retired and retiring baby boomers. On top of this, millennials will have to save more to support themselves within their own retirements and other situations as communally provided social safety nets come under strain. Moreover, many young are not able to accumulate wealth in the same manner as preceding generations through being effectively excluded from the housing ladder. Whilst many already felt that they had to bear the burden of environmental degradation, they were also adversely impacted by the COVID-19 pandemic as they had their education interrupted and were also further impacted by a reduction in their economic opportunities and the longer-term impact upon their mental health. In terms of employment, youth workers were often employed in those sectors directly impacted by the pandemic notably the informal sector where 80 per cent of young workers are employed. Hospitality and other service sectors which have many young employees were also more adversely impacted.

Intergenerational risks are also created as a legacy of the actions of the preceding generation(s) for succeeding generations. Here the issue is less than one a denial of opportunity directly and more than the preceding generation has caused or negated a problem that the succeeding generation must deal with. This will include issues such as the sustainability of welfare provision and climate change. The need to deal with these issues places a constraint upon the opportunities and outlook for succeeding generations. This creates uncertainty for these future generations that previous generations have not dealt with despite an awareness that there was an issue to be addressed. Indeed, many see issues such as climate change as issues to be deferred where risks are by their very nature passed on to future generations. Alternatively, there is the view that this risk created was a direct legacy/externality of preceding generations creating a foundation upon which their prosperity can be secured. This reflects that these preceding generations also took different types of risk as a means of attaining these foundations which generated these new types of risk.

These differences between the generations are also underscored by variances in attitudes between them with regard to risk. One telling factor is that millennials and Generation Z cohorts are more concerned about the natural environment and climate change. This awareness of such risk has been heavily shaped by these generations' proactive engagement with social media and its capability to shape attitudes and belief systems amongst this cohort. There is also less of a belief in the government to solve things than there is amongst baby boomers and a general lack of confidence in state-based capabilities. The desire and capability of baby boomers to vote and to have higher degrees of representation within political systems. Whilst younger generations can feel excluded. This all leads to millennials feeling like losers across a range of issues facing problems that the preceding generation did not.

Taken together these economic, social, and political pressures are giving rise to social tension between social groups that could erode social cohesion. In so doing it can lead to the long-term erosion of the social contract between generations which maintains social stability. These trends have created what has been termed a widespread 'youth disillusionment' with many feeling the system is skewed against them. By 2020, the youth were two thirds of the global poor a position entrenched by a lack of intergenerational social mobility. This has fostered disenfranchisement and led to rising political risk as social issues have erupted in widespread social unrest. This has reflected that their concerns were not being adequately addressed not just in terms of opportunity but also in terms of actions with regard to long-standing grievances in areas such as discrimination and climate change. These concerns can be fuelled by reactionary actors such as organized crime, militias, and extremists who may prey upon these groups to foster widespread instability both within and across states. The rise of radical youth movements could also generate more intergenerational instability and create rising social instability. This tension could cause widespread social instability if it leads to migratory flows into both neighbours and other more distant states

▬ Migratory flows

Where working-age populations are declining, a response by governments—at least over the short term to address this demographic challenge—is to promote immigration to alleviate the skills and labour shortages. Indeed, in the US, migration accounted for 50 per cent of the increase in the workforce in the decade to 2020; in Europe the figure was over 70 per cent. This economic migration—i.e., those flows of people who move for the purposes of seeking enhanced economic opportunity/security—comprises about 80 per cent of total international migration flows. Economic migration is logically a market-based process created by the inequity of and imbalance between different national labour markets. The logic is that an undersupply of labour in one state can be mitigated by an oversupply elsewhere. Of course, such a simple narrative is undermined by the notion that labour—irrespective of source—is fully interchangeable. Of course, mobility and interchangeability of labour are not a simple process as labour doesn't move people do and this migration is both impeded by social factors and can have consequences for social risk in host societies. These trends in the rising economy reflect not just push factors from a lack of opportunity at home but also pull factors. With over 90 per cent of young Africans, three quarters of Young Middle Easterners and over 80 per cent of young Latin Americans all expressing a desire to work abroad at some point of their career. These reflect flows of talent where there is an implied choice rather than a simple economic need to move.

Economic migration between states is not always voluntary as increased economic insecurity within home states can be a direct stimulant to these flows. Whilst there are seen to be direct and indirect benefits from allowing economic migration (to both home and host states) in both alleviating labour shortages in one and promoting development in the other. Whilst most of this migration takes place between low- and middle-income states, there have also been evident flows into leading industrialized states. Within many host states concerns are growing with regard to rising social risk especially where the flows of migrants increase pressure upon and competition for public services. In other cases, the lack of integration is potentially limiting social cohesion and the formation of social capital. These concerns reflect populist resentment towards these flows in times of austerity but also of economic and political insecurity within host economies.

As of 2022, there were estimated to be 281 million international migrants globally (some 3.6 per cent of the global population). Of these, some 169 million are labour migrants. When viewed through the lens of economic migration, then the largest flows (other than internal flows) tend to be between developing states and those of higher level of economic development such as the corridors between the UAE, US, Germany, Saudi Arabia, and other less developed states. The trend over the past 50 years is reflected in ◘ Fig. 7.5. As of 2022, Europe is the single largest destination for international migration (some 31 per cent of the total), closely followed by Asia (30.5 per cent) and North America (20.9 per cent). Though the growth rate is highest in Latin America and the Caribbean. Oceania has the largest share of international migrants as a share of population at just below a quarter; North America is about 16 per cent and the Europe about 12 per cent. The US though is the single largest destination of international migrants with over 51 million with Germany and Saudi Arabia next with 16 million and 13 million, respectively. India has the largest emigrant population (18 million) flowed by Mexico at 11 million. With regard to migrant workers, two thirds of the total stock of migrants were located within developed states; 29 per cent were in middle-income states.

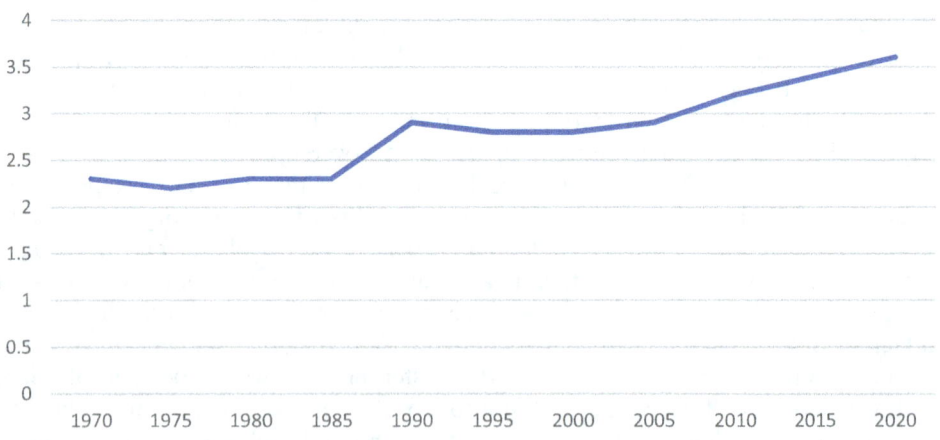

◘ **Fig. 7.5** International Migration 1970–2020 (Percentage of Total Global Population) (*Source* IMO 2022)

Whilst the full depth and range of the issues that can potentially emerge because of this process is beyond the full remit of this section, it is undeniable that as intuitive as the logic is of facilitating such migratory flows, it is something that does raise the potential of increased risk within national social systems. At the macro level, migration can fuel processes of broad-scale social change through the creation of new norms, beliefs, and processes at the level of the state. This, in turn, reflects broader meta processes where these migrants create stronger interconnections between states because of relocation. These links create uncertainty with respect to the community within which a migrant belongs. It can also inhibit integration. This risk comes through three main channels:

- National identity: where migration begins to undermine a long-standing sense of identity and a binding sense of national self as plurality within national social systems increases which can contravene those norms held by the existing population. There is also the risk that as societies grow more diverse so the logic of social cohesion as an underpinning behind welfarism is eroded as social fragmentation that erodes the consensus behind welfarism. This can place pressure upon public services especially where they are already under pressure and where competition for access to these services increases because of migration. Moreover, where these cannot easily be absorbed the opportunity cost placed upon the existing population can feed popular resentment.
- Integration: where divergent groups have their ability to establish a place within common economic, social, and political systems over several generations. This reflects the ease and extent to which interconnections are formed between migratory and indigenous populations. In practice, this is a two-way process of adaption between the host society and the migrant. This isolation is only increased if the migration is temporary. There is also the fear that social and economic exclusion could lead to increased deprivation and lead to increase crime and social disruption. It is accepted that integration can take as long as two or three generations for roots fully to be established within a state. These risks are perpetuated by indirect discrimination where migrants and their decedents are pushed to the margin of society operating within casual employment often outside formal employment processes. This could further erode integration preventing them from accumulating human capital which reinforces their sense of social exclusion.
- Cohesion: the interconnections (social, political, and economic) formed across different groups within a shared space to enable the creation of social capital thus enabling their absorption into the wider population. The fear for social cohesion is that social capital developed solely within limited social groups could lead to the parallel development of social systems within a single state. The fear is that lower social cohesion leads to lower trust within a community and that this leads to economic stagnation as investment declines.

Mitigating this social risk is based upon integration through assimilation which means adapting to the main focal point of the culture into which they are seeking to be absorbed. Whilst host societies are not homogeneous there are key cultural norms and symbols around which citizens are expected to gather to promote cohesion. Thus, cohesion does not mean homogeneity just common points of identity around which diversity can be mitigated. This is seen as a necessity for developing social order and lowering social risk. Systems are based on multi-cultural systems reflecting both ancestry of migrants but also bonds with the host state. Thus, state-based strategies to mitigate this risk are based upon promoting interconnectivity between groups to facilitate social capital and cohesion.

Extensive diasporas in enabling integration and the existence of social systems into which new arrivals can embed can create new forms of social capital. In so doing governments might seek to use this social capital to exclude new arrivals from access to public services. This social capital could erode social cohesion if it leads to marginalization and less community emerges. Indeed, this social capital emerges in the face to counter popular hostility to migrants. In short, social capital is created not by cohesion but as a response to the absence of or lack of progression attaining it as support groups emerge to counter hostile environments.

There is also reciprocal risk upon those states exporting labour. The not least of which is that those that are more migratory tend to be the better educated, the young, and the more entrepreneurial. The result is that large-scale migration from a single state can lead to an erosion of its human capital and erode its ability to sustain its path towards economic development or to even keep it in a state of underdevelopment. Where there have been migratory flows in many developing states rely heavily upon remittances (payments made by migrants to their families/communities in their home country) from migrant labour to support their economy. In 2020, around $ 700 billion was by migrants back to their home states with over 70 per cent of this going to low- and middle-income economies. India, China, Egypt, the Philippines, and Mexico are the top states for receiving remittances. Of the states receiving these flows some do rely heavily upon them. For example, Tonga has nearly 40 per cent of its GDP based upon remittances and Somalia around 35 per cent. These flows are mainly sourced from developed states notably the US and Western Europe. The risk is that an increased perception of social risk from large-scale migration could lead to increased levels of economic risk within developing states when—because of this hostility of immigration—flows of remittances are either cut off or severely curtailed.

Inequality and Social Risk

An overlapping theme with many of the issues raised above are those threats to social cohesion and the development and maintenance of social capital that emerge from the existence and persistence of inequality within social systems. The notion of inequality rests upon the notion of the uneven and/or unfair allocation of resources and opportunities within a social system. Within this section, the focus will be upon three major forms of inequality. The first reflects an uneven equality of opportunity between generations that results in persistently high levels of youth unemployment. This inequality of opportunity is extended through risks of social instability created by variations in human rights between different social groups within a given space. The third reflects inequality of distribution of resources as reflected in the risk of a livelihood crisis which impacts upon the ability of households to be financially sustainable. Whilst these themes directly eschew issues of income and wealth inequality, they are nonetheless often indirectly related to such themes.

Youth unemployment

Youth unemployment is defined as that segment of the working population between the ages of 15 and 24 who are unable to find employment of any kind. This segment of the working population tends to suffer (globally) from higher rates of unemployment than other groups. Even as economic growth has increased across all states this has not easily been translated into rising employment opportunities for young workers. The rate of youth unemployment does demonstrate a wide degree of variability with—across 181 states—the rate of unemployment standing at (as of 2020) 20 per cent (see ◘ Fig. 7.6 for a regional breakdown). These figures are even higher for young women where over a third are unemployed compared to less than 15 per cent for men. Many of these unemployed (especially female) young people have familial responsibilities. This compares to around 8.5 per cent of the working population. Within these figures, there is a wide range of youth unemployment rates with Djibouti possessing a rate of over 80 per cent and Qatar just 0.63 per cent. Nonetheless across all major states unemployment is higher amongst the young than it is across the working population generally. In the Euro Area, it is over 20 per cent (it is especially high in Southern Europe), in the US it is over 15 per cent and in Japan it is 5 per cent. These figures exclude those that are underemployed and those who have deferred entry into the labour market through education and training. Indeed, irrespective of the level of the development this is a social group that does persistently badly in terms of opportunities for employment and personal development. Moreover, where these workers do find employment, it is often in low skilled and insecure positions. Indeed 80 per cent of young people globally are employed within the informal sector. This problem is only expected to get worse as an extra 1 billion young people enter the global labour force with only around half of this increase being able to find formal employment. Moreover, those

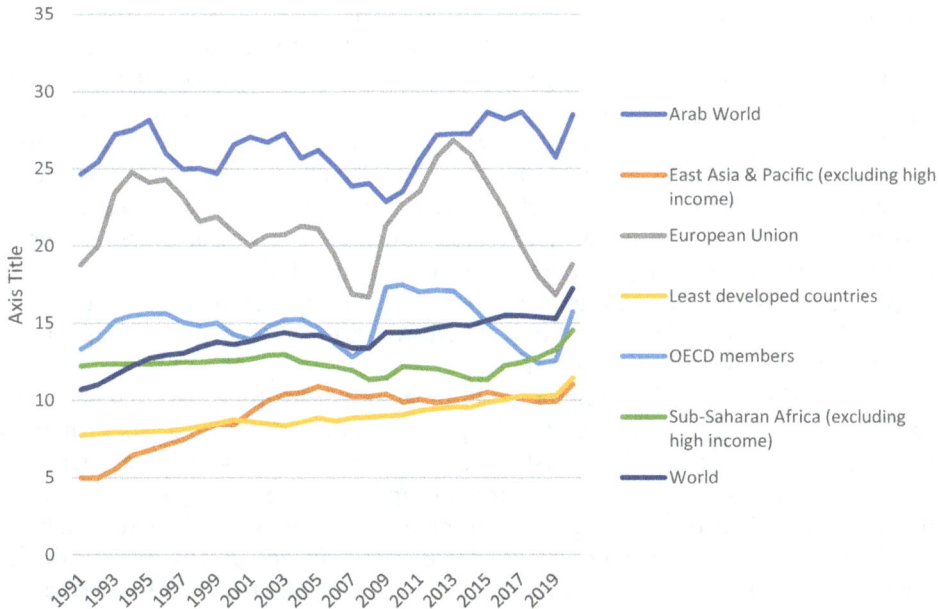

◘ **Fig. 7.6** Youth unemployment (UN, 2022) (*Source* UN Population Division)

that fall into this economically excluded category tend to be amongst those groups that are already marginalized or in households already experiencing poverty. Thus, this process can only be expected to increase levels of inequality of opportunity, income, and wealth between generations.

The reasons for this sustained level of economic exclusion for young people from the labour market is manifold but are mainly driven by:

- Lack of opportunities within the economy generally.
- Bulge of youth workers increasing faster than the ability of economy to create employment.
- Lack of work experience creates a vicious cycle of labour market exclusions.
- Concertation of opportunities in low skilled, informal employment with low levels of security.
- Better educated workforce with higher expectations found these expectations unfulfilled.
- Austerity measures limited opportunities within public sector.
- Corruption and nepotism limited the level playing field for opportunity.
- Limited safety nets to support unemployed.
- Youth work is concentrated in sectors with more automation.

These in combination mean that young workers are often unable to develop the necessary human capital to become fully integrated into national labour markets. This is also true of graduates with some states (notably China) who end up in non-graduate positions due to an excess supply of graduates. Overall, the main social (and related) risks created by high rates of youth unemployment are as reflected in ◘ Table 7.4.

The legacy of these risks can linger within a social system for decades. They cannot merely produce short-term political and economic consequences but can have longer-term social effects. These can create long-term scarring due to young people caught in situations where a combination of employer responses to unemployment, the development of individual human capital, decreased expectations, the problems of searching for employment as well as other extraneous factors can all lead to longer-term sustenance of social risks. These are compounded by potential political risks created by disaffections with an absence of opportunity. This disaffection with opportunity amongst the young was seen to be a key factor behind the political instability that was the Arab Spring between 2010 and 2012. In this case, it was felt that job creation within this region had tended to favour older workers to the detriment of the young. The relationship between political risk and youth unemployment is often two way as the former can cause the latter as much as the latter can cause the former; though only where youth unemployment is coupled with lower levels of education attainment.

Overall, the high and sustained youth unemployment threatens social cohesion creating further barriers between those operating within the formal labour markets and those on the outside of the system. This is compounded by the fact that youth unemployment can often be higher within groups that were already struggling to integrate such as first or second-generation migrant communities. This ties high and persistent youth unemployment into issues of social justice in that the young view the right to earn a living as a human right (see below) and that this being absent is an injustice. It also means that the absence of secure employment erodes the capa-

Global Social Risk

Table 7.4 Main types of risks created by high and sustained youth unemployment

Risk Type	Impact
Social	• Rising levels of social exclusion and longer-term scarring • High level of social ills and lower mental wellbeing • Increased levels of poverty amongst young segment of population • Unemployment reduces life expectancy • Further erosion of social contract • Attain dignity and self-actualization • This means young cannot engage as fully functioning citizens and build social capital
Economic	• High and sustained youth unemployment could lead to the migration of young and skilled workers • Loss of productive capacity of economy • Erosion of skill based as trained workers struggle to find position • Young become 'outsiders to formal labour market'
Political	• High migration could lead to rising political risks in home state • High youth unemployment could lead to rising levels of political unrest • High number of over-qualified young people increases the risk of popular frustration • Lack of opportunities could attract youth to extremist ideologies
Environmental	• Indirect effects as states adapt to rising youth unemployment with a dash for growth which impacts upon the quality of the natural environment • Effects caused by large-scale migratory flows
Technological	• Unskilled employment undertaken by young often more readily subject to automation

bility of operating as an effective citizen and attaining self-actualization (i.e., the realization of one's potential).

▬ Human Rights

Human rights and the uneven manner with which they can be secured and guaranteed across the global economic system represents another source of inequality of opportunity. These rights can work to deny any human being the right to express their belief and/or the same opportunities as other humans within and across space due to an intentional action made by the authority to purposefully deny them the opportunity of these rights and even to coercively work against any security of rights for any individual, community, or other groups. Prejudice against human rights is a denial of human capacity through design.

Human rights are those to which all human beings are entitled and are defined by a set of international conventions, treaties, and organizations to which all states are expected to adhere. There are 30 core human rights included within the 1948 UN Declaration upon Human Rights. This covers areas such as the right to life, social discrimination, employment discrimination, poor employment conditions, freedom of assembly, freedom from persecution and discrimination, health and safety issues, and impacts upon communities. These pressures are typified by contemporary debates based around modern slavery where there is a severe violation of human rights where coercion, physical threats, deception, and other such methods are used to violate individual rights to discretionary action and freedom. This term can involve a range of actions from the use of forced labour, the utilization of trafficked labour, the use of misleading techniques to ensure recruitment of labour, and the use of child labour, slavery, forced marriage, and debt bondage.

Human rights violations directly impact upon the capability of citizens to engage with and from human interconnections to form and/or maintain social capital. In these cases, forms of social cohesion could be seen as a threat to the stability of the state. Thus, human rights could be violated. Where there is a discrepancy in the application of these rights across space creating a social risk for business. Human rights risk emerges as an issue for social risk largely through three main channels:

- Macro level: where the firm undertakes activities in a country where there is known and acknowledged violation of human rights.
- Meso Level: where the firms are engaged in relationships with firms that knowingly violate human rights.
- Micro Level: where the firm itself directly (either intentionally or unintentionally) engages in actions that are seen to violate human rights.

Normally it would be expected that respect for human rights and corporate financial sustainability might appear to be in conflict as adherence to the protocols might impact upon profitability. This reflects that a failure to adapt to these protocols could be bad business as they can impact upon the business through several interfaces each reflects a broad set of corporate social responsibilities. These interfaces between the business and human rights can create a risk for business through several channels stressing the micro level of this risk. These main channels are:

- Regulatory: where the failure to adopt to acknowledge standards lead to tighter regulation upon the business which in turn leads to increased costs as reporting requirements are tightened and standards of commercial practice become more defined.
- Reputational damage: as with environmental concerns, there is a risk that failure to adopt accepted norms on human rights commercial practices can create reputational damage and lead to an erosion of trust for the business by both consumers and partners.
- Investor scrutiny: the failure of the form could come under pressure from activist shareholders who feel that these actions of the firm run contrary to the investor principles. The investor can then place pressure upon the business to adapt or risk seeing the share price impacted as these investors adapt their investment strategies.
- Worker activism: the firms' actions in particular markets may run contrary to the values embedded within contemporary socially conscious workforces. This opens up the possibility of more fractious industrial relations.

Business actions with regard to human rights are guided by the UN's Guiding Principles upon Human Rights which outline the core expectations for companies with regard to human rights. Through adherence to these principles, the firm should be able to manage the degree of social risk attached to activities in localities where there is less than strong adherence to acceptable human rights. These cover activities by states and businesses to ensure adherence but also outline a list of appropriate remedies.

At the macro level, human rights risks are shaped by inter-state activity where one or more states seek to discriminate against individuals or communities within a given territory. State action could exist along a spectrum of implicit discrimination towards outright genocide of a given sub-group or ethnicity. In this case, human rights risk is shaped by the nature of the international community's response to these violations of the agreed international norms and protocols. For businesses operating within states where there is a deterioration of agreed rights existing and legacy activity could be exposed by the actions of others who seek to impose constraints upon the violating state to ensure that there is a change of behaviour by this state with regard to the violations. This can happen through the application of political and economic sanctions (i.e., measures that inhibit the state from fully integrating into and benefitting from proactive engagement within the global system) to seek to change the behaviour of state with regard to its violation of human rights. The impact upon business could be substantial if these sanctions prohibit the business from operating normally within this state and between the violating state and other states. Indeed, an impact of the sanction could be enforcing a divestment upon the business leading it to write down or even write off the assets that the business has within the violating state.

– *Livelihood Crisis and economic inequality*

Whilst economic inequality created by vast disparities in wealth and income has been a perennial feature of the contemporary global system equating the notion that social and economic cohesion are intimately linked and that the greater the disparities the larger these represent an inhibitor to social cohesiveness and to the ability to form social capital. These livelihood crises operate on both a long-term and short-term basis and reflect how different groups have been impacted by the process of globalization. In 'non-standard' forms of employment, globalization has placed pressure upon wages and terms of conditions as competition has intensified between states especially within low-skilled segments of the labour market. These were workers who were less able to adapt to the process of globalization by upskilling. For these workers, globalization seemed to create an on-going crisis of existence as their rights and wages were suppressed. Thus, for these workers the livelihood crisis was an on-going economic pressure upon them created by hyper-global forces.

In a global system, the notion is that livelihoods to be sustainable need to be resilient to shocks to the economic system, be independent of the need for external support, and do not undermine the livelihoods of—or options for livelihood open to—others. In this sustainability depends upon the individual's human capital and wellbeing, social assets (such as status and networks), and physical and financial assets. This can be extended to political assets which may enable the individual to be supported during an emergency. Thus, the extent to which an individual (and their dependents) are at risk reflects the tangible and intangible assets at their disposal.

The notion of someone's livelihood is indicative of broader systemic inequality especially for those at the lower end of the income distribution. In this context, livelihood reflects the capability of a citizen to be able to afford the necessities of existence for themselves and their dependents. This implies that citizens need to possess the capabilities, assets, activities, and opportunities for them to be able to generate an income to be able to pay for these social necessities. Expressed in these terms' livelihood is linked intimately to notions of inequality and this is shaped by the availability of both resources and potential access to resources to enable the citizen to provide these necessities for both themselves and their dependents. The danger is that periods of uncertain employment and unstable income could lead to the development of a social underclass that becomes dislocated from the broader social system. This has been reflected within narratives surrounding the 'left behinds' who exhibit limited social capital development and low social cohesion and endure welfare dependency and consequences become embedded within a culture of poverty.

The threats to livelihoods within an economic system reflect the key vulnerabilities exhibited by those workers who undertake non-standard work. This is work that tends not to confirm normal patterns of employment so can be part-time, irregular, fixed term contracts with multiple employers. It can also include forms of self-employment. Overall—globally—it is estimated that some 2 billion workers are deemed in non-standard forms of employment These non-standard workers reflect the very fragmented nature of the labour market. In many developed states, the uncertainties over income to sustain a livelihood have led to the provision of social safety nets to ensure that erratic income does not undermine the ability to afford necessities. However, this has been eroded and is non-existent in some (mainly developing) states. In many cases, this welfare support mechanism can work against any social risk that could possibly emerge because of livelihoods being undermined by events and/or processes. These workers are in vulnerable occupations with limited—if any—security offered should there be a sudden downturn. These are workers who—if they do not work—they do not eat.

Within the context of the global system, the more the system tends towards political and economic instability the greater the threat there is to the ability of those at the lower ends of the income spectrum as well as those in unstable employment can sustain their livelihoods. The danger is that these uncertainties with regard to the ability to access necessities can spill over into rising levels of social risk as the social cohesion is undermined leading to rising levels of political and economic risk.

Whilst there have been long-standing issues with regard to livelihood risk, the COVID pandemic brought the issue to the fore as there was a fear that national lockdowns would prevent those doing non-standard work were less able to undertake the work necessary and to gain support from employers to cover them during the period of lockdown. Moreover, these workers generally had less savings, lost their jobs, or faced pay cuts because of the lockdown. There was an estimated 500 million working hours lost in 2020 (some 14 per cent of the total). These impacts were felt within marginalized groups such as the young and women. These workers were in a situation where no work means no pay. For standard workers, government schemes were available for support to sustain incomes. These were also made available for many non-standard workers. However, these payments were ad hoc and not long-standing meaning that non-standard workers still face uncertainty over income. Non-standard workers were not a priority for governments the support was less generous and more difficult to obtain. Indeed, in many cases, these non-standard workers find themselves outside of conventional forms of state support. These measures were deemed necessary to ensure that any social vulnerability does not spill over into broader levels of social risk.

Table 7.5 The multi-scalar nature of global health and wellbeing

Level	Events and processes
Meta	Global Pandemics/Epidemics, Health legacy of demographic change, Illicit narcotics trade
Macro	Localized peaks in illness, Failure of health systems. Health governance failures leading to outbreaks/addictions
Meso	Community-level outbreaks, Community isolation from mainstream, localized centres of addiction
Micro	Individual mental and physical wellbeing, familial vulnerability

Whilst this livelihood crisis was something that was only highlighted by the COVID pandemic. It is something that both preceded and will extend beyond the pandemic period. The extension of the livelihood crisis is a direct and indirect challenge to social cohesion. Directly through exacerbating pre-existing inequalities and—indirectly—through stimulating migratory flows. This latter process could extend a livelihood crisis across borders through migration placing pressure on existing non-standard workers within a host economy. This crisis also reflects that the economic crisis hit very unevenly across the social system. This further erodes social erosion cohesion. This can be a powerful factor driving political unrest within states with extreme positions at either end of the political spectrum blaming globalization for the uncertainty associated with this process.

Global Health and Wellbeing

The inter-related Issues of health and wellbeing are not normally issues that generate systemic social risks as these are normally of concern to the individual, family, or of a more limited social group. There is an increased awareness that issues of health and wellbeing can be scaled up to create a broader degree of social risk where they challenge the creation of social capital and social cohesion. If these issues penetrate deep into specific social groups, then they can contribute to the fragmentation of social groups either by self-isolation or through stigmatization. These impacts across multiple scales are reflected within Table 7.5. At the core of this analysis is the essential role of social relationships in maintaining health and wellbeing.

Global Public Health

Global health revolves around those issues that impact upon the physical and mental wellbeing of a population that transcend the formal boundaries of the state. This does not simply reflect how the increased mobility of peoples can spread communicable diseases but also how this mobility impacts upon the treatment of common health issues. As reflected within the Millennium Development Goals and more latterly within Sustainable Development Goals (see Table 7.6), healthcare system maturity and coverage are very asymmetric across states. It is this asym-

Table 7.6 The public health dimensions of the UN's sustainable development goals

Global health sustainable development goals

By 2030, the UN's aims are to:

- Reduce maternal deaths in childbirth to less than 70 per 100,000 live births
- End preventable infant mortality
- End the epidemics of major communicable diseases such as AIDS, tuberculosis, and malaria
- Reduce premature deaths from non-communicable diseases by one third
- Strengthen the prevention and treatment of substance abuse
- Ensure universal access to sexual and reproductive healthcare services
- Achieve universal health coverage
- Reduce death and illnesses from human-induced pollution
- Eliminate global deaths and injuries from road traffic accidents

In addition, there are a set of open-ended objectives to:

- Improve the adoption of WHO protocols for tobacco control
- Facilitate and support R&D into vaccines for both communicable and non-communicable diseases common in developing states and ensure that they are distributed whilst mindful of IPR protection
- Increase healthcare funding (especially in less developed states) to enable more uniform quality services
- Enhance capacity (especially in developing states) for early warning systems with regard to emerging national and global health risks

Source UN (2022) ► www.un.org

metry that has formed the focal point of much of public policy debates within the broad domain of public health. In addressing notions of risk created by global health, this section will devote itself to those meta-level processes where the nature of global risk is created by the health implications of intense cross border activity and common meta-level trends.

Whilst health has been an on-going issue with regard to national risk. These have tended to be through:

- Direct effects: where communicable diseases spread across borders due to the mobility of people and other carriers (see below).
- Indirect effects: where for example national health issues such as obesity (see Case Study 7.3) or opioid addiction can create risk for business through the increased potential for regulation and control. There is also the risk that the spread of the consumption of unhealthy products can create the spread of non-communicable diseases like heart attacks.

The trend towards hyper-globality has increased the risk of communicable diseases spreading across borders. This has had its most obvious expression in the rise of global pandemics. The WEF in its annual risk report has been gradually increasing the degree of risk attached to the effects of pandemics over the past decade. The main risk to the global systems was conventionally seen as the risk of chronic diseases in developed states. These reflected concerns with regard to antibiotic resistant bacteria and how these rendered conventional treatments for serious conditions redundant. The concern is that such resistance allowed these conditions to spread within and across states creating disruptive conditions in economic, social, and political systems. Moreover, these could create conditions where common ailments could once again prove fatal. This situation was created by both the overuse of antibiotics in treatments that has allowed the resistant bacteria to evolve but also since the pipeline for new antibiotics is drying up due to other more profitable priorities for pharmaceutical companies and regulatory burdens. In addition, this is compounded by a lack of protection of IPR fuelling an under-investment in these new treatments. Thus, combining systemic risk with commercial risk. Globally it is estimated that only half of antibiotics are used properly. This misuse is creating increased resistance by viruses resulting in an increased number of deaths up to 750,000 from antibiotic resistance. This number is expected to increase to 10 million by 2050. This has the potential to cause a large economic shock. This is compounded by the increased use of these antibiotics in agriculture to increase production. This further increases the risk of antibiotic resistance and threatens livestock production which could see an 11 per cent decline on current trends.

Overtime attention has turned towards pandemics with special focus upon how the increased rate of urbanization within developing states increases the risk of outbreaks of infection where the density of crowded populations combined with poor public health infrastructure creates a breeding ground for the rapid spread of such diseases. Concerns with regard to the potential for globally spreading communicable diseases really began to rise in policymakers' attention with the Ebola virus in 2014 which began to highlight how the interface between demographic change, urbanization, and poor infrastructure combined with globality created a nexus in which infectious diseases could rise and spread through the global systems. By 2016, there were 20 known diseases that had spread globally directly facilitated by the globality of the flows of commodities and people. Early warning was also evident from early coronaviruses notably the severe acute respiratory syndrome (SARS) in 2002–2003 and the Middle East Respiratory Syndrome (MERS) in 2012 that began to indicate how easily coronaviruses could spread globally (see ▶ Box 7.1 for a list). These were compounded by the global outbreaks of Swine flu and Bird flu. Whilst these were not the most infectious of illnesses, there were evident issues where the spread of these diseases began to shut down core urban centres (such as Beijing) as did other places where high levels of interactivity were evident (such as schools). This started to create economic risk as voluntary and enforced aversion behaviour of limited economic transactions. At this point, it was evident that resilient public healthcare services were largely absent as was proactive surveillance.

Up to 2019, there was a steady rise in infectious disease outbreaks. Between 1980 and 2013, there were over 12,000 outbreaks globally impacting 44 million people. By 2018, these rates were increasing driven by five main factors:

— Increased connectivity: not merely between humans but also between humans and other species is increasing the risk. This connectivity to spread diseases is also aided by core 'superspreading hubs' such as airports where humans' mobility is concentrated for a short time allowing rapid transmission.
— Increased urbanization and more intense human interaction across limited space. This concentration of humanity also facilitates the rapid spread of communicable diseases. This is also aided where these urban centres are characterized by poor health and sanitary conditions and where they are close to animals.

- Increased deforestation increases human–animal connectivity which viruses allow to jump species.
- Climate change: changes in climate cause humans and other species into closer proximity as animals move into new habitats.
- Human displacement: as humans move through longer-term involuntary and voluntary processes such as war and famine so there is the increased risk that carriers of diseases could be amongst them. The risk is increased as these carriers may introduce disease into communities where there are low levels of community immunity.

It was already evident that there was a growing risk from pandemics to become a large-scale public health issue. These were created as a negative externality emerging from the process of globalization that allows carriers to mix and spread communicable diseases across a wider space more readily and speedily. Pandemics create a health problem due to low immunity within a population, the speed with which they can be transmitted, and the geographic range over which this spread can occur. In short, it can spread quickly and easily across borders and cannot easily be isolated. The process is also linked to other meta-level trends such as climate change where the destruction of habitats has enabled these viruses to cross species.

Case Study 7.3: Global Obesity and Social Risk

Globally obesity has increased by 300 per cent since 1975. As of 2020, there were an estimated 1.9 billion of the global population that were deemed overweight with a third of these being classified as being clinically obese (that is those with a body mass index of over 30). That is nearly 5 per cent of the global population or 13 per cent of the adult population. On top of this, nearly 400 million children are deemed obese. Overall, more people live in states where being overweight is more of a social risk than being underweight. This rising level of childhood and adult obesity represents a social risk at many levels. At the micro level, it represents a challenge for individual wellbeing and issues for businesses who may have to adapt to the legacy of obesity for the welfare of their workforce. At the macro level, the risk from obesity is created by the pressure upon national health systems from dealing with the consequences of large segment of the population with health issues created by their obesity.

It is estimated that obesity accounts for nearly 5 million premature deaths annually. This is nearly five times the number that were killed in road accidents and 8 per cent of the global total. These deaths exclude where obesity was a contributory factor to the cause of death such as heart disease, cancer, stroke, and diabetes for example. The rates of death from obesity are notably higher in middle-income states where the rising levels of calorie consumption are not matched by improvements in the quality of local healthcare systems. The figures in high income states are approximately half these figures largely due to the prevalence of mature healthcare systems. Generally, though there is a positive link between obesity and economic development. Outliers on this pattern though are the several states within the Pacific Islands where obesity rates are over 50 per cent.

On the flip side, there are several developed states with low rates of obesity notably South Korea and Japan.

In terms of social risk, not merely is obesity a pressure upon public healthcare and individual health but it is also a reflection of broader social problems. Whilst food availability is inevitably a key driver there are a broader set of issues that impact upon the consumption of poor diets. In more affluent societies, the trend has been enabled by a reduction in physical activity associated with better transportation as well and more mechanized and technologically driven lifestyles. This has also been fed by the linked process of urbanization as well as trade liberalization in foodstuffs. High calorific food of poor quality tends to be more widely consumed in areas of high social deprivation. These are areas with lower levels of economic activity and education. Moreover, obesity tends to be highest in areas with a higher level of crime, low social capital formation, social deprivation, and social disorder. The cost to the global economy of obesity is estimated to be around 2.8 per cent of global GDP. This problem is only set to worsen as it is anticipated nearly around half of the global population could be overweight by 2030. Importantly no country has been able to begin to turn this trend around.

With the COVID-19 pandemic this fear became a reality, and the true economic and social costs of pandemic became evident. Whilst COVID-19 exposed inequality and did immense economic damage, it underscored the vulnerability of the global system to complex global processes where they can operate as a spreader for highly contagious, communicable diseases. It highlighted the absence of resilience and sustainability of national systems to global processes. The COVID-19 pandemic exposed how deep pandemics can infuse themselves into the global system and truly disrupt and distort its functioning. That a pandemic has demonstrated how disruptive it can be across all sub-systems there is as a direct legacy an increased awareness of the risks they pose to the evolving system. ◘ Table 7.7 indicates the evident risk to global sub-systems evidenced by the experience of the COVID-19 pandemic. There were also indirect health risks created by the pandemic as dealing with the pandemic led to a downgrading of the treatment of other conditions leading to healthcare systems came under pressure.

The disruptive effects were evident with (by mid-2022) 533 million cases and nearly 6.6 million deaths. Moreover, at its peak some 4.2 billion people were in lockdown. These cascade effects of this pandemic became evident not merely in short-term social and economic risk but also with regard to longer-term effects which have yet to become evident with regard to longer-term adjustments to economic activity and long-term social risks. This risk can also be extended to agricultural pandemics as explored within ► Box 7.1.

Table 7.7 Global pandemic risks to global sub-systems

Type of risk	Indicative risk
Economic	• Sharp reduction in economic activity, the inflationary risk is system returns to normal rise in public debt • Impact upon human resources due to absences • Impact upon logistics systems and connectivity reduced • Potential livelihood crisis—500 million risks of poverty • Tighter migration rules
Political	• Vaccine nationalism • Increased political division in number of cases • Backlash against science anti-vax sentiment
Social	• Uneven impact upon employment • Poorest citizens hit hardest • Health crisis as other diseases re-prioritized • Erosion of social cohesion • Reduction in social capital • Long-term mental health issues created by social isolation
Environmental	• Disrupted climate transition • Short-term reduction in emissions due to lockdown • Reduction in diversity decreases natural resistance
Technological	• Accelerated digitization exposed and enhanced digital divide • Uneven vaccination rates • Increased cyber risk due to increased online activity

Box 7.1: Agricultural Pandemics

There is a widespread acceptance that the emergence of pandemics is created by the transmission of animal microbes to a human. These so-called zoonotic diseases are sourced from the high and increasing proximity between human and wildlife. As populations expand so the pressure upon wildlife habitats increases the proximity between species that had otherwise little interaction. There is an increased belief that these pandemics are also being created by the high proximity between humans and animals that emerges because of agricultural practices. This emerges not simply because these animals are a source of infection but also because they can function as bridging hosts carrying the infection between wildlife and humans. That domesticated animals should be a major source of zoonotic diseases should come as little surprise given the proximity between these animals and humanity. Over the past nearly 200 years, there have been around several major pandemics created by agricultural practices.

— Bovine Tuberculosis: in the late nineteenth and early twentieth century sourced from milk from infested animals which killed 65,000 in England and Wales between 1912 and 1937.
— Q Fever: identified in the 1930s largely because of intensive goat farming this zoonotic illness has persisted with outbreaks as recent as 2016 in the Netherlands.
— Bovine spongiform encephalopathy (BSE): identified in 1985 but became linked to human cognitive decline in 1996 where there was consumption

of contaminated meat. It has been mainly limited to the UK but has occasionally appeared in other states.
- H5N1 Bird Flu: detected in 1997 and was mainly limited to South and East Asia where there was the close contact between humans and the virus within live bird markets. This is an on-going threat with 400 deaths between 2003 and 2019.
- Nipah Virus: identified in 1999 and sourced from intimate contact between pigs and humanity. Mainly limited to South and East Asia. Pigs were in fact a bridge between bats and humans.
- Severe Acute Respiratory Syndrome (SARS): detected in 2002 and was passed to humans through infected meat either through close contact with source, consumption, or in butchering. Again, identified in East Asia with bats to believe to be the initial source which jumped to an intermediate species.
- H7N7 (bird flu): detected in 2003 in the Netherlands via direct interaction with live or dead infected poultry.
- H1N1 Swine Flu: identified in 2009 in the US it was spread from contact with infected meat. Up to 600, 000 were killed because of this viral infection.
- Middle East Respiratory Syndrome (MERS): detected in 2012 in the Middle East from proximity to infected animals. This was believed to be largely due to the rapid expansion in the camel population (kept for meat and milk) since the 1960s.
- COVID-19 Pandemic: detected in 2019 in central China where it is believed it passed from bats via intermediate hosts to humans. There have been over a 6.5 million deaths.

All of these reflect the risks embedded with modern intensive agriculture and how the desire to have a regular supply of food has led to the rise of these zoonotic diseases. Indeed, it is estimated that 75 per cent of new diseases are created this way. There is an alternative view that free range production requires more space which increases the risk of encroachment of wildlife habits leading to an increased risk of transmission. As a result, intensive farming lowers the risk of encroachment and therefore of cross species contamination.

Global Wellbeing

The notion of wellbeing can be a rather opaque concept. Overall—as a broad-based concept—the notion of wellbeing across a range of mental and physical criteria reflects a broad sense of how happy an individual is with their life. This does not merely include mental wellbeing but also the set of social ties and integration as well as economic wellbeing. The World Health Organization (WHO) tends to view it in the narrowest sense of mental health. Consensus seems to be more generic with it being conceived with a broader sense of wellness and quality of life. This is often defined at the level of the individual and their own self-interest and can reflect a range of issues from mental, emotional, economic, and/or physical wellbeing. In practice, these can be interlinked. In its broadest sense, wellbeing reflects an individual's quality of life according to their own expectations and criteria. In turn, quality of life reflects an individual's perspective upon their position in life set within the context of the goals, culture, and value system in which they exist. It reflects an individual's expectations within the context set by their environment. It reflects a relative aspiration of the individual and their current situations. The closer the two; the better the quality of life. Over time, more dynamic treatments of the concept have emerged that tend to treat it as the ability of an individual to successfully overcome any psychological, social, and physical problems that they may face. Thus, their ability to adapt to changing contexts where an inability to adapt would challenge the individual's satisfaction. There is a belief that quality of life is just one part of wellbeing rather than being a synonym for it. Indeed, these focus on the individual and their needs and not that wellbeing might be linked to broader social functioning. This draws in themes of social wellbeing reflecting the interdependence between social and individual wellbeing where the former has having a bearing upon the latter.

Social wellbeing is important to the stability of social systems in promoting a sense of belonging and fostering interdependence and a sense that an individual can develop a sense of belonging to a community and contribute to it. It stresses the notion that—as a social animal—the individual finds meaning in social interactions through family community and interaction with the broader social system. This depends in turn upon two elements namely social adjustment (the notion that fulfilment is created through social interaction) and social support (reflecting the notion that the individual feels protected and less vulnerable through their integration into social systems. The notion of social wellbeing reflects the importance of the role on the social system and how this acts as a stabilising force upon the citizen, the community and upon the social system. Well-developed social connection adds to social trust and acceptance of potentially divisive issues such as diversity as well as creating trust as well facilitating the exchange of information and promoting collective action. These are based upon an objective list of factors that will drive social wellbeing; these are important as these will feed through into areas of social risk. These revolve around five issues of social wellbeing:

- social integration: this reflects the quality of the individual's relationship with the community and to society more generally. Healthy wellbeing is based on strong links to the rest of society with which the citizen can support and feels supported by the broader community. The higher the degree of estrangement and social isolation the lower individual wellbeing will be reflecting a breakdown in links to the community and an erosion of commonality with a broader group.
- social contribution: this reflects the individual's sense of social value believing that they are an integral and valuable part of the social system. This reflects that individual feels responsible for and to make their contribution to society known reflecting a strong sense of personal responsibility to promote social wellbeing.
- social coherence: this reflects a perception of the quality and capabilities of the social system. This reflects a sense that the individual can understand the social system and the manner in which they are evolving. Through this process meaning can be attained.
- social actualization: this reflects a belief that society is heading in a positive direction and that the individual can be expected to be a beneficiary of this process. This benefit is felt through this process of social evolution allowing both

the individual and the broader community developing new capabilities as a result.
- social acceptance: high levels of social acceptance are linked to higher levels of trust within the group reflecting a process of commonly held belief in mutual support within the community. The more the individual is accepted by the community; the higher the degree of contentment they will feel with regard to their position within it. Also, there is expected to be a high degree of overlap between social acceptance and self-acceptance.

These focus upon relational elements of social capital where wellbeing is reflected within the degree of connectedness between social agents. These connections are not simply important for mental wellbeing but also play an important part within the physical dimension. Indeed, social connectivity has been widely accepted as having more positive welfare effects than conditions that require clinical treatment. This ties social wellbeing into access to core public services that promote social connectivity and community sustainability. These depend upon access to basic needs services (such as shelter, water, food, etc.); access to and delivery of education to secure opportunities for advancement, and access to facilities to form and maintain social capital.

The link with risk can be expanded by defining that the more wellbeing is being eroded or is perceived as declining the higher the levels of social risk. At the community (meso) level, levels of social exclusion are associated with lower levels of wellbeing creating the risk of social upheaval. At the macro level, high rates of unemployment and poverty can also undermine social wellbeing creating the grounds for high levels of social instability. The more extensive there is dissatisfaction with wellbeing the higher the degree of social risk within and between social systems. The erosion or even absence of these drivers of social wellbeing can be direct contributors to the state of and/or diminution of social cohesion and can create a scenario where citizens fail to create the resources to generate social capital to become fully integrated into the social system. This can mean wellbeing creates a self-fulfilling prophecy where the absence and/or loss of wellbeing is self and/or socially reinforced. The broader social risk from lower social wellbeing can also be expressed through a lack of trust or of an acceptance of diversity within social systems. These underscore the importance of social division within the system and where wellbeing is undermined where individuals are excluded and that this is symptomatic of violence against this group. This reflects those social relationships can produce both positive and negative results. This reflects remoteness from social services but also how safe and secure the place is. Thus, it reflects the sense that someone's life is worthwhile. This reflects a strong notion here that wellbeing is derived from a broad sense of social wellbeing. These themes reflect and overlap with the notions of inequality expressed above.

Global Health Security

The legacy of the COVID pandemic was an increased focus upon health security. This reflected the degree of preparedness for the on-set of disease within a population. As such, it stands a good proxy for the degree of risk attached to the health system. The focus is upon systemic resilience to large-scale onslaught of a future mass outbreak of communicable diseases and how national health systems can cope with such pressure. Generally, the more able a state can cope with such pressures the more secure the health system is and therefore the lower the risk of cascade effects created by the outbreak and spread of a virulent disease. This reflects not simply that there is the physical capacity to cope with a surge in numbers but also that these responses are not subject to political risk factors. These political risk factors are created through an amalgam of considerations such as public trust in government, anti-science sentiment, and attitudes to the restrictions of social interaction generated as a policy response to curtail the spread of contagious diseases. This was evidenced in the US where there is a substantive minority view on the rights and efficacy of either vaccinations or lockdowns despite there being a high surge in capacity. This underlines the interface between political risk and social risk in the conditions of rising health risk. It was evident that many responses of states to COVID were short term with limited long-term engagement to deal with an on-going risk with regard to a resurgence of coronaviruses.

Overall, Global Health Security is based around six hard and soft components:
1. Prevention through proactive science and research to understand future risks of pandemics and where and when they might emerge.
2. Detection and reporting to ensure effective and on-going testing and effective surveillance.
3. Rapid response to limit spread and to control at source supported by emergency planning.
4. Healthcare system that has capacity to cope with surges and has sufficient resources to engage in counteracting measures (such as vaccine support)
5. A commitment to adopt national norms, financing to support resilience
6. Risk environment dependent upon political and social attitudes to counter measures.

Based on these criteria the top and bottom-ranked states with regard to health security are reflected in ◘ Table 7.8. These reveal the usual developed/developing country split with those states who are facing the most extreme political and economic turbulence showing the least secure health systems. An evident outlier in this analysis is Thailand which scored a high ranking due to its high rates of rapid response and effective testing infrastructure system. No state is perfect with regard to managing Global Health Security. Public debt in the aftermath of the crisis as well as other issues is hampering fully engaged monitoring and surveillance. This has been compounded by a need to direct resources to those health concerns that were neglected during the pandemic and by increased political risk surrounding the re-adoption of such measures again. The vulnerable segments of the population are still not being afforded special protection/treatment and inter-state co-operation remains limited.

Conclusions

Social risk has conventionally been an issue that has been the almost sole preserve of the state. Rising social connectivity created through global diasporas, international migration as well as other forces has rendered social risk an issue of global

Global Social Risk

◧ **Table 7.8** The most and least health secure states (out of 195)

Top 10 most health secure countries	Bottom 10—least health secure states
1. United States of America	186. Venezuela
2. Australia	187. Niue
3. Finland	188. Tuvalu
4. Canada	189. Central African Republic
5. Thailand	190. Nauru
6. Slovenia	191. Equatorial Guinea
7. United Kingdom	192. Syria
8. Germany	193. North Korea
9. South Korea	193. Yemen
10. Sweden	195. Somalia

Source Global Health Security Index—2021

concern. This concern is across three main areas: demographic change, health and wellbeing, and inequality. All of these have the potential to disrupt the operation of both national and global social systems. This was evident during the COVID pandemic where what was initially a public health crisis also exposed issues of inequality and differences between demographic groups. Social issues represent a key risk for many states that could easily spill over into increasingly regional risk issues.

Key Points

- Social risks are an increasingly salient feature within the contemporary business environment.
- As societies interconnect so these social risks spread across borders.
- A number of risks are created by common problems across states that render them global by default.
- Social risks can direct impede social cohesion and the development of social capital

Discussion Questions

1. To what extent do you agree with the proposition that the best way to deal with an ageing population is through increased immigration?
2. To what extent is human health and wellbeing being challenged by climate change?
3. What do you believe the 2020/22 COVID pandemic has taught policy makers about the nature of social risk?

Activities

As a group, explore the main business opportunities and challenges that can be expected to emerge from an ageing society.

Summary

Social risk is created when there is an erosion of social cohesion within a social system. This erosion is often created by an erosion of social capital. Globalization has led to an increased globality of social system as connectivity between them increases. Increasing levels of social risk also reflect common global problems that apply across a number of states. This chapter noted that there were three that were proving especially salient in shaping global risk namely demographic change, inequality, and health and wellbeing.

Further Readings

Bell, J. A., & Nuzzo, J. B. (2021). *Global Health Security Index: Advancing Collective Action and Accountability Amid Global Crisis*. Available: ▶ www.GHSIndex.org

Goodhart, C., & Pradham, M. (2020). *The Great Demographic Reversal: Ageing Societies, Waning Inequality, and an Inflation Revival*. Palgrave Macmillan.

Harper, S. (2016). *How Population Change Will Transform Our World*. Oxford University Press.

Honigsbaum, M. (2020). *The Pandemic Century: A History of Global Contagion from the Spanish Flu to Covid-19*. Virgin Digital.

IMO. (2022). *World Migration Review* ▶ www.imo.org

Mares, I. (2003). *The Politics of Social Risk: Business and Welfare State Development*. Cambridge University Press.

OECD. (2021). *Fiscal challenges and inclusive growth in ageing societies* ▶ www.oecd.org

UN. (2022). *World Population Prospects 2022* ▶ www.unorg

Picketty, T. (2017). *Capital in the Twenty-First Century*. Belknap Press.

Useful Web Sites

1. The World Inequality Database (▶ https://wid.world/) offers range of data measuring and analysing inequality.
2. The Global Demographic Database (▶ https://www.globaldemographics.com/) offers a range of data upon the form and nature of demographic change.
3. The World Health Organization (▶ www.who.int) explores a range of topics on human health and wellbeing.
4. The UN Population division (▶ https://population.un.org/wpp/) offers a range of data on global population.
5. OECD—▶ www.oecd.org—offers range of population data mainly upon developed states.

Technological Risk

© The Author(s), under exclusive license to Springer Nature Switzerland AG 2023
C. Turner, *Global Business Analysis*,
https://doi.org/10.1007/978-3-031-27769-6_8

"It's not technology that does the harm, It's the person wielding it."

Abhijit Naska

> At the end of this chapter, the reader will be able to understand:
> - the form and nature of the global technology system and the role of change within it.
> - that technological change can generate risks to the operation of the global economic, social, and political systems.
> - the form and nature of technological risk.
> - that technological risk is a dynamic process that evolves with the underlying technological system.

Introduction

Technology in its broadest sense is defined as involving the deployment of scientific knowledge for the purposes of enabling, supporting, and enhancing human activity. This involves the manipulation of the human environment to support better fitness between humans and their environment. This reflects that the human environment is dynamic and requires the on-going application and update of technological solutions to ensure that humanity continues to exist and prosper. Expressed in these terms, it is evident why advances in technology are seen as universally socio-economic goods. It is widely acknowledged that there are risks associated with technological change which has the potential to disrupt the operation of the global system. Moreover, the risk from technological change comes not just from the application and widespread deployment of technology but also from attitudes to technology which is broadly representative of an emergent (albeit still limited) ant-science narrative. This chapter—after an initial examination of the form and nature of the global technological system—as well as the risks within it—will move onto examine the main contemporary technological risks in the global system.

The Global Technological System

The technological system emerges around a particular technology to support its development and roll out. By 2022 (and as reflected within ◘ Table 8.1), there were widely accepted to be 30 different types of technology. These can often be overlapping and mutually supportive. This exhaustive list highlights the diverse pattern of technology across a range of activities. Evidently there are some that are very sector-specific whilst others (notably information technology) underpin many of the other technical systems. This reflects a broader technological system based on the interconnections and interdependencies between these different technical systems; to the extent that the health of one can impact upon the performance and functioning of another. Thus, the technological system is a system of systems.

In each of these technologies, a technological system has emerged to support the development of these respective fields. The nature of a technological system is based on a set of interconnected components that are configured to attain a set and defined role. To attain the set function, the technological system will need to pos-

Table 8.1 Recognized types of technology systems

Entertainment	Educational	Forensic science
Assistive	Architectural	Vehicular
Operational	Medical	Environmental
Agricultural	Product and food	3D printing
Superintelligence	Communication	Sports
Robotics	Construction	Military
Artificial Intelligence	Aerospace	Industrial and Manufacturing
Space	Blockchain	Electrical engineering
Information	Hospitality	Quantum
Business	Biotechnology	Marine

sess the capability to alter, control, and move materials, energy, and/or data/information. This is based upon the utilization of seven types of resources integral to any technological system namely:
1. People (designers, operators, and customers).
2. Information (scientific and technical).
3. Materials (natural and human created).
4. Tools and machines.
5. Energy.
6. Capital.
7. Time.

The utilization of these resources reflects that technological systems are based upon interactions between economic, political, social, and ecological systems. This reveals that technical systems also need to reflect prevailing social-cultural norms and to be underpinned by an effective legislative system to promote, monitor, and protect the political, social, and economic sub-systems. The treatment of technology as a system is based upon breaking the system down into five interdependent components namely:

– Goals: what is the defined objective of the technology.
– Inputs: What inputs are required to meet the objectives both in terms of human, physical, and financial capital. These reflect the specialist knowledge to develop and/or comprehend a technological system.
– Processes: from the research and development process through to prototypes and eventual products this component reflects a legacy of the interaction between inputs and stated goals to generate process of invention and innovation. These reflect the transformation process from inputs into outputs.
– Outputs: the result of the processes is development of an intended product that can demonstrably address the stated needs to be addressed at the outset. This stage involves both positive (i.e., the product) and negative outputs (e.g., pollution) that emerge as an consequence of the process.
– Feedback and control: these reflect a desire that the system is still fit for purpose over time and that any changes necessary feed back into the system. Control reflects a desire that the technological system maximizes positive outputs and minimizes negative outputs.

These components stress both hard and soft components to a technological system and that no components exist independently of any other. As a system, each of these components can be the preserve of a given agent thus this system approach comprises a network of agents all interacting to attain a stated goal. At the level of the state, the aim is to create technological systems as a public policy goal to ensure that they are not simply encouraged to address defined goals but that the technology and know-how generated within the system has the capacity to be diffused through a state's social-economic structures. In terms of both research/technology networks and the process of diffusion, it is increasingly the global/international level that is the focus of activity as there is a desire to tap into global know-how and to also spread the outcomes. Underpinning this notion of technology as a system is that it is dynamic and operates as a system for innovation and change (see below). Looking at the technological system as a dynamic entity, there are widely accepted to be five phases to the development of a technological system. These are reflected within Table 8.2.

The key facet of the process is that these technological systems are both functionally and spatially complex. They are functionally complex in the sense that these different systems are integrated through their shared dependence upon common technologies such as software and of the importance of information to making these respective systems work. They are also more spatially complex in that every technological system is based on a global network of competences that are dispersed across the global system. This reflects not just global dispersion of research and knowledge creation but also that these dispersed systems interact based on agreed interoperability and interconnection to create a common platform for

Table 8.2 Phases of development of technological system

Phase		
1	Invention	New and radical innovations stimulate the creation of a new system. The innovation is based upon a perceived and unmet socio-economic need
2	Development	The innovation seeks to become embedded within socio-economic systems to demonstrate utility and commercial value to attract scaling up of innovation
3	Innovation	This is the phase in which the technological system emerges as the innovation matures and a network of companies is formed to produce, market, and develop the product and its links to other components
4	Technology Transfer	The technology becomes larger than one company (or set of companies) and transfers into a larger socio-economic context. This can often require harmonization/standardization of components and may need to be underpinned by regulation/legislation to protect intellectual property and to restrain market power
5	Growth, Competition, and Stabilization	In this phase, the technological system is at full scale which companies exhibiting economies of scale and firms seek to control more aspects of the system

development and future innovation. This creates a common shared system which firms can adapt to allow the benefits of technology to be dispersed throughout the global economy.

Technological Change and the Global System

The embedded logic of the technological system is of the dynamics that are central to the systems operation. These system dynamics are a core driver of change within each of these systems. At meta levels of analysis, the forces of change within each of these dynamic systems and their interconnections and interdependencies work to create a broader system-wide process of change. Thus, as reflected within Table 8.3, the process of technological change is an on-going process of invention, development, and innovation that leads to better products and/or processes that can be readily dispersed and absorbed across the global system. This links technological change to socio-economic and ecological change. Integral to this process are broader system dynamics and the need of humanity not merely to retain fitness to their environment but also where necessary—though technological change—to improve it. Thus, the notion of technological change is not just based on the existence of technology per se but the rate at which it is adopted to the extent that it generates new forms of or alters human activity. Technological change can involve the development of new processes and/or products but also the development of new designs and functions for pre-existing products. These changes create a transformation in both social and economic structures as not just of firms and industries change but the occupational and lifestyle habits of workers/citizens can also be impacted by these processes.

Technological change is endogenous to technological systems as they adapt to changes within the global system. This reflects that the logic of the technological system is being altered by a shifting context and that the system needs to adapt products and/or processes accordingly. In simple economic terms, technological change is linked to improvements in productivity. That is the ability to deliver more

Table 8.3 Impact of technological system upon other global sub-systems

Sub-system	Indicative technological system impact
Economic	• Promote efficiency in existing industries • Promote emergence of new high technology industries
Political	• Promote widespread political engagement • Promote better reach for political messaging • Promote political stability through closer monitoring of dissident groups
Social	• Use of information technologies to promote social interaction • Provide better access to critical public services • Offer improved healthcare • Online learning facilities • Anti-ageing technology
Ecological	• Use of geo-engineering to mitigate effect of climate change Expansion of green technologies that are less resource intensive in production and consumption

Table 8.4 Overlapping innovation cycles and industrial revolutions

Innovation Cycles		Industrial Revolutions			
Innovation wave (date)	Associated Innovations	Industrial revolution	Underpinning technological system	Geographic scale	Commercial logic
First (1785–1845)	Waterpower, Textiles. Iron	Industry 1.0	Mechanization and steam and waterpower	Industrial cities	Substation of labour by capital
Second (1845–1900)	Steam power, Rail, Steel,	Industry 1.0/ Industry 2.0	Mechanization and emergent mass production	Industrial regions	Attaining scale economies
Third (1900–1950)	Electricity, Chemicals, Internal Combustion Engine	Industry 2.0	Mass production and adoption of electricity as energy source	Industrial regions/wider value systems	Attaining scale economies
Fourth (1950–1990)	Petrochemicals, Electronics, Aviation	Industry 2.0/ Industry 3.0	Widespread mechanization, automation, and emergent digitization	Global Production Networks	Minimizing input costs
Fifth (1990–2020)	Digital networks, Software, new media	Industry 3.0	Electronic and IT systems, increased automation	Global Value Chains	Attaining extra value added
Sixth (2020–?)	Artificial intelligence, internet of things, Robots, Drones, Clean tech, autonomous vehicles, 3d Printing	Industry 4.0	Cyber physical systems, robotization, On-demand availability of computer system resources, Cognitive computing	Global virtual system of value creation	Value creation based on ubiquity of knowledge

output with less input. These processes of technological change at the system level occur in waves (these are reflected in Table 8.4). These highlight the spread of technology throughout a system and that whilst technological change is an on-going feature of the global system it is by no means constant. Indeed, the adoption of technologies is uneven over space and time and this unevenness is due to temporal variations in external pressures at both the micro and the macro-economic level and the capabilities to adapt are uneven between states. These trends reflect those technological changes that have system wide effects and whose impact will be largely universal. Technological change is built upon the pre-condition of a set of hard and soft technical infrastructure (see ▶ Chapter 9) to support and enable this process. At the soft end of the process, change requires a series of institutions that facilitate and embed technological change. This includes the protection of intellectual property rights and contract law that facilitate the cycle of change noted within ◘ Table 8.4. This must be supported by a physical system across social and economic infrastructure such as research facilities, high speed communication channels, etc.

Being embedded within a global technological system shapes the form and nature of technological change. The result is that the most technological change is the result of imported technology with few states being active in innovating. Consequently, adaptation can be costly with the result that there is resistance to the process with government intervention often necessary to act as a catalyst to the process to overcome national-level inertia. This reflects the potential for the technological change to be disruptive upon existing socio-economic structures. This change can be resisted at the micro and macro levels which limits the process of change. Increased competition (both political and economic) could be a catalyst for states to seek to stimulate the process.

The Nature of Technological Risk

Within contemporary narratives, technological risk is shaped by the interface between activity within and across the global sub-systems and the rapidly evolving information system. This reflects that technological risk is historically contingent. Thus, at this stage of the innovation cycle—as reflected within ◘ Table 8.4—the increasing level of embeddedness of information and associated technologies is creating a new, emergent set of risks. Ultimately, the nature of the risk created by this process of technological change rests less upon the existence of technology per se and more upon how and the extensiveness with which it is used within and across global sub-systems. Broadly, technological risks can be subdivided into several types:

- Generic technological risks: these are risks that are a general consequence and legacy of any form of technological change.
- Technology-specific risks: these are risks that are created through the embeddedness of technology within global sub-systems.
- Sub-system-specific risks: these are risks created within a particular sub-system and that are normally limited to that system.

In broad terms, technological risk reflects the perception that the adoption of new technologies creates an adaptation problem in that the new technology has the potential (both known and unknown) to disrupt activity within and the performance of the global system or a component of it. In part, the stimulation of technological change will have some anticipated consequences as the technology is adopted to improve system performance and fitness. In these instances, there is often a time lag between technological change and the ability of any given system to readily adapt to its consequences. In many cases, the impact of technological change creates risk by agents losing fitness with their environment. Throughout history there have been numerous incidents of labour-saving technology being deployed and a lag between redundant labour and its ability to be redeployed in other activities. These actions have shown to create rising social and political risks. Whilst technological change is seen as a socio-economic good, these impacts are not universal across the socio-economic strata. Technological risks are not solely shaped by the pattern and process of adaption they are also generated by technology failing or not operating in the intended or predicted manner.

These themes reflect the above point that technological risk is shaped not by the existence of technology per se but by how it is used and how this deployment impacts upon other sub-systems. These risks—as noted below—can be transitory (that is as systems adapt to the on-set of the new technology with the risk shaped by the period of adaptation) and long-term where the systems do not adapt in the anticipated manner. Broadly, technology has been widely assumed to create five types of risk:

- Unintended and unwanted consequences from the utilization of an otherwise beneficial technology. This could be due to the technology usage being difficult to control.
- The known and understood (and therefore acceptable) risk from the deployment of a technology where such negative externalities are more than compensated by positive effects.
- The risk created through the intended use of a technology where such technologies are designed to impact negatively upon human activity.
- Transition risks created as new technologies are adopted at uneven paces across a socio-economic system and where different parts of the system adapt at different rates creating short-term problems areas of the labour force for example.
- The ability of society to continually develop, accept, and absorb new technologies with its implications for socio-economic structures.

Technology risk can therefore be created by perception as to whether adoption is too fast or too slow, whether impact upon pre-existing systems is too radical, or if the negative externalities can be too great to bear.

The main technological risk associated within the current rapidly evolving global information system is addressed later within this chapter. This section will deal with the main generic risks that can be applied across all forms of technological change. In many cases, these themes will be reflected within many of the specific risks associated with the current wave to technological change. However, it is worth noting their generic salience at this juncture. These technological risks operate across each of the identified global sub-systems.

Economic

Whilst technological change is seen as an economic good promoting competitiveness, long-term growth, and sustainable employment, there will inevitably be losers from the process. The structural change within the economic system because of this process will render some firms obsolescent and expose the activities of others as senescent. The economic risk created by this process of change is a function of ease of adaptability of economic structures. This reflects how quickly workers can be retrained and redeployed and how quickly an impacted firm can adapt processes to shifting context. There is also economic risk created by other vulnerabilities created by the deployment and absorption of new technologies such as efficacy of usage and/or misuse by users. There is also economic risk created by choosing the incorrect technologies upon which to promote change especially where that technology can be rapidly superseded by a better newer form of the technology.

Social

Where innovation has the power to disrupt economic structures, then there is often a direct legacy for social structures especially where economic systems are not quick to adapt. Where socio-economic systems do no adapt rapidly to technological change there is the risk of the social fabric and therefore social capital being eroded. Moreover, as any technological change produces both winners and losers so levels of inequality could also increase further eroding the coherence of social systems. The legacy of social risk in these incidences is created not merely by the legacy of unemployment and social fragmentation but also through the emergence of social alienation where varied tasks are replaced by repetitive and mundane tasks. There is also the risk that technological change could increase fragmentation by accident as technological change alters the form and nature of social interaction. This has the potential to alter many aspects of the operation of social systems. Ultimately, the impact upon social risk of any technological innovation is uncertain at the point of its adaptation and absorption. These risks become evident as the pattern and form of usage become evident and how they reshape socio-economic life.

Political

In many cases, political risks created by technological change feed off the socio-economic processes identified above. The political risks created by this process reflect, first, the extent to which these changes can generate political unrest. There is a risk where new technologies are introduced into highly unionized and labour-intensive activities there could be a political pushback at local and national levels as a large-scale loss of employment in localities with mono-economic structures. The result could be civil unrest and an emergent anti-technology sentiment. Anti-technology sentiment could also be driven by higher levels of social conservatism and anti-modernity sentiment. This could lead to the rejection of new technologies.

Ecological

Successive innovation cycles and processes of technological change have repeatedly introduced technologies that have been widely adopted that have increased the levels of ecological risk over the long term. This was evident across all the first four waves of innovation that involved products created from processes that involved the extraction and mass burning of fossil fuels. This was especially evident in the production of iron and in the evolution of mass transportation systems. Other than localized pollution and other forms of ecological degradation, these issues were either ignored or not fully understood at the time. The legacy of these ecologically harmful technological changes has become widely understood and is at the forefront of the latest innovation cycle as these innovations seek to mitigate these legacy risks.

Technological

There is also the risk that technological change creates its own technological risks. These are created through technological failure or where investment in research towards the development of technology proves fruitless. There is also the risk that technology develops at a rate where it begins to pose a risk to humanity. This remains a fear with regard to artificial intelligence or of military capabilities.

Technological Risk in the Fourth Industrial Revolution

Much of the contemporary narrative with regard to technological risk is shaped by the on-set of the so-called 'Fourth Industrial Revolution' (4IR) and its evolution from the preceding 'Third Industrial Revolution' which developed and deployed many of the technologies upon which the succeeding revolution is based. A common feature of much of the current technological paradigm is the interconnected nature of the technology system underpinned by the sheer pervasiveness of digital technologies as a processing tool or simply as a means to store and move information globally. This is based upon the current innovation cycle based upon the fusion of digital, physical, and biological spheres and its application to manufacturing. It is accompanied by the rise of artificial intelligence and of the penetration and absorption of internet-based technologies into an ever-increasing range of everyday activities through the evolution of the so-called 'internet of things (IOT)'. This process of change is based on seeking to increase the efficiency and effectiveness of human activity through:

- The Interconnection of all components (tangible/intangible, human/machine, different modular devices) to enable effective communication via an embedded internet system.
- The ability of information to be transparent, collectable, and accessible to all users to facilitate more informed decisions and improve system functionality.
- The ability of the technical system to support human engagement in the use and deployment of this information.
- The increase in decentralized decision making by both humans and automated systems.

The risks embedded within Fourth Industrial Revolution are seen as especially risky to human activity. This is due to the belief that:

- They contain a destructive potential that can be both powerful and difficult to control.
- These technologies have penetrated deep into many socio-economic which have become dependent upon certain technologies which could render them vulnerable.
- The failure of a single component could create cascade effects throughout the global system.

Technological Risk

The 4IR is associated with 12 technologies in particular—3D Printing, geo-engineering, advanced materials and nanomaterials, AI/Robotics, Biotechnologies, energy capture and storage, virtual and augmented realities, space technologies, new computing technologies, neurotechnology, IOT, and blockchain technology (see
 Fig. 8.1). The 4IR is a fusion of these technologies. These technologies are all underpinned by digital innovation within the global system where this allows the rapid processing and utilization of data, information, and technology. Of these technologies, the following section will focus upon those where there is the greatest evidence of risk. This risk can often overlap between these technologies but nonetheless each poses an actual and potential threat to the system both in terms of transitory and long term. The focus in this section is upon those technologies where the systemic risk is most evident.

 Fig. 8.1 The main fourth industrial revolution technologies

Technological Risk as Digital Risk

The common theme across all these technologies and the one that underpins each of them is digitization. Evidently this link is more obvious in some than others but in each the technology exists either as a form of digital technology or is one where digitization is a core enabler of the development, deployment, and utilization of this technology. This digitization process is embedded within the global technological system as these processes are based upon the global exchange of digitized content based on global connectivity. Thus, within the 4IR it can be credibly argued that technological risk is largely synonymous with the risks to and within digital systems. Indeed, all the risks addressed below are directly derived from the development and deployment of digital technology. Therefore, in this context, digital risk is defined as the expected and unexpected multi-scalar consequences of the widespread utilization of digital technologies and processes. The pervasiveness of digital technologies within socio-economic strata means that the impact of these technologies can be extensive. However, the scope of this chapter only allows room for the examination of the major anticipated risks from the process.

As for a form of technological risk, digital risk can be categorized into two overlapping types (■ Table 8.5):

— Structural Digital Risk: these are risks posed to socio-economic and political systems due to the failure and/or malfunction of the physical digital capital that supports human activity. This can be due to simple physical capital failure or human activity (accidental or through explicit intent) to damage the physical infrastructure supporting the digital system. These risks are also created where the physical system is absent and/or not performing as expected.

— Usage Digital Risk: this risk stresses that the risk created within the digital system is created by the nature of how the deployed technology is used and/or abused to alter the functioning of socio-economic and/or political systems in manner that can be anticipated or unanticipated. Often this 'usage' based digital risks can be indirect effects upon the system as a result of their deployment and utilization.

The following risks cut across both these broad typologies.

Automation/Robotization

A first key trend (which overlaps with the rise of AI—see below) which poses a risk for the global system is the more expansive use of automation and robotics within the manufacturing sector. Contemporary robotics are characterized as intelligent machines that can comprehend and react to their operating environment largely independently of human instruction. This ability to act autonomously separates these technologies from others. This technology has become increasingly widespread with their deployment increasing markedly with their usage in manufacturing increasing at over 20 per cent per annum. Not only is their usage increasing but robotics is growing increasingly sophisticated with more flexibility and adaptability with many being able to mimic biological structures. Moreover, the spread of cloud infrastruc-

Table 8.5 Major multi-scalar 4IR Technological Risks

	Micro	Meso	Macro	Meta
Cyber Risk	• Loss of IPR • Theft of intangible resource Promotion of extreme perspectives • Loss of privacy through data theft IPR Theft • Loss of personal data privacy • Indirect—damage to systems impedes upon health of citizens	• Disruption of logistics systems • Create risk of community disruption • Erosion of social capital/cohesion • IPR theft of collaborative research • Damage to health of community form attack on major facility	• Hinder activity through disruption of energy systems • Theft of military intelligence • Cyber attack on security capabilities • Corruption of autonomous hardware • Increased social risk through international erosion of social capital Attack on critical infrastructure • Cyber attack on security capabilities • Corruption of autonomous hardware • Increased social risk through international erosion of social capital	• Economic contagion between states through hindering resource and trade flows • Lack of regulation of cyber currencies • Can trigger international conflict • Create transnational social movements—disruptive to state management • Attack shared systems through multiple denial of service
Technological Fragmentation	• Users have to choose given standard • Can limit functionality within firms • Hinder cross border communication • Limit global market for technology	• Hinder intra-partner data flows • Limit cross border multi-party	• States compelled to choose a system • Limit access to latest innovations • Hinder scaling up of new technologies	• Create conflicting technology systems • Limit global interoperability and interconnectivity
IOT Risk	• Increased scope for security breaches • Conflict between data owners and data collector	• Security breaches can erode trust between partners • Lack of agreed principles on privacy and security protocols	• Security risks • Control of data by supplier from rival power	• Fear of control of technology creates fragmentation • Limit movement of data

(continued)

Table 8.5 (continued)

	Micro	Meso	Macro	Meta
Digital Inequality	• Reinforce social exclusion • Limit human capital skills • Limit social	• Erosion of social capital • Limit social connectivity	• Sustain rural–urban divide • Regional inequality • Feed social risk as reinforce social exclusion	• Uneven development of technological system • Promote uneven economic development • Limit flows of data across borders
Techno-scepticism	• Limit personal corporate access to key enabling technologies	• Create social disconnectivity between and within social and economic groups	• Limit level of technological development • Limit system functionality • Create social and political risks	• Create uneven development of technological system • Limit interoperability and interconnection

ture and AI is enabling robots to access information and eschew the need to be programmed via an autonomous device. The drivers behind this trend towards the increased use of robotics are manifold but the core common drivers are:

1. Improving the quality and consistency of products through enhanced precision, reliability, and monitoring. These are compounded by erosion of bad practices.
2. Enhanced productivity by increasing speed and length of operation as automated robots do not require breaks or shift changes.
3. Better safety as there is less scope for human error and injury especially when production must occur under conditions which could be deemed hazardous. Moreover, robots can be managed remotely.
4. Lower labour costs reflect lower variable costs from the on-going deployment and utilization of industrial robots.
5. Manufacturing becomes less driven by the lowest labour costs and more by skills. This reflects the ability of developed states to restore competitive advantage in manufacturing.

These changes must be counterbalanced by the high initial costs involved, the need for expertise to maintain this capital equipment and on-going costs of operation. Nonetheless these perspectives reflect that the rise of automation is an economic good. AI is a development that will enable the economic system to work more effectively and to improve the allocation of resources within it. This process reflects a long-standing process of technological change which has seen capital replace labour within the production process. This has been a perennial feature of the successive cycles of innovation. The most evident impact both over the short and long term is the impact of automation on employment. As highlighted within ◘ Fig. 8.2, there are jobs at risk from the process of change and many of these tend to be in the low-skilled, low-wage segments of the labour force. These are areas where the

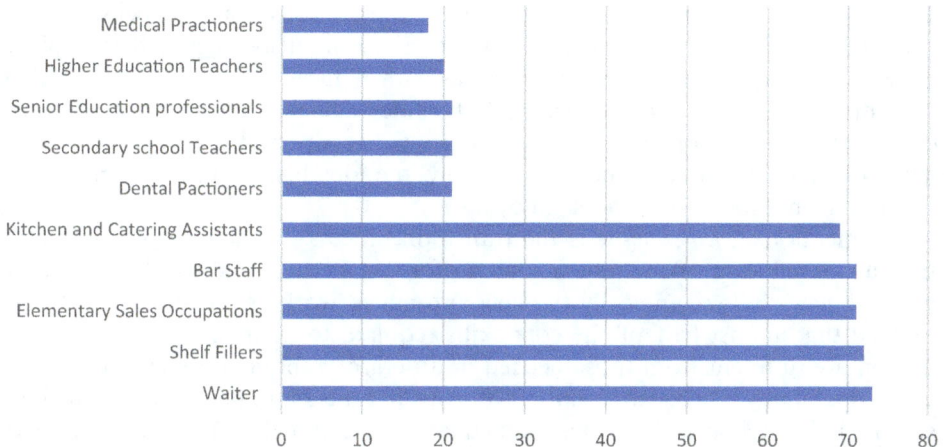

Fig. 8.2 Jobs at risk from automation (*Source* Office of National Statistics)

occupation is also repetitive and simple. This impact upon employment is not solely linked to the physical action of labour that is to be replaced but also increasingly the mental and processing capabilities undertaken as part of the production process. This impact where automation destroys employment for those workers with little alternative forms of employment often allow these changes to be treated as a zero-sum game. Those that advance the cause of automation argue that the process can also be job creating in allowing new forms of employment to emerge. This means those jobs that remain within manufacturing production will be more highly skilled and better paid. The new forms of work required an adaptation that can often be problematic. This reflects the often transitory and potentially long-term impact of these changes upon social system as lack of adaption leads to social isolation. This process could also lead to increased inequality between those that can adapt or are ready for the new technology and those that are simply left behind by the process. Overall, it is estimated only 5 per cent of jobs are fully automatable with an estimated 30 per cent of any job could be done autonomously. The OECD estimates that 14 per cent of jobs are at high risk from automation.

Automation was meant to be of benefit to humanity through relieving the workforce of the need to do routine, dangerous, and heavy work. Its extension into more areas where workers have little fallback for other forms of employment that require an upskilling does create new social risks. Thus, something that was meant to improve human existence could worsen it. This reflects the on-going belief that it is not technology that is detrimental; it is how it is applied and utilized. The need for human endeavour to maintain, sustain, and repair these machines can lead to alternative forms of mental pressure given the demanding working conditions.

Automation has the risk of meaning that some workers lose fitness with their environment. It is estimated that up to a third of workers will be impacted by the on-set of automation by 2030. As suggested within ◘ Fig. 8.2, this is not just production tasks within manufacturing but also within the service sector too. Notably in areas such as driving where the rise of autonomous vehicles opens the prospect of truck drivers being rendered obsolete. Evidence also suggests that displaced workers also suffer long-term health issues with reduced life expectancy and high mortality rates. These social effects can also filter down to family structures where displaced workers also suffer increased risk of diversity and their children's lower levels of educational attainment. Ultimately, the jobs lost to automation are very different from those that are created by it.

As mentioned, a key issue is the transition process. In the case of automation this can be reflective of the time the labour force (especially that which is displaced) gain the new skills required by the new automated working environment. It is estimated that almost half of the core skills required to flourish in an era of automation are different from those needed in an era of robotic automation. In many cases, this simply reflects an evolution of skills in others it requires wholesale repositioning. These issues also exacerbate equality as automation falls more upon unskilled occupations which tend to employ otherwise excluded groups. Thus, reinforcing social divides. Those occupations most at risk tend to be those done by women and young people. Traditionally welfarism has mitigated these effects through education and training systems. These systems have been eroded overtime. Human wellbeing could also be eroded through the possibility that through eliminating task it increases level of human inactivity and leads to an erosion of mental stimulation. The resultant boredom could also increase health and wellbeing problems. This is compounded by the potential risk to social capital and cohesion if it leads to social fragmentation.

Artificial Intelligence

Whilst many of the themes within the legacy of automation reflect a long-standing process of technological change where capital replaces labour within the production process on the pretext of enhancing productivity, this trend towards automation is also reflective of the rise—as mentioned—of artificial intelligence (AI). Expanding upon the foregoing analysis, this section briefly examines in more detail the systemic risks that could emerge from the widespread deployment of AI. AI is based upon the creation of software that is fully capable of undertaking autonomous thought process and being able to interact with human conversations and pre-empt human decision making. This is based upon the software being able to identify patterns and as a result being able to automate processes. Through these processes AI can mimic human mental processes. AI is finding an increased range of uses within both manufacturing and service sectors. This has led to the long-mooted development of driverless cars, drones, and virtual assistants. The rise of AI has not merely been enabled by the development of more sophisticated software that can pre-empt human decision making but also by the sharp increase in the quantity of data that enables these autonomous decisions to be made with increased accuracy. Machines have the capability to learn from this vast amount of data to form decisions based upon patterns that predict how humans would have behaved. This allows self-programming and for these devices to find the optimal solutions to given problems.

The benefits of the deployment and development of AI exist mainly at the micro level through enhancing the performance of business. Indeed, many of the benefits of AI are broadly true of those that are available to the deployment of more advanced technology generally such as improving efficiency of the production processes, replacement of routine tasks, and lower production costs. Additionally there are advantages from AI that are unique to this form of technology namely that:
- It is scale and efficient and can be trained to both routine and complex task repeatedly without tiring operating 24 hours a day seven days a week.
- It can reduce and even eliminate human error through its inability to replicate human frailties such as a lapse in concentration, becoming tired or through having their mental health adversely effected by ecological conditions in so doing it further lowers human risk.
- They can improve human decision making and workflows through the ready identification of patterns that would not be easily acknowledged by human capacity thus enabling better.
- It can improve the efficacy of machinery.
- It can handle volumes and types of data that are beyond the ready comprehension and processing by humans.

In addition, in knowledge-based organizations AI can provide permanency by compensating for the loss or absence of an individual. Moreover, the learning capacity of the system can allow the product life to be extended.

With regard to the negative effects, there are evident expected impacts with regard to loss of employment within routine tasks being undertaken by autonomous technology. There is the fear that the extension of AI deeper into economic structures could extend its impact beyond these areas where technology conventionally has an impact into more professional occupations. There is also the fear that the resultant technological employment could be permanent as AI proves that it is more than capable at doing jobs better than humans across an increasingly diverse range of occupations. Indeed, AI could be better at doing the jobs that technological change is meant to create. This could create a long-standing lack of fitness between citizens and the evolving technological system.

A deeper fear with regard to the embeddedness of AI reflects a long-standing fear that autonomy of machines based on AI could lead to increase independence from humanity leading to a diminished degree of control over these technologies. Thus, over the long term, there is a fear that these machines could diverge from human control. This reflects a belief that AI machines could become dangerous when either they are programmed to be destructive or this destruction happens as an unforeseen side effect of the utilization of AI. This also reflects that—in delegating decisions to machines—we are doing so to devices that have no emotions and which lack the spontaneity that can drive innovation and change and that over the long term these devices can become divorced from human control. This means there has to be a clear alignment between human goals and the goals of machines with AI programmed in such a way that the machine may not be able to find a way to achieve these goals that are not undesirable. This represents a 'value alignment' problem. On top of this there are ethical considerations with regard to when machines become sentient and when they become subject to specified rights but also a belief that machines undertake and formulate moral and ethical decisions.

These reflect that there are long-standing concerns with regard to security and safety issues in the deployment of AI. This could be especially salient where machine learning enables devices to develop their own prejudices and act upon them. This reflects what is seen as the fear that the deployment of AI creates an existential risk for humanity. The increase in autonomy by these devices creates the risk that become super intelligent; that these devices do not merely operate autonomously of humanity, but they do so independently and this creates the risk that the higher degree of intelligence and lack of moral and ethical behaviour could be a supreme challenge to humanity. There are also security risks as allowing military hardware to be driven by AI could lead to adversaries corrupting the data upon which these devices act. This reflects that AI is only as good as the data upon which they act. This reflects there are a number of operational risks from the utilization for AI namely:

- That data can be compromised by poor use and can contravene user confidentiality and create reputational damage.
- That poor data leads to blind spots in AI decision-making.
- That these devices and their operating algorithms could be disrupted and insecure.
- AI models may be operating on poor information causing their behaviour to be erratic and unplanned.
- Humans and AI may interact poorly leading to humans overriding the system possibly mistakenly or when humans dot spot cases where the AI device needs to be overruled.

There has been increased concern that the development of AI can create a 'Turing Trap'. This results from the advent of AI creating new inequalities of wealth and power due to the fact that the process replaces rather than augments labour. The trap emerges due to the belief that these workers replaced have no means to improve their economic, social, and political outcomes due to an embedded lack of power. This is the risk as the potential and actual role for AI within both manufacturing and service sectors increases. These workers whose tasks cannot easily be replaced with AI will benefit from the process. A direct replacement creates losers who are difficult to reabsorb within the labour market. These workers become marginalized as the increase in wealth to those who benefit from this process is coupled within an increase in their political power at the expense of the marginalized.

Cyber Risk

Arguably the greatest technological risk at both the micro and the macro level are those related to the increased dependence of both states and businesses upon cyber systems. The fact that so much activity within each of these levels now depends upon the efficiency of the supporting and enabling Information and Communication Technologies (ICTs) creates a strategic vulnerability for both states and businesses when these systems are disrupted due to both accidental and malicious human activity. These vulnerabilities increased the degree of connectivity between different systems that allows the risk to cascade throughout the system. These attacks exploit vulnerabilities within cyber systems to gain illicit and/or illegal access to

these systems to either destroy, alter, or pilfer this information. This can be attained via attacks on one or more of the following:
- Confidentiality: where the attack seeks to obtain otherwise restricted or confidential information.
- Integrity: there the attack seeks to lower the value of information through its alteration, manipulation and/or its open release to public fora.
- Availability: these attacks seek to deny the owners/users of a system and/or data access to this resource.

Of greatest concerns are cyber attacks which are intentional attacks upon states and commercial cyber systems for the purposes of inducing vulnerability within other agents. These attacks upon micro- and macro-level systems tend to come from four major sources:
1. Nation state actors: these are well-resourced actors seeking to steal IP and/or collect other forms of intelligence to advance their strategic interests.
2. Organized Criminals: these are focused upon financial benefits through using assorted software to penetrate information systems to either extort or directly steal money.
3. Terrorists and/or 'hacktivists': these are groups or individuals who use cyber systems to push a political agenda to both generate fear and disruption within the global system.
4. Insiders: either through incompetence or malevolence insiders can use and misuse networks to destructive effect.

At the criminal level, these attacks can be made to access, manipulate, and control data from other organizations or to undermine the efficacy of core commercial and state infrastructure systems upon which the other agent depends for the effectiveness of their operation. Moreover, from attacking one company's or state's system they can gain access to other systems to create endemic failures.

Whilst there are many types and forms of cyber risks, ENISA has identified that there are eight main types of threats (as of 2021). These are as follows:
1. Ransomware: this is where an agent's data is attacked and encrypted and will only be unencrypted on payment of a fee.
2. Malware: this is software of firm ware that gains unauthorized access to an agent's network and in so doing causes the system to operate in a manner that impacts upon the security, availability, and performance of the system.
3. Crypto jacking: this is where a criminal covertly uses a victim's hardware to generate cybercurrency.
4. Email-related threats: these involved the use of unsolicited emails to introduce viruses and other malware into a network.
5. Threats against data: this can involve data breaches and leaks that lead to the release of sensitive information into unsafe and insecure environments. These can be generated through both intended and unintentional user behaviour.
6. Threats against availability/integrity: these attacks intentionally seek to restrict access to a network and can involve a denial-of-service attack or an attack upon a web site. The net effect is the same namely to reduce the functionality and efficacy of the online resource/capability.

7. Disinformation/misinformation: this is where the system is used to spread false information and alter user behaviour in manner that is not conducive to system stability. This can often occur through phenomena such as social media.
8. Non-malicious attacks: these may involve a direct financial loss or operating difficulty but can be done so as to create a nuisance to the victim and to simply inconvenience them.

This issue of cyber risk has been steadily rising up both state and business agendas. By 2020, it was estimated that the cost of cyber attacks was close to $ 1 trillion. This is almost a 300 per cent increase since 2013. By 2021, the cost of these cyber attacks to the global economy was estimated to be in the region of $ 6 trillion per annum. The seriousness of this threat to all agents is reflected within ◘ Fig. 8.3 which reflects how these risks exist across multiple levels at all scales. This reflects the sheer pervasiveness of cyber risk and how it can have both direct and indirect impacts upon the operation of the global system. Whilst—as mentioned—this risk can impact upon all scales, it is (arguably) at the micro and macro level where these risks are seen with the greatest degree of impact, thus for reasons of brevity these will be the focus of the analysis within this section.

◘ Figure 8.3 indicates the rise in serious cyber attacks over the past decade. This indicates an upwards trend in those attacks that have or had a potentially seriously disruptive impact upon the operation of the global system or of a significant section of it. Of course, by looking at the serious attacks it ignores the high volume of low-level attacks upon individuals and small and medium-sized businesses. These groups are especially vulnerable due to low levels of protection and the sheer volume of attacks to which these agents are exposed. Indeed, it is estimated that nearly half of all attacks are targeted at SMEs. Looking across the business sector more generally, there are widely accepted to be a number of major impacts upon business of the increase in cyber risk.

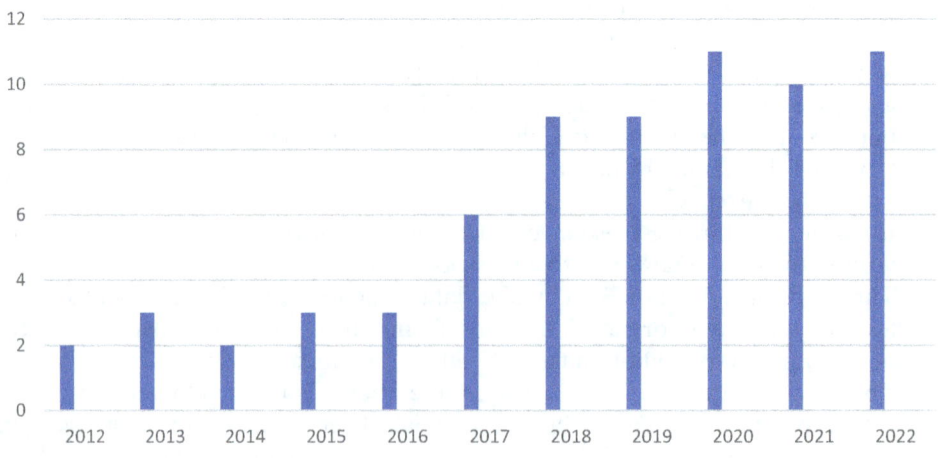

◘ **Fig. 8.3** Average monthly number of serious cyber attacks (*Source* Centre for Strategic and Information Studies)

Increased Cost: the threat of a cyberattack compels business to increase expenditure upon protection. These increased outlays do not merely include the spending upon cybersecurity measures but also those direct and indirect costs that emerge as a result of the cyber breach such as public relations, increased insurance premiums and compensation to victims. These costs are especially evident when Ransomware is deployed against the business and the firm needs to buy off the attacker to resume normality upon its cyber system.

Disrupted operations: the embeddedness of cyber systems within operational systems means that a disruption to the former disrupts the latter. The attack can undermine those systems that operate consumer transactions, relations with key suppliers, and logistical systems.

Adapted Business practices: the actual and/or perception of a cyber threat can lead to businesses adapting their business practices. The obvious example of this is the manner with which they engage with customers especially with regard to the way in which they store their data. In response businesses could become more selective in the type of data they choose to store and how they choose to store it. Some business may also alter their online presence as a response to the risk that they may encounter through such operations. The dependence upon cloud storage is seen as an especial vulnerability for businesses as they move data into server farms (see ▶ Chapter 9).

Reputational damage: this is a much more indirect impact, but the long-term impact of a cyber attack could be to erode the firm's brand equity as it becomes seen as a threat or at least insecurity with regard to customer security and privacy. This can also apply to intra-firm relations which could also be damaged by data breaches by one party.

Erosion of revenue base: a legacy of the reputational damage noted above is that the loss of trust by customers erodes the revenue base of the business as they switch to more reliable and trusted businesses. This reflects a natural desire by these businesses to protect themselves against cybercrime by eschewing any dealings with those who might be insecure.

Loss of intellectual property rights: this is an area where state and business rights overlap. These intangible assets are often a business' most valuable resource. As much of this resource is stored online it becomes vulnerable not just to theft by rivals but also to ransomware where hackers access and control this resource and insist upon a fee to return this material.

Overall, these attacks are becoming more common across a wider range of firms of all sizes and industries than ever before. Sectorally, healthcare, utilities, higher education and banking, and other financial institutions are seen to be especially vulnerable to cyber attacks. Macro-level risks have been to increase in prominence as state security and military infrastructure as well as critical infrastructure are underpinned by their dependence upon cyber systems. The result is that inter-state rivalry and, in some cases, conflict are precluded and often include direct attacks upon a state's cyber systems to render them vulnerable to direct physical attack. These attacks are through:

— Sabotage: where there are direct attacks upon the cyber systems that enable critical infrastructure.
— Espionage: where there are attempts to gain hold of military and other security-sensitive and confidential material.
— Subversion: this aims to facilitate internal dissent to weaken the state form within thorough remote methods through for example viruses or social media.

This security threat is not just created by inter-state relations but could also be shaped by non-governmental actors who could apply to states the very same pressures they apply to corporate actors with regard to the use of ransomware for example. These technologies can also be used to undermine internal security where external agents could use social media to recruit and to ferment social and political unrest within a state through direct attacks or through indirect attacks through campaigns of disinformation for example. These actions by both state and non-state actors being to redefine the nature of the security threat. The security is further threatened when key industries (for example those that provide key technologies) are attacked. At the macro, an issue that is of especial concern is the potential for cyber attacks upon critical infrastructure. These themes are addressed more fully within ▶ Chapter 9.

This trend is only expected to increase as hackers increase in their degree of sophistication. This is no longer a lone wolf attacker. Hacking is now a sophisticated operation that has been scaled up. This increased level of risk has also been enabled by the fact that there is an increased level of activity that now occurs online. This is especially so in the aftermath of the COVID pandemic when more activity moved online, and it became more common. This is further compounded by the fact that regulations and control of cyber risk lag behind the innovativeness of the cyber criminals.

Fragmentation of the Global Technological System

One of the drivers behind the on-set of the information economy is interoperability and interconnectivity between the diverse technologies that underpin its establishment and evolution. It is agreed on common standards across parts of the global system and for tangible and intangible components to move and operate seamlessly across it. It is this seamlessness that allows network effects to be realized that drives the demand for these technologies and allows the production of these technologies to attain economies of scale that facilities their spread and penetration across the global system. Underpinning this process is the existence and acceptance of a set of internationally agreed standards and protocols. These are often agreed though multilateral, multi-sector standards bodies. This system though complex has generated a set of internationally agreed standards that secure both consumer and producer interests and ensure that these interests are aligned with those of states. This seamlessness is increasingly being challenged as the strategic interest of states stares to see a virtue in limiting interoperability and interconnectivity. In part, this does not merely represent diverging interests but also of state competing to gain control of the evolving technological system.

The fact that there is expected to be substantial growth and employment in these technologies means there is a race between states to gain a lead in the development and deployment of these technologies. Indeed, AI is expected to generate $15 billion to the global economy by 2030 and the IOT 13 billion and 22 million jobs by 2035. This has branched over from simple geoeconomics considerations into geopolitics. This reflects that the power of states can increasingly be shaped by their ability to control flows (in this case data) around the global economy. The control and use of data are leading to the fragmentation of the global technology system as states seek to both to expand the access to these technologies domestically and to limit the access to and decrease the efficacy of these technologies to rival states. This leads to an intentional erosion of interconnectivity between states. This interconnectivity does not merely extend to the flow of data between states but is also shaped by the limits placed upon the mobility of IT professionals, technology, and services. This will impact business through increasing IT costs, reducing system functionality, more limited system functionality, and increasing complexity of IT system operations.

These systems are developed by high-technology companies and states will increasingly seek to control and influence their behaviour to seek their geostrategic objectives. These constraints will also reflect divergent attitudes to issues such as personal privacy and security. Reflecting geopolitical themes, larger states are seeking to create technological dependence by smaller states within this fragmenting technological system by encouraging them to adopt a particular system that has limited functionality with other systems. In so doing, they aim to generate a critical mass quicker than their rivals to enable them to become the dominant player in a given technology. Often this is done through granting favourable terms of access to these technologies by the states. This is compounded by the larger states seeking technological independence by limiting access to rival technologies and data into domestic markets.

The danger is that states could use this to not merely extend their influence but could also seek to use it to extend the reach of its values into states who become dependent upon its technologies. This China—for example—is doing through its Digital Silk Road strategy (see ▶ Chapter 9) which is built upon China extending its digital governance to these states where it helps finance local technological infrastructure. For many, this covert intrusion can represent a security threat. The larger states are not just in competition with regard to reach but also with regard to domestic deployment and penetration especially with regard to maintaining a competitive edge not just in economic capacity but also in terms of security capabilities where relative advances can undermine each of these states. For these reasons larger and more powerful states (notably China and the US) are placing restrictions both domestically and within their sphere of influence with regard to the accessibility and availability of 4IR technologies. Inevitably such disputes hinder the capability of the system to develop harmonized norms.

Control and influence over the standards for the emerging technologies underpinning 4IR is a core strategic risk for states. Traditionally the western states took the lead in the development of standards. Over the past two decades, there has been an increased Asian influence over this process notably in Japan, South Korea, and China, where the development of standards by one power could act as a trojan horse for other states. Thereby utilizing these technologies could provide a way for potentially rival states to attack—when and of conflict emerges—to attack critical infrastructure of rival states. With regard to the emerging rivalry between China and the US, there is a fear of the links between some Chinese tech businesses and its government as a direct security threat. For China, these links mean that standards are a route through which it can implement industrial policy. There is a fear that Chinese control of these could lead to digital autocracy. Whether such fears are justified or not, it is leading a western push back to develop rival standards that counter this potential security risk.

The longer-term legacy is the possible creation of a bipolar global technological system. This is created by a coalescence of technological system with military, political, and economic security. One system will be based around western states with the US as its leader and the other around eastern states (Asian/Eurasian states) with China as its leader. The former will be based upon private sector big technology companies; the latter by state-driven development strategies. China's approach to standardization is characterized by the following strategies:

− Protecting and securing the domestic market while accessing the international systems.
− Market-driven whilst being state-led.
− Improve the quality of Chinese products to push them further up industry value chains.
− Aiming to become standard market and exporter than a simple standard taker.

This power to drive the standards of the evolving technological system represents not simply its role in the production in the technologies underpinning this system but also the emerging ownership of the IPR that also underpins its development. To China, this stance simply reflects the market reality of its emergence as a technological powerhouse and that—accordingly—it should have an influence over these processes. To the west, proximity between state and private interests within China has led it to push back against this process pushing for the development of standardized technologies that are more aligned with their interests than those that might source from alternative systems.

One aspect of the technological system where this fragmentation is already evident is in the increased division of the internet. The so-called 'splinternet' is being created by the gradual dissolution of the single interoperable global system into a series of regional networks based upon a divergent set of rules, processes, and protocols. The effect of these divergences is that it is directly hindering the movement of data across the global system. This system is leading to different availability of information across the system and with applications forms in one system being curtailed or even banned in other systems. These are driven largely by state, business, and personal security and privacy concerns due to divergent principles between states on the use and access to such data. Broadly—as per the narrative developed above—it is anticipated that the internet will evolve into two separate systems—one based around US technology and the other around China's. It is expected that each state will have to choose with which system to align. Alongside these broad-based geopolitical trends there are also increased actions by individual states to seek to restrict the flows of data across borders. In other cases, states are seeking to restrict the domestic usage of social media where the utilization of such services could pose a political, social, and/or economic risk. Some states are deeply unsettled upon the global nature of the internet and the potential impact it could have upon domestic stability. Broadly this fragmentation of the internet is of three types:

Technical Fragmentation: These reflect the erosion of common standards that inhibit the ability of modular hardware and software to possess full interoperability and limit end-to-end interconnectivity. These drivers of technical fragmentation are in areas such as internet addressing, interconnection, naming, and security.

Governmental Fragmentation: these are as mentioned the intentional and discretionary acts by government to limit access to internet-enabling technology and to the flow of data within and between states. These actions are across a range of areas including controls of e-commerce, limits to accessible content and censorship, national security, personal privacy, limits on cross border movement of data and divergent national strategies to promote internet penetration and usage.

Commercial Fragmentation: These are actions by businesses to intentionally (for commercial reasons) seek to limit access to specific uses of the internet especially with regard to the creation, distribution, and access to information. These include a range of actions such as developing non-interoperating standards, limiting flows by third parties over infrastructure due to issues of network neutrality, limiting universal access to ensure preferences for subscribers, limiting access to content to specific geographic markets and IPR protection.

The salience of these respective forces as a driver of internet fragmentation depends upon its occurrence (whether it is a theoretical or real action); intent (whether the splitting is an accidental by-product of this action or an intentional strategy); impact (whether the act has a substantive or minimal impact upon internet functioning); and character (whether this fragmentation is to lower political, social, and economic risks). This latter point is important for it reflects that the desire for fragmentation is not always a socio-economic bad as it could be a force for positive social cohesion. Thus, not all free flows of data are positive for all states and there is a need to reflect local sensitivities in the process of managing the evolution of this technological system. These restrictions are not just state-driven. They are also being created by private interests as they seek to protect and monetize their IP. To do so these businesses are looking to close down parts of the internet that are seen to infringe these rights.

At the corporate level, these trends mean that technology businesses have to have an adaptive offering across the different markets in which they operate. It will impact upon operations as well as it will restrict the form and types of data that can be moved across borders so as to support and enable their international activity. It will also facilitate the emergence of regional tech giants rather than companies with a global reach. This reflects that some states do not like the conventional open, multi-stakeholder system of internet governance and would like to see it replaced with one based on inter-state agreement. Creating proprietary standards that limit the efficacy of the global internet is also something that can be labelled at western system whereby the large technology companies have created a network of private networks. Complete separation would be difficult in practice due to the intensity and depth of the interconnections within the global system. On top of this, it is expected that the severing of links could lead to civil unrest. This position is not so much isolation but more an on-going fragmentation as new technologies emerge that do not offer sustained interoperability and interconnection. Moreover, states can still restrict flows of data at their discretion.

Internet of Things (IOT)

The IOT is one of the primary technologies associated with 4IR. It is based upon the interconnection of computer devices (such as smart phones, autonomous vehicles, home appliances, and personal electronic devices) which are embedded within notionally non-IT physical devices which facilitate the gathering and utilization of data from usage without the need for direct human intervention. All of these devices collect data both about users and the environment in which they are operating. By 2020, there were over 50 billion devices connected with an extra 5 billion devices expected to be connected by 2025. These technologies are expected to be especially effective in the retail, residential and home goods, automotive and healthcare industries. These are expected to allow mass customization of services and better consumer experiences. It will also be seen to be of benefit to industry in allowing them to collect more real-time information upon the performance of products and allow them to be improved. It can also allow for improved product maintenance and performance. This reflects a broader view from the industry of a connected life with ubiquitous mobile and physical connections between devices. Broadly the benefits from the spread of IOT are:

- Enhancing technology: improved access to data and its sharing will allow both new and existing technologies to perform better and evolve to customer needs.
- Improving customer relations: IOT allows on-going engagement and feedback to manage and improve customer engagement.
- Better information capture: all information can be captured and directed to the most appropriate body.
- Lower levels of waste: the use of data allows for the more efficient use of resources.

These benefits reflect the core facets of IOT namely that it allows remote monitoring thereby reducing the need for physical trips; allows automation and control through machine-to-machine communication and predictive analysis which allows users to know things in advance.

The risks created by the spread of IOT are a result of largely micro-level processes. Thus, it is at this level where many of the identifiable risks are evident. In many ways, the risk from the IOT represents a continuation of generic internet-based risks embedded within IT systems. The challenge for IOT risk represented is created by the sheer ubiquity and intensity of data flows and how this reshapes the IT risk environment. The categories of risk driven by IOT are highlighted below. These often reflect a number of blanket concerns with regard to IOT namely these devices interact with the physical work in a different way to conventional devices, that they are managed in different ways to conventional devices and that—as a result—the risk within their usage is different.

Ethical IOT Risk

These are created by the expected and unexpected ethical issues created by the deployment of IOT systems. For example, software could be programmed to circumvent environmental laws on emissions.

Security IOT Risk

As per the definition above, this includes those actions via malicious individuals/groups and/or systems that seek to exploit vulnerabilities within the system for the purposes of causing harm to other users. At the micro level, the constant data exchange is open to breaches of security as a lot of data enter the IOT system unencrypted. These security risks are also challenged by the poor monitoring and management of connected devices. This could allow a hostile actor to take control of a device without the user being aware. This is compounded by the fact that under IOT the expansion in the number of attack and data collection points increased this vulnerability. In the automobile industry, there is a fear that hacking could render an autonomous vehicle dangerous as safety procedures are turned off. These could leave the operator vulnerable to ransomware attacks and other forms of cyber attacks. Security seems to be a special problem with nearly 90 per cent of early adopters suffering from some degree of security breach.

Privacy IOT Risk

The rapid and constant exchange of data between devices could lead to an erosion of personal and/or corporate privacy. The erosion of this privacy would be detrimental to the interests of the user. It is often the case, that the frequency and volume of data exchange within the IOT system can mean that privacy breaches can often go unnoticed. The level of data that can be collected from IOT-linked devices is immense as any individual can give away more detail than ever before about the minutiae of their everyday life. These fragmented pieces of information can be agglomerated by government, non-governmental bodies or by criminals. Moreover, the sheer volume of data generated means that the reach of surveillance and tracking of users is also extended enormously. It is widely expected that these privacy threats evolve with the technology underpinning IOT. As with broader use of data to drive e-commerce rights over the use of data are a core driver. This is an especially difficult issue as the intimacy of the data collected from the IOT can be a direct contravention of privacy. As such, these need to be supported by effective data governance.

Technical IOT Risk

This is due to failure of a component of the IOT system (either hardware or software) due to poor design evolution, etc. This risk can be sourced from the connected device itself where vulnerabilities possibly created by its senescence can leave the system open to hackers. Attack can also happen through communication channels connecting IOT devices. The remote deployment of IOT devices leaves them especially vulnerable to attacks.

***

The legacy of these micro-level risks is that they could limit the ability of these IOT technologies to really transform the technological system. It could lead to a suspicion of the development of new technologies and lead to limitations of the on-set of the technologies and furthermore limit the development of new marketplaces. Looking beyond the micro level, these risks can scale up into macro-level risk if it impedes state-level economic transformation. These debates over the supporting (5th generation) mobile technology that underpins the IOT and how this is controlled at the state level has been a factor driving the fragmentation of the system where the lead by Chinese manufacturers (ZTE and Huawei) of this technology has led to some western states either denying access by these suppliers to domestic systems or in some cases actually removing already deployed technology. This reflects both a security concern with regard to the deployment of this technology and also a measure to seek to allow the deployment of 5G technology from either domestic suppliers or suppliers from those states that are deemed friendly. Thus, the risk associated with the deployment of IOT can scale up into a meta-level risk operating as a catalyst to fragment the global technological system.

The Digital Divide

There are long-standing concerns with regard to technological change and inequality especially where the technology becomes general purpose which impacts upon all sections of the global system and its dynamics. In the third industrial revolution, there was inequality in the deployment of digital technology due to inequalities of access usage and outcomes. These continue into 4IR, where during the installation phase—due to technological unemployment—income inequality (due to uneven benefits) and existing social divides are accentuated. Given the centrality of digital technology to the evolving technological system, the unevenness of the digital system across both space and social groups is seen as a core source of risk. In many ways, these reflect a long-standing trend that any technology does not diffuse itself evenly across any system. The pervasiveness of and necessity to access the digital system has given added impetus to erode these inconsistencies across social and economic systems. Importantly it is widely accepted that this uneven technological development can also spread to other sub-systems notably there is a long-standing concern that this digital inequality/digital divide can act as a catalyst for rising levels of social and political risk and hinder economic growth. There has been much debate with regard to differentiating between digital inequality and the digital divide. The former tends to stress unevenness with regard to physical access to the digital system (i.e., limited internet access) whereas the latter is a more evolved concept tending to focus less upon physical access and more upon variations in the benefits to users from accessing the digital system due to differences in what they are able to access and benefit from with regard to the digital system. Thus, the digital divide is informed by four themes namely:

- Motivation and attitude to digital technology.
- Physical access to the technology.
- Digital skills.
- Divergent usage pattern amongst groups.

These differences reflect the gap between individuals, businesses, households, and geographic areas with regard to income, knowledge, relationships, and social capital. These four themes have created a focus upon three types of digital divide within the global system.

- Global Divide

This is the divide between states with regard to the disparities of access to the digital system. Overall, it is estimated that around half the world's population—around 3.7 billion people—do not have access to the internet. Around 80 per cent of these offline communities are in Africa and Asia–Pacific. This compares to 90 per cent of the population being online in developed states and less than 60 per cent in developing states (see ◘ Fig. 8.4); a figure that falls below 30 per cent for the least developed states. These figures are compounded by the fact that these—as we shall see below—mainly comprise of those groups who are already at the periphery of mainstream socio-economic structures. On a geographic scale, the gap demonstrates an evident rural–urban split with around twice as many urban households having access to the internet than rural households. Again, this rural–urban split is especially

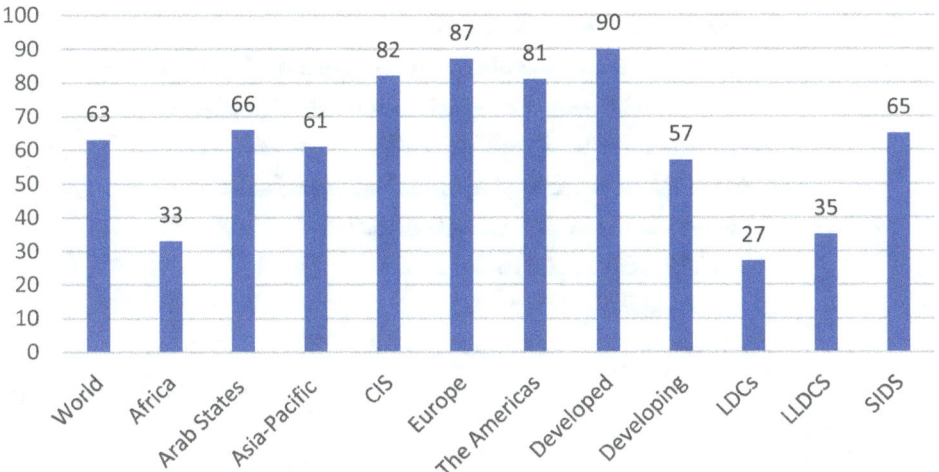

■ **Fig. 8.4** Intenet usage by individuals 2021 (%) (*Source* ITU [2022])

marked within developing states where—in Africa for example—only 6.3 per cent of households have internet access. This is compared to nearly a quarter of households in urban areas across Africa. The coverage of key digital technologies is also very uneven across the global system. Mobile internet access is approaching universality in developed states while in Africa the coverage is less than 80 per cent. This is also true with regard to internet usage where South Asia and sub-Saharan Africa have usage rates of around 20 per cent compared to 80 per cent in the leading developed states (2020). The rapid increase in mobile technology is beginning to close this divide.

More broadly, this inter-state divide is also reflected within the extent to which a state is ready to adopt and absorb many of the digital-based technologies associated with the 4IR. Again, UNCTAD's Digital Readiness Index is a reflection of five criteria namely ICT deployment, skills, R&D activity, industry activity and access to finance. On this basis, it is the leading industrialized states (the US, Western Europe, Japan, and South Korea) that will be the speediest to develop and deploy the technologies associated with 4IR. These stand in contrast to the lack of preparedness in many developing (especially sub-Saharan African) states. There are some states such as India whose readiness outranks their level of economic development as does China across a number of criteria. These are helped by big domestic market and cheap labour.

– Social Divide

This reflects the differences in access to the digital system within a state's social system. This has a number of dimensions. One of the most immediate reflects the social legacy of automation and how this effects particular groups with economic class remaining a big predictor of the source of the digital divide within states. Such inequalities are frequently expanded into a reduction in life chances. The rise of digital platforms are also a means of social interaction and economic engagement. These platforms have also fed inequality in shifting the power from labour to cap-

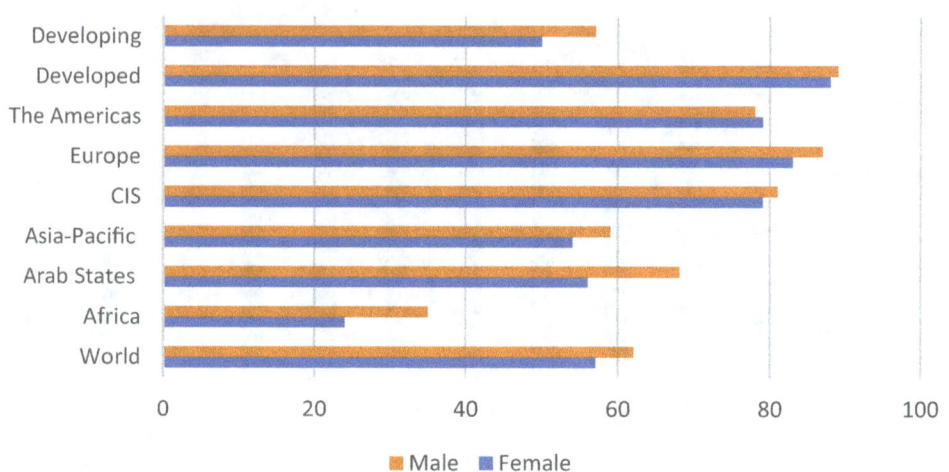

Fig. 8.5 Usage of internet by gender (*Source* World Bank [2022])

ital and thereby allowing employers to pick and choose workers and also to offer minimum levels of worker protection.

Looking beyond class and the impact of automation, it is also evident that there is a long-standing gender divide in digital access and usage. Globally, 48 per cent of women used the internet compared to almost 60 per cent of men. This gap is highly varied between states dependent upon development. Wherein some developed states the gap is 3 per cent whereas in some developing states, the gaps are over 40 per cent (see ▸ Fig. 8.5). These gender divisions reflect the broader role of each within a social system. Thus, whilst the gaps have closed within developed states, women tend also to understate their skills. In developing states, these gaps persist due to contextual issues where social norms, expectations, and institutions can drive these differences. This divide reflects a persistent inequity with regard to female access to digital technology. This extends to the most basic and common forms of internet access namely mobile connectivity. There are over 300 million less women in possession of a smart phone than men with women over a fifth less likely to use the internet than men; a figure that appears to be growing. These may reflect the absence of the autonomy of usage within patriarchal societies and lower level of skills and education for female users within such societies. This is reinforced by lower levels of support to encourage female users.

The rise of social media has highlighted the role that digital technology plays in the development and sustenance of social capital (see ▸ Chapter 6). The unevenness of access to technologies with different environments (urban versus rural, educated versus uneducated, etc.) all underscore how the ability to use this technology to form social connections is limited for certain groups. The ability of these technologies to promote and sustain social (and economic) connectivity became evident during the 2020–2022 COVID pandemic where social vulnerabilities created by the digital divide between and within groups were highlighted where segments of groups with poor broadband became more socially isolated with potentially long-term consequences for mental and physical health. This was also evident when

COVID and its shift towards online working promoted easier adaptation amongst those who were better educated and with higher digital skills than those at the lower end of the economic spectrum. This was also compounded by unequal access to the education system during this period which hints at long-term disparities being sustained.

- Democratic Divide

The salience of the digital divide is underpinned by notion that accessibility to the digital system is a human right. As more public services are accessed through this channel there is increased risk of social exclusion because of digital exclusion. This in turn will shape the pattern of human development and the creation of social capital. This reflects not just access to training in the use of digital technology but also being aware of proactive means of engagement with civil society. Thus, even in conditions of universal access to the digital access divisions can still be evident due to a mix of lower capacity technology or other user constraints/restraints (such as physical disability or the absence of skills). These limit proactive engagement with public services. These issues of digital engagement were also exposed during the COVID pandemic where there were big differences in the ability to access health services. Areas with good broadband connection were more able to access public services as well as engage in routine economic activities online. It was also important for the purposes of enabling otherwise isolated and vulnerable people to maintain social connectivity.

***

All of these digital divides reflect and accentuate the broad structural inequalities pre-existing within socio-economic systems. The fact that the internet has spread and has attained near universality globally yet is still characterized by these digital divides reflects endemic weaknesses within the socio-economic system that allows these differences to persist. These are true both across states at all levels of economic development These endemic weaknesses with regard to allowing the persistence of these digital divides are:

- Low literacy levels that hinder and broader educational inequalities that feed the digital divide both within and between states.
- Income disparities are major factor influencing the degree of digital engagement and the quality of user experience. This is compounded by the cost of access technologies which for some income groups can be prohibitive.
- Spatial divides where user intensity drives network development which can leave rural areas under-served. This can also reflect that there is a residual unevenness with regard to the availability and capability of physical infrastructure.
- Low engagement in the digital system by a number of excluded groups could be either by older techno-sceptic generations or social groups who choose to consciously exclude themselves from the digital system.
- Persistent digital illiteracy within economically and socially excluded groups.

The means of closing these divisions has conventionally been left to market forces. This presumes that all have the same capability and tendency to utilize the digital system for their own personal and professional wellbeing and development and that—as mentioned—digital technology does not spread throughout a socio-economic system in a stable and predictable manner. The salience of these divisions became evident during the COVID-19 pandemic when there was an evident gap between those higher-skilled jobs that were able to do through home working with a high degree of connectivity. This represented a new aspect to the digital divide where those less able to work from home and thus who were more exposed to the risks of the virus were those with low digitization skills and competencies and those whose jobs simply could not be done from home. These were often low-skilled jobs. This reinforced the notion of digital inequality as those at the lower end of the income scale were more exposed during the pandemic. These lower-income groups were also not able to engage in e-commerce. In short, there was marked increase in the degree of digital autonomy between groups reinforcing social division and inequality. The fear is that this creates a digital underclass who feel excluded from the evolving digital-based technological system.

The Emergence of Widespread Anti-Science Sentiment

Given the concerns over AI and long-standing issues with regard to the social impact of automation as well as emerging concerns with regard to privacy, there is a long-standing concern that the fitness (or lack of) between social and technological systems could read to a pushback on or at the very least an emergent resistance to the process of technological change. These processes could seek to limit deployment and take-up of new technologies, seek a ban upon those advancements that infringe upon social norms and protocols and set limits upon how the technological system evolves. This reflects that as much as technology can be a source of optimism and human advancement, it can also be a tool of oppression and fear creating increased uncertainty and accentuating prejudice, and inequality. These are often created when the technological advancement has a more disabling than enabling impact upon specific terms of human activity. The emergent techno-scepticism reflects concerns with regard to the social impact upon technology.

These reflect differing views upon the role of the evolving technological system upon human advancement and development. One is techno-optimism-based technology enhancing human existence and enabling it to retain fitness with its environment as it evolves under a multitude of pressures at all levels of analysis (micro, meso, macro, and meta). This view sees technology as the core of human advancement enabling the species to continue to control the means of our existence. Contrary to these views is the aforementioned techno-scepticism which argues that technology is advancing faster than humanity's capability to deal with its consequences with the result that the process begins to run out of control. These can often reflect that the trajectory and development of any given technology can be complex with its ultimate impact unknown at the point at which it is introduced into the technical system. This unpredictability can be both a boon and a curse to humanity. This can often require the careful balancing of the regulation of technology as has been evidenced in areas of human privacy and security and technological change especially where too much information given with regard to an individual could fuel interventions by AI devices. This could create a dilemma between investors who will fund these technologies but will not do so should their technologies be restricted or shunned.

Often this techno-scepticism reflects what it means to be human. Thus, technology tends to be resisted more when they substitute rather than augment their humanity. This reflects a desire to humanize technology. Moreover, technology is also resisted more when it is evident that the benefits from the development and deployment of the technology offer benefits to a very limited number of the population while the risk from this process would be more widespread. This resistance is also evident where the costs are felt over the short term and where any benefits are felt over the very long term.

In other cases, the pushback against science could be due to the sheer power that control of this technology hands to a relatively few bodies within the global system. This has been a common complaint with regard to the big technology companies and how their ability to collect and process data gives them an outsized power within the global system. The fear is that this power could enable these businesses to outpower governments and also control the individual for corporate gain. The ability of these businesses to control the increasingly socially, politically, and economically important online environment is seen as core source of power enabling them to influence social and political narratives as well as patterns of economic development and performance. This is compounded by the fear that these platforms could operate as conduits for the spread of socially and politically destabilizing misinformation.

These anti-tech views are a sub-set of a broader anti-science movement. The movements are fed by a mix of factors from those with genuine concern with regard to humanity and its interface with science, those with a high degree of religiosity and spirituality and of humans playing God to broader conspiracy theories. For a long time, these anti-science views have been peripheral to the mainstream with limited political traction. With the rise of national populism (at either ends of the political spectrum) these perspectives are finding increased voice where such views become aligned with an anti-elite narrative. This reflects a perception that scientists can be political authorities. On top of this are a group of consumers who are also sceptical with regard to the value of advancing technology. These tend to be older consumers and/or those upon lower incomes and are more fearful of the role of technology in the development of future generations. These are largely socially conservative individuals who feel the technological system is evolving too fast and fear with regard to how their data will be used. This fear is also evident amongst younger groups who are aware of the risks of technology.

The legacy of these movements is difficult to predict and depends upon whether any such movements can spread across borders. Generally, these narratives have been at the periphery of mainstream debate though there has been an evident growing resistance to the power of big technological groups. Thus, these opinions are likely to stay as having minimal impact upon the operation of the global technological system other than at the local level. The power of technological change within the global system is so strong that is unlikely to be curtailed. What is more likely is sustained constraints on the types of technology and how it is to be used and therefore of users pushing back against particular types of technology especially where they might infringe core rights.

Box 8.1: The Dark Web

Whilst there are many socio-economic and political risks sourced from the usage of internet, arguably the greatest dangers lie within its more obscure corners. The Dark web refers to a collection of web sites that are not readily accessible through conventional internet browsers. They are hidden from normal users through complex overlayers. These overlay networks are normally a positive force within the use of cyber technologies as they allow for the protection of personal data and allow for user privacy. To access sites, users need access to a particular browser. The dark web is often referred to as the 'wild west' of the internet. Indeed, it is much like the internet within its formative stages before the system became effectively governed and controlled. It is an area that is beyond law enforcement with no rules or aspects of user protection. Users tend to use the dark web for one or more of the following reasons: anonymization, accessing hidden services, and illegal activity. As such not all activity on the dark web is illegal in every territory as it can simply be used by some to circumvent local rules.

Nonetheless the usage of the dark web for less well-meaning uses poses an evident social risk. The dark web has become especially notorious for its virtual bazaars where a diverse array of products is sold. The products that tend to be sold upon these bazaars are those that infringe universally held rules and beliefs such as drugs and those materials gathered illegally (such as social security numbers). In addition, the dark web can be a site where hackers can be hired, and ready-made viruses can be purchased. An example of this was the Silk Road. This was a business closed by the FBI and was a marketplace that operated like many other e-retailers but where anonymous sellers could sell their products (often narcotics) to similarly anonymous buyers. Closing these businesses down is simply akin to a 'whack-a-mole' strategy as these operations simply emerge elsewhere.

The risk from this to social system largely stems through the facilitation of access to products that contravene social norms. The ability to access illegal drugs, child pornography, and other illegal matters poses a challenge for the legal system. For businesses, the risk from the dark web is created by the ability of rivals to gain hackers for hire. These could lead to rivals seeking to steal Intellectual property or simply to disrupt a firm's IT systems.

Case Study 8.1: India Moves up the Tech Value Chain

Like other emerging economies, India is seeking to move up industry value chains as it seeks to transform itself from an economic system largely based upon agriculture towards higher end manufacturing. Whilst India has a long-standing IT services sector (through companies such as Infosys) its positioning in high-end manufacturing has been less developed. With the fragmentation of the global technology system India is becoming an increasing attractive location for inward investment for hi-technology manufacturing.

Typical of this emerging trend was the switch by Apple towards the manufacture of its latest iteration of iPhone (iPhone 14) in the country. This process was launched in late 2022, when three of Apple's leading assembly partners (the Taiwanese firms Foxconn, Pegatron, and Wistron) began operations in the South of the country. It is expected that Apple will be making around a quarter of its iPhones in the state by 2025. This represented a move by the company to lower the risks associated with large-scale manufacturing in China due to the sustained policy of zero COVID (with its frequent lockdowns) and the on-going geopolitical friction between China and the US. In this context, investment in production looks like a rational strategy to avoid the risks associated with sustained Chinese production.

These efforts to entice this investment into India have been facilitated by supporting investment in supply chain infrastructure to enable the development of a fully supported local commercial ecosystem within this region of India where both the product is assembled and where also many of the components are also to be manufactured. At the moment, these plants are simple assembly plants based upon imported components. This reflects a long-standing strategy of the Indian government to 25 per cent of GDP by 2025 up from the current (2022) 15 per cent. Moving beyond assembly into component manufacturing will be more difficult especially where there are long-standing protectionist measures within the state. This reflects a desire by the Indian government that supply be internalized (i.e., all in India) rather than stretching across borders. On top of this the government also favours supply chains when they are run by nationals rather than foreigners.

These internal issues are compounded by external pressures. The not least of which is that other states (notably Vietnam and other ASEAN states) will also be seeking to compete for this investment and have friendlier business environments. In addition, this strategy is set against increasingly hostile relations between India and China. This is important as the latter produces many of the components necessary for the assembly of Apple's products. India has already banned many Chinese technology products and services. For example, it has limited access to Chinese apps and has taken legal action against Chinese mobile phone manufacturers. Thus in seeking to create a domestic high-end manufacturing sector control that China has over this could be a problem.

Case Study 8.2: Google and China

Google initially entered China in 2006 but departed in 2010 amid concerns over the control exerted by Chinese authorities over its activities. Nonetheless China remained a lucrative potential market and, in 2018, it emerged that the company was working on a new product that adhered to the requirements of the Chinese market that addressed its demands for censorship in search results. When this activity—the so-called project Dragonfly came to light—the company faced a range of pressures from NGOs and politicians in existing markets to cease such activities. For many, these activities could legitimatize human rights abuses and condone censorship. This was pressure to which the company acceded. This does mark the last phase of this technology giant's engagement with China.

With its initial entry into China in 2006, Google was just entering another market. At the time, China was still a relative technological backwater. In entering, Google agreed to censor results. In acceding to this demand, Google engaged in the necessary internet diplomacy believing that even a limited exposure to content via a censored search would be positive for Chinese users and help create a more open culture. Nonetheless highlighting that content had been removed from the searches upset Chinese regulators. This was a public acknowledgement that censorship was occurring. Despite there was little pressure to remove the notice of censorship as it was felt that China needed the expertise that Google was providing. As a result, local search engines followed but the disputes between Google and Chinese resistance to openness did not diminish though Google still manged to gain around a third of China's search market by 2009.

Google's position within China was ultimately undermined not by these censorship disputes but by a large-scale hacking incident which stole a great deal of its intellectual property. With the source of the attack being China, Google felt no longer obliged to censor its search results. China though refused to cede ground and stressed the need for technology companies to adhere to Chinese law. Indeed, around this time, China began to more aggressively police the 'Great Firewall' around its internet system in the fear that it was fuelling unrest in certain provinces. China was making a statement—it no longer needed US big tech. Google retreated from China and offered a service based around a Hong Kong-based search engine.

In the intervening years, the Chinese internet sector took off as the state developed its own indigenous internet ecosystem based around the emergence of national champion across all domains of the sector from hardware through to many forms of software and applications. This was based on aggressive push by China to recruit technologists back from the US and then to use a big domestic market as a push for tech exports. This was also supported by a very proactive attitude by the Chinese state towards technology entrepreneurship with the state often providing seed capital for these businesses. On the back of this success, China decided it no longer needed Google at all and blocked all remaining services it offered within China.

Finding itself blocked out of a lucrative market, Google looked to find ways back in. This was against a background of a further tightening of control by China over the internet. In 2017, Google announced the launch of a research centre in Beijing which reflected on-going ef-

> forts by the business to adapt to the conditions of operating in China. The result of this was Dragonfly, a search engine that aggressively filtered content and which was to be developed in collaboration with a Chinese partner. Moreover, the app also allowed for active surveillance of users' searches opening up the possibility of arrest should these not meet with the censor's approval. Google rationalized these actions as trying to fully understand the nuances of the Chinese market and to learn from this. To outsiders, it looked like a case of the necessary adaption that Google needed to undertake was in direct contravention to the principles of openness that lie at the core of its value proposition.

Conclusions

Technological change is an on-going process of change within business systems. As much as these processes create new opportunities for business, they also generate new sets of risks that stretch across an array of global systems. In part, this reflects that technological change is filled with a great deal of ambiguity with regard to the end point of the process and also with regard to the anticipated consequences of this process. The latest iteration of this process linked to the so-called 'Fourth Industrial Revolution' has the potential to create new risks related to the wider use of data and also to the extension of automation. These risks are right across the socio-economic spectrum.

Key Points

- Technological change represents an evolutionary process within the global system.
- Every phase of technological change creates new sets of risks.
- The advent of latest phase of technological change can introduce new risks related to automation and wider use of data.
- There are also issues related to the geopolitical dimensions of this process of technological change.

Discussion Questions

1. How does the Fourth Industrial Revolution change global business?
2. Why does the fragmentation of the internet ecosystem matter?
3. What are the major barriers to the widespread adoption of Fourth Industrial Revolution technologies?

Activities

How do your account for the rise of technophobia in global systems? Are such fears ever justified?

Summary

Technological change has a long-standing and long-understood impact upon risks within social, economic, and political systems. The latest iteration of this process is the technologies associated with the Fourth Industrial Revolution and these are creating new (actual and potential) risks from the deployment of technologies that depend on highly intense data usage. These create concerns with regard to cyber risks, artificial intelligence, and the reinforcement of pre-existing socio-economic divisions.

Further Reading

Ford, M. (2015). *Rise of the Robots*. Basic Books.
Gawdat, M. (2021). *Scary Smart: The Future of Artificial Intelligence and How You Can Save Our World* Bluebird.
Kaplan, F. (2016). *Dark Territory: The Secret History of Cyber War*. Simon & Schuster.
Mueller, V. (2015). *Risks of Artificial Intelligence*. Chapman, and Hall/CRC.
Scwaub, K. (2017). *The Fourth Industrial Revolution*. Penguin.

Useful Websites

1. The OECD Science and Technology website (▶ https://www.oecd.org/science/) offers a range of material upon technology and technological change.
2. The World Bank (▶ https://data.worldbank.org/topic/14) offers up to date data upon a range of technological indicators.
3. UNCTAD Science and Technology sub site (▶ https://unctad.org/topic/science-technology-and-innovation) offers a global analysis of the state of technology.
4. Office of National Statistics—source for range of UK focused but also comparable data from other states (▶ www.ons.gov.uk).
5. The Centre for Strategic and Information Studies offers material upon global system impact of wider adoption of new technologies (▶ https://www.csis.org/topics/cybersecurity-and-technology).

Infrastructural Risk

The highly functional infrastructure that surrounds us… is a gift from our ancestors: the comparatively incorrupt political and economic systems, the technology, the wealth, the lifespan, the freedom, the luxury, and the opportunity.

Jordan Peterson

By the end of this chapter, the reader will be able to comprehend:
- The multiple forms of infrastructure.
- The form and nature of risks to businesses created by infrastructure.
- The major global bottlenecks within the global logistical systems.
- How geopolitical issues can shape infrastructure risk.

Introduction

Infrastructure risk (that is those business risks created by the failure and/or absence of infrastructure) has conventionally not been treated as a risk on its own but as a secondary risk whose performance can directly impact upon the operation of the separate global sub-systems and on the global system as whole. Infrastructures are conventionally issues of state territoriality, but increased integration of national systems and the increased salience of the global commons as international transmission routes underscores the interdependence between systems at different levels. This chapter will look at the increased salience of infrastructure risk, focusing upon an examination of trends at the macro and meta levels (and the interactions between them). The chapter will examine the form of nature of infrastructure and the risks associated with its usage. The chapter will then move onto to the major global challenges posed by the infrastructure system both at national and global levels.

The Nature of Infrastructure

Notions of infrastructure tend to revolve around the concept of large-scale systems that promote the enablement of resources in network form. The conventional conceptualization of infrastructure is of physical structures that reliably and securely store, transmit, distribute, process, and consume raw, semi-finished, and finished tangibles and intangibles around national and international systems to support and enable human activity and its flourishment. Infrastructures create the conditions to allow other objects to operate and in so doing they have become critical to the operation of everyday life. Importantly infrastructures are relational in the sense that they foster connectivity and human inter-relationships and enable the creation of human economic and social capital. These enable human activity to be conducted securely and reliably over longer distances where the infrastructure offers continuity of access, capacity, and quality across space. These facets place infrastructure at the core of human development and as a direct enabler of human (economic, social, and political) activity. To this end, notions of infrastructure have evolved to be split into two broad categories.
1. Hard Infrastructure: these are the physical structures and systems (such as transport, energy water, and information systems). These can be further subdi-

vided between economic infrastructure (i.e., those that support and enable economic activity) and social infrastructure (i.e., those that offer social services and promote social wellbeing such as hospitals, schools, etc.).
2. Soft Infrastructure: these are the institutional systems that underpin the operation of hard infrastructure (both economic and social). These include formal (for example rules and regulations governing usage and development) and informal (for example those derived from social groups) rules/structures that shape user interface with infrastructure.

Moreover, infrastructure is as much a verb as a noun. This reflects that all agents (at all levels) must acquire and build around themselves structures to enable them to not simply exist but to also form interconnections with other agents of relevance to their activity. In many cases, leaving this provision to commercial forces would lead to an under infrastructure or—where externalities exist—mean that one agent cannot exclude another from infrastructure usage. Thus, infrastructure systems have a strong public good component of collective provision to prevent socio-economic exclusion from the under-provision of infrastructure. These public systems (such as public communication and energy systems) exist alongside private infrastructure operated frequently on a very localized basis (such as a household, office, or neighbourhood systems) that services a particular agent's need but which connects into public networks for wider area connectivity (see ◘ Table 9.1). Moreover, no single infrastructure is a standalone entity. Each is enmeshed within a network of supporting and/or enabling infrastructure. Thus, for example, transport relies upon an effective energy system with its flows increasingly enabled by data systems. This complexity makes the behaviour of infrastructure systems increasingly difficult to predict and increasingly subject to breakdown.

◘ Table 9.1 Multi-scalar infrastructure system

Micro-level Infrastructure	Local/personal private systems are used to support interactions within a limited enclosed facility which connects into public networks for connectivity across a wider space
Meso-level Infrastructure	These are shared facilities including those that allow for interaction to create social capital. Also included could be private shared facilities such as research facilities or third-party logistics systems
Macro-level Infrastructure	These are state-wide infrastructure systems to support and enable transport, data, and energy flows within the borders of the state. This also applies at social context based on state-wide network of social facilities
Meta Level Infrastructure	These are infrastructures/channels that are either located within a single state, but which are global conduits or parts of the global surface/atmosphere which are important to global connectivity, but which lie out with the control of a single state

The Global Infrastructure System

At the core of the global system is international connectivity. This connectivity is directly enabled by universal access to the interconnected, interoperable global infrastructure system (GIS). In a global system of territorial states, the global infrastructure system is based upon the interconnectivity and ease of flows between separate national infrastructure systems (NIS). It is this interconnectivity and interoperability that fosters international interactivity through cross border tangible and intangible flows. Conceptualizing the global system as just the interactions between national system simplifies the complexity of the process of global infrastructure and of the movement of flows across it. Broadly, the global system has four interacting components.

- Inter-NIS Flows: these are flows across contiguous spaces where these transactions flow directly between respective national systems. These flows directly cross borders with no third-party state involvement nor without the need to cross the global commons. The ease of flows is derived not simply by the capacity of the system at the borders by also by the capacity of soft infrastructure to enable the rapid transmission across borders by adoption of common standards for example.
- Transit infrastructure: these are those parts of a state-based infrastructure system that are used by other states for the purposes of gaining access to tangibles and intangibles produced by a third state. Transit infrastructures can also be used by states to ensure their products are able to reach their customers when such interactions occur across non- or semi-contiguous space. Such transit systems can be used where a state is landlocked, and needs access to major logistics systems or in the case of long-distance energy pipeline systems. In addition, there are global pinch points which are operated by a state which are central to the operation of international logistics, energy, and data systems. These are explored more fully below.
- The Global Commons: whilst these are not direct physical systems (high seas, cyberspace, and airspace) they are a core component of the global infrastructure system. These are parts of the global system that are not under the power of a sovereign entity and can be accessed by any agent with the requisite capability. As these lie beyond the control of any states, their control is normally secured by international agreement though this is often attained by the hard power of globally powerful states.

Whilst the GIS exists as an informal system, it does nonetheless reflect interdependencies within the global economic system. It also reflects the complexity of the operation of the global system where all flows are underpinned by a network of networks where the failure of and/or the interruption of flows within or across a state can cause a disruption to global connectivity. In a global system of flows this mutual dependence can (as noted later on) pose a grave risk to the global system. Such concerns focus upon the notion of criticality within infrastructure systems.

Critical Infrastructure

Before moving on to examine the nature of infrastructure risk it is important to recognize that—within any given infrastructure system—not all of its components are equal in terms of their value to support economic and social activity. There are

those infrastructures whose proper functioning and operations are central to human activity and whose failure (or even destruction) would represent a serious (and possibly) existential risk to human activity both within and across countries. Without these infrastructures working in their anticipated manner, territories would be more difficult to govern as these infrastructures are core to the state being able to:
- Assert control over a given domain.
- Secure a territory from external threats.
- Promote economic growth and/or development.
- Attain popular legitimacy and socio-economic cohesion.
- Promote ecological security and sustainability.

This has been reflected upon within the concept of Critical Infrastructure Systems at the state level. These are public systems whose failure would hinder socio-economic wellbeing and inhibit the state from asserting its territorial rights and responsibilities. There is no single definition of what is critical as it depends not simply upon physical feature of an infrastructure but also on the priorities and values of those who deem an infrastructure 'critical'. Whilst there is no definitive definition of critical infrastructure, most identify the following sectors (and sub-systems) as vital to sustaining human activity.
- Energy systems (including electricity, gas, and fuel).
- Digital and non-digital communications (i.e., digital communications postal services, and broadcasting).
- Transport systems both terrestrial and non-terrestrial including aviation (including space), maritime, rail, and land transport.
- Emergency public services (ambulance, fire and rescue, marine, and police).
- Financial services (such as payment, clearing and settlement systems, markets and exchanges, public finances).
- Food systems involving its production, processing, import, distribution, and retail.
- Government at all levels both central and devolved administration/functions, regional and local government.
- Public Health and social care systems.
- Water Infrastructure that promotes distribution and recycling of safe drinking water, wastewater disposal and those structures that inhibit the negative impact of excessive fluctuations in water quantity such as dams, flood defences.

As reflected within ◘ Table 9.2, there is within and across these interdependent sectors a hierarchical approach which reflects the different scales at which critical infrastructure operates. The system level reflects that critical infrastructures are often dependent upon and have other critical infrastructures embedded within them with the result that one cannot function without the other. Next are those clusters of firms within the same sector (or sub-sectors) (see above) that are mandated to supply a component of the critical infrastructure system. The final level is the individual components both within and across sectors which are pivotal to that sector's (or sub-sectors) operation.

These critical systems are characterized by operational complexity due not only to their own operations but also due to the interdependencies between them. This creates a critical infrastructure within a critical infrastructure. This all underlines

Table 9.2 The hierarchy within critical infrastructure systems

Hierarchical Level	Features
System	This has two mutually dependent components: 1. Technical infrastructure: these are sector producing specific commodities (e.g., energy, water) 2. Socio-economic infrastructure: these are sectors that provide socio-economic services (such as health or education) These depend upon each other especially in crisis situations
Sector	These are sectors and sub-sectors within any given infrastructure system. For example, energy consists of gas, oil, and coal as well as various parts of the value chain. Transport has five different modes (road, rail, maritime, inland waterways, and aviation)
Element	These are individual components of an infrastructure system such as hub airport, oil refinery, etc. The criticality of any given element depends upon their role in sustaining national and/or international flows. These are critical points whose failure could undermine entries sub-system

Adapted from Rehak and Hromada (2018)

the complex interactions and mutually dependent operation of these infrastructures. These interdependencies (i.e., bi-directional relationship between infrastructures) can be through three main channels:
- Physical: where the output of one infrastructure depends upon the output of another infrastructure for example water and power infrastructure.
- Cyber: the increased level of embeddedness of IT systems within all systems to manage flows but also that cyber systems depend upon other systems (notably energy).
- Geographical: this occurs when a local event can create changes in a number of elements of an infrastructure system due to the close physical proximity of these systems.

The notion of criticality when applied to the global system reflects that there are some infrastructures whose sustained operation and evolution is central to the smooth operation of the international system and that any of these elements ceasing to operate in a normal fashion, failing or ceasing to evolve in manner that responds to user trends can all pose issues for the operation of global systems. These are not merely those systems that are international by design (such as global logistics systems) but also those parts of the global system that are national by design and which either by intent or through the evolution of traffic have morphed into critical global infrastructure. Overall, critical global infrastructure tends to be one of the following types:
- Global hubs: these locations where the movement and management of global traffic is concentrated (such as international sea or airports, server farms, or large oil refineries).
- Global transit points: these are territorial links that operate as key transit points for global or international flows. This includes major logistical bottlenecks (see below) and national airspace.

- Global Commons: these—as suggested above—are parts of the global system beyond state control but which could be disrupted through human and/or natural activity.

Consequently, when assessing risk within the infrastructure system, it is evident risk varies with the degree of criticality of a single element, system, or sector. It is the nature of this infrastructure risk that this chapter now turns.

Infrastructure Risk

Infrastructure risk is a Graduated phenomenon where the degree of risk is derived from the extent to which human activity (either intentional or accidental) and naturally occurring processes cause infrastructure to fail or be disrupted leading to meaningful disruption to socio-economic systems. ◘ Table 9.3 offers examples of infrastructure risk across each of the global sub-systems. For business, infrastructure risk is created through undermining of the conditions of operation within any given locality. Without a reliable supply of energy, transport, and information as well as certainty over the rules with which they can be used then infrastructure continuity and certainty represents a major business risk. Whilst the vulnerability of any given infrastructure will vary with a number of factors such as its condition, capacity and use, its dependence upon other infrastructures (see below) and location, it has been widely accepted that natural and human causes of infrastructure risk can be accounted for within the following categories of risk.

1. Climate-based risks: these are created by singular events (such as floods, snowstorms, etc.) or a long-term process of change in anticipation created by long-term processes of climate change.
2. Geological threats: these emerge due to vulnerabilities exposed by alterations (both sudden and long-term) in the earth's geological activity. This can include phenomena such as earthquakes, volcanic activity, and landslips.
3. Biological risks: these emerge from activity within the earth's biosphere, but which can impact upon infrastructure functions by altering the ease and capability of flows. Such threats can include pandemics and other probes created form biological materials.
4. Technological threats: these could be created as a result of the human activity or through the degradation of the physical technological systems that cause infrastructure to fail. These include not just the cyber threats mentioned above but also damage to the physical components of the system such as rail/road accidents, breaching of flood defences.
5. Criminal threats: this is where intentional human activity seeks to disrupt the system for political and/or economic reasons or simply through random act of sabotage/damage. This can include terrorism, vandalism, and armed conflict.

Either on their own or in combination, these threats can impact upon the infrastructure system by inhibiting and disrupting the flows that make normal human activity more difficult to initiate and complete. The impact of the event and/or process upon socio-economic activity depends upon the centrality of the impacted in-

Table 9.3 Examples of infrastructure risks across global sub-systems

	Transport	Energy	Information
Political	• Links could be subject to human interferences through terrorism or piracy • Landlocked states vulnerable to exclusion from global logistics system	• The risk for pipeline systems passing through states • Use of energy as a geopolitical tool due to absence of diversity of supplies	• Terrorist and/or foreign state attacks upon core information systems • Use of information systems to undermine political stability
Economic	• Power of global hubs and their disruption to hinder global flows • Ability of core links to be disturbed and blocked	• Restrictions on supply increase prices and erode competitiveness • Risk to business from energy transition (see ▶ Chapter 7)	• Theft of data from in secure systems • Attacks on data centres causing loss of data
Social	• Infrastructural violence created by underdevelopment • Underdevelopment of local transport systems reinforces social exclusion	• Rising prices causing energy poverty • Risk to energy accessibility and affordability	• Information poverty/digital exclusion leading social exclusion • Social disruption caused by misuse of social media
Technological	• Cyber attacks upon traffic management systems • The rise of bigger ships requiring more port investment	• Cyber attacks upon energy facilities • Risks in deployment of new energy infrastructure	• Cyber attacks upon key links and hubs • The rise of new AI infrastructure raises new risks
Ecological	• Climatic events damage transports links and hubs • Use of transports systems degrades	• Pipelines damaged through melting permafrost • Climatic events damage energy facilities	• Increased use of power in data centres where threats to supply hinders capability • Risk of events to global data system (e.g., earthquakes)

frastructure to a specific pattern of flows and/or the extent to which it has other systems embedded within it that can create new types of failures. These failures can be:
— Cascade failures: where the failure of one infrastructure causes another to fail which in turn causes another to fail.
— Escalating failure: where the failure of one creates a more severe failure within another which has a wider more long-lasting impact.
— Common cause failure: where a single event causes simultaneous failure in one or more infrastructures.

These risks and their ability to spread underscore that these impacts are not simply operational but also spatial. This latter point highlights that interdependence be-

tween systems across space can cause disruption across multiple national systems (or components of that system); it can also more obviously impede the global flows around the international system even though the events are localized. Thus, looking at risk within the global system, infrastructure risk reflects mutual dependencies across space even where immediate impacts are local. Thus, within a global system (and reflecting the global typology above).
- Hub risk: where cascade effects in global systems are created as a result of disruption of flows through a core global hub.
- Transit risk: where a transit route is disrupted within a third country or the global commons which disrupts flows between the source and destination of a flow.
- Border risk: where border systems are disrupted either creating congestion or a free unchecked flow creating potential security risks.

The degree of risk within any given component of the global infrastructure system is a reflection of the degree of resilience within it. This reflects the extent to which there is spare capacity within the system to cope with and adapt to the disruption to flow and/or the extent to which there are alternative facilities to cover the loss of capacity. This resilience reflects the degree to which the system can return to normality after an event disrupts its operation. Within the conditions of spatial complexity, there is likely to be a temporal gap between the event and impact upon global flows. Thus, other than in cyber systems, the effects will not be simultaneous across space.

Much of the narrative with regard to infrastructure has focused its failure and/or its absence. There are also scenarios where the provision of infrastructure itself can—either by design or accident—lead to an increase in risks. One of the more evident is that the provision and maintenance of infrastructure can act as an enabler of civil unrest. In a number of states widespread digital infrastructure led to insurgencies notably the role of social media in the case of Arab Spring. In other cases, insurgents have used infrastructure for economic development within a state as a tool against the state enabling them to move rapidly around a territory. In other cases, social risk can be created by inequality in infrastructure access and provision. The intent by states to intentionally underprovide or to overprovide to targeted, preferred groups can lead to increased socio-economic risks and undermine cohesion. This can often mean that when infrastructure fails it fails unevenly across space and social groups where the system is more poorly maintained within social groups/classes than others. In short, infrastructure quality is not universal across social groups.

Infrastructure Risk Within Global Systems

The complexity of global system and of the infrastructure that supports and enables global interaction means that any single infrastructure can fail for a multitude of reasons. As such global infrastructure risk covers a wide range of potential disruptions. For reasons of brevity, this section will focus upon those aspects of the three main economic infrastructure sectors (i.e., transport, energy, and information) which have the greatest impact on international interactions. By its nature, these tend to focus upon those hard infrastructures (mainly those operating as global hubs or offering international transit) that are deemed critical to sustained operation of the global system. The risk at the macro level can also be shaped by the absence of infrastructure and/or failure of infrastructure at this level. The focus of this section will be upon those infrastructures with self-evident international/global dimensions. The key risks are summarized in ◘ Table 9.3.

Transport

The risks created by the transport sector to the operation of the global system are shaped by the role of the global logistics system in enabling inter-state connectivity. The global logistics system connects the processes of production and consumption together over an ever-expansive geographic space. This is a function of the interconnecting of national transportation systems which promote internal and external movement of products to points of processing and consumption. This process depends upon global hubs (to coalesce, process, and distribute products) and links (that is those physical connections between hubs (both national and global) that channel flows around the global value system. The underpinning enabling facility of this process is that both links and global hubs have sufficient, continuous, and sustained capacity to cope with anticipated flows of traffic. As such, infrastructure as a risk to global logistical systems emerges when there is physical restriction upon the capacity of these global hubs and links to cope with the traffic directed at or across them. Whilst there are two major conduits for international logistics—maritime and aviation—it is the former that is by far and away the most important as it covers around 80 per cent of international trade in goods. Risks are greater in international logistics systems when compared to domestic systems due to the increased number of interconnections within the former where there are multiple systems of governance where any single failure can cascade through the system. These can disrupt the global supply of products throughout the system. As such, this will be the focus of the analysis within this section.

Whether it is a transport hub or link, what determines the risk attached to a given infrastructure is the extent to which it can be considered a system bottleneck. Bottlenecks are points within the global transport system where transportation flows are concentrated and where any disruption to flows is likely to have an outsize effect. These are points within the global systems where reliability and resilience of the system are under the greatest pressure. Thus, risk within transport infrastructure is shaped by two factors:
1. Complexity and efficiency: this reflects the scaling up of transportation into larger volumes via larger ships, aircraft, etc. and to enable increased flows within the constraints imposed by the physical capacity of the system which the global system is designed to operate at maximum potential with limited scope for extra capacity.
2. Vulnerability: these critical nodes are always but therefore maintenance is difficult with the result that increased use means increased risk of failure.

In part, the infrastructure risk for businesses reflects the nature of how they conduct and operate their supply chain. Where there is a focus upon minimal inventories, any disruption is likely to have an outsize effect upon firm operations as they will exhibit little resilience to adapt to disruption to their supply chain. Thus, local events in local infrastructure system can have global impacts where it impacts on global supply chains with little resilience. Thus, this creates a problem where congestion and/or restriction in capacity in one point can have knock-on effects throughout the system (see below). A restriction in a core hub causes traffic to back up elsewhere within the system causing delays in traffic flows and leading to supply chains breaking down.

Global Bottlenecks

Bottlenecks can be supply or demand driven. In the former there is usually a disruption to the supply chain which—as noted above—creates restriction in global flows. These will be the focal point of much of the analysis here. Demand side bottlenecks are created where demand increases beyond anticipated levels causing points within the global value chains to be overwhelmed leading to congestion and flow restrictions. This was a driving factor in the post-COVID era where a bounce back in demand for consumer goods placed increased pressure upon supply chains. There were—for example—restraints upon motor vehicle supply due to a shortage of microchips generated by a surge in demand. This reflects that demand and supply bottlenecks can be interlinked where there is limited slack within the system. The core characteristics of choke points are:
1. Physical: these are locations with limited physical capacity where traffic converges and where capacity has limitations.
2. Usage: the salience of a choke point is linked to the amount of usage and the availability of alternatives.
3. Access: its universal value to all users based on limited capacity means that rules must be established to regulate and control usage.

Within the global system, the combination of rising demand and limited capacity created global bottlenecks within global logistical systems. These bottlenecks tend to be of two types of hubs and link-based constraints. These are compounded by issues within the global commons which can also increase risk within the global maritime system.

Hub Bottlenecks

These are places where flows terminate, are collected, processed, or transited for onward transmission to their final destination. Within the global logistical system these bottlenecks are major ports on the primary global logistics routes. Across the global system, the key ports are those that are focused upon the handling of container traffic and the volume of traffic that passes through them. Containers are central to the global system carrying 35 per cent of trade by volume and 60 per cent of trade by value. These have rendered container ports as central to the operation of the global logistics system. The biggest ports in the world are not necessarily the busiest. It is those that are the busiest and where congestion and/or disruption of traffic is likely to have the greatest effect upon the flow of goods around the global system. These are places where container traffic is concentrated before it is dispersed to other points within the global logistical system. As of 2022, the busiest ports globally are all in East Asia with seven of these ports being on the eastern seaboard of China with the others being Singapore, Busan in South Korea, and Port Klang in Malaysia. This Chinese dominance reflects the importance of China as a manufacturing hub and how this activity is spreading elsewhere in East Asia.

The risk to container ports is manifold and can be created by a multitude of factors such as:
- Limitations in space relative to demand.
- Poor operating efficiency.
- Limits in maritime and landside access.
- Poor port governance.
- Poor co-ordination between agencies involved in port management.

That container ships operate in tight schedules across the global logistical system with times of arrival and departure carefully planned can mean cascade effects with increased costs and inhibition of trade. These concerns are especially acute in landlocked states and in small island developing states. The risk of the hub ports within the global system became evident during the COVID pandemic where congestion in many of these major ports within East Asia and beyond became increasingly common. The tight zero-covid restrictions (resulting in labour shortages) placed upon some of the busiest Chinese ports as well as surging consumer demand for manufactured products in the US generated a loss of capacity within these ports creating longer waiting times for ships. As a result, shipping companies lowered available capacity. In Hong Kong, over two thirds of ships faced significant waits for berths. These problems were also evident in US ports notably Los Angeles, Long Beach, and Charleston. At times, these ports reported yard utilization (i.e., where the containers are stored) of 100 per cent when 80 per cent is considered capacity. These problems were compounded by China's 'zero-covid' policy which resulted in labour shortage within ports as infected workers were forced to isolate for 14 days at the peak of the pandemic. This was also evident within hub airports where congestion also arise due to labour shortage due to worker isolation. This impacted not just on activities such as baggage handlers at airports but also left logistics warehouses understaffed. Indeed, the disruption to schedules was such that the reliability of the system fell from nearly 80 per cent in 2018 to less than 40 per cent in 2021. In other areas—notably within the food value chain—the issue was not so much capacity restraints from sheer volume of traffic but more that the infrastructure is of poor quality meaning that it is unreliable and liable to fail disrupting flows through it. It can fail due to damage or simply due to obsolescence. In dry goods (such as cereals), the absence of storage and processing facilities is an endemic problem especially within the US and the Black Sea ports.

Link Bottlenecks

The link bottlenecks are those places within the global logistical system where flows converge and become concentrated to the extent that flow congestion becomes the norm and where any disruption to the capacity of this link will create cascade effects throughout the rest of the global logistical system. As suggested above, as the majority of global trade goes through maritime channels, these choke points lay largely within the core shipping routes for the main east–west logistical channels. That is the route from China to Europe, the US and back to China. These concerns have most frequently been expressed with regard to the sustenance of the global energy system which depends upon maritime transport especially for oil flows from the Middle East to both Europe and East Asia. There are also emerging implications for the increasingly globalized nature of food supply too. Within the maritime system, these choke points are narrow points within the global transmission channels with restricted capacity which are essential and difficult to circumnavigate should they be disrupted. These are channels and narrow straits chosen for speed and cost reasons. The main maritime choke points are identified in ◘ Table 9.4.

The oil industry is seen as especially vulnerable to these chokepoints as nearly two thirds of global output flows through these channels. For gas (or more especially liquefied natural gas) the figure is around 30 per cent. These vulnerabilities are also evident within the global food system where nearly 3 billion people are dependent upon the transmission of cereal and other crops (Rice, Wheat, Soybean, and Maize). These account for 65 per cent of global protein supply. The international fertilizer trade is also vulnerable to these choke points. The hazards to these chokepoints are of four types:

- Climatic Threats: where extreme weather events lead to a disruption of flows due to rising sea levels, excessive rain, or tropical storms.
- Security Threats: many of these choke points transit through or close to politically unstable states this can disrupt flows through issues such as piracy, armed blockades, or terrorism.
- Political threats: these emerge due to intra-and/or inter-state disputes leading to these chokepoints restricting traffic. This could be due to the effects of sanctions, trade embargoes, labour disputes, or levels of administration required.
- Cyber risk: these systems increasingly rely upon automated system any disruption to these will have cascade effect through disrupting traffic flows.

The food security issue with regard to infrastructure highlights further infrastructure risk namely those internal systems that are central to getting the raw material to the hubs notably in those major crop-producing regions where there is distance between the point and production and point of export. In energy, this is usually done by pipeline (see below) but in food it is done by inland transportation infrastructure. In the case of food, the infrastructure involving US inland waterway, the Black Sea Rail network, and the Brazilian road network are all seen of vital importance. These risks reflect that the export of core grains is highly concentrated within three regions of the global system namely Latin America, Eurasia, and the US. The issue in Brazil is the poor quality of the roads of the hinterland between the main coastal ports and the grain-producing regions. In the US, its inland waterway is old and congested and the Black Sea rail system has been impaired by long-standing conflict between Russia and the Ukraine. This was on top of long-standing under-investment in this infrastructure system.

A further aspect of the risk created by infrastructure is more evident at the macro level notably with regard to landlocked states. These are states with no

■ Table 9.4 Global bottlenecks in international logistics

Choke point	Main sector impacted	Risk
Maritime Choke Points		
Panama Canal	Containers, Grains	Connecting Atlantic and Pacific Oceans, this suffers from both narrow and shallow in parts, it is vital for all form of maritime traffic
Dover Strait	Grains	Connecting North Sea and the Atlantic Ocean, it is major strait to access key global hub ports for entry into European marketplaces and is 33 km at its narrowest point
Danish Straits	Oil	Key for Russian-based oil exports connecting the Baltic and North Seas through three narrow channels
Strait of Gibraltar	Oil, Container traffic, Grains	Connecting the Mediterranean Sea and the Atlantic Ocean,. it is 13 km at its narrowest between the European and African land masses
Suez Canal	Oil, gas Container traffic, Grains	An artificial waterway connecting Mediterranean and Red Seas avoiding a long detour around southern tip of Africa. The Canal is narrow and shallow in parts. Key to food and oil trade and gas trade
Strait of Bad-al-Mandab	Oil, Container traffic	Between Red Sea and Arabian Sea, this is 18 miles wide and is vital for both food and hydrocarbons towards Europe and Asia
Strait of Hormuz	Oil, Gas	30 per cent of Global oil and 30 per cent of LNG flow through narrow waterway between Iran and Oman in Persian Gulf. There is no alternative maritime route
Turkish Straits	Oil, Grains	This comprises both the Bosporus and Dardanelles Straits. The former connects the Black and Mediterranean Seas but is very narrow and has difficult geography. 80 per cent of Eurasian exported grain passes through these straits
Malacca Strait	Oil, Gas	Connecting the Indian and Pacific Oceans via South China Sea whilst being long (800 km) it is at its narrowest at 2.3 km and it is also shallow. Vital for not just hydrocarbons but also for broader freight flows

coastline and therefore have no direct territorial access to the major global logistics channels or at least a secondary route that provides access to these channels. As such these states rely upon access to the infrastructure system of neighbouring states to gain access to these core commercial channels. There are currently 44 landlocked states. Twelve of these states are relatively affluent (such as Luxembourg and Slovakia) and exist in a stable geopolitical context with the result that there are limited degrees of risk as access to neighbouring infrastructure systems is secure and those systems are reliable. The greater risk is based around the 32 developing landlocked states (such as South Sudan and Afghanistan). This not merely limits trading opportunities but makes the states dependent upon the quality and quantity of neighbouring infrastructure systems as well as gaining access to these systems. These states become heavily dependent upon their neighbours and a stable geopolitical context. Should this deteriorate or if there is damage to the processor connectivity due to damage from human activity or natural processes. These states have an absence of other easy-to-utilize alternative routes to replace any routes which have become difficult to access. Whilst the risk impact of these events is likely to be very localized or at worst regionalized, there is the risk that these disputes could spill over into disruptions into global systems depending upon their proximity to major bottlenecks. Many of these states are remote and the biggest risk to global economic systems is where these states are key points within global overland transit routes such as those states on the 'New Silk Road' between China and Europe. There are also cases where internal links can be a source of disruption to the global logistics system when the state or local government imposes constraints upon internal movement for reasons of security and/or public health. This was evident within the COVID crisis where the Chinese state—as a means of seeking to limit the spread of the disease—sought to limit inter-regional movement within China. This created internal borders which slowed the traffic to international ports down from the inland Chinese manufacturing hubs. These restrictions were also evident when the Chinese state restricted cross border trade flows.

The Global Commons

Broadly the global commons are those segments of the Earth's surface (notably air and sea) that are beyond the control of a single state or entity, but which have a pivotal role in the transmission of goods around the global system. As a global common, the benefits of the system are greater as a whole than if it was subdivided into smaller parts, where anybody with the necessary capabilities can access these areas for economic, political, scientific, and cultural purposes.

As they are beyond the control of any single state, these areas are governed by international agreement. These define a state's territorial waters as being 12 miles from the coastline of the state and the state's airspace is up to 60,000 feet above its territory. The main risk within commons—with regard to the operation of the global logistics system—exists largely at the margin of the state territorial system and the communal areas. These are points where operations can be disrupted where traffic begins to converge and where threats to flows can be disruptive. Whilst the commons can be seen as an expansive space, in practice, traffic (both aviation and maritime) tend to be focused upon dedicated paths so that the passage of flows can still be monitored. Not all parts of the commons involve expansive space, flows within them do converge and where they do there can be issues with regard to sustaining flows. This risk is created not simply by states who might seek to restrict flows across these commons for their own reasons but can also involve pirates operating from failed or failing states that can also disrupt maritime flows across the global commons. In the period 2007–2008, there was a sharp rise in piracy largely sourced from states within the Horn of Africa that converge upon the maritime commons as ships approached many of the important bottlenecks identified above notably the Malacca Strait and the Strait of Bad-al-Mandab. Whilst the figures have reduced since 2010 when there were 445 incidents (they were 132 incidents globally in 2021) the area impacted has extended beyond Horn of Africa and the Malacca Straits to include the Gulf of Guinea.

Increases in piracy result from macro-level failure but lead to an increase in micro-level risks as shipping businesses pass through these areas where piracy is a risk (notably the Horn of Africa where traffic converges on two bottlenecks). These businesses need to pass through these zones where piracy has had to endure higher insurance risk premiums. At its peak in 2008, the premiums increased ten-fold though these have settled down as increased security measures across the Gulf of Aden have been deployed. The alternative is for ships to be re-directed via the Cape of Good Hope which increases fuel costs which is passed on to the end user. There are also broader ecological risks created by piracy should it result in a ship being scuttled or its contents being emptied into the oceans. There is also evidence these increased costs associated with this risk has a deterrent effect upon trade that can spread beyond the impacted state into the broader region.

Increasingly powerful states are seeking to assert control of main maritime channels to goods are able to continue to flow through them but also to seek to control these channels as a passive form of action against adversaries. Powerful states have conventionally seen as the guardian of these channels to ensure free flows. These states have also been important in forging a consensus between states to create the common rules that facilitate the free movement across these sections of the earth's surface. Where this was under the power of a single hegemonic state the system had stability. With the emergence of a bipolar system based around China and the US there is a long-term risk for fragmentation of the global commons.

Case Study 9.1: The Ever Given's Disruption of the Suez Canal

On March 23, 2021, the Ever Given—220,000-tonne mega ship was blown off course during its transit through the Suez Canal: a major shortcut for trade between Asia and Europe. The resultant blockage of the Suez Canal lasted six days and caused significant disruption to global logistics. Nearly 19,000 ships transit through the canal annually. This traffic represents some 12 per cent of global trade by volume and 10 per cent of global oil flows. Indeed, one of the more immediate effects of the blockage was a short-term rise in the price of oil. This blockage of the Suez Canal occurred against a background where global supply chains were already under severe constraint as they emerged from the COVID pandemic, and a long-term rise in traffic driven by increases in global trade.

The losses were both to businesses and governments from such a blockage. It is estimated that each transit costs $300,000 thus Egypt was keen to have the Canal unblocked as soon as possible as the Suez Canal is a major source of foreign earnings. In terms of the cost of the blockage to the global economic system, it is estimated that the blockage would cost between $5 and 10 billion per week. The exact cost is difficult to estimate as the follow-up costs for logistics businesses are difficult to know. In addition, there was a cost to Egypt not just from the loss of transit revenue but also for the cost of repairs to the damaged section of the Canal. Arguably the biggest impact was upon the operation of global supply chains. It was estimated that up to 30 per cent of global container traffic was disrupted by the blockage with up to 400 ships having their transit delayed by the blockage. As many of these are charter ships, the daily cost of the delays in charting costs for both the ships and the containers as well as the costs of diverting these ships was estimated to be between €50 and 100 million a day. There were also costs to destination ports where there was resultant congestion and other problems due to a lack of rail facilities. The actual impact of this is difficult to assess. As many of these products are timebound due to just-in-time production systems production of certain goods was halted due to key components being delayed. This was evident in the automotive sector where a chip shortage appeared as a result of the blockage. Overall, it is estimated that the 6.5-day blockage caused a net loss to the global system of €2 to 2.5 billion.

In sum, what is learned from this experience is the fragility of global trade and of the logistics systems that underpins it. All it took was one sudden gust of wind to temporarily derail the global trading system. The events of the Suez Canal blockage underpin the vulnerabilities of the global shipping industry to not just closure of key bottlenecks but also of emergent challenges in areas such as geopolitics where there could also be challenges with regard to the sustaining of flows.

Energy

Energy faces many of the same natural- and human-driven risks that face any physical asset. They are subject to adverse weather, cyber activity, and simple negligence for example. The nature of the international energy system is that these localized events could have global impacts not simply in terms of the physical performance and capabilities of infrastructure system but also on the attitudes of different states to different forms of energy. This was notable in the case of state's response to nuclear power after the Fukushima incident in Japan in 2011. The infrastructural risk within an energy system reflects the ability of the infrastructure system to enable and sustain systemic energy security. This is based around the '4 As' of energy security mentioned in ▶ Chapter 6 namely affordability, acceptability, accessibility, and availability. Based upon this framework, infrastructure risk in energy is created by a system which inhibits the attainment of one or more of these objectives. Thus, infrastructure risk within energy systems is created where there is disruption to flows which impacts upon availability, where there such disruptions impact upon affordability, limit accessibility, and result in less acceptable forms of energy being utilized.

The main infrastructural risk for the energy sector parallels directly with the main logistical challenges noted within the transport sector noted above. These reflect that the global energy system is based around the transmission of energy from the point of production to the point of consumption involving maritime transmission of these flows often through the same bottlenecks as other forms of international trade. This reflects that risk within energy system is based upon a global imbalance between its demand and supply. These logistics problems are also compounded by the low energy density of the fuels transmitted which stresses particular modes of transportation which are more vulnerable to disruption. Not surprisingly, the main thrust of the risks is based around the transmission of hydrocarbons (notably oil and gas). Nearly two thirds of oil and a third of gas are moved through these maritime channels. The main maritime bottlenecks revolve around the transmission of these hydrocarbons and are based upon the channels and straits between the Middle East and Europe in one direction and east Asia in the other. The international transmission of gas can be especially problematic as it is highly flammable and ethereal. Any small leak could lead to a big loss in capacity and also create a large risk of explosion. These issues are also evident in the long-distance transmission of gas which needs colling to render it liquid which compresses the gas 600-fold. As LNG gas expands—as a source of energy—there needs to be a rapid upscaling in the LNG processing capacity.

Aside from these previously explored maritime channels for disruption, the other main source of transmission risk for energy systems comes from the international pipeline systems. These pipelines transmit oil and gas from those locations for which maritime access is more difficult and the transmitted commodity sufficiently valuable to warrant the large sunk and operating costs involved in pipeline development. These—for both oil and gas—are over shorter distances and tend to be regional (as opposed to global) in nature. The risk within such systems is compounded by the fact that many of these regional-based energy systems are based upon transnational transit energy pipelines. These are pipelines that transit between the producer of energy and the consumer which often have to traverse the sovereign territory of another state. This can cause risks where there are bad relations between neighbours and the transit state (i.e., the state between the producer and the consumer) which could decide to interrupt the flow of energy across its territory. This need not be due to conflict but can also result from disagreements between states over the terms of transit. Western Europe (see below) has become a focal receiving point/destination for many of these transit pipelines for both oil and gas from North Africa, Eurasia, and Russia. There are transit pipelines elsewhere within the global energy system notably in the Middle East and Latin America though these are often concerned with getting flows of inland sourced energy to major export terminals.

These concerns are especially acute within Europe which relies upon gas supplied from Norway, North Africa, and Russia to meet its energy needs. That the sustained flow of energy through these complex systems depends not solely upon the physical capacity of the system but also on the prevailing geopolitical context represents a key strategic challenge for energy-importing states. This latter point highlights the danger not simply of energy exporting states using oil as a geopolitical weapon but also of resource nationalism, where the state will want to seek to enhance domestic control over key critical infrastructures to ensure its own priori-

ties are met within the evolving energy system. In the Eurasia landmass, there are a number of pipeline systems that exhibit an on-going risk to the smooth operation of the international energy system. The major international pipeline systems in the major European market which exhibit the greatest degree of risk are as follows.
- Druzhba Pipeline. This carries oil between eastern Russia over 4000 km to central and eastern Europe. Dating from the early 1960s, it can transmit up to 1.5 million barrels of oil per day.
- Yamal Pipeline: This is 4000 km gas pipeline between eastern Russia and Central and eastern Europe.
- Nord Stream pipelines. These are two underwater gas pipelines operating directly between Russia and Germany. These are both over 1000 km long and were designed to mitigate transit risk (see Case Study 9.2).

Whilst there are oil and gas pipelines from North Africa and from sources that can by-pass Russia, it is the links with Russia that exhibit the greatest degree of risk largely due to rising level of geopolitical risk. This risk is acute within Europe where over 60 per cent of EU's energy is imported. Whilst there are diverse sources for both gas and oil (which together represent 58 per cent of Europe's energy supply), the long-standing links with Russia led to this state being the major supplier; a state which has had an especially troubled relationship with transit states (notably in Poland and the Ukraine) as it sought to get its oil and gas to main markets in Western Europe. This Russia sought to get around via the Nord Stream set of pipelines that went direct to main markets by-passing transit states. In 2021, Russia supplied the EU with 43 per cent of its gas (it was as much as 60 per cent in the case of Germany). This is more than double the share of the next biggest source from Norway (21 per cent) and Algeria and Qatar (with 5 per cent and 4 per cent respectively). This is coupled with the fact that Russia is also the single largest supplier of crude oil at 30 per cent of total supply; it also comprises 44 per cent of EU imports of coal. This created a dependence by Europe upon Russian energy. Germany felt that proactive engagement through trade would create a benign geopolitical environment. On-going disputes between Ukraine and Russia which had been emerging for the best part of decade spilt out into open conflict in early 2022. In this conflict, the EU and Russia found themselves on opposing sides. As Russia gradually began to assert the EU's dependence upon its energy it tightened supply of gas to get it to change its behaviour, so this dependence spilt out into the global energy systems. The EU's need to replace Russian oil and gas led it to go to alternative sources which led to a further increase in energy prices which were already increasing as a direct legacy of the expansion of the global economy as it recovered from the effects of the COVID-19 pandemic.

The case shows an example where one state was prepared to use another state's dependence upon its energy to shape another state's or group of state's behaviour in a way that suited its own interest. The exporting state showed that it was willing to lower the flows of energy coming through a pipeline to create economic pressure upon other state(s). The restriction upon flows caused energy prices to rise sharply. This placed economic pressure upon businesses and households with the exporting state hoping that this political pressure would cause a shift in geopolitical behaviour. This short-term geopolitical use of energy could have longer-term economic impact as the exporter (in this case Russia) becomes known as an unreliable supplier of energy and therefore finds markets closed off to it as the previously importing states look to alternative supplies (both domestic and foreign). In Russia's case the big risk is that it becomes beholden to China as the sole large-scale buyer of its oil and gas.

This is only the latest example where geopolitical risk has been conflated with energy systems. The same happened in 1973 when Saudi Arabia lowered energy flows to force a change in the west behaviour with regard to the Arab–Israeli conflict and—to a lesser extent in 1980 when Iran sought to restrain and constrict flows by restricting movements in an out of the Persian Gulf. These state-based actions to increase infrastructure risk across energy have also been evident with energy systems becoming a primary focus of terrorists' attacks. Rebels from Yemen have made a point of attacking Saudi oil facilities. In 2019, these rebels attacked two facilities that process the bulk of Saudi Arabia's oil exports. Whilst the effects were not massively disruptive it did highlight how vulnerable such systems were to such measures. This group of rebels also attacked Saudi Arabian oil facilities in March 2022 which again offered a temporary slowdown in production.

It is a fact that energy infrastructure is a system that has been a common target for terrorism. Increasingly through cyber attacks upon those systems that underpin energy system operation but also more often—as noted above—by a direct attack upon physical structure itself, these are done to reduce the energy security of both domestic and foreign states. Often these attacks are not upon the physical system itself but upon aspects that impede its operation such as kidnapping of staff, etc. They are attractive to attack as they are often in remote areas and a single attack can have outsize effects upon the operation of the global system.

These risks underline how infrastructure both for transmission and processes drives the global energy system. These states with exporting power know that closing down transmission routes disrupts these systems. Also, non-state groups know that disrupting these assets can also be effective in disrupting the activities of those mainly state-based actors who are the target of their actions. As energy security goes to the heart of state security there is a trend within states to seek to increase freedom from these international flows of energy and create energy security based upon domestic generation. In many ways, this is a secondary theme within the long-term objective of climate transition where energy-importing states replace these domestic sources or from sources which are less risky.

Expropriation Risk Within Energy

Energy nationalism can create a further infrastructure risk namely what can be termed infrastructure nationalism where the state in which a key resource is located seeks to control ownership of all parts of the system involved in the processes and distribution of that resource within an economy. For some businesses this creates the risk of expropriation as energy security goes to the heart of state territoriality, energy is a sector that is especially vulnerable to such pressures. These measures seek to exclude non-domestic (or investment by non-aligned states) in the critical infrastructure of the state (see also ▶ Chapter 4). This is related to the designation of energy infrastructure as critical infrastructure and therefore is core to state territorial functioning and must be under direct state control or under the con-

Infrastructural Risk

trol of trusted party. Resource nationalism is something that has ebbed and flowed over time usually with the price of the hydrocarbons. Rising nationalism across the global economy increases the risk of resource nationalism and of states. In the case of energy, these risks can take the form of:
- Changing or nullifying existing contracts.
- Altering frameworks to allow more local input into a process in which local firms were otherwise excluded.
- Nationalization where the state takes a majority controlling interest in the energy business often against the wishes of the existing foreign owner.
- Outlawing foreign ownership of energy production or simply demanding a national share in any joint venture within an international oil company.
- Increase the tax payable by energy companies to undermine viability of investment or to make sure state gets its share when prices are rising.
- Strict local content rules covering investment.
- Limits on exports of energy products.
- Controls on what can be exported on ground of national energy security.
- Policies to proactively increase domestication of energy sector.
- Mandatory payments to be made by energy companies towards social and ecological spending.

The rising nationalism with regard to energy is not merely shaping the relationship between states and businesses but is also shaping relationships between states themselves. As states seek to secure their own supplies of energy many are looking into maritime territorial environments. This has led to disputes between states as to the extent of territorial waters and others of the rights to the energy that is under the seabed. This increases the risk of conflict between states as each seeks to assert their territorial rights and business could be caught in the centre of such disputes. Energy expropriation could also work not simply through the lens of resource nationalism but also for reasons of energy security where consuming/importing nations begin to take control of domestic energy systems to secure delivery of energy to homes and businesses. It can also encourage its businesses to go out into the global system and seek to acquire resources that can be sent back to the home state.

Case Study 9.2: The Nord Stream Pipelines

Nord Stream are two separate gas pipeline projects running under the Baltic Sea directly connecting Russia and Germany. These are approximately 12,200 km long. Each of these two pipeline projects consists of two pipelines (thus there are four pipelines in total). The first pipeline—Nord Stream 1—was completed and started delivering gas in 2011 with the second pipeline project brought into service in 2012. The second set of pipeline—Nord Stream 2—was completed in 2022. Due to the Russia–Ukraine conflict it has yet (and maybe never will) to begin delivering any gas between these two states.

The development of these pipelines has always been controversial. First, it was felt that it was leading to increased German/European dependence upon Russian gas which could give the latter geopolitical power over the former should disputes between them emerge. Second, the pipeline system and its management could be used to contravene the security of those states who border the Baltic Sea. Third, in by-passing transit states (such as Poland and the Ukraine), the pipelines erode these states' capability to generate transit fees. Whilst this may lower the cost of the gas, it does represent a significant revenue loss for those states who operated as transit points for this gas. Fourth, in delivering more gas cheaply the pipeline system implicitly encourages the consumption of hydrocarbons and delays the on-set of the energy transition.

With the development of Nord Stream 2 these issues were brought more broadly into focus. Whilst the development of Nord Stream 1 was problematic enough to many observers to double down on the dependence on Russian gas with Nord Stream 2 was an outright mistake. Germany defined the project but many of its allies warned it about the trap it was being led into. For Ukraine, Nord Stream 2 was a means to deprive it of transit revenue and of the supply of gas into the state. The fear was that Russia would divert gas to western Europe and undersupply gas to the Ukraine to assert power over it. Whilst Russia always denied it would use gas as a geopolitical tool there was little doubt that these pipelines gave it increased leverage over several states. Germany dismissed these concerns arguing that engaging with Russia through trade meant that it had a vested interest in sustaining flows.

These fears came to fruition and Germany's naivete was exposed with the outbreak of conflict between Russia and the Ukraine. With the EU siding with the latter, Russia threatened then actually cut off supplies through the Nord Stream system. At the point of the conflict beginning, the EU was dependent upon Russia for around 40 per cent of its gas. Thus, reducing then turning off the supply left European states exposed especially with storage levels reduced after a hot summer led to increased use of electricity for the use of air conditioning. Russia clearly hoped that this process would lead to western states reconsidering their use of sanctions. This they did not do. The result was that—as western European states sought to find alternative sources of energy—the price of gas spiked. As flows across the Nord stream system slowed to dribble, the Nord stream system was sabotaged with two of the four pipelines damaged by a series of explosions. The act of sabotage (for which Russia is suspected) was not merely done to put these pipes out of action for a sustained period but also to signal that other gas pipeline infrastructure is also vulnerable.

Ultimately, the future of the Nord Stream system is in severe doubt. It seems unlikely that flows will resume through the system anytime soon. Not merely are these systems out of service due to damage but the hostile geopolitical climate looks very difficult to enable flows to resume. Moreover, even if these two large impediments are removed, it is likely that the energy shock of 2022/2023 will accelerate the trend towards the green transition in Europe as well as it seeking to switch and diversify its supply towards partners it sees as more reliable. Thus, without any radical change in the geopolitical context the Nord Stream pipeline system looks more and more like a stranded asset; a piece of infrastructure rendered obsolete by its changing operational context.

International Risk in Electricity Grids

Whilst there is long-standing trade in primary energy (i.e., coal, oil, and gas), trade in secondary energy (i.e., that which is obtained from transforming primary energy notably electricity) is a more recent phenomenon. In this case, there are increased number of transnational grids often developed on a regional basis. Such regional systems are well established in Europe, East Asia, and North America. These regional systems are motivated by a range of factors such as:
- Promoting security of supply.
- States need to build less space capacity into a domestic system.
- Balancing supply and demand for electricity across different systems.
- Enabling widespread access to renewable energy sources especially where the large generating areas are far from the main centres of consumption.
- Seek to diversify energy sources.
- Accessing remote energy resources.
- Lower cost of system development by sharing capacity.
- To foster deeper interconnection to breed wider co-operation.

The drivers are a degree of infrastructure sharing and mitigating a need for states to invest fully in infrastructure where capacity can be shared across borders. These do not come without risks as disruptions can easily and quickly spread across borders. There have been several minor incidents in transnational electricity grid systems where failure in one state has led to a cascade failure across multiple national systems in both Europe and North America. In the US, it was a case of a tree falling across a power line. In Europe, it was a ship hitting an overhead wire across the German section of the Rhine. Of course, these were not single events but an event that led to a multitude of events based on widescale under-investment in transmission infrastructure. These grid problems can also be caused by exceptional usage due to extreme weather vents placing too much pressure upon the grid and of the simple failure of the grid to adapt to its shifting context.

The European blackout in 2006 reflected cascade effects within the continent's electricity systems due to the high degree of interconnectivity between national grids. In less than a minute, overload within one part of the system (in Germany) led to a cascade failure in grids from Romania to Portugal. Overall, 15 million households were impacted. The failure went so far as to disrupt links to North Africa notably Algeria, Morocco, and Tunisia. Thus within a few seconds of a system failing in Germany the lights went out in parts of North Africa. These international events within electricity grids also had precedents in the North American blackout (between connected Canadian and US systems) in 2003 and in the same year there was a failure within the Italian system that spread to Austrian, Slovenian, French, and Swiss systems. This reflected that these international ties were created with low capacity in what were still overwhelmingly national systems. Thus, the links could not cope with the traffic once one part of the system failed and increased flows were pushed through it.

Aside from these operational issues, states can often be reluctant in the presence of cascades to build links where the failure of one can spread to many others. This is especially true where these systems have proven especially vulnerable to cyberattacks. The Ukrainian system was subject to a cyber attack in 2015. This reflects that grids are increasingly dependent upon cyber systems for their management. Within these enabled transnational grids, where there are uneven cybersecurity measures there can be a strategic vulnerability to the whole system. This could create an atmosphere of mistrust between parties involved. Interconnections are difficult to run and manage and they can involve different standards as well as a multitude of operating companies.

Information Infrastructure

▶ Chapter 8 identified that one of the main risks associated with changes within the technological environment were risks associated with the global system's increased dependence upon cyber systems. Such dependence underpins the vulnerability to the core infrastructure that enables these cybers which is focused upon two sets of facilities—global server farms and the trans-oceanic cable systems—both of which represent vulnerability to the operation of the global system.

▬ *Server Farms*

These server farms are clusters of computer servers that are co-located in a single location. In a cloud-based computer system (based upon remote storage and access to data), these farms enable the collective holding of data and processing capabilities within these locations. These arrangements are typically used for web applications through the backing up of corporate data and are attractive to business as they lower upfront costs of capital spending and delegate the management of these systems to specialists. As of 2022, it is estimated that there are nearly nine million data centres of assorted sizes globally; this is up from just 500,000 in 2012. These have a universal reach but have an overwhelming focus upon locations within large, industrialized states that are also—not surprisingly—the largest users and collectors of data. Across this large number of farms, there is a process of consolidation occurring with the sector with the average size of server farms growing. The largest server farms (both located in China) are more than 5 million square feet with the largest being over 10 million square feet. Of the largest data centres (so-called hyperscale centres—which exceed 5000 servers), there are around 700 of which nearly 40 per cent are in the US and 10 per cent in China. The increased salience of these data centres to all sectors was underlined within the COVID-19 pandemic as more activity moved online and as more activity became dependent upon these facilities. The legacy of this is that up to 50 per cent of corporate IT spending is upon such facilities.

One of the big controversies surrounding these centres is their levels of energy consumption. Overall, these data centres use 40 per cent more electricity than the UK as a whole. They account for three per cent of total energy consumption and two per cent of total greenhouse gas emissions. This demand for electricity is created not simply by the need to power these systems but also by a requirement for air conditioning to keep these facilities cool. Overall, by 2025, it is estimated that these facilities will represent nearly a fifth of total electricity demand and nearly 15 per cent of global emissions. This represents the increased use of data created by new

applications such as the Internet of Things which will see the energy use of these facilities double every four years. Aside from these longer-term, ecological consequences there exist other risks associated with the widespread utilization of these data centres. These risks are stemmed from an essential issue that in order to co-locate data, this data is now concentred in a limited number of sites across the global system rather than being more dispersed. This means that any large-scale disruption to these flows of data can have significant effects upon the operation of the global system. The main identified risks are:
1. Security: this could be through a mix of cyber attacks where there is denial-of-service attack upon the system or through social engineering attacks (where the psychological manipulation of personnel takes place to make them commit security errors). There are also the threats of more direct attacks through terrorism and other forms of malign human activity. This need not necessarily be a direct attack upon the centres facilities but could also involve an attack upon energy supply upon which the centre depends.
2. Natural Disasters: not only do these centres represent a major contributor to climate change they are also impacted by it. Inevitably increased levels of moisture (and in an extreme case flooding) would cause immense damage to these facilities. Moreover, given the amount of electricity used within these centres, then fire is another real risk again whether through malfunction or through malicious acts.
3. Infrastructure failure: this will be due to power loss and/or the failure of the installed hardware leading to a potential loss of data.

– *Trans-Oceanic Cables*
  Linking these data centres together—as well as enabling the international transmission of data between states—is the global trans-oceanic cable system. These are the backbone of the global information infrastructure facilitating the rapid transmission of data globally. Currently, these cables carry 99 per cent of all international data traffic. These cables are a network of submarine cables laid upon ocean floors connecting land stations. As of 2022, there were 530 active or planned submarine cables. These represent some 1.2 million kilometres of deployed cable which are varying degrees of length of between 100 km (between the UK and Ireland) to 20,000 km (the Asia-America gateway cable). Inevitably, these cables are mainly located to enable connectivity between the world's major financial and service sector hubs. There is a lot of capacity across the Northern hemisphere's oceans notably reflected in the proliferation of trans-Atlantic and trans-Pacific cable systems. As such the main cables routes are:
– Trans-Atlantic: mainly between New York to London.
– Trans-Pacific: This includes several routes between Los Angeles to Tokyo, Hong Kong, Singapore, and Sydney.
– Americas: These are routes between North and South America notably Miami to São Paulo and Fortaleza (Brazil) and New York to São Paulo.
– Intra-Asia: these are links between Singapore and Tokyo, Hong Kong, and Mumbai.
– EMEA-to-Asia: These are routes connecting Europe to Asia via the Middle East such as links between London and Singapore and Marseille to Mumbai.

These cables are mainly privately owned with many of the major tech companies (i.e., Google, Facebook, Amazon, and Microsoft) also becoming increasingly involved in the development of these cable infrastructures often to support their extensive data centre activities. Like the server farms (which these links often connect) these undersea cables are also subject to a number of issues that could disrupt the flow of data across them. Threats to these cable systems have been an issue for almost as long as these cables have been in existence which these systems often being seen as a legitimate target in times of conflict. Broadly these threats can be threefold.

1. Unintentional human interference. It is estimated that 70 per cent of all damage is accidentally created by the human maritime activity. The activities of trawlers (notably in East Asia) can—through certain types of trawling—snag cables and represent about a third of all reported incidents. A further 25 per cent of cable damage is caused by ship anchors notably where they are dragged along the sea floor.
2. Intentional human interference. As these cables are a strategic asset to states they become a key legitimate target in times of conflict shutting off communication channels. Alternatively, states could tap into these cables to collect information.
3. Natural events: it is estimated 14 per cent of damage is caused by natural hazards (current abrasion or earthquakes).

The impact of any single event and the extent to which it can cascade through the system depends upon the extent there are alternate routes for channelling traffic should any single route be disrupted; the more any state is dependent upon a single or limited channels to connect into the global system.

Infrastructural Splintering

The final issue to deal within the notion of infrastructure risk is related more to themes that can endanger the universality of uniformity and universality of the global infrastructure system at the macro level. These are decisions and actions made by states that undermine the ability to act as a common resource for all both within and between states. Thus, the notion of infrastructure splintering reflects a force that inhibits the access to infrastructure by groups either through economic, political, social, or ecological forces.

1. *Uneven Development*
Not only are there wide variations in the quality of infrastructure between states, but there are also wide variations within states. This represents a risk to business if they are unable to get their product from the point of entry to the point of consumption within a state. This does not merely reflect the relative state of logistics within a state but also reflects the extensiveness of the development of energy and information networks. The WEF Global Competitiveness Report in assessing business perceptions of infrastructure quality (across transport, energy, and water) highlights the sustained divergence between developed and developing states with

small open, developed states possessing the best quality infrastructure with universal coverage of high-quality systems. This contrasts with the performance of these systems in much of sub-Saharan Africa where quality is often poor beyond cities. Even in urban areas these systems can be poorly developed with power shortages common and transport infrastructure congested. This pattern of uneven development is also evident within the infrastructure components of the World Bank's Logistics Performance (which focuses upon the trade component of the national infrastructure system).

Of course, examining, the legacy of uneven development simply through the economic risks created by dislocation from the global trading system and the security and reliability of economic flows. Uneven development of infrastructure systems is also salient to macro-level forces of social and political risk. States need extensive infrastructure to assert political control over their territory. There is also risk that infrastructure underdevelopment in specific sections risks undermining social cohesion with sections of a territory. This can have consequent implications for levels of social risk within a state where segments of the population are under-served or even denied access to essential public services (such as energy and transport). There has been increased policy narrative regarding the erosion of infrastructure universalism within states with users within the same proximity having different infrastructure experiences.

2. Infrastructural Violence

There are also circumstances where states may seek to lower levels of political and social risk through intentionally underproviding infrastructure. Narratives upon infrastructural violence have stressed how these systems can be used as a tool of repression where limiting access to infrastructure can act as a tool for limiting political risk from specific social groups. This is based on notion that the universal provision of infrastructure can act as a platform for disruption of the operation and efficacy of the state especially where there are rival groups vying for power and control. This was evident throughout the Iraq conflict between 2003 and 2016 where insurgents used these infrastructures to target the state and also destroyed these systems to disrupt the operation of the state. In times of internal conflict and unrest, sides will attempt to size and shape the infrastructure systems as a means of asserting territorial control; in other places, will seek to control and lower social unrest through denying access to infrastructure.

3. Infrastructure Nationalism

Another force for fragmentation (as mentioned in the case of energy above) is where states seek to overtly discriminate between who can own and use infrastructure within a given state. Given the increased salience of critical infrastructure as a policy narrative there is an increased desire to control ownership on this structure to ensure they support state strategy. This can often mean that the state places direct ownership constraints upon given critical systems to ensure they do not run the risk of ownership by a business from a potentially hostile state. These concerns have been evident over ownership issues regarding transport, energy (see above), and information infrastructures.

4. *Ecological Disruption*
A further dimension that could create more splintered effects within the global infrastructure system is the impact that climate change has upon these physical assets. Infrastructures that are exposed to weather are developed with a specific set of conditions in mind to enable these assets to be resilient to weather to which it would be exposed. The effects of climate change are making extreme weather events increasingly common thereby increasing the risk of disruption to these systems. These climate-based risks are also compounded by the increased severity of climatic events. These are likely to not merely increase the disruption to these physical structures but will also increase the rate at which these infrastructures degrade. These in combination undermine the resilience of these systems. In addition, to climatic events, infrastructure can also be disrupted by events such as earthquakes and volcanic activity. The impact of these ecological events upon infrastructure does tend to be highly localized. These events can have cascade effects as the infrastructure disrupted leads to a disruption of flows into the global systems. For example, the melting of permafrost in the Arctic could erode the stability of pipelines within both the US and Russia. There is also the fact that much of the US' oil refining capacity is in the Gulf of Mexico which is subject to the disruption of tropical storms. There are also the widespread effects of 2011 Tōhoku earthquake of the coast of Japan which triggered a powerful tsunami which caused damage to the Fukushima nuclear plant which led to a reassessment of the role of nuclear power within not just Japan's energy mix but within other states too.

5. *Soft Infrastructure Risk*
The themes within infrastructural splintering hint at broader issues with regard to infrastructure risks namely those related to soft infrastructure systems. Much of this chapter has dealt with the risks created by the operation of hard infrastructure systems (the physical channels, hubs, and other facilities) that enable the flow of tangibles and intangibles around the various global sub-systems. The operation of these hard systems depends very much upon the existence of enabling soft infrastructure. This soft infrastructure is the underlying governance systems that shape the operation and usage of hard infrastructure (see above). These define who can access the infrastructure within a given territory, they also define who can own infrastructure and who it can be used. The issue of soft infrastructure becomes increasingly salient when infrastructure develops under polycentric infrastructure systems. In this case, there is a desire to ensure that these systems operate as a national and international resource and do not develop in a manner that hinders interconnectivity and systemic interoperability. As such, these soft infrastructure systems create the interface between the user and the physical, hard system. Typical of such soft infrastructure issues include planning processes, user preference/discrimination, measures that restrict cross border flows (such as customs processes) and interoperability created by divergent standards.

Case Study 9.3: China's Malacca Dilemma

The Strait of Malacca is the quickest route between the Middle East and China (see ◘ Table 9.4). Its importance to the global trading system lies not simply in the export of manufactures from China but also in the fact that the Strait is a major conduit for the flows of energy to east Asia (especially China). It is estimated that—daily—some 16 million barrels of crude oil and 3.2 million barrels of liquefied natural gas (LNG) are moved through the Strait of Malacca rendering it the second busiest route for the oil trade globally. China is very dependent upon the imports of oil and gas (especially from the Middle East) with some 70 per cent of its imported hydrocarbons being moved through the Malacca Strait. Its significance to China extends beyond energy to trade itself where—it is estimated—60 per cent of its trade flows also through this narrow channel.

In recognizing this 'Malacca Dilemma' in 2003, the then Chinese Premier (Hu Jintao) underscored this as a vulnerability for China especially with regard to the external dependence upon external energy supply. This was a location where actions by rival states could—through blocking this channel—cause significant damage to the Chinese economy. On that basis, China was seeking to push back against any attempt by any rival state to seek to control the navigation through the Malacca Strait. This position is worsened through China's deteriorating relationship with India which—via a rapid Naval build up—also has the potential to disrupt flows through the Malacca Strait.

One response from China has been to increase the amount of domestically generated energy. To that end, China has begun to diversify its supply of energy through not simply seeking alternative suppliers that by-pass the Malacca Strait (such as LNG from Australia and both oil and from Russia) but also through increasing the share of domestically generated renewable energy. China is also seeking to develop overland routes which enable the state to by-pass the Malacca Strait without having to go the long way round via longer maritime channels via Indonesia. To this end, it is developing or has developed overland energy systems in Myanmar, Pakistan, Russia, and central Asia. For example, China is using the developing China–Pakistan Economic Corridor to bring gas into western China and by-passing any pinch points. Though this is proving difficult due to the unfavourable geography which means any pipeline must pass through the Himalayas, China has also been exploring the possibility of using the Northern Sea Route (via the Arctic Ocean) to reach both Europe and Russia. However, these flows remain marginal. Indeed, despite the range of militating action undertaken by China to seek to alleviate the Malacca Dilemma, it remains an issue of large geostrategic concern.

Conclusion

Infrastructure risks are generated by a global system where there is a physical dislocation between the point of production of a resource and its point of consumption. This requires extensive international transmission systems of which the global logistics system is arguably the most apparent. Within this system, there are a number of key bottlenecks that have the potential to disrupt the global flow of goods and commodities. These risks are also evident—though to a lesser geostrategic salience—with energy and information infrastructures. In the former, this has been driven not only by its dependence upon the global logistics systems but also by regional pipeline systems. In the latter, the vulnerability lies within the oceanic cable system.

Key Points

- Infrastructures are central to creating and maintaining international connectivity.
- Disruption to infrastructure systems inhibits global interconnectivity across transport, energy, and information infrastructure systems.
- The global logistics systems are seen as especially vulnerable to the concentration of flows around several bottlenecks.
- Energy systems are increasingly prone to geopolitical risk.
- Information infrastructures can be disrupted via the extensive network of web farms and trans-oceanic cable systems.

Discussion Questions

1. How do you think geopolitical risk can shape infrastructure risk in global transportation?
2. Do infrastructure risks underline the strength of the argument for the localization of production?
3. How big a threat in infrastructure splintering to the operation of the global system?

Activities

Using the example of the third-party logistics business, undertake an analysis of the major infrastructure risk these businesses face.

Summary

International infrastructure underpins the operation of the global economic system. Such dependence creates a number of risks for the sustainability of the system. This has its most obvious manifestation within global logistics where there are a number of bottlenecks whose disruption would impose a direct impediment on the flow of goods. These concerns overlap with risk in the transmission of energy which often depends upon the same bottlenecks but is also subject to risks associated with pipeline transmission. An emerging concern is the evolving information infrastructure where server farms are increasingly seen as a key strategic risk for both states and businesses.

Further Readings

Greenstein, S. M., & Fang, T. P. (2020). *Where the Cloud Rests: The Economic Geography of Data Centres*. Harvard Business School.
Kandiyoti, R. (2007). *Pipelines: Flowing Oil and Crude Politics*. I.B. Tauris.
Rehak, D., & Hromada, M. (2018). *Failures in a Critical Infrastructure System: System of System Failures* (pp. 75–93). IntechOpen.
Thomas, A. R., & Vaduva, S. (2016). *Global Supply Chain Security*. Springer-Verlag.
Turner, C., & Johnson, D. (2017). *Global Infrastructure Systems*. Edward Elgar.

Useful Websites

Telegeography, this is a guide to the major global trans-oceanic cables. ▶ https://submarine-cable-map-2021.telegeography.com/
World Bank Global Logistics Performance Index, this is a global ranking of state's logistics systems across a range of indicators. ▶ https://lpi.worldbank.org/
The Global Energy Monitor, which is a good source of data for the global energy system. ▶ https://globalenergymonitor.org/
The World Economic Forum, this offers a global competitiveness report that assesses relative infrastructure performance. ▶ http://www.wef.org

Conclusions: Analysing Global Business In a Complex Environment

Globalization is not a monolithic force but an evolving set of consequences—some good, some bad, and some unintended. It is a new reality.

John B. Larson

At the end of this concluding chapter, the reader will be able to understand:
— The evolving role of risk within a global business.
— The rising concern with regard to the emergence of Polycrisis.
— How resilience is core to risk mitigation over the short to medium term.
— The role of sustainability as a broad-based concept in dealing with long-term systemic risk.

Introduction

This book has attempted to navigate students around the major forms of risk that inhabit the current phase of our contemporary global environment. Of course, in choosing the main risks, the focus was upon those about which there is both widespread evidence and a consensus upon those which have had the greatest known impact. Inevitably, such an analysis has—by its very nature—to ignore those risks which are possible but essentially unknown such as threats to the planet's systems from non-terrestrial sources such as asteroids. This final chapter brings together the main themes addressed within the book to reflect upon the evolving risk environment and what it means for our understanding of the development of global/international business. The chapter also seeks to revisit issues of sustainability and resilience within global systems as a means of seeking to militate the effects of the known risks within the global system.

Understanding Risk in Global Business

For much of the late twentieth and early twenty-first centuries, there was widely accepted consensus upon the seeming inevitability of globalization. This was seen as on-going process of change that induced change not simply across economic systems but also had long-lasting implications for political, social, technological, and ecological systems. This was an era where the change to the commercial operating environment would render all agents within it (states, consumers, MNCs, etc.) subservient to global forces. This sense of powerlessness found its most apparent manifestation within the period of hyper-globalization borne of the period of the great moderation (see ▶ Box 4.2). This reflected a belief that globalization offered inherent benefits to all agents within the interconnected global sub-systems and that the connectivity between agents meant that any problems within the system were best solved through international co-ordination and co-operation.

This global consensus on the benefits of globalization reflected that the speed, extensiveness, impact, and interconnectedness within the global system was a stabilizing force within it. There was a belief that states that traded did not go to war with each other. Thus, there was a logic that the system tended towards stability as every agent benefitted from it and therefore had an interest in promoting its stability through international consensus. This was seen as true for political and social systems as it was for economic and technological systems. This era saw a period of rising interconnectivity between micro, macro, and meso levels within all of the global sub-systems, and that all agents were actively encouraged to interact and interconnect across borders as a means of sustaining and enhancing the stability and widespread socio-economic and political benefits from the global system. Moreover, as a lot of the value creation within the global system is created by human—as opposed to natural—capital so there was less of an incentive for states to start wars for territorial expansion to gain control over natural endowments. This trend is reflected in that some states seek to undermine other states' competitive advantage through hacking and IPR theft than military conflict. Thus, globalization has meant that it is easier to acquire resources through the market than it is through conflict. Indeed, it is a moot point as to whether much international conflict could have been avoided had global trading systems exhibited greater maturity.

Successive shocks to the global system (see ▶ Box 1.1) began to erode this global consensus. There was a growing feeling that interconnectedness as well as the depth, speed, and extensiveness with which events could cascade through the system was working to undermine the stability that was at the bedrock of the global consensus. Moreover, the belief that states would not seek to destabilize the system because of a vested interest in its stability and consensual governance has also come under threat. There is a tendency by some states with economic power within commodities, technologies, and/or manufacturers or in some other part of the global value chain to use this power as a source of political strength. These states seek to erode the consensus of liberal internationalism to shape the system to their own political ends by exploiting systemic dependence upon their position within global value chains. This created a geopolitical vulnerability. The notion that trade would bring change in all states as they accept political liberalism as a natural bedfellow of economic liberalism has—as of 2022—been debunked. China has shown that autocracy and economic liberalism can co-exist. Moreover, the integration of these states into the global system has—it can be argued—increased the risks within its operation. Thus, the supposed benefits of the 'great moderation' have proved to be largely illusory.

Alongside this geopolitical risk created by interconnectedness and interdependence is a growing recognition that whilst there have been systemic benefits to globalization, it has increased (and often neglected) social risks. These social risks were neglected in the belief that over time the benefits of globalization would 'trickle down' throughout social structures allowing all parts of the social system to benefit. This trickle down is increasingly disputed as inequalities have persisted and become embedded. This provided a narrative whereby social risk became political risk which eventually morphed into economic risk. Thus, as inequality fuelled national populism, so this fed a zero-sum mentality to global interaction which has legitimized protectionism and a more hostile attitude to globalization. As the risk levels have increased so there has been a tendency for states to lower the extensiveness of their global reach. This highlights a trend at micro, meso, and macro levels for increased disconnectivity/decoupling as a means of dealing with the risks associated with the global system.

Ultimately interconnectivity within the global system tended to magnify and accelerate risk as the interdependence this created led to the spatial spread of any singular event. States could not isolate themselves from global events and trends as they were too embedded within the global system to resist this pressure. This reflected that globality was far deeper than was otherwise supposed. It was a process that was both geographically extensive (with more states proactively engaged within the global economic system than before) but also that within these states its effects penetrated deeply into socio-economic structures. In the 2020s, these interconnectivities and their consequences have led to cumulated effects of singular events which are creating enhanced system wide risks and creating an unstable and unpredictable system. This has led to an increased focus upon the global system as one characterized by Polycrisis.

The Rise of the Polycrisis

Whilst the global system is littered with problems created by its operation, many of these can be dealt with the normal degrees of flexibility within the system that can often render these issues temporary. Thus, bad weather, unemployment, flu epidemics, and shifts in political sentiment can all normally be dealt with via adjustments within the system as these events are all anticipated, and which are expected to occur within the normal operation of the global system. When events either occur simultaneously or overlap in their duration and impact they have the capacity to overwhelm the capacity of the system to cope. Where such shocks to the system are heterogeneous and disparate but they interact, and negative feedback loops are created so that the combined impact is more than the sum of the individual shocks a Polycrisis is created. These are driven by the interconnectivity between global sub-systems which cause the operation of each to begin to work in a mutually damaging manner driven by links between these systems allowing any single crisis multiple paths to spread throughout the global system (see ◘ Fig. 10.1). The result is an accumulation of interacting crises and a more unstable global system.

Thus, the difficulties and instability within the global system cannot be attributed to a single cause nor can there be a single answer to the Polycrisis. Issues of more limited socio-economic development are coinciding with emergent irreversible changes within the global system notably with regard to climate change such that normal fixes

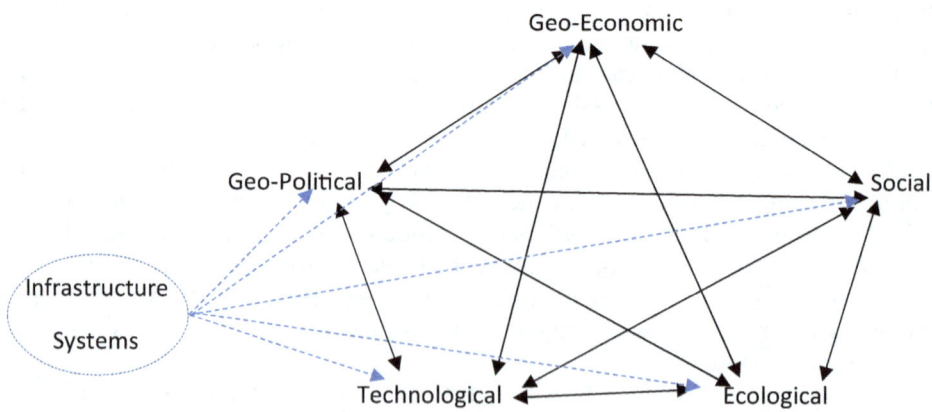

◘ **Fig. 10.1** The complex links between the global sub-systems

can no longer work as they worsen other conditions in other sub-systems. This is notable with regard to issues like the political need to sustain economic growth but to do it in a time frame that is politically expedient without accelerating climate change. This reflects the need to account for the time horizons of an event with the time horizon of the outcome. Thus, extreme weather is a short-term event with short-term outcome as the system adjusts. Whereas climate change reflects long-term actions with long-term effects. A crisis therefore has to:
- Require a response that necessitates a great deal of disruption to the allocation of resources.
- Have a wide scope that its effects are directly and widely felt.
- Have a sense of duration which implies that can be anticipates but can impact in short bursts but for whom adjustment requires a long-term set of actions.

The problem is that these crises can create conflict between states as they seek to resolve their respective problems. This reflects that the nature of the Polycrisis is that entanglement of shocks within each sub-system is such that the impact and legacy of these disturbances are felt simultaneously at multiple levels (micro, meso, macro, and meta). Thus, these are crises that leave no agent untouched. This complexity means that there is no direct measure that any actor in any sub-system can take as the outcome of the event is unknown.

The notion of the Polycrisis has become a more widely used term within the evolution of the global system. In 2018, the then-President of the European Commission used it to describe the simultaneous raft of crises impacting upon the EU from the sovereign debt, refugee influxes, Brexit, and the rise of the far right in both western and eastern Europe. More recently the term has been strongly suggested by IMF which refers to a 'confluence of calamities' across the global systems created by the COVID pandemic, global inflation, and the Ukraine–Russia conflict. These have created a mix of rising prices, food and energy security issues, lower growth, and falling wages. Over time—if these conditions persist—these can be expected to morph into rising levels of social and political risk which could then further economic risk as states turn inwards and seek to compete for diminishing resources.

The notion of the Polycrisis within the global system may not simply reflect short-term events but can also indicate long built-up tensions within the system that create events that require a short-term adaptive action but a long-term solution to restore the system to a new state of stability. This has its most obvious manifestation in climate change. The need—therefore—is to push the global system towards a more sustainable path over the longer term to reflect the new operating conditions of the system (see below). The inter-relationships between these systems mean that the system is characterized by a high degree of uncertainty. There is no real degree of certainty as to how any single event will play out. For example, the Russia–Ukraine war whilst being a largely localized event occurs against a background of economies recovering COVID. Thus, as an example of this process, this conflict was felt through a number of channels such as:
- Geopolitical: as it increased division between leading global powers as they responded to the resultant European energy crisis.
- Geoeconomic: as Europe used its economic power to buy energy it pushed up energy prices for all states notably for developing states who can ill-afford the rising prices.

- Social: the rise in energy prices (causing a sharp rise in fertilizer prices) as well as restrictions on food exports from these food exporting states caused food prices to rise and increased the risk of social unrest.
- Ecological: to meet the shortfall in Russian energy supply and its impact on prices many states turned to hydrocarbons which meant delaying the on-set of the energy transition as well as more fully degrading the ecological environment.
- Technological: states pushed the deployment of renewable technologies to solve their long-term energy crises. This created new pressure upon energy value chains and enabled the rise of new energy powers.

The issue is that any one of these events can function as a catalyst to cause further crises. Where for example, energy price rises cause an inflationary surge which leads to rising interest rates and austerity which then spreads to rising political and social risk. This is just one of a multitude of channels through which one crisis can fuel another crisis. As of 2022, the global system was facing a crisis after crisis within and across the sub-systems namely increased poverty, food insecurity, energy shocks, debt crisis, climate change, Inflation, and conflict. There is—at this stage—no real means to determine how this overlapping risk will play out to the stability of the global system. Indeed, one cannot rule out the prospect that it creates an existential crisis for the operation of the system as it operates at the moment especially if it feeds into broader, escalating conflict which could turn nuclear. The capability of systems to resist these crises and to inhibit the global system from entering a period will depend upon systemic resilience and sustainability. These were concepts addressed within the first chapter. However, it is worthwhile reflecting upon these issues in the light of the embedded risk and potential on-going instability within the system.

The Resilience of Global Systems

As reflected within ▶ Chapter 1, the nature of resilience renders it integral to our assessment and understanding of business risk within global systems. An event and/or process only becomes a risk to the system when that event/process impacts markedly upon normal systemic functioning and operation. If an event/process has no tangible impact upon this system and/or sub-system, then it poses no direct risk to it. In part, this reflects that the event/process is irrelevant to the global systems functioning so that it offers minimal disturbance to it. Thus, events in economically and/or politically globally peripheral states might disrupt a local system but will be largely incidental to the broader system. Alternatively, where an event/process is anticipated system designers and agents operating within it can take mitigating measures to ensure any events will not disrupt their actions or the actions of agents at meta, macro, meso, and micro levels. Of course, these actions are all vulnerable to unexpected events where the ability of the system to cope is ambiguous.

Resilience therefore reflects a mitigation strategy for known risks. As mentioned in ▶ Chapter 1, this risk mitigation is often shaped by the existence of capital (in all its iterations) within the system to absorb the impact of these events/processes. Looking across the various sub-systems strategies for resilience offer an interesting range of options with regard to how the assorted agents operating within the global system deal with the risks that are evident within the range of sub-system that form its structure.

Geoeconomic

At the micro level, the most common form of risk mitigation is through the accumulation of financial and physical capital to enable the agent (be they a consumer or a business) to absorb the impact of an event. The agent will seek to draw upon these reserves until conditions within the sub-system have normalized. At the meso level, the business will seek to build as extensive a value network as possible to ensure that any disruption in one part of the network does not lead to a direct impediment to the normal functioning of the business model. It is widely assumed that globalizing the value network would create a less risky operational basis as the firm would have a wider network of businesses to draw upon. Increased pushback at macro and micro levels towards globality with value networks is seeking states to make them less extensive. For some, too extensive networks can be difficult to control and can create new types of risk through for example reputational damage where the partner's operations diverge from those of the rest of their operations. At the macro level, there was also a narrative that globalization would mitigate risk through the diversity of markets and similarly states have begun to believe that a resilient macro system is based upon diversity and choice and more upon the ability to control to provide certainty and security. These reflect that meta-level interconnectivity can create system wide risks that cascade down through the other levels, and which need to be protected against through the process of economic decoupling.

Geopolitical

At the micro–macro interface, states will engage in non-market strategies to ensure their interests are represented within national political systems. The efficacy of such actions does depend upon the degree of openness and transparency of the political system in which they are operating. The inability to influence these processes or where these processes have been captured by rivals does heavily shape the risk context for businesses both in terms of their internal value chains within the state as well as the value network that the firm is embedded within at the state level. Of higher profile interest has been how geopolitics has come to shape business risk and its mitigation. Within geopolitical systems, the overlap with the geoeconomics system is evident through the process of decoupling. This process essentially seeks to render national systems more able to resist global risk through a process of either domesticating the production of critical material/products or through facilitating or encouraging the move towards sourcing from friendly states. Both of these seek to assert greater control over this aspect of the system. This will sacrifice efficiency for control as transaction costs are likely to increase as a result. This process reflects the perceived commercial risk as well as political pressure upon businesses to adapt to changing political sentiment. Increased geopolitical tension will place pressure upon firms to reconfigure operations to focus upon those states where inter-state relations are at less risk of fracture.

Social

Social resilience is based around the notion that any social system is able to absorb any process and/or event without threatening social cohesion and/or undermining embedded social capital. In more developed states, this can often be based around the collective provision of safety nets and the existence of universal welfarism so that all are cushioned by any event/process that has a common impact. Moreover, where these disturbances to the prevailing social system are asymmetric, there is the provision of state activism to ensure any given community can begin to adapt to the negative impacts. These can be financial support and extend to broader community-based measures to counteract incidences or risks of social exclusion or marginalization. In other states, resilience is based upon social networks centred upon familial systems. These—again—are focused upon allowing specific parts of the family network to cope with an erosion in their physical and/or mental wellbeing. In both cases, the act of resilience is born of the existence of social capital that generates social cohesion at micro, meso, and macro levels to allow social systems to stabilize when they come under stress.

Ecological

Resilience within ecological systems reflects largely how quickly these natural systems can recover from human-instigated or naturally occurring events to the extent they can retain their capacity to operate as an effective habitat for all species which depend upon it. This reflects an in-built store of natural capital within such systems to enable them to cope. Thus, resilience in this context is shaped by the interface between human and natural systems and how the interactions between them can reflect the resilience of both. Left alone with limited damage these systems would tend to recover through endogenous processes. As suggested sometimes these events are out with human influence or control such as earthquakes and all humanity can do is monitor ecological conditions to assess and predict the likelihood of any given event. Where an event is deemed likely humanity can take pre-emptive measures to ensure any disruption to its own (or other threatened species). Increasingly where human activity has to exist alongside natural systems an on-going risk means focusing upon mitigating these disruptive ecological effects through new practices and technology. As such, the adaptation is more upon human activity than on the ecological system per se. Such actions are only feasible where events are known with climate change extreme weather events render this natural environment more unpredictable which means a legacy in terms of human resilience where the known impact is uncertain. This could mean that human adaption to control such risks seeks more to control the natural environments through new practices (such as those linked to geo-engineering) than through simple adaption of human structure and activity.

Technological

Technological resilience is defined by the underlying technology that underpins and supports human existence and advancement at a given point in the innovation cycle. In the current era, this is defined by the capacity of digital systems to respond rapidly to challenges caused by human activity (both intentional and unintentional) and—less frequently—natural events. The most evident means of mitigating known risks within such systems is to build redundancy into the physical capacity of these systems so that should one component fail or be disrupted then there is sufficient space capacity to cope. Resilience can also be built within such systems by their designs which can build in fail-safe devices to mitigate against erroneous human behaviour. The embeddedness of these technologies into human systems underscores that simply building in extra capacity is no longer simply enough the generate resilience. The links between technological systems and state and business interests underscore that resilience has a distinct security element and that this component of the state and/or business architecture can be subject to hostile activity. In this context, resilience is defined less by physical capacity and more by its capability to resist these attacks upon these cyber systems without there either being damage to the efficacy of such systems or through the theft of sensitive material from such systems from online attacks. This depends upon the existence of both human, physical, and financial capital as a key enables of this resilience.

Infrastructural

As these systems both support and enable the main sub-systems, infrastructural resilience is often seen as underpinning this aspect of the global system. When viewed as a global system in its own right it is evident that resilience is frequently based upon hard infrastructure systems possessing sufficient redundancy to cope with any disruption to movement across and between these systems. ► Chapter 9 illustrated this with regard to the main physical systems notably how resilience with logistics systems depended upon capacity within or alternative capacity to the main physical bottlenecks. Looking across the main infrastructure sectors, resilience reflects the capability/capacity of any given transmission system to sustain flows through it especially where there could be a restriction on capacity within a single component of that system. Less considered within such debates are the risk created by soft infrastructure systems where a divergence of the governance of infrastructure systems between states can create impediments to flows which increase the transactions costs of securing interconnectivity and reinforce a splintering process within these notionally global systems.

***

The nature of the emergent Polycrisis alters the nature of resilience and what is required to make any single sub-system resistant to the forces of disturbance that are intensified due to the high intensity and velocity of interactions between these sub-systems. The immediate legacy for the management of risk is to understand that one sub-system's vulnerability can easily spill over into another and that just because one sub-system exhibits resilience it does not mean that all components of the global system are. As such, resilience in the era of the Polycrisis will increasingly need to be seen as a systemic—rather than sub-systemic—need. Rendering one sub-system resilient to an event does not mean that the sub-system and/or agent will not be affected as feedback loops from other systems can work to erode this resilience. This micro-level resilience can be undermined by an absence of resilience at the meso and macro levels. Looking across the respective systems, it is apparent that resilience within each of the sub-systems and at each of the scales (micro, meso, macro, and meta) is a direct derivative of the capital available be it physical, financial, natural, human, and social. Such resources are not always inexhaustible thus there is a need within strategies to cope with rising levels of risk to address what makes each of these systems sustainable over the longer term.

The Importance of Sustainable Global Systems

In ▶ Chapter 1, there was a brief acknowledgement with regard to the importance of sustainability to system stability and viability. The notion of sustainability reflects the notion of the global system (and the sub-systems within it) to persist in a form that enables it to fulfil its core functions. This reflected—building upon themes in the section above—upon the need for stable sustainable systems to be self-renewing and be able to generate sufficient resource capacity to allow these systems to demonstrate longevity. Thus, where resilience reflects a characteristic of being able to absorb an event without posing a risk to system functioning over the short term, sustainability reflects the ability of that sub-system to persist in the face of known trends and risks and the events and processes that emerge as a legacy of these risks. In an era of the Polycrisis, the analysis of any attempt to promote sub-system sustainability in isolation from the global system as a whole seems to create a mere pyrrhic victory. Sustainability has to reflect the state of the system as a whole. In this sense, themes of sustainability based upon enabling the preservation, restoration, and evolution of all systems begin to make sense. Sustainability within this context represents an on-going process of co-evolution between these sub-systems and that any disruption within any sub-system creates an adaptive tension within others.

Sustainability as a process of adaption is based on the notion that each system is interconnected to every other sub-system. This process of co-evolution reflects that change within each of these sub-systems is perpetual and that each of the sub-systems is subject to known and unknown risks that can alter the trajectory of change. Thus, sustainability is an oxymoron of being in a state of perpetual change where that known process of change can be subject to known and unknown events that cause this process of change to adopt a new trajectory. In assessing risks within such system to useful to reflect upon that these risks can be endogenous and/or exogenous and can—through altering anticipated trajectory—render a previously sustainable system unsustainable or create new conditions under which existing notions of sustainability can be attained. There are of course 'positive shocks' such as technological innovations that open up the possibility that sustainability is now more easily attainable.

Again, the pattern of evolution is linked to the available resources and the constraints faced by agents within the sub-system. These constraints will dampen the

10 Conclusions: Analysing Global Business In a Complex Environment

system of anticipated change within any system due to the limited capacity to adapt to the anticipated change. This reflects that adaption to the changing context of the sub-system comes up against contextual constraints reflecting on limits with regard to resource availability to adapt to the shifting conditions of operation. There is a risk that change happens faster than the system or an agent within it can adapt causing a shift in system functioning possibly as the population of agents within the system diminishes as a result.

The notion of sustainability within the main recognized sub-systems examined throughout this text reflects a large degree of overlap with notions of systemic stability. This stability reflects sustainable themes in allowing each sub-systems to have a high degree of predictability in terms of its operation and allowing links between the sub-systems to be non-disruptive. Of course, stability does not mean status it means that the nature of systemic evolution is stable, consistent, and predictable. Looking across the main sub-systems addressed within this text, the notion of sustainability as a proxy for stability tends to reflect the following themes.

Political: sustainability within political system reflects a trend towards political systems towards consensus within the polity with a clear set of rules with regard to governance which enables political processes to be transparent and predictable with no sudden unexpected deviations in public policy and/or state strategy.

Economic: the notion of sustainability within economic systems is based upon broad macro-economic performance that is free from large and rapid oscillation in macro-variables such as economic growth, inflation, exchange rates, government debt, etc. This reflects consistent and predictable economic management with a clear focus upon long-term-stated economic objectives.

Social: social sustainability reflects the capacity of a social system to maintain and where necessary seamlessly evolve social capital so as to maintain social cohesion. This means managing demographic change with no rapid changes in population causing a disturbance to social structures, it means policies of assimilation and non-discrimination, proactive welfarism, and other social policies/services to maintain social health and wellbeing.

Technological: this form of sustainability is largely driven by its links with other systems. Thus, technological change as a sustainable force should at best enhance stability within other sub-systems and at worst do not cause a disturbance within such systems. Thus, this process should not cause mass unemployment, promote political unrest, or damage ecological processes for example.

Ecological: this is perhaps the most widely accepted notion of sustainability and refers to the ability of natural systems to maintain existing natural capital when subject to usage patterns of human activity. The latter utilizes natural systems to support its development and can degrade the system such that natural and human systems become involved in a zero-sum game. Sustainability seeks to reconcile this conflict through notions of green growth where human activity can co-exist with the preservation of natural systems.

Infrastructural: in this context sustainability refers to these physical systems' capacities to maintain the tangible and intangible flows that underpin the major sub-systems. This means that these physical systems need to evolve with these systems, be free from disturbance, and be maintained and upgraded to ensure they enable the smooth and secure operation of the global system.

All agents will be aware of how sub-systems are changing but how they need to evolve with these changes are less well known. This pattern of evolution reflects that these agents are unable to influence the broad process of change but can merely seek to adapt to it. This presumes that they know the trend and can comprehend what the trend means for them. This then suggests that there are trend risks for agents to face. This suggests the failure of sustainability in the face of anticipated risks is created by one or more of the following.

- Poor human capital. This reflects that sustainability was not enabled due to poor leadership either in government, the firm or at some other level of operation. This means simply not taking the necessary decisions, failing to accept a trend, or simply not having the capacity/capability to understand the form and nature of the trend and of the risks that it creates. This failure of the human dimension could also include those actions by human activity that intentionally or unintentionally disrupt the adaptation process.
- Senescence. This reflects that the agent simply does not have the resources to adapt to the process or to the risks that are evident within these processes due to the level of development, maturity, etc., and as such are simply unresponsive to change these are sub-systems and/or agents characterized by sclerotic processes and structures that simply cannot adapt.
- Complexity catastrophe. There is a risk that the system grows too complex that it becomes difficult to understand the process going on within it and thus evolution/adaptation becomes more ambiguous. This becomes an special problem in an environment characterized by Polycrisis.
- Divorce from operating context: this is created by an absence of adaptive tensions in the business thus the processes that are evident within the operating environment are either simply ignored or not considered relevant to the agent. In this case, the agent stops evolving with its environment which runs the risk of the agent being rendered obsolete by this disconnection.

All this indicates that sustainability is driven by the interaction between systems and that all agents within these systems are on an on-going process of adaption to changes within their external environment. This then raises the notion of risk from endogenous sources where the adaption is either too slow or that the agent loses fitness with its environment. In this case, there are known risks with regard to ecological change and those are created by a failure to adapt to the trends and processes that are on-going within it. There are also incidents where single agents possess a lot of power within a single sub-system such as a hegemon within a geopolitical sphere though even then these cannot ignore evolution within this and other systems.

Ultimately sustainability reflects the capability of the system to persist through possessing sufficient resources to enable the system to evolve with its environment where that environment is characterized by both known and unknown risks. There are evident trends within the system and risks as a result of these trends are often created by a failure to adapt. Sustainability is also impacted by events that undermine the longer-term resilience of the global system to persist in anticipated forms. Thus, whereas resilience allows for short-term mitigation repeated events that erode resilience and create longer-term sustainability issues. Like resilience, sustainability depends upon the sustained availability of resources to allow agents to adapt to the

Conclusions: Analysing Global Business In a Complex Environment

process of change within the global system. The emergence of multiple crises and the need to deal with them simultaneously threatens to erode the adaptive capacity of agents.

Conclusion

Risk is embedded within the complex global system. The pressure is upon agents (firms, states, etc.) to adapt to this change based upon anticipated risks and the likelihood of unanticipated events and the potential disruption of such incidents. This draws in themes of resilience and sustainability. These reflect how the underpinning resource base of agents within a given sub-system can cope across the short and long term with the legacy of embedded risk. This process is rendered more difficult in an era of Polycrisis where agents are subject to multiple simultaneous and interconnected risks.

Key Points

- Risk is integral to the modern global business environment.
- The system is veering towards a state of Polycrisis.
- Systemic resilience and sustainability are key public policy and corporate strategic issues in such a context.

Discussion Questions

1. How valid is the concept of 'Polycrisis'?
2. How does a business seek to secure resilience in a dynamic environment prone to crisis?
3. What do you understand with regard to the notion of systemic sustainability?

Group Activities

Taking one of the recognized sub-systems, map the links between this sub-system and the other sub-systems to identify the linkages between them and the mutual causation of risk.

Summary

The intensity and extensity of interconnectivity between sub-systems have increased the impact of singular events upon the global system. This has given rise to the notion of the Polycrisis where a series of simultaneous, mutually reinforcing risks has increased markedly levels of systemic uncertainty and instability. This has again drawn attention to the countervailing measures undertaken by all agents to ensure their respect part of the global system is both resilient over the short term and sustainable over the longer term.

Further Reading

Bostrom, N. (2001). Existential Risks: Analysing Human Extinction Scenarios and Related Hazards. *Journal of Evolution and Technology, 9.* ▶ https://www.nickbostrom.com/existential/risks.pdf

Citi GPS (Global Perspectives and Solutions) and Centre for Risk Studies, Judge Business School, University of Cambridge. (2021). Systemic Risk: Systemic Solutions for an Increasingly Interconnected World. ▶ https://www.jbs.cam.ac.uk/wp-content/uploads/2021/04/crs-citigps-systemic-risks-report.pdf

Folke, C., et al. (2021). Our Future in the Anthropocene Biosphere. *Ambio, 50*, 834–869.

Krishnan, A. (2022). The Uncertain Future: A World in Crises. *Development Advocate Pakistan, 9*(2), 37–40. UNDP Pakistan.

Tooze, A. (2021). *Shutdown: How Covid Shook the World's Economy*. Penguin.

Supplementary Information

© The Editor(s) (if applicable) and The Author(s), under exclusive license to Springer Nature Switzerland AG 2023
C. Turner, *Global Business Analysis*,
https://doi.org/10.1007/978-3-031-27769-6

Index

A

Afghanistan 140
Ageing 197
- population 203
Agent adaption 16
Anthropocene 154–156
Anti-biotic resistance 217
Anti-biotic resistant bacteria 216
Apple 261
Aquifers 171
Arab Spring 210
Artificial intelligence 236
Asset bubbles 113
Authoritarian model of country risk 77
Authoritarian nationalism 143
Automation/robotization 238

B

Biofuels 187
Border risk 273
Born global 46
Business ecosystem 33
Business model 3
- adaptation 40
- component and risk type 38
- conceptualisation of 39
- embeddedness of 33
- endogenous risk framework 39
- framework 31
- global, types of 47
- globality 41, 42
- hyperglobal 43
- introduction to 30
- nature of 30
- reconfiguration 41
- resilience 40
- risk 36
- simplified value network 34
Business risk 44
Butterfly defect, the 16

C

Capital interconnectivity 97
Carbon dioxide emissions 155
Cascade failures 272

Change 230, 231, 233–236, 240, 243, 263
Climate change 154, 156–164, 166, 167, 169, 170, 187
Climate risk 156, 157, 160, 185
- adaptation 160
- physical 159
- scenarios 163
Cohesion 190–192, 197, 207, 208
Commercial fragmentation 251
Commodity markets 107
Common cause failure 272
Comparative energy security 174
Compensation hypothesis 61
Competition state 69
Competitive advantage 69
Competitiveness 73
Complex chain of events 8
Complexity 2, 4, 6, 8, 9, 13–16, 22, 24, 26
Complexity risk 18
Concentration 13–17
Concentration risk 18
Contextual risk 5
Corporate social responsibility (CSR) 4
Corporate strategy 32
Country level risk 124
COVID-19 pandemic 21
Credo-nationalism 143
Critical infrastructure 268
Customer intimacy 43
Cyber risk 239, 244–246, 248, 264, 277

D

Dark Web, the 260
Data interconnectivity 98
Decoupling 104, 106, 107, 109, 110
Demographic change 190
Demographic dividend 199
Demographic transition 199
Dependency ratio 201
Developed states 62
Developing states 63
Diaspora 195
Digital Divide 254
Digital risk 238
Discretion 60
Discretionary risk 3
Distributed generation 175
Distribution of resources 208
Dominant state performance 102

E

Ecological connectivity 128
Ecological risk 20
Ecological system 11
Economic connectivity 128
Economic globalism 94
Economic globalization 90–92, 94, 96, 120
Economic migration 205
Economic nationalism 110
Economic risk 20, 90, 98, 99, 103, 113, 117, 118
Economic system 11, 91
Economic wellbeing 221
Efficiency hypothesis 61
Emerging economies 63
Endemic instability 135
Endemic stability 134
Endogenous risks 5
Energy 267–269, 271, 272, 281–288, 290, 291, 293–295
Energy nationalism 284
Energy security 173
Energy transition 164, 175
- risk context of 178
Equality of opportunity 208
Escalating failure 272
Ethical IOT risk 252
Existential risk 5, 37
Exogenous risks 5, 37
Exporters 47
Expropriation 112
Expropriation risk 284
External risks 3
Extinction 155

F

Feedback loops 8
Food security 182
- risks 184
Food sovereignty 182
Food-water-energy nexus 154, 188
Foreign Direct Investment (FDI) 52
Fourth Industrial Revolution (4IR) 236–239, 249, 251, 254, 255
Fracturing connectivity 197
Fragmentation 125, 138, 142, 150
- of global technological system 248
Freshwater resources 167
Friction of distance 60
Fulfilment risk 37

G

Generic technological risks 233
Geo-economic risk 90
- and its cascade effects 99
- nature of 98
- sources of 101
Geo-economy 91, 99, 101
Geopolitical risk 20
Geopolitical states 134
Geopolitics 132
Global/standardisation strategy 49
Global bottlenecks 275
Global civil society 129
Global commons 268
Global decoupling 106
Global economic interconnectedness 96
Global economic system 92
Global Financial Crisis 8
Global food system 182
Global governance 130
- architecture 131
- failure 149
Global health 215
Global hubs 270
Global infrastructure system (GIS) 268
Globalised business 93
Globalised markets 93
Globalised production 93
Globalised technology 93
Globalism 66, 141–143
Globalist 61
Globalist strategy 67
Globality 9, 30, 40–43, 46–51, 55, 59–61, 66–70, 75, 77
Globalization 10, 65
- drivers of 94
- four dimensions of 93
Global logistical systems 274
Globally obesity 218
Global pandemic risks 220
Global risk 16, 17, 22, 24
Global system 2, 9–18, 20–23, 26
- operation of 13
- structure of 11
Global technological system 228
- bi-polar 250
- fragmentation of 248
Global transit points 270
Global Value Networks (GVNs) 49
Global warming 155
Governmental fragmentation 250
Great Acceleration 154
Great Moderation, the 105
Greenhouse gases 156
Growth, conditions for 75

H

Habitat destruction 155
Hard infrastructure 266
Health and wellbeing 190, 191, 195, 196, 215, 225

Index

Health risks 191
Health security 223
Hegemonic power 136
Hegemony, erosion of 136
Home bias 69
Hub bottlenecks 275
Hub risk 273
Human capital 210
Human rights 208, 211
Hydroelectricity 177
Hyperconnectivity 100
Hyperglobalism 10, 60
Hyper-globalization 10

I

Increasing polarization 197
Inequality 190, 196, 197, 202, 208, 210, 213, 219, 223, 225
- of opportunity 211
Information 271, 272, 290, 294, 295
Information infrastructure 288
Infrastructural splintering 290
Infrastructure 266, 267, 273, 274, 277, 284, 287, 290–292, 294
- critical 268
- hard 266
- information 288
- nature of 266
- soft 267
- transit 268
- water 269
Infrastructure risk 20, 266, 268, 271, 273, 274, 277, 281, 284, 290, 294
Innovation cycles 232
Innovation driven adaption 40
Intangible international business 43
Intellectual property rights 233
Interconnectedness 10
Interconnectivity 8, 13, 90, 96–101, 104, 106, 107, 109, 117
Intergenerational dependence 202
Inter-generational division 202
Inter-generational income inequality 203
Inter-generational issues 197
Intermittency 180
Internal risks 3
International energy system 283
International – export-based strategy 49
Internationalization 44
International Monetary Fund (IMF) 130
International water systems 171
Internet fragmentation 251
Internet of things (IOT) 236
Inter-state conflict 147
Iran 139

L

Left behinds 214
Liberal capitalism 76
Liberal internationalism 137
Liberal internationalist order 137
Link bottlenecks 276
Livelihood 213
Livelihood crises 213
Logistics 268, 270, 274, 275, 278, 279, 282, 290, 294
Low carbon economy 160

M

Macro-economic instability 104
Macro level risk 50, 124
- multi-scalar nature of 127
Malacca Dilemma 293
Managed globality 76
Mandatory risk 3
Market risk 2, 37
Mental wellbeing 221
Meso level risk 124
Meta level risk 124
Micro level risk 124
Migratory flows 197
Millennial generation 204
Millennium Development Goals 215
Modernity 11
Multi-domestic strategy 49
Multilateral system 66
Multi-national corporations (MNCs) 47–53
Multi-scalar nature of risk 7
Myanmar 117

N

National infrastructure systems (NIS) 268
Nationalism 60, 129, 138, 141–143, 145, 150
Nationalist strategy 70
Nation state 58
Natural resource extraction 155
Negligible risk 37
Net Zero 177
Non-governmental organizations (NGOs) 130
North Korea 139
Notional risk 6

O

Ocean acidification 155
Operational model 31

Operational risks 244
Organizational learning 44

P

People interconnectivity 97
Peripheral risk 6
PESOE framework
- categorisation of state risk within 80
- for state based risk assessment 79
PESOE Pentagon 84
Political connectivity 127
Political globalization 129
Political interconnectivity 126
Political risk 124–128, 132, 135
- multi-scalar nature of 125
Political system 12
Polycrisis 300, 301, 305, 306, 308, 309
Populist nationalism 143
Primary fuels 176
Privacy IOT risk 253

R

Race to the bottom 59
Radical uncertainty 4
Rare earths 112
Regulatory risk 160, 188
Remittances 208
Renewable energy sources 176
Renewable technologies 176
Replacement rate 198
Reputational damage 212
Resilience 10, 298, 302, 304–306, 308, 309
Resource nationalism 111
Retreat of the state 59
Revenue model 32
Risk 266, 271–274, 277, 279, 282–284, 291, 295, 298, 299, 301, 302, 304–306, 308, 309
- mitigation strategies 60
Rogue states 138
Russia-Ukraine conflict 21

S

Sane globalization 62
Sanitation 168
Scales of analysis 6
'S'- curve hypothesis 45
Secondary fuels 176
Security Crisis 2001 20
Security IOT risk 252
Security of supply 173

Semi-globalization 67
Server farms 288
Shadow economy 90
Singular events 8
Singularity 16
Sino-American dominance 103
Social capital 191–194, 196, 197, 203, 207, 208, 212, 215, 223, 226
Social cohesion 192, 193, 197, 205–208, 214, 215, 226
Social connectivity 128, 191
Social interconnectivity 192
Social justice 210
Social media 194
Social movements 194
Social networks 192
Social risk 20, 190, 195, 199, 200, 214, 223, 224
- conventional 191
- demographic change and 197
- globalizing 194
- global obesity and 218
- impact of 191
- inequality and 208
- interface 192
- level of 191
- meta level 194
- mitigating 207
- nature of 190
- social media and 193
- within global system 196
Social stability 191, 200
- risks 191
Social system 12
Social wellbeing 222
Soft infrastructure 267
Solar power 178
Sovereignty 58
Spheres 236
Splinternet 250
State based risk 65
- mapping 84
State-based risk 76
State competitive development, stages of 74
State failure 78
State power 62
State risk 61, 80
States 58–64, 67–69, 71–74, 76, 78, 79, 81, 84–86
State strategy 63
- spectrum 67
- types 68
State success 72
'Steps' model 44
Strategic trade-off for states 67
Strategy(ies) 60, 63–67, 69, 70, 72–74, 78, 86
Structural digital risk 238
Sub-systems 11
Sub-system specific risks 233
Super-spreaders 17

Supply side shock 115
Sustainability 298, 302, 306–309
Sustainable Development Goals (SDGs) 215
Syria 139
Systemic geopolitical instability 136
Systemic inequality 213
Systemic instability 134
Systemic resilience 22
Systemic risks 5
Systemic stability 134
Systemic sustainability 24

T

Taiwan Semiconductor Manufacturing Company (TSMC) 140
Technical fragmentation 250
Technical infrastructure 233
Technical IOT risk 253
Technological change 231–233
Technological connectivity 128
Technological independence 249
Technological risk 20, 233
Technological system 11, 229
Technology 228–231, 233, 234, 237, 238, 243, 249, 251–254, 256, 257, 259
Technology specific risks 233
Techno-optimism 258
Techno-scepticism 258
Territoriality 6, 58, 61, 63, 64, 68
Third Industrial Revolution 236
Thucydides Trap 138
Tipping point 15
Total factor productivity 73
Trade interconnectivity 97
Transit infrastructure 268
Transition risks 160
Transit risk 273
Transmission risk 282
Transnational civil societies 59

Transnational strategy 49
Trickle down 299
Turing Trap 244

U

UN Declaration upon Human Rights 211
UN's Guiding Principles upon Human Rights 212
Upskilling 213
Usage digital risk 238
US hegemonic strategy 137

V

Value 30
– creating system 35
– creation 31
– network 33
– proposition 31
Variety of capitalism hypothesis 61
Vector risks 17

W

Water scarcity 170
Water security 167
Welfarism 60
Worker activism 212
World Bank 130
World Trade Organization (WTO) 130

Y

Youth unemployment 209

GPSR Compliance

The European Union's (EU) General Product Safety Regulation (GPSR) is a set of rules that requires consumer products to be safe and our obligations to ensure this.

If you have any concerns about our products, you can contact us on

ProductSafety@springernature.com

In case Publisher is established outside the EU, the EU authorized representative is:

Springer Nature Customer Service Center GmbH
Europaplatz 3
69115 Heidelberg, Germany

www.ingramcontent.com/pod-product-compliance
Lightning Source LLC
LaVergne TN
LVHW081537070526
838199LV00056B/3691